CHEKHOV

OBSERVER
WITHOUT
ILLUSION

DANIEL GILLÈS

CHEKHOV

OBSERVER
WITHOUT
ILLUSION

TRANSLATED BY
CHARLES LAM MARKMANN

FUNK & WAGNALLS
NEW YORK

TO MY WIFE

CONTENTS

I A CHILDHOOD WITHOUT CHILDHOOD 3

II ALONE IN TAGANROG 30

III A STUDENT IN MOSCOW 44

IV MEDICINE, MY LAWFUL WIFE, AND LITERATURE,
MY MISTRESS 68

V "I LACK PASSION" 91

VI A SEASON IN HELL 131

VII ESTRANGEMENT FROM TOLSTOY 153

VIII MELIKHOVO, "MY DUCHY" 175

IX THE SEA GULLS 203

X TOO ILL TO LIVE 245

XI THE LAST PAGE OF MY LIFE 281

XII LIVING BY LETTER 333

XIII THE AXE IN THE CHERRY ORCHARD 379

BIBLIOGRAPHY 425

INDEX 429

CHEKHOV

OBSERVER WITHOUT ILLUSION

I

A CHILDHOOD
WITHOUT CHILDHOOD

> Our grandfather was beaten by the landowners, and the lowest
> functionary could smash his jaw. Our father was beaten by his
> father, and we by our father. What nerves, what blood we have
> inherited!
>
> CHEKHOV

Like so many writers in their declining period, at the age when
the exhausted imagination is as it were invaded and fed anew
by memories, would Anton Chekhov have ended by writing his
memoirs if tuberculosis had not killed him so young? It is hardly
likely, for, to judge as much by his correspondence, for all its
abundance, as by the recollections of his friends, there has rarely
been a writer more reserved, indeed more secretive, than he. Not
only did he never bring himself into his stories, not only did he
speak very little of himself in his letters; even with his intimates
he rarely engaged in confidences. In contrast to many Russians,
unconscious Freudians who love nothing so much as talking about
themselves and dwelling at length on their failings, Chekhov always avoided giving confidences, to say nothing of making confes-
sions or complaints.

Hence it is all the more startling to read a letter that he wrote in
January, 1889, to his eldest brother, Alexander, and in which, by
way of motivating him not to follow the lamentable example of
their father, Anton reminded Alexander in a few words of the experiences of their childhood. "I ask you to remember," he wrote,

"that it was tyranny and lies that destroyed your mother's youth. Tyranny and lies also darkened our childhood to such a degree that it is impossible to think of it without shock and revulsion. Remember the horror and the disgust that we felt in those days when our father made a scene at dinner because the soup was too salty, or when he treated our mother like an imbecile. . . . Tyranny is threefold criminal. . . . Remember that it is better to be the victim than the executioner. . . ."

Anton Chekhov was twenty-nine years old when he wrote this letter. So he was no longer in that stage in which adolescents, especially when they are talking with one another, exaggerate their grievances against their parents. He was never, furthermore, a rebel, and his smiling tolerance, which was one of the basic traits of his character, embraced his father as well as others, perhaps even more so. But though he almost always refused to recall the darkest aspects of his childhood for others, he could not prevent his memory—his poet's memory—from being haunted by certain recollections, certain scenes of violence and hypocrisy, that had marked him permanently.

Often, in the first shock of awakening in the morning, he found himself once more for a fleeting moment the five-year-old who wondered every morning when he got out of bed: "Am I going to be beaten today?" Or he saw himself again as a little eight-year-old grocer's boy, taking his father's place in the shop and, as the evening dragged into an eternity, crushed, like one of his future heroines, by "the need to sleep." And he admitted that whenever he passed a church he habitually walked faster, "seized with terror. . . ."

One day he was to explain to his friend Shcheglov why "he no longer had any religious belief": throughout their childhood he and his brothers had been "little galley slaves" of religion. Their father, who was a fanatic, though not so much in religion itself as in the observances of its forms, in its pomps and its music, consistently forced them to share his tastes. When they were not in school, and while their schoolmates were playing in the fields or the streets, the Chekhov children had to run to church. What was more, their father was not satisfied with this compulsory attendance at services; he had formed a choral group, which was his pride, and of course he had forced his sons to become members of it. The two eldest, Alexander and Nikolai, were the sopranos; as for Anton, he was enrolled in it at the age of seven as an alto. Rehearsals were held in the evenings, often lasting from ten o'clock to midnight.

It was Sundays and holidays that little Antosha dreaded most. On such days his father aroused him and his brothers at two or three in the morning and, regardless of rain or snow, took them with him to church. As a rule they went to the Greek monastery, more rarely to the Palace chapel,[1] the setting for "the elegant Mass attended by the aristocracy of the city." The little boys took their places in the choir. There they remained for hours on their feet, trembling with weariness and fear; in growing desperation their eyes followed the clouds of blue incense, the tapering flames of the candles, the golden reflections of the holy ikons, the waxen tears that dripped unceasingly on to the stone floor. But when under the leadership of their father, at once imperious and glowing, they stood alone in the middle of the church to chant the trio "May My Prayer Be Granted" or "The Voice of the Archangel," "everyone looked at us sentimentally and envied our parents, but we ourselves felt like little galley slaves . . ." as Chekhov was to write later (March 9, 1892).

Their feeling was all the stronger when, on their return from these endless Masses, they had their tea and their father repeated the religious service in little at home. There was no end to his burning of incense before the ikons, while his family, ordered to gather round him, sang prayers and psalms. Then, when the church bells announced the second Mass, everyone had to rush back to church.

This suffocating religious despotism, mingled with so much hypocrisy, was to imbue Chekhov forever with "the fear of religion." It would not be the seminarists alone of whom he was thinking

---

[1] The Palace was what the people of Taganrog called the house in which Tsar Alexander I had lived and where he died in 1825. There was a stubborn legend, which Tolstoy took as the inspiration for one of his last stories, that held that instead of dying in this house, the Tsar had left a soldier's corpse in his place and secretly fled the city in order to live a hermit's life in Siberia.

when one day he wrote: "It is not for nothing that so many atheists have come out of the seminaries and the religious institutions" (March 17, 1892).

"The little galley slave of religion," little Anton was also too often the little galley slave of the grocer's shop. His father, whose business was in the suburbs, was not content to rely on his children's help; quite regularly he turned over the entire shop for a whole evening to one or another of his sons. Always reserved, Anton Chekhov was to restrict himself later to a passing confidence to a friend: "I was a proletarian; I sold candles behind the counter of our shop in Taganrog. Oh, how damned cold it was! . . ." But his brother Alexander, in his recollections, added details to what was concealed by these excessively discreet little remarks. Here is his account of one of the evenings spent by Anton at the age of nine:

Anton has just come home from school. In the yellow circle of a candle's light he was concentrating on his homework, his Latin grammar open beside him. Suddenly his father entered, enveloped in his heavy winter overcoat and his leather boots. Framed in its dense black beard, his face was severe. "I have to go out on business," he said. "Antosha, you take care of the store, and see to it that everything goes right."

The little boy looked up. There were tears in his eyes. "I haven't stopped shivering since I came home from school. And it's so cold in the store . . ."

"Never mind. Dress warmly and you'll be all right."

"But I have so much homework for tomorrow . . ."

"Do it in the store," the father commanded with mounting irritation in his voice. "Come on, and don't forget to keep an eye on everything. All right, hurry up!"

Father and son set out for the shop, which was not far from their house. When they arrived, two little Ukrainian peasants, apprenticed—or, rather, sold—by their mother as salesclerks in the grocery, stopped stamping their feet and clapping their hands, which were blue with cold, and froze in postures of deferential attention. Antosha's father told him to go behind the counter and be careful with the ledger; then, having crossed himself several times in front of the ikon—for there was one in the store, too—he went out.

Fighting back his tears, Antosha took a crate of Kazan soap as a seat and established himself behind the counter. He tried to go back to his schoolwork, but soon he had to give it up. The little apprentices, Andryushka and Gavryushka, had begun playing and jabbering; customers came and went. It was almost as frigid in the unheated shop as it was outdoors, and Antosha was stiff. He knew that he would be there for hours, because when his father went to visit friends or to church or to see Uncle Mitrofanos, he always stayed away the whole evening. His arms crossed, his icy hands thrust into his sleeves, Antosha thought sorrowfully of the bad marks that he would get at school next day . . .

The shop sold everything, including, semi-illegally, vodka, "for consumption on or off the premises," as a placard announced. Hence, as the evening wore on and in spite of the peeling walls, the darkness, the disorder, and the penetrating cold, the customers became more and more numerous. Most of them were old clients who met there to drink and gossip, often until very late at night. The little apprentices fell asleep, but Antosha had to continue waiting on the customers, go down to the cellar to fetch more vodka, and keep his ledger. The drinkers chatted and exchanged the latest stories—a charming minor sin of many Russians—and when one of them grew too bold, they shouted to the little boy watching them out of his large dreamy brown eyes: "You, Antosha! Don't listen, eh? You're still too young."

He learned many other things, however, behind his counter, child grocer that he was. Honesty was one of them, for example. His father had ordered him to keep close watch on the apprentices, whom he suspected of stealing from him. But from other sources—the mouths of Gavryushka and Andryushka themselves—Anton learned that his honest father, so quick to suspect others, had trained them to cheat the customers: he insisted that they weigh their thumbs with the merchandise. And Antosha himself had heard certain curious remedies recommended to the *babas*.

The evening dragged on. To go to the outhouse, which was in a vacant lot, Anton had to walk a verst.* "Sometimes it happened that when I got there," he was to write, "I found myself face to

---

* About two-thirds of a mile.—TRANSLATOR.

face with a tramp who had taken shelter there for the night. What panic gripped both of us!"

Finally, one of the apprentices, who was keeping watch, would see Pavel Yegorovitch coming round the corner. "Papa's coming!" he would shout. Quickly Antosha would stand erect behind his counter and pretend to be checking the accounts.

In the shop as in church he was indeed in a school of hypocrisy and despotism. Freedom, frankness, and tenderness were too often forbidden him, and he had the feeling that he had been robbed of his childhood. "In my childhood," he later wrote, "I had no childhood."

"I like life on the whole," Chekhov was to say, "but Russian provincial life, that mean, petty life, is something I detest and despise with all my strength." When he wrote that, he was undoubtedly thinking of his native town, Taganrog. Once prosperous, it was now an old town fallen into lethargy, one those little "hollow towns," as they said in old Russia. A rather brilliant past lay behind it; now it was as if cut off from the world and drugged with indolence, indifference, and lassitude.

Taganrog, lie Petersburg, was a creation of Peter the Great. It was in 1687 that the founder of modern Russia decided to build this port on the border of the Don steppe and the northeast coast of the Sea of Azov, and Taganrog very quickly became a major center for the export of wheat and other farm products. Still quite prosperous at the beginning of the nineteenth century, the city was overshadowed, however, as its harbor slowly silted up, by its rival, Rostov on the Don, which was better situated and which from the outset had been linked into the new railway network. Forsaken by ships, gradually deserted by trade, Taganrog had thereupon withdrawn progressively into itself. In 1860, the year of Chekhov's birth, Taganrog the Dead had no more than thirty thousand residents. When he paid a visit to his native town in 1887, after eight years spent in Moscow, Chekhov wrote: "Taganrog has the same effect on me as Herculaneum or Pompeii. . . . I have had the opportunity to recognize just how dirty, empty, lazy, ignorant, and dull the town is. There is not a single shop sign without a spelling mistake. The streets are empty and laziness is universal. . . ." (April 9, 1887).

This decaying little town caught between sea and steppe had nevertheless retained some traces of its past. While its outskirts were wretched, in the center of the city there remained a "fine neighborhood," still rich and elegant enough to create illusions. Through it ran an "almost European street" traveled by splendid carriages and by ladies in hoop skirts, and it possessed five-story houses, a fine park, a theater, clubs, and a cemetery full of marble monuments. This was the millionnaires' quarter, occupied almost exclusively by foreigners—who, moreover, made up almost half the city's population—who had done well in business. There were Englishmen, Germans, a large number of Italians, and, above all, Greeks. In Taganrog the Greeks, rich shipbuilders and grain dealers, were the cocks of the walk, and the "great families" were named not Pavlov or Ivanov but Mussuri, Kondayaki, or Valiano.

This rich neighborhood was surrounded by a town of poor people, like an overgrown village in its shabbiness and disorder. The streets, being unpaved, turned into mudholes in autumn and dust paths in summer. At night the residents went about with lanterns, for only the two main streets were lighted, and feebly at that. Among the wooden houses, the vacant lots, and the dreary fences there was a constant movement of tattered dock workers, ragged peasants, prisoners pulling wagons, a few uniformed officials, and innumerable stray dogs. On meat days the town stank of cabbage soup, on fish days there was the smell of sturgeon frying in sunflower oil. Every Saturday a public crier, a huge brushwood broom on his shoulder, went through the streets chanting: "Bath day, bath day! Municipal bath day!"

It was in this shabby setting that Anton Chekhov was born on January 17, 1860—one year before the abolition of serfdom. His father, Pavel Yegorovich Chekhov, was not a native of the town: he came from a family of serfs in the province of Voronezh. The writer's grandfather, Yegor, had been the first of his clan to attempt to rise out of his wretched condition. Stubborn, intelligent, hard-working, he had taught himself to read and write and he had abandoned the land in order to become a foreman in a sugar refinery belonging to his lord and master, Count Chertkov.[2] The great dream of his life—to buy his freedom—had finally been realized in 1841, after he had saved up kopeck after kopeck. Thanks to the thirty-five hundred rubles he had saved—a very large sum for that time—he had been able to redeem, at the price of seven hundred rubles per "soul," his wife, himself, and their three sons. He had not had enough money to buy his daughter's freedom as well, but the Count had "generously" thrown her into the lot of redeemed serfs. Once free, Yegor had become overseer of the tremendous estates between Taganrog and Rostov that belonged to Countess Platova, the stepdaughter of the ataman* M. I. Platov, who was a famous hero of the patriotic war of 1812.

Notwithstanding the fact that he had bought his children out of serfdom, Yegor was not, however, a loving, understanding father. On the contrary, he was the incarnation of that paternal despotism—a reflection of the social despotism—that often prevailed at that time among the Russian people. Violent, authoritarian, subject to excesses of lunatic rage, he often beat his children, and it was he who determined their futures for them. Thus he sent his eldest son, Mikhail, to learn bookbinding in Kaluga and placed his second son, Mitrofanos, as an apprentice to a merchant in Rostov. As for Chekhov's father, Pavel, who was born in 1825, for three years he was an apprentice salesclerk in Rostov until at the age of nineteen, on his father's decision, he was sent to join the clerical staff of a merchant named Kabilin, who was Mayor of Taganrog.

For ten years Pavel Yegorovich endured his wretched, servile existence. He bowed his head when he was slapped, he suffered hunger and abuse, he slept on the floor. But he too was very ambitious and he had made up his mind that one day, following his father's example, he would have his revenge on life and even climb a step higher and become his own master. Furthermore, he had educated himself, and, having been taught reading and writing in his childhood by a village priest, he had subsequently studied, without a teacher, solfeggio, singing, and the violin. When his

---

[2] Count A. D. Chertkov, grandfather of Vladimir Grigorievich Chertkov, Tolstoy's famous disciple and executor, as faithful as he was tyrannical.
* A Cossack chief.—TRANSLATOR.

brother Mitrofanos moved to Taganrog and opened a little grocery store there, Pavel saw an example to be followed: it was through trade that he would "arrive." But first he married: through Mitrofanos he had come to know the Morozov family, which like his own was of serf origin, and in October, 1854, he married the Morozovs' daughter, Yevgenia Yakovlevna.

In 1857 he was able to realize his first ambition: to open his own grocery store in a little house that his father had bought for him. At last he was his own master! Unfortunately, one does not become a grocer by wishing, and Pavel Yegorovich, who was given more to fantasy than to tenacity, endowed more for dreaming than for turning pennies, more a chatterer than a bookkeeper, soon proved to be a poor merchant. His ill-managed business brought in very little, and his resources were far from increasing in proportion to his needs.

For his family was growing. The first son, Alexander, was born in 1855, during the Crimean War: since the Anglo-French fleet was shelling the harbor, Yevgenia Yakovlevna, who had fled the city, gave birth to her child in a village in the steppe. Alexander's birth was very quickly followed by those of three other sons: Nikolai in 1858, Anton in 1860, and Ivan in 1861. Then a daughter, Marya, was born in 1863, and another son, Mikhail, arrived in 1865.

Because Pavel Yegorovich was unstable, there was a succession of domiciles. The first move was made in 1859: family and store were set up in Politzeiskaya Street. It was there, in a one-story wooden house consisting of three rooms and a kitchen, that Anton was born. This white cottage with its green shutters and zinc roof was situated at the end of a courtyard filled with wild bushes and overshadowed by the drooping branches of large acacias. A barrel set beneath the corner of the drainpipe collected rainwater, which was most precious during the long weeks of summer drought. This house, however, was given up in 1861, and six years later, after another move, the Chekhovs occupied a house in Monastirskaya Street. Finally, in 1874, the family emigrated again, this time to make itself "at home" in a house built by Pavel Yegorovich himself in Elisavetinskaya Street.

For the Chekhov children the setting might change, but their existence—that unfortunately real melodrama—remained unaltered. It was totally dominated by that all-powerful being, their father. Physically, Pavel Yegorovich was a solid peasant with square shoulders, a severe expression under bushy eyebrows, a face engulfed in a great dark beard. Psychologically, like his father, he was a domestic tyrant who, having been treated as a slave by those more powerful than he, played the despot in turn toward his family. It is beyond question that he loved them in his fashion, but convinced that he owed his position to God alone, he demanded absolute submission from his wife and children, and the slightest contradiction sent him into towering rage. Implacable and brutal, he whipped his children, and if his wife dared—however seldom—to raise her voice in timid protest, he replied: "This is how I was brought up and, an you can see, it hasn't hurt me too much." To him this was the natural order of things.

Anton was never to forget in how brutal a fashion he was taught morality. "I remember," he was to write in 1892, in one of those infrequent letters in which he allowed himself an intimate disclosure, "that my father began my education, or, more simply, my beatings, when I was not yet five. Every morning when I awoke, my first thought was: 'Am I going to be beaten today?'" And after this dreadful degradation, he was obliged, according to custom, to kiss the hand that had struck him.

Beneath his brutal exterior, however, Pavel Yegorovich was also, paradoxically, a sensitive person, much drawn to art, beauty, and mysticism. He had an excellent voice and sang well, he played the violin with passionate clumsiness, and he painted bad but beautifully colored holy pictures.[3] For it was in religion above all that this frustrated artist, never quite resigned to the grocery trade, found the way to satisfy his feeling for beauty, mystery, and poetry.

The orthodox religion was indeed Pavel Yegorovich's passion. In his way he was quite pious, and he often went to the church nearest to his shop to say long prayers before the holy ikons. At the same time this piety, which we know he forcibly compelled

---

[3] Some of these ikons from the hand of Pavel Yegorovich were piously preserved by his family and can be seen today in the Chekhov Museum in Yalta.

his family to share, was in his case much less a deep religious sentiment than a kind of primitive lyric devotion to the ceremonial of the church. If he went there so often, it was much less from the love of God and his neighbor than because he loved the slow, solemn rituals of the liturgy, the golden shimmer of the ikons and the chasubles, the smell of the incense and the candles.

This failed artist, this potential priest, was determined, for lack of anything better, to be respected in his little town. He managed his business badly, but he devoted all the more attention to the acquisition of standing: proud of having become a member of the second guild of merchants, he wore its emblem on a ribbon round his neck, and he never went out except in a silk hat and a white shirt. He was present at all public occasions, solemnly discussed local politics, and often played host to the priest. He was also an inveterate reader of newspapers, which he read aloud for the edification of his family; subsequently he bound them in volumes with his own hand.

"Our talent," Anton Chekhov was to write with his usual lack of bitterness, "came to us from our father, our characters from our mother." Completely the opposite of her husband, who perhaps was talented but who was also vain and tyrannical, Yevgenia Yakovlevna was a "tender and tranquil" and self-effacing person who most often was silent. Her six confinements in ten years had worn her out, but she still loved her husband in spite of his despotism and his savage scenes over nothings. She bowed before him in that "serf" attitude traditional in ordinary Russian households of the time. On the rare occasions when she attempted to stand up to her husband, it was in order to defend her children, whom she adored. Besides, she never had time to think of herself, obsessed as she was by the cares of the household: where to find money for shoes for Nikolai, how to make Anton's overcoat last a little longer.

The shop brought in little, much too little, even though it was simultaneously grocery store, dry-goods shop, drinking place, and dispensary of religious objects. Above the door there was a black sign with golden lettering: "TEA, SUGAR, SOAP, SAUSAGES, AND OTHER COLONIAL PRODUCTS." Actually one could buy anything in that dark, dirty store: there were boxes of tea and packages of candles on the shelves; sacks of coffee, rice, olives, and sunflower seeds were on the floor; sausages and candies on strings swung in the empty space above the counter; in the cellar there were casks of vodka and Crimean wine. In winter the store was bitter cold and in summer it swarmed with flies. The grocery was open from five o'clock in the morning until eleven at night.

It was in this miserable shop that Alexander, Nikolai, and Anton, when they were not in school or church, spent the better— and the worse—part of their time. "When there is no boss, the goods weep," their father loved to repeat sententiously, but since he himself preferred to spend his time elsewhere, it was his sons whom he chose to represent him in the shop. And if their mother sought to win them a reprieve from this painful forced labor, he replied, always in the same peremptory manner: "I work, so let them work too. Children should help their fathers."

At home as in the shop the father's tyrannical presence burdened the children's lives. He had his private domain in the house, the "big room": there a missal lay open on a lectern and a whole corner was hung with ikons before which a light burned night and day. While there were evenings when he was more cordial and played his violin while Nikolai accompanied him at the piano, normally he never stopped grumbling and moralizing. Everyone in his little world trembled before him: for the slightest infraction—a bad mark at school, a clandestine escapade with other children— he applied to his children, as he did to his miserable little apprentices, those "means of improvement" that, according to him, were represented by the slap and the whip. "Like my brothers," Chekhov was to write, "I was forbidden all play and all amusement." Pavel was one of those fathers whose children must be taught from birth to "take life seriously."

Little Antosha had become so enured to this school of hard knocks that he could not even conceive of anything different. One day when a schoolmate said that he was never beaten at home, Anton called him a liar. But the blows and the wounds molded him permanently and made him a man incapable of abandoning himself to the impulses of his emotions. He himself, moreover, was to admit as much when at twenty-nine he wrote: "When I was a child, I was so rarely caressed that even now, as an adult, I react to caresses as something unheard of, unknown. . . . Our childhood was poisoned by terrible things."

It was virtually only when the father was absent that the family atmosphere could be relaxed. Then the children abandoned themselves to the forbidden games—lotto, pantomine, cards—and Anton, who had a natural and infectious gaiety, unchained himself and let himself go in all kinds of amusing jokes, mimicries, and preposterous farces. On such evenings he and his brothers enjoyed with their mother—who was in retreat when their father was present—that tenderness and that warmth of which normally they were deprived. Grouped round her, they loved nothing so much as to hear her tell "stories" and recollections of her youth. There were two stories that were requested again and again: the tale of her flight from Taganrog under the shells of the Anglo-French fleet when she was expecting Alexander, and that of a remarkable, endless childhood journey that had taken her and her mother across the whole of Russia.

The strange odyssey that Yevgenia Yakovlevna related was in fact something to make one dream. Still a small child, she was with her sister and mother in a little village in northern Russia, in the province of Vladimir, when they received word of her father's death during a business trip in the southern part of the empire, in the area of Novocherkask. It was known that he had been the victim of a cholera epidemic, but it was not known where he had been buried. So his widow decided forthwith to set out in search of his grave. She rented a carriage and, taking her two small daughters with her, she began to range in this primitive vehicle through the whole country.

The fantastic journey, which went on for weeks, was forever etched in Yevgenia Yakovlevna's memory, and she recalled it in such clear and vivid terms that her children listened spellbound. She told of going through forests to which there seemed to be no end, of meeting frightening wanderers on deserted trails, of stopping at inns with barricaded doors and closed shutters where one lived in constant terror of highway robbers. Then she described how she had discovered the south: the endless steppes, empty beneath the great naked sky, the broad rivers, the torrid, dusty days, the warm nights glowing with stars. The travelers slept in the fields, amid the scents of the wild, in total silence broken only by the sounds of flights of ducks and the noise of crickets.

"What about the grave?" the children would ask, even though they had long known the answer. "Did you find Grandfather's grave?"

"Never! We traveled all over Russia, from Marshansk to Taganrog. When we reached here, we found the sea, which prevented us from going any farther. My mother had friends in this town and they took us in. Little by little we grew used to it, and we stayed here. Then, one day, I met your father . . ."

Clustered round the oil lamp, the children never wearied of hearing it. Antosha, his imagination on fire, could visualize the endless forests, the tramps, the green and yellow surge of the steppe . . .

The rich Greek merchants dominated the city, so it was a Greek school to which Pavel Yegorovich, in his ingenuous social climbing, decided to send his children. When his wife timidly argued in favor of a Russian school, he replied curtly that he was thinking of his sons' futures: if they went to the Greek school, they would learn the language of business and easily find good jobs with one or another of the big local importers. Very soon they would be earning as much as a thousand rubles a month, and if they were intelligent, they would not stop there. On the other hand, where would they get with the Latin that they would learn in the Russian school? Besides, his friend Nicholas Vutchina—a regular customer in his store—who was a teacher in the Greek parochial school, had made it clear to him that this was what he must do and had promised to give his particular attention to the Chekhov boys. True, it would cost twenty-five rubles a year, but he had just had a large payment from one of his big customers. So the decision was made, and in 1867 Nikolai and Anton were enrolled in the Greek school.

It was indeed a strange school. It had only one room, broken-down and dirty, in which seventy little Greeks between the ages of six and twenty were huddled together. They shared five rows of desks, each row representing a "class"; a sixth row, in front, was set aside for beginners. Nicholas Vutchina himself was the entire pedagogical staff, imparting everything from the alphabet sing-songed in the front row to the rudiments of arithmetic, syntax, modern Greek, and history for the five "classes."

Nikolai, who was nine, and Antosha, who was only seven, were terrified, if their brother Alexander is to be believed, when they entered this strange room for the first time. And even later they never succeeded in acclimating themselves to this new environment, in growing accustomed to hearing only Greek spoken round them, and in accepting the fact that they were regarded as curious, badly trained animals by dubious youths who were much older. No more could the teacher, Vutchina—that heavy man with a fiery red beard who went from "class" to "class" distributing cuffs and blows with a ruler—restore their confidence. Furthermore, after he had given them a Greek alphabet book on their first day, he virtually never looked at them again.

But the weeks went by. Every day Nikolai and Anton went to school, and from nine in the morning until three in the afternoon they sat quietly, their arms crossed, on their "beginners'" bench. Neither Vutchina nor his new assistant, Spiro, seemed to take any interest in them. But they dared not complain to their father or let him know of the punishments that were inflicted on them: slaps with a ruler on the palm of the hand, the ribs, or the head, prolonged genuflections on coarse salt, or deprivation of lunch. Anyway, Pavel Yegorovich was convinced that everything happened for the best in the best of all possible schools. Did not Vutchina assure him that he was very satisfied with the boys? And they brought home excellent marks: Nikolai was described as "pious" and Anton as "studious."

It was only when the Christmas vacation arrived that the elder Chekhov learned the sad—and shattering—truth. One evening he invited some Greek friends; eager to show them what progress his sons had made, he ordered the boys to read aloud from Greek text. It was a catastrophe: neither the "pious" Nikolai nor the "studious" Antosha could spell out more than two or three words. Feeling that he had been made a laughingstock, Pavel Yegorovich flew into a violent rage. But he had paid the year's fee in full and so, after the vacation, his sons went back to the Greek school and completed their year, though without penetrating any farther into the secrets of Homer's language. Hence it was not until the next autumn that, as their mother had always wanted, they entered the Russian school.

Anton was now eight years old, chubby, pale, round-faced, with thick hair and large, rather dreamy brown eyes. Full of pride at having for the first time put on the regulation uniform—a blue cape with metal buttons, and a flat cap—he entered the doors of the Taganrog school for the first time on August 23, 1868. It was a big dirty-white barracks with an emerald-green zinc roof; long, filthy corridors were punctuated with classroom doors, each of which had a peephole, the better to permit supervision of the pupils. Institutions typical of Russian provincial life, these "gymnasia" were the foundation of the educational system of the time: the pupils spent eight years there, devoted mainly to the study of Latin, Greek, Church Slavonic, and Russian. On their graduation they acquired certain privileges; they could enter the lowest of the fourteen classes of officials established by the famous *Table of Ranks* of Peter the Great,[4] they were exempt from military service, and they were eligible for admission to the university.

Enrolled in this school at the age of eight, Anton Chekhov was to require eleven years to complete its course of studies, which he finished in June, 1879. He failed twice and had to repeat the third and fourth years. Moreover, he was never a brilliant student. Undoubtedly the long hours spent in the shop and the church had much to do with this, but it must also be said that he was hardly enthusiastic about his studies. Put off by monotonous teaching methods and mediocre instructors, he showed no sign of zeal and was satisfied to follow the routine. In contrast to other writers, who began by learning everything from books—and some of whom never went beyond books—Chekhov preferred direct attendance in the school of living.

It was with untiringly alert curiosity that Anton observed the

[4] Published in 1714, the *Table of Ranks* created a systematic hierarchy of all ranks in the army, the navy, and the civil government. It contained such surprising titles as "full general" and "incumbent privy councilor." Aside from a few simplifications, this structure remained intact until the Revolution of 1917. It also prescribed the honorary titles of the various ranks. A "full general" must be addressed as "High Excellency"; a state counciler was "High-Born"; but a lieutenant colonel should be addressed only as "High Nobility."

school world around him and with humor that he noted its characteristics. Instead of Greek and Slavonic, he learned a great deal about people. His teachers were either mediocrities or half-savages, like Kramsakov, the history and geography instructor, who never wearied of insulting his students; or else they were suspicious men who watched one another as closely as they did their pupils. Diakonov, the vice-principal, was constantly spying on his students; his habit of noiselessly appearing where he was least expected had earned him the nickname "The Centipede." The Latin teacher, a Czech named Urban, smelled political conspiracies everywhere and carried his buseness to the point of writing to the police: "My colleagues smoke during the meetings of the teachers' council. They are not interested whether the walls of the rooms in which they happen to be are adorned with an ikon and a portrait of His Majesty the Tsar."

Anton's reserve amazed both his teachers and his fellows. First at home and then in the Greek school he had learned to hold himself aloof, to make himself inconspicuous, and he continued to do so. He was—or at least he seemed to be—timid, withdrawn, fiercely secretive. He did not mingle with the little groups of his fellow students, who, rubbed raw by pitiless discipline and surveillance, were already playing revolutionary and clandestinely reading Bakunin, Pisarev, and Herzen. He was at the age for deep friendships, but he made none, and far from regarding them as real "masters," he kept his distance from his teachers, whose insignificance and pettiness he had quickly penetrated. The only one who would have a certain influence on him, when he reached the upper classes, was his teacher of religious history, F. P. Pokrovsky, who loved literature and talked to him of Shakespeare, Goethe, and Pushkin with an enthusiasm that was infectious. It was obviously these sorry mentors of his youth whom Chekhov was to address in The Man With the Case: "Are you pedagogues and teachers? No, you are miserable functionaries, and your temple of knowledge is a police station, which, furthermore, it smells like."

This quiet, highly independent, and even rather distant boy was capable, however, of making his whole class laugh when he wished. He had no equal in devising hoaxes, ridiculing a teacher or a student, telling funny stories. But though he much enjoyed making others laugh, here again it was as if he were withdrawn, and when he conceived the idea of some joke to be played, he left it to his fellows to carry it out.

Besides, the poor boy had little time in which to amuse himself. We know already that our "little galley slave" had to spend countless hours in church, in the store, and in rehearsals of the choral group directed by his father. But Pavel Yegorovich required still more: he had Anton taking French lessons from a lady named Chopet and music lessons from a bank clerk who was a melomaniac. And even this was not enough: believing that his sons should also have "a trade in their hands," he made them take courses at a vocational school; and so at the age of thirteen Antosha began to learn how to be a tailor. His brothers were soon expelled from this institution for "excessively rowdy behavior and excessively slow progress," but Anton demonstrated more application. When he thought that he had advanced far enough, he made a pair of trousers for his brother Nikolai that was supposed to be in the latest fashion. The legs were so narrow that Nikolai had terrible trouble getting into what the aspiring tailor himself called the "macaroni pants."

Later Chekhov was to write to his architect friend F. Shekhtel: "Taganrog is a very beautiful town. If I were as talented an architect as you, I would tear it down." At the age of fifteen, however, emerging from the insipid hours in the *gymnasium* or the tailoring course, he was fascinated by the spectacle of Taganrog's streets. For Anton this was the real school of life, full of motion, sunlit, and joyous. For he could be amused by a trifle and, in contrast to the severe and solemn policeman whom he passed, he saw everything: an idling dog, a funeral procession dragging along behind an open coffin, a quarrel among longshoremen or old women.

As often as possible he took the "European" main street so that he could watch the passage of "the aristocrats (the Greeks) on the left, the democrats on the right," and the elegant maidens, dressed in the fashion of Moscow or even of Paris, "with leg-of-mutton sleeves and figures, all dressed in olive green one season and in chocolate brown the next."

However dreary and provincial the little city, Anton and his brothers found places to play everywhere, even in the most unlikely spots. They went hunting for goldfinches in the empty lot near their house, and, excited by reading James Fenimore Cooper, they pursued "scalps" in Elizabeth Park. They had merely to follow Politzeiskaya Street to reach the harbor, where they watched the barge traffic, swam, or sat on the jetty and fished for hours. Anton, too, went for long walks in the cemeteries, which indeed he was to love all his life. Rather than the Greek necropolis, in which the black flames of cypresses alternated with the white columns of marble, he preferred the humble graveyards of the nearby villages, planted with cherry trees, where in summer the fruit fell on the graves "like drops of blood."

In order to improve their defenses against their father's despotism, the Chekhov children formed a kind of "clan" that was held together by a deep mutual affection and that had its own rites and secrets. It had as well its unrestrained laughter, for all the children shared a very keen sense of humor and they were skilled at parodying the absurdities of their intimates and teachers. Inside this clan Anton's reserve vanished: it was almost always he who was the leading spirit, the instigator of merry games, the inventor of magnificent jokes. Thus one day he decided to fool his good Uncle Mitrofanos: disguised as a beggar and followed at a distance by his brothers, he limped his way across the whole town and knocked on his uncle's door to ask for alms. Deceived—or playing along with the boy—his uncle gave him three kopecks.

All the children, for that matter, but especially Antosha deeply loved their Uncle Mitrofanos, who had done much better in the grocery world than his brother. He too was deeply religious—Alexander called him "the holy man"—but he also practiced the Christian virtues that he professed. He forbade physical punishments, he treated his wife and children decently, and he was very good to his nephews and his niece. So for them it was a holiday when he invited them to dinner.

The real holiday, however, the big holiday, which, when one was ten or twelve, seemed to have no end, began with the last days of June and the start of the summer vacation. Paternal discipline was somewhat eased, and then for long weeks there were swimming parties, fishing, little dinners in the garden. Barefooted, because the summers were often hot in Taganrog, Anton and his brothers roamed through the public parks and the vacant lots. Since the nights were too stuffy, they slept in huts that they had built for themselves under the trees in the garden. Antosha had erected his beneath an acacia, and in the bad verses that he scribbled in those days he described himself as "Job under his fig tree."

The climax of the vacation—as happened in 1872 and 1873—was the children's visit to their grandfather, Countess Platova's overseer, at Kniazhaya. This little village in the Donets steppe was seventy versts from Taganrog, and going there was very like an expedition. For the young Chekhovs it was an unforgettable adventure that lasted for days and enabled them to discover or rediscover all the enchantments of the steppe, "a fantastic country that I loved," Anton was to write later, "and in which in those days I felt at home, for I knew every nook of it" (1888).

The family rented a peasant telega, and the mother and the six children piled into this unsprung wagon, made of planks laid directly on the axles; they bade Pavel Yegorovich farewell—fortunately his business kept him in Taganrog—and *lay on the whip, izvoshchik, off on the great adventure!* Mikhail has left us a detailed account of one of these memorable junkets. The telega moved slowly across the limitless plain in a cloud of dust, the sun burned down, but in spite of the heat and the jolting, the children did nothing but laugh at the paper hat worn by Alexander and the stage opera hat that was Nikolai's pride. They stopped along the road, fetched the picnic food from the wicker basket, tumbled one another among the haystacks, and then set out again, stopping again farther on to swim in a pond or filch apples from an orchard. The nights were spent in Cossack inns or outdoors, beside a glowing fire. Drunk on dust, tiredness, and laughter, intoxicated with the scent of the steppe, the children fell asleep . . .

At Kniazhaya, Grandfather Yegor Mikhailovich—who had mellowed with the years—held holiday for them. Since he could not accommodate the entire family in his little peasant *izba,** he established some of them in his employer's house, a vast, empty, uninhabited structure with so many rooms that the children slept

* The typical Russian peasant hut, built of logs.—TRANSLATOR.

badly there. But during the day what mad runs they had in the huge park, what joyful swims in the pond! It was during one of these aquatic tourneys that Antosha managed to knock off Nikolai's opera hat, which filled with water and "drowned."

But Kniazhaya was not only fun and games. It was harvest time, and grandfather had no hesitation about exacting labor from his grandsons in the fields. Anton would long remember having had to interrupt his play for whole days to supervise a threshing machine and keep a written record, from morning to dusk, of the number of *poods*[5] of grain that it processed. Fifteen years later he was to write: "The machine's whistles and gasps and snorts, muted like those of a spinning top when the work was going hardest, the squeaking of the wagon wheels, the lazy motion of the cattle, the clouds of smoke, the sweating, blackened faces of some fifty men, all that is as firm in my memory as the 'Our Father' . . ." (August 29, 1888).

Thus steeped in the "works and days" of peasant life, the future author of "The Steppe," though he had as yet no idea that he was doing so, was storing up pell-mell his images, his scents, and his musics, everything that one day would finally, slowly be deposited "at the bottom of the filter" of his *Georgic*.

In the autumn of 1873 Anton had just returned from his vacation in Kniazhaya when he suddenly discovered a "game" for adults that was going to excite his enthusiasm far more than his childhood games: the theater. He had walked past the little municipal theater in Petrovskaya Street hundreds of times: this time he went in, saw a performance of *La Belle Hélène,* and was dazzled and enchanted—dazzled in spite of the wrinkles in the blue cloth "sky," enchanted in spite of the bad performances. He had just discovered a world—a world of mysteries, of rituals, of pretenses, of dichotomous life, ephemeral and eternal—and already he was enthralled, and for life, by its magic.

After that he went back to the theater as often as he could: thus he saw, in succession, *Hamlet,* Gogol's *The Inspector General,* an adaptation of *Uncle Tom's Cabin,* melodramas, and skits that imitated the French. But in Taganrog it was not proper for a school-

[5] A Russian measure, equivalent to slightly more than thirty-six pounds.

boy to frequent that hotbed of perdition (as his teachers viewed it), the theater: this required the express authorization of the headmaster and the promise to go only when accompanied by a parent. In order to penetrate, in spite of these bans, into the shrine of their dreams, Anton and his friends, who were as excited as he by the theater—the future actor, Vishnyevsky, and a boy of good family, Andrey Drossy—found an ingenious solution: becoming actors themselves, they resorted to disguises. For Anton the pleasure—with great poundings of the heart—began as soon as his make-up, supplemented by artificial sideburns and dark glasses, got him past the monitor sent by the school to flush out any students present in the audience. Anton was a good actor and the stool pigeon did not recognize him. He found a seat in the top gallery, sensing the intensification of his happiness as the house lights dimmed, the seats filled, the boxes were taken by pretty women . . .

Insinuating oneself in disguise among the crowd of spectators was fun, but how much more exciting still must it be to take the stage oneself! Anton was a born actor: he loved to make up and dress up, to imitate with some exaggeration the eccentricities and the idiosyncrasies of people whom he observed with his smiling but unpitying eyes. With the help of his brothers and his sister, Masha, he formed his own acting company. It was a well-disposed audience, composed of relatives, friends, and neighbors, that attended the première of the Chekhov children's theater, which consisted of repertory plays. Having seen *The Inspector General,* Anton staged it in his own fashion, and he did so with so much originality and humor that he scored an unquestioned success. He himself took the part of the fat mayor: his abdomen enlarged by three pillows, his chest ablaze with medals of cardboard, he threw the audience into gales of laughter. He was in ecstasy, for, like many lonely, sad children, this was what he loved more than anything else: making others laugh, making them laugh at what had made him suffer.

Anton was hardly going to stop once he had started on so good a road. Why not turn those imitations of teachers and town "characters" in which he indulged at school, and that sent his companions into guffaws, into sketches that he could add to his repertory?

So he put on mocking skits that caricatured the charlatan of a dentist, the headmaster of the school, some crotchety teacher, or even—though one may be certain that this sketch was reserved for Papa's absence—a doddering old priest. Anton always had his biggest success with a pantomime that made fun of the Mayor of Taganrog presiding, complete with uniform and saber, over a church ceremony and then taking the salute of the Cossack guards. Carried away by the laughter of his audience, spontaneously reinventing the *commedia dell'arte*, he added new variations to his pantomime with each performance.[6]

In the summer of 1875 the parents of his friend Andrey Drossy, who shared his love for the theater, staged various benefits for charity; by this time Anton's reputation was already so firmly established that he and his "company" were asked to take part. In a drawing room divided by a curtain he put on a scene with stage sets, wings, and dressing room. He played sketches of his own composition, inspired by the life of the little town and also, among other works, by Grigoryev's *The Coachman*. This play was so well received that Anton, who had taken the main part, was given several curtain calls. "It is impossible," Andrey Drossy was to write, "to imagine the Homeric laughter of the audience every time Anton Pavlovich came on the stage. And it must be said in all honesty that he played his part in masterly fashion."

Unfortunately, it was in this same year that the time of gaiety and games was to be abruptly interrupted and Chekhov's "company" was to be disbanded.

For Anton, in fact, this year of 1875 had begun badly. His marks at school had been so bad that he had had to repeat his fifth year. In addition, his health was impaired, and through his own doing. Invited to spend part of the summer at the country home of a schoolmate, Glivanov, he had had the wretched notion, as he crossed the steppe under a burning sun on his way there, of taking a swim in an icy river. After a night of horrible suffering in a tavern, he had been fetched back to Taganrog with peritonitis. His

---

[6] These first sketches by Chekhov were recorded in school notebooks, none of which has been found. It would appear that a few years later the author himself destroyed them.

life had been saved only through the devotion of the physician attached to the school, a Russian-German named Strempf. During Anton's convalescence the doctor talked enthusiastically to him about the profession of medicine, and it seems quite likely that as a result of these conversations Anton made up his mind to become a physician. But in order to do so, he must get down to serious work in a favorable atmosphere.

At this time the climate of the Chekhov household was that of revolution. The two eldest sons were in outright revolt against their father's despotism. A year earlier Alexander had left home to go to live with the headmaster of the school, where he paid his way by tutoring the children. Pavel Yegorovich had written to him, in a tone of wounded dignity: "I regret only that you have begun so soon to forget your father and mother, who are devoted to you with their whole hearts and have spared neither their efforts nor their health in order to educate you," but Alexander had proved insensible to such noble discourse. He had just finished his studies of the humanities with great distinction, and without seeking his father's counsel, he had decided to go to Moscow in order to take up the study of mathematics at the university. His brother Nikolai, even though he had not yet finished school, was determined to go with him, and since he felt that he had an artistic vocation, to enroll in the School of Fine Arts in the capital. They left Taganrog in August.

For poor Antosha, deprived henceforth of the brothers and accomplices whom he adored, abandoned by his "company," and alone now in his struggle against his father's tyranny, the shock must have been brutal. When school resumed, there was only Ivan to accompany him. He did not allow himself to be discouraged, however, and as much to maintain his school reputation as an entertainer as to keep up communication with his elder brothers, he began to put together a little satirical magazine in manuscript, for which he was at once editor-in-chief and copyist. Amusingly, he called it *The Stammerer*.

At the age at which other boys are pouring out the loves or the sorrows of over-sensitive hearts in bad rhymes, he, with his crafty eye and his mocking pen, was recording little "things observed" in the streets of Taganrog. His manuscript publication, when it had

been read by one schoolmate after another, was sent to his brothers in Moscow. But Alexander, alas, whose literary judgment Antosha highly esteemed, proved to be a harsh critic and, discussing
the September issue, he wrote brutally to his parents: "Tell the
publisher of *The Stammerer* that his sheet is not so interesting as
it was. It lacks salt."

Poor "publisher"! Should not Alexander, rather, have congratulated him on still having the courage to laugh? In the Chekhov
family, where the father's business was taking an increasingly dis-
astrous course, the atmosphere was one of pessimism. A year earlier, however, in 1875, the vainglorious Pavel Yegorovich had
thought he had reached his goal: being an independent, respected
merchant, a man of substance. On a plot given to him by his father he had had a house built that could serve as both residence
and shop. But he had aimed too high, and in order to complete the
building he had had to borrow five hundred rubles; now, a year
later, having continued to mismanage his business in the same
way, running out to attend to so-called important matters more
often than he stayed behind his counter, he could no longer pay
even the interest on this debt.

Between the father, who had lost his arrogance, and the sons,
who had acquired a certain assurance during their residence in
Moscow, a strange correspondence sprang up during that autumn,
a correspondence of deaf-mutes made up of intersecting lamenta-
tions and reproaches. Pavel Yegorovich wrote to Alexander: "Day
after day our affairs slide into worse peril. I am in the dumps; I
have lost all my nerve, and I don't know any more what your
mother and I are going to do. Oh, money, money!" This brought
Alexander's angry response that he and his brother too were having a great deal of difficulty in merely existing and that his parents
might long ago have thought of sending a coat to Nikolai, who
was walking about in rags. To which his father retorted either
with the inevitable "at your age, I . . ." or with counsels of piety.
"When the heart is heavy," Alexander answered in exasperation,
"and the mind is full of unhappy thoughts, one looks at least for a
bit of friendly comfort and a word of sympathy, instead of which
one is advised to go to church!"

It was a fact, however, that the paternal business was going from bad to worse. Pavel Yegorovich had his back to the wall and he was trying to scratch out survival in any way he could. He kept his younger sons at home for the whole of October in order not to have to pay their school fees, and then, to reduce the number of mouths to be fed, he sent Mikhail and Ivan to spend a few weeks with their grandfather. The family doubled up and the rooms thus made available were first rented to a widow and then turned over to a family friend, Selivanov. Since Selivanov had a niece, Alexandra, Anton was ordered to tutor her with her schoolwork—a few more rubles coming in. But nothing could save Pavel Yegorovich any more, and in the spring of 1876 the final disaster struck.

In April he filed as a bankrupt, but fearing imprisonment for his debts, as was then usual in Russia, he ran away, and in a rather shameful manner. Since he was afraid of being recognized if he took a train from Taganrog, he went to the station of a nearby village in order to embark for Moscow. The journey must have been filled with bitter thoughts: Taganrog was the city where he had dreamed of being "somebody" and here he was in flight from it like a thief after twenty years of wasted effort, abandoning wife and children. And how would he be received in Moscow by his eldest sons—he, the discredited "despot" who was nothing but a failure at the age of fifty?

Remaining in Taganrog with the children, Yevgenia Yakovlevna tried during the first weeks to keep up a front. But it was in vain that she sent word to the members of her family: none of them came to the rescue, and even good old Uncle Mitrofanos begged off: what with the state of his own affairs, he could do nothing for her. And then the Chekhovs' "friend" Selivanov stepped forward: since he worked for the court, he made a great show of settling the problem of Pavel Yegorovitch's debts. Unfortunately, it was to his own advantage that he settled them: he paid off the five hundred rubles and thus obtained a court order giving him title to the Chekhovs' house. The court decided in addition that in order to meet the arrears of interest, the family's furniture should be sold at public auction.

Homeless and stripped of everything she owned, Yevgenia resigned herself to going to Moscow to rejoin her husband. She took Mikhail and Masha with her. Ivan was turned over to his mother's sister, a Miss Morozova, and he was to stay in Taganrog for a few months before he too would go to Moscow. In their father's house, which was now Selivanov's, there was only Antosha. He was sixteen and a half, and while he had decided with a heavy heart not to go with his mother, it was because he was firmly resolved to complete the three years of study that he had still ahead of him in the local school, no matter what it would cost him.

For him, surely, there was now an end to the "lies and the despotism." But he was going to have to serve his harsh apprenticeship to freedom and truth in a sharp and total loneliness.

II

ALONE IN TAGANROG

One thing (in your letter) displeases me: why do you call yourself the mediocre, insignificant little brother? Do you admit your
mediocrity? . . . Do you know the only place where one should
acknowledge one's personal insignificance? Before God, of course,
and before the mind, beauty, nature, but never before men. Before men one must be aware of one's own dignity. . . .
CHEKHOV in a letter
to his brother MIKHAIL, April 8, 1879

Left alone in Taganrog, Anton went on living in the house in Elisavetinskaya Street that had been his father's. But now he was
only a despised tenant. Selivanov, cynical and triumphant now
that he was the master of the house, had made him a proposition:
Anton could have room and board—not a room, really, but a bed,
a "corner," as the Russians called it—and in exchange he would
tutor Selivanov's nephew, Petya Kravstov, who had also come to
live with his uncle and prepare to take the examination for admission to the military school, the "Junkers' school." Wounded in his
pride but already clear-thinking and eager to complete his studies,
Antosha had accepted.

But what about school fees and clothes? In order to pay for
these he became a tutor, and he remained one for three years. For
the sake of a few rubles a month he had to run through the city
from one section to another, often going to quite distant suburbs,
always on foot, through mud or blizzards. He had no boots, and as

he gave his lessons he hid his mud-covered shoes under the table as well as he could. What was harder still was to have to listen without visible reaction to the ill-tempered scenes made by his pupils and the humiliating rebukes of their parents, to feel that it was charity that made them offer him a glass of sugared tea.

Chekhov was later to acknowledge that his poverty in those days hurt him "like a perpetual toothache." But at sixteen he was too proud to complain to anyone, even to his family. This rigorous apprenticeship, however, did not make him hard; on the contrary, he always had sympathy for those who were poorer than he. Thus, having learned that one of his schoolmates, a young Jew named Isaac B. Strulev, was in difficulties, Chekhov suggested that they work together: they would divide the lessons to be given to a pupil who lived far from the center of town and they would also divide the monthly three rubles. And when he spent the Easter vacation of 1877 with his parents in Moscow and saw in what deprivation they were living, he did not hesitate to help them out.

With his schoolmates and in his correspondence with his family he continued to be the adolescent full of humor and imagination that he indeed was, but that did not prevent him from taking life very seriously now. In school he worked with greater effort, and his marks had never been so high. He still found time for reading, much and very selectively. He spent Sundays and holidays in the municipal library that had just been opened, and there he discovered one after another, with so much excitement that sometimes he forgot to have lunch, the great Russian authors, and Victor Hugo, and Cervantes. Schopenhauer's pessimistic thinking impressed him and remained with him: for he knew too much about the world and its inhabitants not to find himself in frequent agreement with the philosopher and to be tempted to embrace his doctrine of renunciation of life and action. But since Chekhov would rather smile than weep, he also made it a point in his weekly visits to the reading room to go through the humorous magazines of Moscow and Petersburg—*Grasshopper* and *Alarm Clock*. He also continued to write *The Stammerer* and send it to his brothers.

An amazing boy! It would have been completely understandable if, left to his fate by his parents as he was, he had revolted and broken with them. But what occurred was the opposite. He wrote to them frequently and, far from being the one to reproach them, it was he who felt sorry for them and comforted them. During these first few weeks he also carried out as well as he could the task with which his mother had entrusted him: the sale of the few things left to her after the auction that she had abandoned in her departure—a chest of drawers, a few benches, some pots—and the dispatch of the proceeds to Moscow.

His mother's letters to him were full of complaints; they were artless notes, written as she spoke, full of errors and devoid of all punctuation. "We have had two letters from you, full of witticisms and puns," she reproached him, "and here at that time we had only four kopecks to buy bread and candles."

Was his poor *Mamushka* really unaware that this joking manner of her son's was the finest kind of courage and perhaps of precocious wisdom? To his parents' letters, which were nothing but inventories of miseries and discouragements, then, he continued to reply with comforting notes full of amusing little tales about their old friends in Taganrog. Alexander wrote: "Things are going very badly with us. . . . We have eaten up all our money. . . . No news, still the same old thing. There's nothing left to pawn." And Anton answered with the latest manuscript issue of *The Stammerer*.

He never complained. How alone, though, he must have felt, and how lost in that town his family had left! Very rarely he saw Uncle Mitrofanos, "that good soul"; his school friend Andrey Drossy often went with him to the town library, trudged through the streets with him, and invited him home, but that was not what could gratify his desire to be surrounded and loved. He was sixteen; he was at the age at which one needs to talk about oneself to someone for hours, to confide one's dreams and one's disillusionments—the age of friendship. So, deprived of his dear *Brüder*, who had been his intimates until then, he enthusiastically embraced the friendship offered by Mikhail Chekhov, a first cousin who was ten years older, whom he had never seen, and who lived in Moscow. Anton guilelessly wrote to him that he "would clasp with pride" the proffered fraternal hand, adding innocently: "One of my first ideas and one of my plans was this friendship" (December 7, 1876). In spite of the difference in age, a correspondence developed between the cousins that, though rather stilted in the beginning, soon became open, confiding, and friendly.

Anton's letters were charming, ironic, amusing. Now that he had a new "*Bruder* once removed," he felt like a man who had everything—everything "except money and common sense." But he did have common sense, indeed to a remarkable degree for a boy of his age. It is true, however, that with his cousin he relaxed somewhat. He asked him for a photograph and solemnly put foolish questions to him: "Write and let me know whether you smoke or don't smoke. I very much need to know." And he was eventually to acknowledge to Mikhail that he was bored to death in Taganrog, and he would announce too that he was an "advocate of polygamy" (November 4, 1877).

Through his mother's plaintive letters and Alexander's violent ones Anton was kept informed of developments in the lives of his relatives in Moscow. They had quickly sunk to the depths of misery there and, abetted by fatalism, they were not making any great efforts to climb out. Living in a furnished room, they had only one mattress—rather large, it was true—and, laid directly on the floor, it served as the bed for the whole family: when night came, the father, the mother, and the children slept in a huddle on it, crowded further by Aunt Fedosya Yakovlevna, who had gone to Moscow to be with them, and little Misha's dog. Rising before dawn and wearing a man's old overcoat, the mother chopped wood for the stove and hauled heavy buckets of water, while little Marya, who was barely eleven, swept, cooked, and washed everyone's clothes. The poor child did not go to school because it cost twenty-five rubles; she spent long hours knitting woolen shawls for which she was paid fifteen or twenty kopecks each.

Yevgenia Yakovlevna never stopped complaining, and God knew she had reason enough. Her only resources were what she received from her two eldest sons, who, though very grudgingly, shared with their parents the little money they earned by giving a few lessons, transcribing lecture notes, and scribbling or drawing for little illustrated papers. Alexander, furthermore, had other, private concerns: he had seduced a married woman, who had done him the disservice of leaving her husband, and so he had to provide for her needs and her child's. As for Nikolai, he was more diligent in the bars than in the Institute of Fine Arts.

Pavel Yegorovich had rapidly become himself again: as if nothing had happened, he was once more the despot, the holy man, the proper burgher. He made a show of looking for work. "Every day, every day we go to church," Alexander wrote of him in a fury, "and, like the former merchant we are, we go to the Stock Exchange, where we listen to discussions of the war in Serbia, and then, as usual, we come back home without having found a thing." Returned to the house, Pavel Yegorovich consoled himself for his rebuffs by reading aloud, for the instruction of his family, the sermons that his friend the beadle had sold him for a few kopecks. Everyone pretended to be listening, and if by chance Nikolai yelled at his little brother Misha, who was acting as his model, to sit still, their father would scold: "Speak more softly, heathens!"

Could he have been unconscious of the fact that he had lost face in front of his children or was he, on the other hand, trying to take his revenge on them for his failures? The fact remains that, far from relinquishing the paternal power "that comes from God," he grew more rigid than ever. Beneath the holy ikons he had posted a code of regulations for the household, very carefully written out and drafted for the edification of his children. This "regulation," intended for Nikolai, Ivan, and Masha, specified the hours at which they were to rise and retire and the manner in which they were to employ their leisure: the youngest were instructed to attend church at seven o'clock every morning; on holidays they must also go to Mass at six-thirty and again at nine. At the bottom of the paternal ukase there was one sentence: "Derelictions in these duties will be punished on the first offense by a severe reprimand and on subsequent offenses by correction during which it is forbidden to weep." The document was signed: "The head of the family, Pavel Chekhov." The code was rigorously enforced, moreover, and sometimes Ivan was so savagely beaten for his infringements of it that his cries brought the neighbors to protest.

It was only in religion, however, that the father set the ideal example. He abandoned himself to laziness and no longer even tried to find work. By way of self-justification he quoted the Gospel with relish: "Behold the fowls of the air: for they sow not, neither do they reap, nor gather into barns; yet your Heavenly Father feedeth them." As for himself, however, it was always his earthly sons on whom he relied for his food. "Papa and Mama have to eat," [1] he would frequently repeat solemnly, stroking his great beard, which was now all gray.

Papa had also to drink, for the holy man had become a drinker. There was no money to buy shoes for little Misha, but it could be found for Crimean wine or vodka. There were evenings when the table was loaded with "an incalculable number of bottles," and in the company of relatives and little shopkeepers from the neighborhood, good solid drinking was undertaken. These were curious bouts, in which the drinkers formed a chorus to intone the chants of the Church "that pleased the ear and touched the soul." Everyone got drunk, everyone forgot his sufferings, and indeed, in the midst of the "philosophizing" in the Russian manner, everyone found excuses for his drinking. As Alexander, himself a journeyman drinker, wrote to Anton: "When one drinks, one dies, and when one does not drink, one dies also. So it's better to drink" (April 23, 1877).

Anton, who went to Moscow to spend his Easter vacation in 1877, must have had a terrible shock, in spite of all the letters, when he saw the state of wretchedness and abandon in which his family was living. Alexander had paid for his railway ticket, and he had traveled more than seven hundred miles to learn that his family was mired in an existence in comparison to which its "little life" in Taganrog had been paradise. The entire family was living in one room, sleeping on the floor, doing without the most rudimentary amenities; Nikolai was occasionally compelled to steal wood in order to keep the fire going. Hence, though Anton's parents, brothers, and sister made a celebration for him, he found it difficult to conceal his deep grief from them. More than anything else it was the condition of his mother, whom he loved very much

---

[1] Chekhov, who was to bear the burden of supporting this family as long as he lived, would often repeat this sentence in a bitter-kindly tone. It occurred again in his letters in 1897.

and found "half dead from suffering," that cut him. No, Alexander had not lied to him when he wrote: "Mother, like a candle, is growing a little smaller every day."

His horrible disappointment, however, was partly dissipated by the discovery of Moscow. His younger brother, Mikhail, had been disillusioned with the big city, and in his nostalgia for Taganrog, he often went to the Kursk station to meet travelers who came from there and to talk with them. But Anton was immediately fascinated by the capital, which "stunned" him with the noise and the activity of its streets. He wanted to see everything: he stopped in front of the luxury shops, he admired the picturesque rags of the cab drivers as much as the splendid uniforms of the Guard officers, he followed the splendid carriages with his eyes. Guided by Misha, he discovered the heart of the city, the crenelated red walls of the Kremlin, the patinaed onion towers and the golden crosses of the churches, the remarkable blue and green mosaic of the Cathedral of St. Vassily, the neo-Greek façade of the Bolshoi Theater, and the little streets running down to the Moskva River.

He experienced a great joy in Moscow: at last he met his dear cousin Mikhail Mikhailovich. Far from disappointing him, Mikhail delighted him: not only was he a brilliant young man who already held an important post with one of the city's important merchants, I. E. Gavrilov, but he also lavished great attentions on Anton's parents. The little provincial was extremely flattered when his cousin invited him to meet friends and to go to the theater. Anton had hardly returned to Taganrog when he wrote to thank Mikhail for everything, adding: "I rejoice with all my heart that we parted intimate friends and brothers . . ." (May 10, 1877).

Back in his country province, Anton felt that now that he had explored the great city, "his head was turned." Oh, how mean Taganrog was, how boring life was in that isolated backwater! "I went to the theater in Taganrog recently," he wrote to his cousin, "and compared it with the theater in Moscow. What a vast difference! And what a difference too between Moscow and Taganrog!" Oh, just let him finish his schooling quickly and he would fly like an arrow to Moscow. Unfortunately, there was no question of another flight to the capital for a long time: "The Finance Ministry," he mocked, "will explain the reasons to you."

Happily, the summer vacation was not far off. After he had almost "lost his mind" because of his examinations, Anton passed them quite creditably, thus assuring his promotion to the "seventh" class. Now he was more alone than ever in Taganrog, because his brother Ivan had just left for Moscow. But since he was an ingenious and pleasant companion, Anton was invited to the country by friends. He spent some time with his landlord's brother, a rich landowner who took him along on business journeys across the steppe. But he enjoyed himself particularly in the home of his pupil Petya Kravtsov, whose parents had a farm in the Don steppe.

Life among these Kazakh squires was again rather primitive and very rustic, and this enchanted the young city boy. He rediscovered what had so much delighted him in the past during his visits to his grandfather: the vast plains merging into the horizon, the wild rivers, the scent of the warm grass at midday, and at night the incomparable silence beneath the swarms of stars. In addition, Petya, who was almost his own age, initiated him into the pleasures of Cossack life. Anton learned to use a gun, to ride, to course the plain in quest of game, to beware of the half-wild dogs. He watched how the Cossacks tamed the horses they captured, and it amused him to note that when his hosts wanted to cook a chicken, they slaughtered it by gunfire.

Left to himself, but also developing in a freedom that he had never known before, the adolescent had quickly become an adult. What was astonishing was the fact that having had to earn a livelihood so early, to take his first steps alone in the world of men and women, while it had precociously matured him, had in no way turned him toward bitterness or revolt. He knew already that man was weak (his father) and greedy (his landlord, Selivanov) and that he found it easy to slip into aimless existence (his elder brothers); but Anton had not drawn from this knowledge the conclusion that he must do likewise and that only selfishness could claim a reward. Quite to the contrary, he was firmly resolved to keep his distance and at the same time to be generous and to smile no matter what happened to him.

His age was that of intransigence, but he gave evidence of a rare indulgence. Instead of being angry at his parents, he felt pity for them and even loved them more perhaps than when he had lived in their house. And it was not the result of the enchantment of distance, for it was particularly after he had seen them again in Moscow, miserable, degraded—and, for him who had so keen a sense of humor, grotesque—that he showed tenderness toward them. He often sent them something out of his meager tutoring wages. He even pampered them at times, sending them parcels of coffee, olives, and *khalva*.[2]

What Anton felt toward his mother was much more than indulgence: it was a profound tenderness. When he left Moscow, he had charged his cousin with taking his place beside her, consoling her, helping her, and he reminded Mikhail of this in his letters. "I beg you," he wrote, "to continue consoling my mother, who is physically and spiritually shattered. . . . Mother's character is so constituted that a moral support coming from someone else has a beneficial influence on her. This is a rather stupid request, isn't it?" But his cousin would understand, because for him, Anton, "in this world full of unhappiness, there exists nothing dearer than his mother." He also asked Mikhail to make quite certain that his mother had received the money that Anton had frequently sent her and to be sure to put certain letters secretly into her hands, because, he explained, "there are things in life that one can tell only to someone reliable" (May 10, 1877).

He had good companions in school, notably the studious Andrey Drossy and the fat and jolly Vassily Zembulatov, nicknamed Makar, but he had no real friends. Even if he was often the life of his class, his jokes and laughter were, as in the past, really only the mask that covered a certain withdrawal, a "complete indifference," as one of his fellow students, Samkovich, was to put it, adding: "He kept aloof."

It was only his cousin Mikhail who received his affection and certain confidences—"I like all kinds of Russian celebrations, with dancing and drinking"—as well as his dreams of the future.

[2] An Oriental candy made of nuts, sugar, and oil.

"I will make a fortune," Anton wrote to him, "and that I shall do this is as certain as that two and two make four (and also that I shall reach the top). Then I will feed you on cakes and honey exclusively and regale you with the best wine to thank you for the brotherly affection with which today you repay my esteem and my attachment to you. In many respects you are a remarkable person, and I say this without flattery, in a fraternal spirit" (June 9, 1877.)

On the subject of women, even with his dear *Bruder*, Anton exercised an extraordinary discretion. While he did mention the "maidens of Taganrog" whom he met during his walks in the elegant part of town, he did so only to make fun of them: they were so limited, so affected, their speech was "vulgar and their thoughts worse." Later, in an ironic tone, he was to write in a short biographical note: "I was initiated into the secrets of love at the age of thirteen," but is this to be seen as anything other than a joke or the admission of a fugitive experience of youth? Girls liked him, however, for he was a good-looking boy and, besides, he was now attracted to them. If, for instance, he always enjoyed visiting the Drossys, it was also because he hoped to encounter his friend's sister, young Marina. He and Marina went for walks in the public park, and by plying her with delicacies, he won the right to enter her room. And too, even when there was a storm, he would wait for her at the gate of her school so that he could have the pleasure of walking home with her. One day, too, he was to confide to his brother Mikhail that during these last two years in Taganrog he had a number of "gay and happy" love affairs.

If the confidences that he gave his friend Suvorin much later are to be believed, it was during his vacations in the steppe that he discovered one day what love could be—in fact, love at first sight. He was sitting by himself, near a well, when he saw a little fifteen-year-old peasant girl approaching to fetch water. She was so extremely beautiful that he was at once enchanted with her; he took her in his arms and began to kiss her. The girl put up so little resistance that she completely forgot her water bucket, and for a long time they remained in close silent embrace beside the well, looking down at their reflections within it. "He did not want to leave, and she had forgot that she had gone there for water. . . ."

In reality, his sudden solitude and the prematurely encountered contradictions of life had already shown Chekhov himself.
He was a man without great passions or seething revolts, a spectator of life rather than an actor in it. At eighteen he was amazingly
wise, with a precocious wisdom compounded of skepticism and
irony mixed with tenderness, and he had an unalterable will, the
determination to rise at any cost from the wretched level into
which his father's incompetence had thrown him. Perhaps he did
not have overmuch respect or admiration for the adult world, but
he was resolved, all the more, to earn self-respect. As he wrote to
his brother Mikhail: "Before men one must be aware of one's own
dignity" (April 8, 1879).

With the months and the years that passed in that Taganrog in
which, since he had known Moscow, he felt like an exile, Chekhov
drew closer to the goal that he had set for himself. When his com-
rades asked him what career he was going to adopt, he told them
very gravely that he was going to be a priest. In actuality, as he
had confided to his cousin, he was indeed determined to "reach
the top," but without traveling by way of either the "black" of the
Church or the "red" of politics, or even the gold of trade, of whose
horrors he had seen only too much. His aim was clear and relatively easily attainable: a career in medicine.

He discussed this career with the school physician, Dr. Strempf,
who had saved his life when he had peritonitis in 1875 and who
advised him to go to Switzerland or Germany to study. His
mother too was urging him to become a physician. "Since you
have some respect for me," she wrote to him in February, 1879,
"try to get into the Medical Institute; that is the best profession.
. . ." Besides, Anton had already decided on it. Was this, as
some have said, for humanitarian reasons, a desire to ease the
sufferings of others? It would seem not, because he never gave any
such indication either to his mother or to his cousin Mikhail,
whereas he made no secret to either of them of the fact that he
was hoping above all for a certain material security and the respect attached to this profession.

It is certain, too, that at that time he had not yet thought or even dreamed of a literary career. And yet there was already in him a need to write, and he was writing. In 1877 his school paper published one of his short tales, "Life in the Seminary," and he sent his brother Alexander "little nothings" that he asked him to appraise and, if his judgment was favorable, to pass on to this or that humorous periodical where he had friends. Alexander kept two little stories, which he sent to *Alarm Clock*, in which it seems probable that they were never published. "The others are weak," Alexander wrote to his brother. "Make them shorter and more biting."

A year later Anton began to write as well for the theater, which fascinated him the more now because, thanks to a school comrade, he had occasional access backstage and was meeting actors. Then he wrote a sketch and sent it to Alexander: *Why the Hen Cackles;* it was followed by a comedy, *Tit for Tat,* and a gloomy drama, *The Orphan Girl,* with horse thieves, attacks on trains, and abductions of young girls. His brother considered the drama very bad— "unforgivable"; as for the comedy, he read it to friends, including a playwright, and their reactions were encouraging. "The style is excellent," they said; "it's intelligent; but it lacks acuteness of observation and the feeling of experience. With time, *qui sait,* a good writer will come out of this."

Otherwise there was no special variety to life in the "hollow city." There were always the same walks in the empty streets smelling of horse dung, dust, and roses in summer and of rain and wood fires in winter. In the summer Anton and his friends often went to a place called The Quarantine—in memory of an epidemic of plague—four versts outside the city, on the seashore. "Arriving," he wrote, "one sees the blue sea to the left and the endless, cheerless steppe to the right." He was also reading a great deal and his taste was taking shape. *Uncle Tom's Cabin* had pleased him on first reading, but now Mrs. Stowe's book gave him the feeling of "having eaten more dry grapes than was wise" and he advised his brothers instead to read good authors: Cervantes and Turgenev. The only events in his life were the letters that arrived from Moscow—thanks to Cousin Mikhail, Pavel Yegorovich had got a job with Gavrilov and was earning thirty rubles a month; Nikolai was getting drunk more and more frequently—or the death of a relative or an acquaintance: in March, 1879, Grandfather Chekhov died of heart disease.

Later that spring Anton had the pleasure of facing the last of his examinations, after which he would graduate. He passed creditably, with high marks in religion, Russian, logic, geography, and German, doing less well in Greek, Latin, and mathematics. He was given a handsome diploma bearing the Imperial eagle: conduct, excellent; punctuality, very good; effort, very good; interest, very good. But with that practical sense he already possessed, and in spite of his eagerness, there were still two matters he wished to settle before leaving Taganrog. One was to obtain a municipal scholarship—twenty-five rubles a month—which required long-drawn-out negotiations; the other was to persuade two of his schoolmates, the good fat Makar and D. T. Savelyev, who were "going up" to Moscow with him, to board with his mother, who would feed them "divinely well."

He left Taganrog without regret and indeed with that elated excitement young men feel when it is time to turn a first important page in their lives. His farewell to the house on Elisavetinskaya Street was to be put later into the mouth of little Anya when she left her cherry orchard: "Good-bye, house. Good-bye, past." Moscow, the great city, was pulling him, and he promised himself that he would enjoy life there, but that wisdom—excessive for his age —that he had learned from circumstances prevented him from having too many illusions. Yes, he was happy to leave his vulgar, cramped provincial town, but at least he had been free and independent there, whereas in Moscow he would be going back to his family, misery, and his father . . .

Finally, with his first stipend of twenty-five rubles in his pocket and his two friends beside him, he left Taganrog on August 6, 1879. He was carrying the passport that was mandatory for every Russian who was changing his residence: "Age: nineteen; height: two *arshini*, nine *vershoki*;[3] hair and eyebrows: light chestnut; eyes: brown; nose, mouth, chin: regular; shape of face: long and pale; distinguishing marks: scar on forehead." Undoubtedly he

---

[3] One *arshin* = twenty-eight inches and one *vershok* = one and three-quarters inches; Chekhov was thus just short of six feet tall.

was thinking of what his mother had written a few months earlier: "Hurry and finish your schooling in Taganrog and, I beg you, come to us quickly. I am waiting impatiently for you. . . . I can't keep myself from thinking that everything will be better for me when you are here."

III

A STUDENT IN MOSCOW

What writers of the nobility acquire "gratuitously," by right of
birth, commoners buy at the price of their youth. . . . Try, then,
to write the story of a young man, a serf's son, a former shop clerk,
church chorister, schoolboy, university student, trained to bow his
head and kiss priests' hands, subjugated to the ideas of others.
. . . Tell how this young man tries to rid himself, drop by drop,
of the slave that is within him and how, awakening one fine morning, he becomes aware that it is no longer *slave's blood* that runs
through his veins, but a real man's blood.
CHEKHOV in a letter to
A. SUVORIN, January 7, 1889

Chekhov arrived in Moscow on August 8, 1879. After so many
years of separation his little brother Misha asked who he was, and
even his mother found it difficult to recognize her Antosha. The
chubby little boy whom she had left behind in Taganrog in 1876
had been transformed into a man who imposed his presence by his
height, his bass voice, and his confident manner. True, his tight
jacket and his absurd little round hat still betrayed the provincial
—who, however, thought that he was declaring his independence
by wearing his hair too long—and his long, very pale face, broken
by a small mustache, was certainly that of a Russian peasant. But
this gentle face of a young Christ with its deep soft brown eyes
masked a strange resolution, the energy and the ambition of a
Rastignac. And Anton made no secret of it. Had he not written to

his cousin: "I will make a fortune . . . that is as certain as that two and two make four"?

Anyone else, however, would have been cast down by what he found when he arrived in Moscow. The family he had been so eager to rejoin was living in an unbelievable state of misery and abandon. Having changed residences a dozen times in three years, it had finally sunk to the brothel quarter and was living in a filthy four-room apartment, half ground floor, half basement, beneath the Church of St. Nikolai. It was exceedingly dark, and through the transom windows one could see only the feet of the people on the sidewalks; the penetrating odor of its dampness was mingled with that of laundry that never dried.

The eldest sons, Alexander and Nikolai, had left this wretched hole in order to live by themselves, but not for a moment did it occur to Anton to follow their example. Whipped at the age of five, abandoned by everyone, this strange youth had a sense of family, and in contrast to his brothers he was firmly resolved to repair his family's state. The most urgent task was to find the means to live decently; later would be time enough to see to the eradication of the apathy and to the revival of a sense of dignity and duty in the whole family. Since neither his father, who worked some distance away and came home only once a week, nor his elder brothers seemed to wish to assume the function of the head of the family, then it would have to be he, Anton, who would take it on. At the same time as he was completing his own education, he would see to his family's.

The gentle dreamer could be extremely realistic. He explained to his mother that in order to have the money the household required, boarders would be taken in: the two schoolmates who had come with him from Taganrog and a third student, whom he soon found: each of them would pay twenty rubles, to which he would add the twenty-five of his stipend, and thus the family would be able to survive. But it was important also to get out of this sordid hole as quickly as possible: a month later that was an accomplished fact, and the amazing Antosha had installed his family in a building in the same questionable street, but on the third floor.

There was also the problem of re-educating this family to a certain discipline, a certain code. "Who knows," Mikhail was to write, "what would have happened to our family if Anton had not come from Taganrog when he did?" Anton did not attack these problems as his father did, and he was most careful not to post written moral codes on the door of the new apartment. He preferred to preach by example, and far from being a sermonizer, he began with open discussion. For instance, since he wanted each member of the family to make some contribution to the household chores, he announced that he himself would do the housework on a given day of the week, so the next day it would be Ivan's turn. Little Misha, to whom no one had paid any attention for months, could not get over this; here was his rediscovered brother giving him counsels that he had never heard: he should not tell lies and his appearance should always be neat and clean. But Anton said these things kindly, and soon the entire household—with the exception of the father—had meekly accepted the authority of the boy, whom Alexander jokingly called "Father Antosha." Whenever a decision had to be made, there was always the same question: "What does Anton say?" or "What does Anton think?"

Little by little order was restored. Yevgenia Yakovlevna stopped complaining; Masha and Misha, who had long ago stopped going to school because of the lack of money to pay for their tuition, resumed their studies. Ivan, the least well endowed of the children, a quiet, rather heavy, stubborn boy, continued studying to be a teacher and also began bringing in a few rubles by carrying spears in theatrical productions. Nikolai, who had returned to the bosom of the family, was selling caricatures to satiric publications. Misha was also earning a little money by copying university lecture notes; later he was to say: "It was a touching union of all the members of the family round a center, Anton."

A few days after his arrival in Moscow, Anton enrolled in the School of Medicine and began to attend its courses regularly, for he had made up his mind to obtain his diploma as quickly as possible. He was disappointed, however, both by the university itself, which he had pictured as a majestic "temple of learning" and which was only a motley collection of gloomy buildings, and by its teaching methods. "We repeat by rote," he was soon to write, "like schoolchildren, only to forget everything afterward as fast as we can."

But the discovery of the sciences and their disciplines was to fascinate him and to make a deep impression on him, and in spite of his disillusioned skepticism, he was to retain a great respect for science as long as he lived, as well as a certain faith in "the future of science," of science that would benefit mankind.

His companions in the university consoled themselves for the monotony and the routine of their lives by devoting themselves to political and social problems, all the more because under the tsarist system these represented forbidden fruit. They talked endlessly in their clubs and cafés, reforming the Slavic world, trying to develop conspiracies, catching fire from reading Dostoevsky and Gogol, playing their traditional part as the shock troops of opposition. But Chekhov took no part in these aspects of university life. As he had done before in the academy in Taganrog, he held himself aloof, and though he was always polite and ready to be of help, he had nothing to do with the activities of the others, of whom, for that matter, he saw very little, with the exception of the three friends who were living in his house. He had enrolled in the university in order to become a physician, not a revolutionary.

He remained remote and alone, apparently indifferent to the pleasures and passions of the other students. "He had nothing to do with the clubs of the 1880s," his friend Naradin was to write; "he did not plunge into feverish reading of Lavrov, Mikhailovsky, and Bakunin, he took no part in the discussions of the terrorist activities in Russia. He was closed in, withdrawn." His individualism, too, was already making itself manifest: he did not like the herd instinct, the student propensity for the cheek-by-jowl. He was perfectly willing to pay the price, which was his youth, but what it was most important to him to buy with it was the riddance of his "slave's blood" as quickly as possible.

No more was it a need to "express himself" that made him start to write and seek publication: he simply wanted to earn money. As we have seen, he had sent some of his work to Alexander in 1878, asking him to try to sell it to a humor magazine. When he went to Moscow, he learned that Alexander had been able to sell some of his own work to the illustrated papers and that Nikolai was selling cartoons, and this gave him hope. Since he wrote with great ease—almost mechanically, he was to say later—he soon had several stories ready, and he began to make the rounds of all the humor publications in Moscow and, by mail, in Petersburg.

He encountered a few rejections and some harsh criticisms: "Too long! Lifeless!" In March, 1880, however, his first story, "Letter from a Don Landowner to His Scholarly Neighbor," appeared in *Grasshopper*. Thus, under a pseudonym, which was merely the letter V preceded by a few dots, Chekhov made his entrance into literature by a side door, with amusing notes written on the run. He was not yet twenty.

The publication of this first story and the first "honorarium" that he collected were the joy of the Chekhov family. Anton used this first money earned by his pen to make a proper party for his mother's birthday: he bought her a tremendous cake.

Spurred by this first success, Anton was thereafter to devote much of his free time to writing. Embarking on a real journalistic career, he accepted all assignments and adapted himself to the public tastes, of which the editors of his publications forcefully reminded him. He signed his work with various pseudonyms: The Man Without Spleen, My Brother's Brother, Ulysses, Hot Iron, and, chiefly, Antosha Chekontey, a pen name he was to employ until 1885. He was remarkably prolific: in 1880 he published 9 stories, in 1881, 13, and in 1885, 129 stories, articles, and news reports.

He wanted money, and he got it. He began by earning a few rubles a month, then twenty, then fifty, and finally seventy-five. But how hard it was sometimes to collect what was due to him from the fly-by-night little rags that hired him! Sent to an editorial office by his brother, little Misha would be told: "Three rubles? Where do you think I'm going to get them? Won't you take a theater ticket? Or don't you need new trousers? You can go to my tailor and order them." On other occasions Anton himself and a group of his friends would descend on an editor, cold-bloodedly prepared to lay siege. One day, after a two-hour wait, they lost patience and began to bash their fists against the walls. Finally, they were admitted—only to learn that the editor had run out by way of the kitchen in order to avoid them.

There was, however, an interval of suspension in Chekhov's career in journalism. At the end of 1880 *Grasshopper*, which had previously published nine of his contributions, refused two of his manuscripts in succession and the outraged young author refused to do anything more for it. He turned then to the theater and spent the winter enthusiastically writing an interminable play— *Platonov*—that he did not hesitate to send to the famous actress M. Ermolova, who was with the Malyi Theater and who naturally turned it down. Chekhov filed the manuscript with his others and never looked at it again;[1] but he was not at all discouraged and went back to writing for the press. This time it was two satiric weeklies, *Alarm Clock* and *The Spectator,* that agreed to buy his prose at six kopecks a line.

He wrote with disconcerting facility and adapted himself to all forms, enjoying himself and "gamboling like a young calf." Short-story writer and chronicler, he also attempted the serial novel and the detective story. In 1882, as the result of a bet with a colleague, he gave *Alarm Clock* a serial novel "in the manner of" the Hungarian writer Jókai Mór,* who was well known at that time, and the imitation was so effective that it deceived the readers. Two years later he published another serial, *A Drama of the Chase,* in *News of the Day;* this was the delight of the first Russian enthusiasts of the detective story.

His work as a chronicler of "Moscow life" gave him access everywhere, in courts and police stations as in literary cafés and theaters. But while he was often content to sketch a few characters and catch bits of dialogue on the fly, he also came to engage, almost without being aware of it, in dramatic criticism. One evening toward the end of 1881, when he had been assigned to cover a performance by Sarah Bernhardt in a play that had all of Moscow excited and in tears, he wrote an article about her for *The Spectator* that was much more than a mere review. "There were times," he wrote "when her acting moved us almost to tears. Our tears did not flow, however, for so much charm was virtually erased by artifice. . . . This highly intelligent lady employs methods rich in effects. . . . Her art consists in impressing, astonishing, dazzling."

---

[1] Contrary to what his brother Mikhail said, Chekhov did not destroy the manuscript. But it was not until 1920 that it was found in his literary archives in Moscow and subsequently published as "an untitled play."

* Hungarian names are customarily given surname first.—TRANSLATOR.

In theatrical dressing rooms and in the *traktiri* of which his brother Nikolai, who often illustrated his articles, was an old customer, Chekhov came to know the artistic and journalistic bohemians of the capital. Though consistently keeping a cool head and a rather severe manner, he took pleasure in the company of this young, effervescent intelligentsia; indeed, he formed friendships with two of the most picturesque specimens of the fauna.

The first was a poet, Lyodor Palmin, a kind of warm, enthusiastic vagabond who spent his days bartering increasingly inspired ideas for glasses of vodka and who was always followed by five or six limping one-eyed mongrels he picked up in the street and tenderly cared for. He was extremely cultivated, knew many languages, and translated the foreign classics. Anton and he had endless Russian-style conversations, which, in spite of the vapors of alcohol, never lacked tone or dignity. "He could obviously drink enormously," Chekhov was to write, "but in three or four hours of conversation you would never hear a single lie, not a single coarse remark, even if your own sobriety was his butt" (February 1, 1886).

The other friend whom Chekhov found in this bohemia was Vladimir Giliarovsky. A journalist on the staff of *The Russian News*, he was recognized by his colleagues as "the king of the reporters," and in his hours of meditation he was also a poet. He was a blustering man, a force of nature, who would invite one to feel his iron muscles on first meeting and who sometimes diverted himself by breaking up a chair for sport; he told stories as spicy as curry, but he was also one of the kindest men in the world. He had worked at every trade, and since he was on as intimate terms with aristocrats as with porters and was as much at home in the very stuffy English Club as in the lowest dives, he was the mentor for Chekhov, who was still very new in the trade of journalism.

For Anton, however, the center of his emotions was still his family. He maintained courteous relations with his father, who had finally accepted him as the head of the family, and he was full of little attentions for his mother. With his eldest brother, Alexander, who was marvelously gifted though of unstable character, an inveterate drinker and spender of money, he could not establish any real intimacy, in spite of a shared interest in science and literature, the latter of which Alexander too attempted, though sporadically. On the other hand, Nikolai was perhaps his closest friend in these years.

Their joint enthusiasm for art, nature, and music and their common sensitivity was the basis of the alliance between these two brothers, who often worked together and who circulated in the same bohemia. Anton persevered unremittingly in his efforts to instill some self-respect in his affectionate, generous brother, who was also weak, a drinker, and thoughtless. Anton exercised the greatest patience with him and was especially careful not to criticize him for living with a woman to whom he was not married. "Everyone has the right to live with whom he likes and as he likes —that is the right of a civilized man," he wrote to Alexander (February 20, 1883). But when Nikolai turned up dead drunk in the family circle after days and nights in the lowest depths of Moscow and threw himself down on a couch without undressing to spend the next twenty-four hours sleeping off his vodka, Anton, though he may not have assailed him with sermons, despaired of ever seeing him become the great painter he could have been.

For Ivan, the taciturn younger brother, who was not too intelligent and whose character tended toward the commonplace, Anton felt little affinity. But he respected Ivan's earnestness, and though he wrote with a certain irony that Ivan "is one of the most conventional and solid members of the family," he added that "one may be sure of his future. He is hard-working and honest." To the gentle, rather shy Masha, who was attending the Rayevsky Institute for Girls, and the light-hearted, sensitive little Misha, Anton was still "Father Antosha," who was to be unreservedly adored.

He loved to see his family gathered round him and to hear them all laughing and enjoying themselves. There were actually evenings when things were very lively in the Chekhov house, which was always "open" to everyone's friends. Anton brought Palmin and other writers there, such as the Tolstoyan P. Sergeyenko, and Nikolai entertained young painters, including Isaac Levitan, a timid, emotional Jew who rolled his Rs and made everyone laugh by calling Masha "Mafa."

Some played games, Nikolai worked the piano, someone else took up a balalaika, and everyone sang popular songs. But there were other evenings when Anton wanted to write and, held captive in a cage of merry noise, he flew into a rage because he could not concentrate. "I write under the most revolting conditions," he complained. "In the next room some visiting relative's brat is playing . . . in another, my father is reading *The Sealed Angel*[2] aloud to my mother. Someone has wound up the music box and I can hear *La Belle Hélène.* . . . I want to run away to the country. . . . The brat is yelling. I swear I will never have children" (August, 1883).

Meanwhile, with inconspicuous but unshakable consistency and perseverance and without allowing himself to be led astray by literature, Chekhov continued to pursue his goal: to become a physician and thereby assure himself of independence. He did extremely well in the spring examinations of 1880 and 1881, and he maintained his record in 1882. That year he went for the first time to spend the summer vacation in a country village in the Moscow area—at Vosskressensk with his brother Ivan, who had settled there as a teacher more than a year earlier. The whole family, which had discovered immediately that Ivan had a large house to himself, accompanied Anton.

Chekhov was not content to rest in Vosskressensk, to let himself go in "Russian laziness" and the torpor of country life. He devoted himself to his two favorite sports—a poet's sports: fishing and mushroom hunting. A writer's mind is never at rest, and Chekhov, with his curiosity about everything, wanted to learn all there was to learn about this village life that was so new to him. So off he would go to the *traktir,* with its blue signboard and its samovar, or the post office, or the justice of the peace, or the *izba* of some muzhik, or the squires' country houses, or even the officers' mess of the artillery regiment stationed in the little village. In Moscow he occasionally would offer to give ten kopecks to anyone who could provide him with a subject for a sketch, but here he was supplied for nothing. In the autumn he published sketches of this country life over the signature Antosha Chekontey.

---

[2] A famous collection of stories by Nikolai Leskov that was built round the sect of the Old Believers. Obviously Pavel Yegorovich had not deserted his pious readings.

Soon after his return to Moscow he had an encounter that was to mark a turning point in his literary career. He and his brother Nikolai were strolling through the streets one October afternoon when his friend Palmin hailed him from a passing carriage. The poet introduced the two brothers to the friend who was with him. The heavy-set man with the black beard and the little ferrety eyes was the Petersburg author Leikin, who was also the publisher of an important humorous magazine, *Oskolki* (*Splinters*). Leikin had just been telling Palmin that he was looking for an intelligent and not overly demanding contributor for his magazine, and Palmin replied that Anton Chekhov was his man. The business conversation began on the sidewalk and then, because of the biting cold, it was transferred to a nearby café. Puffing on his cigar, Leikin explained what he wanted: short, brisk, light, amusing pieces; but beware of the censor! Anything serious must be avoided. Anton replied that he could at once provide four or five trifles of this kind, but . . . how much would he get? Eight kopecks a line, which would come to four or five rubles an article. Delighted but concealing his pleasure, Anton agreed. It was also decided that Nikolai would provide the illustrations. Somewhat dazzled by this Leikin, who was an author who had "arrived," Anton thought it would be clever to ask him for one of his books: he would guard it as a treasure and have it bound. Flattered, Leikin promised to send him one, and they parted, mutually pleased.

Anton hastened to tell his brother Alexander of the windfall, and this time he made no effort to hide his satisfaction and his pride. "I must tell you that right now *Splinters* is the most popular of the magazines. . . . It is read everywhere. Now I have a right to look down on the other papers. . . ."

He hastened also to provide copy for *Splinters*. On receiving his first effort, the editors replied bluntly: "Write more concisely and we will pay you more generously," but on November 20 it printed the first piece by Chekontey. During the ensuing months the number of his contributions grew: *Splinters* published a hundred of them within a year. Young and gay, Chekhov had an enthusiastic mind and a sharp eye, and what he saw around him was enough to furnish him with material for light stories. Writing, for him, was simple and as natural as talking or breathing. And he was not satisfied to confine himself to depicting the narrow world of students, artists, and solid citizens in which he circulated. "The Moscow public has no taste, no culture," he announced, and he did not hesitate to let his imagination loose and choose as his heroes Hungarian aristocrats or even, as in "The Useless Victory," "the Parisian demi-monde."

Since Leikin was pressing him to do so, he agreed also to take on reportorial assignments: early in 1883 he began regularly contributing "Moscow Notes" to *Splinters*. Although he had little taste for this, he sketched quick pictures of "Moscow life," described street scenes, wrote about unusually daring burglaries, described autopsies, toured theaters, covered the courts that were trying the more notorious cases, and reported on musical and literary events. And he apparently did a good job, since he very soon aroused the jealousy of both his colleagues and his competitors. He complained of this to Alexander as early as February, 1883: "Among us journalists there is a sickness: jealousy. Instead of rejoicing at your success, they envy you . . . and they run you down. How that poisons everything!" (February 20, 1883).

Soon, however, he found that Leikin's exigencies were excessive, and he told him so frankly. Of course he understood that the paper did not accept articles of more than a hundred lines, but as soon as he sat down to write, the thought of those hundred lines paralyzed him. "I cut if I can," he wrote, "I filter, and when I have done so, I begin to count." He did not ask for much: could he not, to overcome his terror of those hundred lines, go to as much as a hundred and twenty? . . . Even more than the hundred lines it was the insistence on "chasing after humor" that irritated him. This lightness-to-order, which can soon become a writing idiosyncracy—Leikin himself had fallen into it—often weighed on him, froze him, and he was not afraid to say so. "Life is not always amusing," he wrote to his editor; "sorrow and misery are real, too; they too are part of life and could be artistically incorporated into fiction." He thereupon took it on himself to send *Splinters* some pieces of a more sober character, and Leikin, though he raised some objections, finally dropped them. For Chekontey had quickly acquired many readers and the editor of the weekly was therefore eager to hold on to him.

Chekhov, from his own point of view, wanted to appear in *Splinters* as often as possible. It was a matter not of literary vanity but of the need for money. He had constantly to pay for this family that "hung round his neck," and often too he had to help needy friends. And he never complained about it. But one day, when Alexander, who was now a customs official in Taganrog, had written to Anton that he was dying of boredom, Anton allowed his rancor to come out. "I am paying bills in all directions," he wrote on May 13, 1883, "and I have nothing left. The family alone eats up fifty rubles. . . ." And he concluded his letter with a selfish observation of the kind that was so rare from him: "If I lived alone, I should live like a rich man."

Money, money—this problem seemed to dominate his life. He mentioned it in every letter he wrote. But how could it have been otherwise? He had constantly to think of earning money for his family, and in addition he lived in a world in which money was the sole way out of the "slavery" into which he had been born. It was because he was always in desperate need of money that he wrote as if the Devil were at his heels, and it was because he needed even more that in the winter of 1883 he accepted a post as tutor to the two sons of a senator. With that honesty that was characteristic of him he was later to acknowledge that money had ruled his youth: "I place great importance on money . . . ," he was to write. "I was corrupted by the fact of having been born, having grown up, having educated myself, and having begun to write in a world in which, shockingly, money held the first rank" (August 28, 1888).

What had become of the fourth-year medical student Anton Chekhov in all this? He still found time to pursue his studies, and with a great deal of application. In fact he took quite a keen interest in them, and there was a time when he thought of devoting a monograph, a scientific thesis, to a subject that for the time was quite revolutionary: *A History of Sexuality*. It has been said that his major medical interest was in theory rather than practice. This is hard to believe of such a man, a born observer, full of curiosity about every aspect of human behavior, and, in addition, indefatigably ready to help others. In any event, whatever his preferences, he spent long hours in the study of medical cases and in attendance at operations. He was also always available to his penniless bohemian friends for unpaid consultations.

In the summer of 1883, when he had passed his examinations creditably, he again spent his vacation at Vosskressensk. There he acted as assistant to Dr. Arkhangelsky, who had a rural hospital at nearby Shikino. Chekhov did little writing during that summer and apologized for the fact to his "boss," Leikin. "All that poets are good for," he joked, "is scribbles, moonlights, and loves." He preferred to spend his evenings with Arkhangelsky, in whose home he was staying; or else, rejoining his family in Vosskressensk, he spent part of the evening gossiping with garrison officers who had become friends of the family (talks that he would remember when later he came to write *The Three Sisters*). As full of reserve and restraint as he was, Chekhov liked to surround himself with people and laughter.

"Moonlights and loves. . . ." That was all that anyone could get out of him by way of confidences. There was no man more discreet, indeed more secretive, with respect to his private affairs and his emotions—and in this refusal to unburden himself there was no man less Russian. Even those closest to him, like Alexander and Nikolai, knew nothing of his inmost thoughts and feelings. The reserve that was to be one of the characteristics of his art was already the dominant characteristic in the young man's life. It was at this time, moreover, that he criticized Alexander for injecting too much personal "satisfaction" into his writing. "Subjectivity," Anton wrote to his brother, "is a terrible thing. It is bad in this sense, that it strips the poor author completely naked" (February 20, 1883).

Was he an adept of "the science of the tender passions"? In the lack of direct revelations, the stories that he was writing at the time must answer for him: no, he had nothing more to learn from women, and perhaps even less from loose ones. Some biographers have mentioned his intimacy with a French actress appearing at the Lentovsky Theater. Occasionally he spent an evening in the

Variety Hall, the then fashionable *café-chantant*, with officers and uninhibited girls, but this kind of little student "debauch," wholly provincial and conventional, seemed hardly to amuse him. On Christmas Day, 1883, he wrote to Leikin from Moscow: "I spent the whole night playing cards with some girls. We played until it was time for Mass, drinking vodka the whole time out of boredom —besides, I never drink it for any other reason. My head is fuzzy."

Without putting any great zest into it, then, he submitted to a kind of conformity to the "young man's life" and furthermore he was apparently the first to make fun of it. He wrote to a friend who had lent him a frock coat: "Without it I should have perished under the women's lack of interest." Looking at love as no more than a theme for pleasantries, he wrote to the same friend's wife that he would go to Taganrog in the summer to fetch the wife whom she had promised him. But, he added, "these are my terms: beauty, charm, and, alas, a little matter of twenty thousand rubles. Nowadays the young have become frightfully materialistic" (February 24, 1884). There was more fire in the admission that he had made to Leikin a month earlier: "I am ambitious" (January 22, 1884).

His ambition soon had the opportunity for satisfaction. In the spring he completed his studies with some brilliance. Now he was infused with confidence because he "felt the physician's passport in his pocket." He went back that summer to the Shikino hospital, but this time as a full-fledged doctor. Every second day he had visiting hours, and he also had occasion to perform coroner's autopsies on "cadavers in red shirts and new underpants." The first fees he earned seemed quite miraculous to him: five rubles from a young lady whose aching tooth he had not even been able to cure, one ruble from a monk whose dysentery he did cure, three rubles from a vacationing Moscow actress with an unpredictable stomach. These first earnings were joyously disbursed at the *traktir* to provide everyone at his table with "vodka, beer, and other medications."

He also experienced for the first time the joy of having a book published, though he paid for it—the joy and the publication. A little eighty-six-page collection, *The Tales of Melpomene*, appeared in the bookshops that summer. It cost sixty kopecks and it was signed "A. Chekontey." Alexander, having given up his job in the customs at Taganrog and gone back to Moscow, amiably assumed the task of offering it to the booksellers, but with limited success.

In July, at his own request, Chekhov served as substitute for the chief of the hospital of Zvenigorod. But although he had to take care of thirty to forty patients a day, he was soon "horribly" bored. Sitting at the window of his office, he watched the unending downpour of rain on the house of the district chief of police and the empty avenue.

Otherwise, when he went back to his family in Vosskressensk, he amused himself as well as he could. He loved nature and took long walks, often as far as the Monastery of the New Jerusalem, which impressed him as "poetic": he would allow himself to be lulled by the chants of vespers while meditating themes for stories. He went to the village *traktir* to read the newspapers, for hours on end he fished for chub and tench with an old man called Prokudin, an impassioned angler, he ate "to bursting," and he drank vodka mixed with currant leaves. In short, he felt that he was a reprehensible loafer.

He was eager to "flee" from Vosskressensk, where the weather had turned bad and "diphtherial," and on September 1 he went back to Moscow, a city he had begun to love exceedingly, to the point of asserting that he "belonged to it forever." He wanted to plunge himself again into its journalistic and literary atmosphere, which he enjoyed, to see the friends "about whom one could gossip while hiding under a pseudonym," to prepare his doctoral thesis in medicine, and to "lick" squibs for Leikin's weekly. He was quickly caught up again in the whirlwind: he reported a notorious trial for *Splinters*—that of the banker Skopin; he wrote theatrical reviews, and he sold "odds and ends" of copy to another humorous paper, *Amusement,* which paid him better: ten kopecks a line. He also worked on his thesis, *The History of Medicine in Russia,* and he found time to spend evenings with his friends Palmin, Gilyarevsky, and other writers, such as Kruglov, who took him to hypnotic séances. As he wrote to P. Sergeyenko on December 17: "Much work, little money, the winter is severe, my health is terrible. . . . We are singing 'Frère Jacques'. . . ."

In September Chekhov had proudly ordered a brand-new brass plate: "Anton Chekhov, Doctor of Medicine." Three months later he would learn that he was himself ill. It was during December that he spat blood for the first time. He pretended to take the matter lightly. "It is not tuberculosis," he assured Sergeyenko, and he remarked what pleasure it had given him to learn how many friends he had as a result of it. The hemorrhage did not prevent him in the least from realizing one of his dreams: he was going to spend the year-end holidays in the artistic capital that he did not yet know, "Peter"—Petersburg. He was a physician, and in addition he knew so clearly that he had a serious symptom on his hands that he wrote to Uncle Mitrofanos that he thought he would soon have to "go abroad for his health."

Meanwhile he took care of the health of others, "masses of people" who lived in all parts of the city and who cost him more than a ruble a day for carriage hire. Though half his patients never paid, the other half paid well—three to five rubles a visit. So money was coming in: he was able to buy new furniture and a piano, to have two maids, to give little "musical evenings." It gratified him above all to be able now to pay cash for everything, even the butcher and the grocer. And since he had not lost family feeling, "Father Antosha" could write proudly to Uncle Mitrofanos: "If my health holds up, my family's future is assured. . . . I have no debts and no intention of incurring any . . ." (March 3, 1885).

He had paid a high price—as high as spitting blood—but it was no longer "slave's blood" that ran in his veins.

During these five years of apprenticeship to medicine and life the man had preserved his guise of a listening angel, but he had profoundly altered. His threefold experience as "head of a family," needy journalist, and hospital assistant, instead of embittering him or driving him to despair, rather had strengthened him in his idea that the world is a spectacle from which it is better to hold oneself aloof. He had just emerged from the age of great passions, mad love, all-absorbing friendship, political fanaticism, and he had not allowed himself to be carried away or even distracted by any of these. He had no more illusions about himself or the knowledge that he had just acquired—"thanks to my examinations, I have forgot all the medicine I ever knew"—than about the men with whom he associated, either his colleagues or his patients. He had already lost his gaiety and his lust for living.

His unceasing solicitude for his family, his kindness to his friends should not give rise to illusions. Unquestionably he was doing—and would continue to do—a great deal for them, but it was not because of surges of affection; there is no cry from the heart in his letters to his brothers, for instance, or in his notes to Leikin, his most regular correspondent during this period. His charity was conscious, his spirit of devotion was deliberate, and through these he was seeking above all to reach what mattered most to him: his "own dignity" and self-improvement. We know that he kept away from love with an amused smile. He did not trust women: "Wherever there is a good woman," he wrote with regard to Nikolai, "it is difficult to exert any influence" (November 11, 1884). An individualist, he was capable at times of being almost a cynic: he wrote to Leikin, describing a writer whom he knew well: "This gentleman of the chamber suffers from angina pectoris and probably will soon provide the subject of an obituary notice" (July, 1884).

He had succeeded—totally without help—in organizing his life reasonably harmoniously. "I cannot earn less than a hundred fifty to a hundred eighty rubles a month," he wrote to Leikin, and now, through the combination of medicine and writing pot-boilers, he was taking in the required amount. He had no thought of abandoning writing for medicine or the reverse; on the contrary he was determined to carry on both, "to course the two hares at the same time." Besides, he did not take himself seriously either as a doctor —"I never have any confidence in myself as a physician," he wrote to Alexander—or as a writer, and he spoke of his writings as "knickknacks," "futilities," or "excrement."

His medical studies had left a mark on him, however; they had given him a scientific turn of mind. He believed in the efficacy of reason, in the necessity for analysis and experiment, and in the worth of the positive methods of science. But he was not one of those who saw an irreducible antinomy between science and art, like Tolstoy and the romantics; on the contrary, he regarded the two domains as complementary. In the future he would write to a former fellow student at the University of Moscow, Dr. Rosso-limo: "I have no doubt that my medical studies have had a great influence on my literary activity." He knew that they had widened his horizons and that they had given him certain kinds of knowledge about people that are essential to a writer. They had also made him a severe critic of his own imagination: "The knowledge of the natural sciences and of scientific methods," he said in the same letter, "has made me cautious, and I have always striven, when it was possible to do so, to take scientific data into consideration. When it was not possible, I preferred not to write at all" (October, 1899).

The gaze this nearsighted man turned on the world about him was one that disciplined itself to impersonality and objectivity. This deliberately cold contemplation occurred again in a letter in which he described an autopsy: there was no ennobling pity, nor were there any great guffaws to hide an emotion. His seemingly vacant eyes saw everything and recorded everything. But when he described what he had seen—that amazing Russian world surrounding him—even though he wanted also to include "sad things," he never sat in judgment.

At the age of twenty-five—thanks to his experience of provincial life in Taganrog, of city life in Moscow, and of rural life in Vosskressensk—Chekhov already possessed an almost complete picture of the Russia of his time. Like Taganrog, it was a "hollow" country, frozen into social and political immobility; after the great wave of expectations thrown up by the abolition of serfdom in 1861, it had fallen back under its ancestral oppression, which had brought on a kind of slow paralysis, a torpor. Emancipated, the muzhik was still what he had always been: not the saint, not the barefoot, flowing-bearded prophet whom the intelligentsia had been busy erecting as a model, but an unlettered, passive, wretched being. The provincial nobility, thrown off balance and half bankrupted by the emancipation of the serfs, was incapable of making the rural administration of the zemstvo function. The real power was in the hands of a narrow-minded and brutal police force and a corps of officials whose corruption had been legendary since Gogol.

Since the assassination of Tsar Alexander II in March, 1881, the situation had grown even gloomier. The immobility had been reinforced by fear and discouragement, for with the beginning of the reign of Alexander III reaction took control. On the orders of Pobyedonotsev, the Tsar's former tutor, who had retained a strong influence over him, the censor mercilessly stifled every trace of free thought. But this sectarian fanatic was not yet satisfied, and in 1882 he wrote insidiously to his master: "I have always been of the opinion that it is impossible to embark on anything solid and essential to the establishment of order as long as disorderly freedom persists . . . for newspapers and magazines. Unfortunately, no one has approached this matter with a firm hand."

During the reign of Alexander II the role of opposition had been played, however timidly, by a certain new élite—the intelligentsia (the word appeared for the first time in 1866)—that was becoming aware of itself. The word included university students and graduates, intellectuals, and artists who occupied a place apart, almost on the margin, in the highly hierarchic Russian society but who, in the absence of a middle class, could play an important part. In the face of the reaction unleashed by the new Tsar, however, this intelligentsia had turned away from politics and was languishing in discouragement and apathy. This withdrawn élite, of which only very scattered elements had thrown themselves into terrorism and revolutionary activity, either took refuge in a fierce individualism or found its excuse in resignation to minor personal virtues. If Tolstoy's pathetic cry—"What ought we to do? Who are we to be?"—awakened so many enthusiastic echoes, it was because it was the same question that so many Russian intellectuals were putting to themselves at the same time.

Young Chekhov, as a physician and a writer, was a member of this intelligentsia on two counts. But his attitude, at least for the moment, was that neither of revolt—there was nothing of the rebel in him, in any case—nor of resignation. As for Tolstoy's plea, even though it had so deeply troubled the student environment from which Chekhov had just emerged, it seemed that he had not heard it—not yet. The man had been too deeply absorbed in ridding himself of his "slave's blood" to take part in public affairs, and the writer's only thought had been to feed his family and himself by amusing others.

Almost without being aware of it, however, Chekhov had constructed, in one little story after another, an almost complete panorama of the contemporary world of Russia. It contained all those "heroes of everyday life"—all those anti-heroes—whom he had known: the students crammed with ideas and the professors who had none, the little shopkeepers, the disabused doctors, the bored judges, the functionaries at once arrogant and servile, the bewildered country squires. This panorama was painted with an extremely light touch and also with an irony that was often savage. But this lightness was suggestive, this humor went beyond humor; they constituted a new method of illuminating the psychology of the characters.

Chekhov himself did not yet look on himself as a writer. There was a vacant place in Russian literature then: Dostoevsky and Turgenev had just died and Tolstoy was turning his back on literature, but Chekhov had never imagined that he could be the new writer for whom the nation was waiting. To him, as to all Russians of his time, a writer was above all a master thinker, and the idea that he could be one had not yet come to him—indeed, it was never to come to him.

At the end of his life Chekhov was to disown, or at least to reject, almost all his youthful output. When in 1901 he assembled everything that he had written earlier for his "complete works," he kept only a few pieces from the period 1880–1884 (although the rest make up three thick volumes in the modern complete edition). And yet this very young writer, who considered himself merely a more or less well-paid entertainer, had already produced such little marvels as "A Daughter of Albion," "The Chameleon," "The Tutor," "The Album," "The Swedish Match," "The Decoration," "The Death of an Official." He had even created a new form—the anecdote told with wit, a touch of poetry, and great vivacity—and he had immediately gained complete mastery of it.

Written at that age at which one is still full of self-confidence, and infused with a fine melodramatic exuberance, the first known play by Chekhov, *Platonov*, is simultaneously *Don Juan* and *Hamlet*. In it the young author tells the story of a provincial Don Juan, but a Don Juan in spite of himself, obsessed much more by himself than by women. Mikhail Platonov, the son of a ruined minor country nobleman, was a student full of lofty ambitions who had resigned himself to being merely an obscure village schoolteacher. Nevertheless he could have lived happily with his wife, a woman compunded of devotion, tenderness, and charming simplicity, if, to his misfortune—and to his fruitless pleasure—he were not the county lady-killer and the prey of the women. As the scenes of the play unfold, we see him succumb in succession—if not simultaneously—to the rather hearty charms of a general's widow, the more passionate lures of her stepdaughter, Sofia Yegorovna, and finally the studied coquetries of a young "emancipated" woman. His wife leaves him, the general's widow nags him, and Sofia Yegorovna insists that he run away with her. Platonov hesitates, lavishes promises and lies, gets drunk, talks too much, and at bottom is interested only in Platonov. Finally, in despair, Sofia Yegorovna shoots him to death with a revolver.

The play is interesting but it fails, and Chekhov knew this better than anyone. At the end of his life, when he was compiling and, with so much attention, revising his "complete works" for the publisher, Marx, he was careful to eliminate *Platonov* as well as others of his youthful works.[3] The play is a failure because it is too long—performed without cuts it would take more than seven hours—badly focused, "wild," composed of the most diverse themes, unbelievable in places, and irreparably wordy. All this could be redeemed if it contained what created the incomparable charm of Chekhov's later plays—that is, a magic atmosphere—but this is strangely lacking in *Platonov*. It is too brightly highlighted, its irony is too cutting, the dialogue is too explicit to cre-

[3] This rejection by the author himself has not prevented certain theaters from adding it to their repertories in recent years and performing it, always in drastically shortened and often in very debatable forms. Jean Vilar was the first to perform it in Paris, under the title *That Crazy Platonov*. It was subsequently performed, variously titled, in Germany, the United States, and England. In the Soviet Union it had its first performance in 1959.

ate the famous Chekhovian climate composed of shaded lights, tender, disciplined rancor, and unfinished sentences.

Appalled, as in his early stories, by the inanity, the hypocrisy, the greed, and the stupidity of the world around him, Chekhov here adopted a tone of biting irony that was often cruel and merciless. No one escaped his lash, and it might be said that in this sense *Platonov* is an astounding collection of caricatures of contemporary Russian provincial life with its enervated landowners, its greedy new rich, its solemn failures, its conscienceless physician, and idle, talkative women. It even contains—and this is the sole instance of its kind in all Chekhov's plays—the profiles of two cunning, grasping Jews. In this gallery of savage grotesques there is only one portrait drawn with a loving hand, that of Platonov's wife, the simple, big-hearted Sasha, but this kind of woman, too, was not to recur in Chekhov's later plays.

In this first play Chekhov was still seeking his tone and his perspective. On the other hand, he had already found his characters and his themes, and one might even say that in this first attempt, with the impulsive generosity of youth, he has given us all of them at once. The play already questions and from its second line—"it is pleasantly boring"—deals immediately with that irremediable and mortal boredom that hung like a pall over the idle Russian provincial society of the period, that shadow that recurs in all Chekhov's other plays. Already these spiritless idlers, disgusted with the mediocrity of their existence, dream of a "new life" that will be happy but that will require work—and so they always put off the fulfillment of their dreams until tomorrow. "After tomorrow," Sofia Yegorovna tells Platonov, "you will be a different man, fresh and new! We will breathe a new air, we will have new blood in our veins. . . ." Already the old family home is threatened with sale, already revolver shots ring out on the stage and sometimes interrupt the idle chatter about the "meaning of life."

The characters of Chekhov's future plays, too, are already almost all present in this first play. They were borrowed from that provincial Russian society bogged down in boredom and resigned inanity but uneasy over its fate, for it felt threatened by the "new men," realists prepared to buy everything, who were produced by nascent capitalism. In *Platonov* these decadents and these upstarts are already mixing, cheating one another, embracing one another. They are surrounded by fashionable women who are bored and who dream of love, by old men who refuse "to be satisfied with memories alone," by lecherous landowners stupefying themselves with vodka, by people who sigh: "How heavy the air is in Russia, how stifling, how musty," by sloths who pose imitation problems to themselves: "Why is it so hot? What could that mean?" *Platonov* is like the wings from which all those Chekhov "types" will go out onto the stage in *Ivanov, The Three Sisters,* and *The Cherry Orchard.*

In Platonov himself, however, the young Chekhov had created on his first attempt a new and very original character with a rich psychological texture. As one of his friends says, he is "a man unlike the rest, a strange type, his face bathed in a noble sadness," who holds remarkable fascination for all women. He himself is the male forever on the alert: "It is enough for a woman to say some trivial word," he admits, "and a storm is let loose within me." But though Platonov plays on his seductive power, he does so almost without wishing to, as if absently, and in any case without believing in it. For women are essentially far less interesting to him than himself, than that species of "disease of living" that rowels him and that is all that remains to him from a youth filled with enthusiasm and talent.

Platonov sums himself up marvelously when, at the point of death, he calls to a woman: "I have Platonov's disease! You love me, don't you?" He wants to be loved, but without giving anything in exchange; he wants to take a hand in the destiny of every woman he sees, but not in order to make her happy; indeed, and quite to the contrary, apparently in order to drive her irresistibly into misery and despair. This "extraordinary swine," as he defines himself, seduces only in order to lead his victims and himself to an inescapable damnation.

In fact that type of Don Juan-in-spite-of-himself seems to have seduced Chekhov himself, for it will be found in almost all his subsequent plays. Ivanov will have the charm of his "noble sadness" and will exercise it on his wife and little Sasha. In *Uncle Vanya* the strange Dr. Astrov will exploit his power of charm as much against the cold Yelena as against the passionate young

Sonya, and in *The Sea Gull,* Trigorin, unthinkingly, out of idleness, will accomplish the conquest—and the doom—of young
Nina. And even in *The Three Sisters* there is something of Platonov, of the charmer, in the fascinating colonel with the graying
temples, Vershinin, who drags Masha into a footless adventure.

Playwrights, in contrast to poets, are seldom precocious. Nevertheless, and even though *Platonov* was a failure, Chekhov shows
us with this first effort that he was magnificently endowed for the
theater. In fact he possessed all the talents of the thoroughbred
dramatist: he knew how to arrange his characters and even to create some who, like Mikhail Platonov, were amazingly individual,
how to mesh speeches—the drunk scene between the general's
widow and Platonov is a little miracle of black animation—how to
write lines that hit home. One might well wonder how this obscure twenty-one-year-old student, barely arrived from his rus-
ticity, could have acquired his knowledge of the world that he put
on the stage—a world that he had never thus far penetrated, for
he wrote *Platonov* before he made the discovery of provincial society in Vosskressensk; one might wonder whether this kind of
psychological divination is not also part of the dramatic genius.

There is more still. This youth barely out of adolescence was
already so surely, so thoroughly a playwright that on his first attempt he tried to overthrow the prevailing dramatic rules and replace them with his own. Not satisfied merely to borrow nothing
from his predecessors, he sought to revolutionize the theater of his
time by writing a play without a real subject and a comedy whose
deepest pattern, in its third dimension, was entirely dramatic.

IV

MEDICINE,
MY LAWFUL WIFE,
AND LITERATURE,
MY MISTRESS

Life is a dirty business for everyone. When I am serious, it seems
to me that those who have an aversion to death are illogical. As
far as I can understand the order of things, life is made up only of
horrors, squabbles, and trivialities that follow one another in regular series. One drudges along without seeing happy people.

CHEKHOV in a letter to
MRS. KISSELYEVA, September 28, 1886

If winters are long in Russia, summer comes early there, and in
1885 it was at the beginning of May that Dr. Chekhov left Moscow for the dacha he had rented in Babkino, five versts from
Vosskressensk and some fifty miles from the capital. This was the
first time he had rented a country house, and it goes without saying that, only too happy at the chance, the whole tribe accompanied him with its cargo of packing cases, luggage, jam pots, and
samovar. The villa stood in a park that was part of the estate of a
family named Kisselyev—whom Chekhov had already met on a
visit the year before—on the steep bank of the Istra River, surrounded by magnificent forests.

Chekhov fell in love with the place on his first evening. Arriving
at one o'clock in the morning, he thrust open the unlocked door
and found "enormous rooms, more furniture than was necessary
. . . everything extremely pleasant, comfortable, and attractive
. . . what a joy to look out the window at the black trees and the

river! . . . I could hear the nightingale singing and I couldn't believe my ears" (May 10, 1885).

He was going to divide his days among three activities: literary work, medical care for the peasants, and relaxation. Fortunately he had no more journalistic "papers" to write at the moment. He had just given up his reportorial column—those little squibs printed under the headline "Echoes of Moscow Life"—which had always been a burden to him and which appeared regularly in Leikin's weekly; besides, his relations with the editor had grown somewhat chilly. Thus he had more time to devote to regular contributions to *The Petersburg Gazette*, with which he had just signed a contract that allowed him more freedom both in the choice of his subjects and in the length of his stories.

"I eat, I drink, I sleep, I fish," he wrote. Actually he worked above all. Rising at seven o'clock, he wrote all morning, making the best of an old sewing-machine table, and then returned to his writing at the end of the afternoon. But he often had to break off, because the local peasants, having learned of the presence of a physician, came more and more frequently to consult him. These peasants, who swarmed round him "like flies," undoubtedly were an intrusion, but he never refused to see them and he was lavish with professional treatment and medication, for neither of which he charged them. "During the summer," he observed ironically, "several hundreds called on me, and I collected a total sum of one ruble" (September 14, 1885).

A great lover of fishing—that sport of poets—he was well provided for: the Istra and the estate's pond were teeming with fish. Not only did he use rod and line, he set out nets as well, and he regaled his correspondents with fishing stories: twenty-nine gudgeon in a single net, a perch so huge that he had to invite people in to help eat it. By his accounts, the whole family was gorging itself on bouillabaisse, fried fish, and jellied fish. His neighbor Mrs. Kisselyeva often went fishing with him, and, sitting on the river bank, they talked for hours. The talk may have scared off the gudgeon, but it provided Chekhov, always eager for material for his stories, with anecdotes that his friend compiled for him from old French newspapers.

At night in the country "what could be more pleasant than to drink a glass of wine on the terrace after supper?" There were gatherings sometimes at the Chekhovs', sometimes at the Kisselyevs', and while the trays went round with the wonderful pastries made by the writer's mother and the vodka Chekhov never drank and that Kisselyev drank rather too well, everyone talked as Russians talk, there was reading aloud, or people played whist or chess. Often too there was music. Through the wide-open windows the Beethoven sonatas and the Chopin nocturnes, splendidly played by the Kisselyev childrens' governess, floated over the terrace and lost themselves in the forest's great dark silence.

Chekhov had barely settled into Babkino when he learned that one of his brother Nikolai's friends—who was also his friend— Isaac Levitan, the painter, had had an attack of neurasthenia that had almost driven him to suicide and that he was now living like a lone wolf in a villa nearby. This "kind of psychosis" having no meaning to him, Chekhov went to fetch Levitan and established him in a building belonging to the dacha. "I brought him home and I am taking him for walks; I have a feeling that he is better already," Chekhov was soon able to write to Leikin. He also went hunting with Levitan and urged him to paint, and his friend, Isaac, who was primarily a landscape artist and was enchanted with the beauty of the place, soon began to do so almost frenetically.

The real remedy for these crises of suicidal depression, during which Levitan refused for days to speak to anyone, lay elsewhere, however: in amatory adventure. He could not meet a moderately attractive woman without falling in love with her, and though he was not handsome, he had an "interesting" look with his deep-set burning eyes and his wild locks, which women liked. His sudden, extreme, and immediately declared passions, however, never lasted long. It was undoubtedly during that summer that he suddenly offered his love to Masha Chekhova.

She was just twenty-two years old. Hers was a lively and emotional nature, but in appearance she was already the schoolteacher she was soon to become: her movements were heavy, and with her drooping eyelids and her large jaw, her face was rather severe. At once a dreamer and a realist like her brother Anton, she knew exactly what she wanted, and while on the one hand she was studying painting with zeal, she was also completing her studies at the Rayevsky Institute for Girls. She had a passion for friend-ships and there was a certain innocence in the way in which she insinuated her friends—that "bouquet of girls"—among her broth-ers and their friends. With his romantic airs, the halo of his suc-cesses with women, and his genius as a painter, as well as his talent for discussing the art, Levitan had everything to attract her.

One fine summer morning they were walking in the forest and chatting pleasantly when suddenly Levitan threw himself on his knees in front of Masha and told her that he loved her and wanted to marry her. Thoroughly upset, Masha fled; she spent the rest of the day weeping in her room. Anton, puzzled, sought her out in the evening and she told him everything: not only their friend's declaration but her own bewilderment. Her brother, very gently, advised her to think about it carefully: of course she could marry Levitan, but in his opinion what Isaac needed was not a girl as young as she but a "woman of Balzacian age." Masha did not quite understand what he meant by that, but she grasped it well enough to know that she must discourage her admirer, and this she did by avoiding further meetings with him. "That was the end on our 'romance,'" she was to write later. "We remained excellent friends." [1]

In September, however, it was necessary to return to Moscow, "in utter dejection." Anton resumed his medical and literary la-bors courageously, but his head was still filled with memories of nets, fishing rods, woodland paths, and cold baths in the Istra. "I have so little lost the habits of the summer," he wrote to Mrs. Kisselyeva, "that when I awaken in the morning, I wonder whether anyone has 'caught anything.'"

He had money troubles: he was in debt to certain weeklies, and others owed him money. Furthermore, in spite of the summer in Babkino, his health was no better and he soon began spitting blood again. He had changed apartments and was now living on

[1] Masha, however, who never married, preserved the consoling illusion that if she had wished to . . . , and Levitan gallantly backed her up in this notion. "He often told me," she was to write, "even just before his death, when he was ill and I went to visit him, 'If I had ever married, I should have married only you, Masha.'"

the other side of Moscow, in a neighborhood that was "a real province: clean, quiet, cheap, . . . and a bit stupid." He had returned to the city with many literary plans, but in the grip of his patients and his thesis, he was writing less than he would have liked and he hadn't even time to go to the theater.

What he did not yet know was that his "knickknacks" were beginning to earn him a real name as a writer. Even in Petersburg, the artistic capital of Russia, which he had never seen, people were beginning to talk of this unknown "Chekontey" who wrote stories that were so alive and so new in manner for *The Petersburg Gazette*. This was how a well-known novelist who had played a leading part in Russian literary history for twenty years, Dmitri V. Grigorovich, had come to know and admire Chekhov's story "The Hunter" and recommended the author to the attention of Alexis Suvorin, the largest newspaper owner of the time. Chekhov was to become aware of this unexpected renown in December, when he made his first visit to Petersburg.

Although his relations with Leikin were not of the best—the publisher criticized him for submitting material to other publications and Chekhov replied that he did so because Leikin paid him poorly—it was Leikin who invited him, at the publisher's expense, to spend two weeks in Petersburg. Chekhov, in new overcoat and trousers and pointed shoes, set out for the artistic capital and was stupefied by the greeting he received. The editorial board of *The Petersburg Gazette* welcomed him like "the Shah of Persia," and reputed authors and journalists, like Buryenin, told him how pleased they were to meet him and how much they admired his writing. "Everyone offered invitations and sang my praises," he wrote to Alexander, "and for my part I was ashamed of having written carelessly until now, off the top of my head. If I had known that they were reading me, I should never have written anything on assignment" (January 4, 1886).

In Petersburg he was also introduced to the press magnate Suvorin—the founder and director of the largest newspaper of the period, *New Times*—who received him most cordially and proposed that Chekhov contribute to his newspaper on a regular basis. No loubt exaggerating slightly for the sake of a joke, Anton described Suvorin to his brother Mikhail as a man of empty promises who counseled him on the excessive length of his trousers and added: "Persevere, young man! I am pleased with you, but go to church more and don't drink vodka" (December, 1885). Encouraged by a contract for twelve kopecks a line, Chekhov a month later sent a story, "The Requiem," to *New Times*, which immediately published it.

On his return to Moscow he was caught up again in the stresses of his double life. For he was a physician as well, and in February, when typhus began to rage in Moscow, he joined his colleagues in the battle against the disease. Nor could he refuse to make a daily visit to some Jewish schoolboy stricken with "Nana's disease"— smallpox—or help some little girl with a bad attack of croup. At the same time he had to correct the proofs of a second collection of stories that he had put together but for which he had not found a title. *Sketches? Notes? Motley Tales?* In the end he chose the third title.

He wrote under difficult conditions. The tranquil "village life" of which he used to speak was definitely over. The second floor of his building was occupied by a restaurant that was forever being hired for wedding and funeral feasts. Besides, what was he to write? It seemed to him that he had said everything he had to say: "I feel drained," he told Bilibin. Furthermore, now that he knew that the good writers among his contemporaries were reading him, he was seized by a kind of fear when he confronted a sheet of blank paper. And besides he still had to go and chat with Palmin, divert himself, spend an evening with the girls. "It was clear and dry this February in Moscow," he wrote to Leikin. "Sun all day, moon at night. . . . Weather for not writing and for talking about love" (February 16, 1886).

Soon, however, he would have no further occasion for self-doubt. On February 14 he had written to Bilibin: "Sooner or later I will say good-bye to literature," but two weeks later he received a letter from Petersburg that dissipated all his doubts. In a spontaneous, generous gesture—reminiscent of his behavior forty years earlier toward Dostoevsky—Grigorovich, the famous novelist, wrote to him to assure him that he had talent, "talent that puts you in the very highest rank of the new generation of writers. . . . If I talk of your talent, it is with deep conviction. I am sixty-

five years old, but I still have so much love for literature, I follow
its progress with so much enthusiasm, I rejoice so much when I
come across something living in it, something gifted, that, as you
see, I could not restrain myself, and I hold out both my hands to
you."

To this certificate of talent Grigorovich added a few counsels
from a well-wishing elder. When one had a gift like Chekhov's—
so rarely received as one's lot—one must respect it. "Abandon all
hasty work!" he wrote, adjuring Chekhov to give up journalism
and "rather endure hunger, as we ourselves have done in the
past," in order to dedicate himself henceforth to a "great work."
Grigorovich also advised him to drop his pseudonym and use his
real name on the forthcoming collection of stories. Finally, but
amicably, the old writer asked him hereafter not to indulge in
such "pornographic shadings" as those that had shocked him. Was
it really necessary to carry realism to the extreme of mentioning
"dirty feet" and "a functionary's navel"?

What was little Chekontey's reaction to this letter from his eminent senior? He at once communicated it to Bilibin, and even
though he assumed a rather mocking tone—his correspondent
must not think that he was carried away—he could not mask the
uprush of joy, of pride, he had felt. "Suddenly, in an unexpected
fashion, like a *deus ex machina*," he wrote, "I have had a letter
from Grigorovich. . . . His handwriting is bad and senile; the
old man insists that I write something long and that I give up
working against deadlines. He swears that I have a real talent (it
is underlined). . . . He writes with warmth and sincerity. I am
certainly happy, even though I feel that G. is exaggerating"
(March 4, 1886).

It was in quite another tone—simultaneously rather stilted, embarrassed, and extremely sincere in its gratitude—that he replied
to Grigorovich, beginning: "Your letter, my good and warmly
loved messenger of joy, struck me like a thunderbolt. It almost
made me weep. . . . May God ease your old age as you have caressed my youth! I cannot find words or deeds with which to
thank you." In the body of the letter the tone changed: he admitted that heretofore he had not "respected his talent." What
reason would he have had to do so, since there was no one in the

Moscow "literary" circle in which he moved who had ever taken him seriously? His five years of "vagabondage" through the newspapers had led him to treat literature casually, to write mechanically, without regard for himself or for his readers. "I do not recall having put in more than a day on any of my stories. 'The Hunter,' which you liked, was written in a bathhouse." And there was a second reason for his lack of respect: "As a physician, I am up to my ears in medicine." But alerted first by Suvorin and now by Grigorovich, he felt that there was indeed a literary "gift" inside him.

It was too late to sign the new book with his real name. Besides, it did not much matter, that was only "a disorderly hash of little student pieces, deformed by the censors and the newspaper editors." But henceforth he would follow his senior's advice: he would give up conspicuous "cynicism" and as soon as he had time —during the summer—he would get down to a serious undertaking. He asked Grigorovich to send him a photograph—the novelist did so at once, inscribing it "To a young talent from an old writer" —and he concluded on a note of fervor: "All my hope is in the future. I am only twenty-six. Perhaps I shall succeed in doing something, although time goes quickly."

But the present counted too. This sudden success intoxicated Chekhov to a certain extent, and by his own admission "the fumes of praise made him giddy." To Uncle Mitrofanos, for whom he had a special affection, he wrote a long letter, affectionate and boastful. He spoke of his successes in Petersburg and announced that he was now a contributor to *New Times*, "the biggest newspaper in Petersburg," which, miracle of miracles, had just sent him a hundred and thirty-two rubles for three little stories, to which must be added the hundred rubles a month paid by *The Petersburg Gazette*. He discussed Grigorovich's marvelous letter with enthusiasm and quoted the flattering passages. He finished with a delightful touch: when in ten or fifteen years he came to write his autobiography, he would use it to thank publicly, "before the whole reading public," his dear Uncle Mitrofanos for everything that he had done for him. And he promised faithfully to go back to Petersburg during Easter week, because, he said, "I am now the fashion there."

As soon as Easter was past—he spent it strolling through the churches, listening to the Kremlin bells, and, returning home at two in the morning with a couple of singers from the opera, drinking and singing—Chekhov did indeed go to Petersburg. He spent two splendid weeks there, praised and sought out by everyone. "I have formed the closest ties with Suvorin and Grigorovich," he wrote to Alexander. Satiated with glory, he set out directly for Babkino, "still completely dazed by the excitement created in 'Peter' " by his five stories printed in *New Times*.

His excitement subsided quickly in the familiar tranquility of Babkino. He returned to the routine of the previous year: writing in the mornings at the sewing-machine table, walking in the woods, dreaming over his fishing rod, raising his nets, taking care of the peasants, the old *babas* and the rachitic children, spending his evenings on the Kisselyevs' terrace. The weather was fine and he accused himself of loafing, of working poorly: had praise made him, like the crow in Krylov's fable, lose his head? And indeed he wrote little during the early weeks. This was because he was harassed by the delay in the publication of his *Motley Tales*—the book did not appear until June and it was not too well received by the press—and because his health left much to be desired.

At the end of the winter he had started spitting blood again. But although he had a good idea of the nature of his disease, he preferred not be certain of it. "I am afraid to undergo a thorough examination by my medical colleagues," he had written to Leikin in April. "They will suddenly find that my breathing is too slow or that there is a dullness at the base of the lung." Since he had no fever, he preferred to tell himself—and above all to tell his intimates—that he was not tubercular and that his trouble came "less from the lungs than from the throat." Since his arrival in Babkino he had also suffered from painful attacks of hemorrhoids, which on some days made it impossible for him to walk or sit. His teeth were also giving him a great deal of pain, to such an extent that on one occasion he had to take the night train to Moscow, where he had two of them pulled at the same time.

What a contrast in this man of only twenty-six between the already deeply damaged body and the heart throbbing with youth and hope! There were even days when he felt that he was "an urchin" again, when, despite his respectable appearance in his dark suits and starched collars, he was once more completely the captive of his childhood memories. To V. Bilibin, the secretary of *Splinters,* to whom he wrote with somewhat less reserve than to others, he admitted: "Sometimes it still happens that I dream of my school, of a lesson badly learned, and I am afraid of being asked to recite by the teacher." In spite of himself, in spite of the tuberculosis that was consuming him, he let himself go in the magic of youth and preferred to believe that there was no limit on the time that lay ahead of him.

Young, handsome, and attractive to women, how could he not have been interested in love as well? When his friend Leikin asked how he was spending his money now that he was beginning to earn decently, he replied: "With women." During the winter he had not deprived himself of the presence and the savor of the "bouquet of pretty girls," friends of his sister, Masha, who often went to his house. It had even occurred to him to give serious thought to marriage.

In January, again through Masha, he had come to know a rich young Jewess, Dunya Efros, and he had been so taken with her that one evening, as he was taking her home, he proposed marriage. "I want to jump out of the frying pan into the fire," he wrote to Bilibin. Two weeks later he was sure of his desire, and he and the girl had a serious talk about marriage. But the problem was not so simple because, although it was not mandatory, it was traditional that Jewish girls who married Russians became converts to orthodoxy. Meanwhile the talks between Dunya and Anton soon became quarrels, and one day, to his amazement, Chekhov saw his Dunya sweep all the papers, pencils, and photographs off his desk. He discovered that she was a shrew, "a terrible vixen." Undoubtedly he would have married her just the same, but he was already talking of his conviction that he would have to leave her "after a year or two of marriage."

A month later he told Bilibin that everything was over between himself and this temperamental girl. But he did not dramatize the matter. "I have not bought a revolver or begun keeping a private diary," he concluded. "Everything in this world is changeable, annoying, approximate, and relative" (February 26, 1886). Soon he declared that he would have no more to say of his "vixen," and he kept his word.[2] Having made the experiment, he recognized that it was still too early for him—"I am rather frivolous"—to think of marriage. When, not long afterward, Mrs. Kisselyeva asked him whether he would marry, he replied: "No, and I'm proud of it. I am above marriage" (September 21, 1886).

Friendship really occupied a greater place than love in his life, even if in any case, at least on his part, it was friendship full of reserve and lacking in intimacy. Rather than friendship properly so called, what he was looking for was companionship, the close presence of others, movement and sound around him. "I need people around me," he was soon to acknowledge to Suvorin. "Alone, I don't know why, I am afraid, as if I were alone in a tiny boat on a great ocean." In his letters, even those to people he barely knew, he insisted that people come to visit him, or better still spend a few days with him in Babkino. And in lieu of physical presence, he demanded letters, many letters.

The chief visitor in Babkino that summer was again Levitan. He spent a great part of the summer in a building belonging to the dacha, and with Nikolai, Ivan, Mikhail, and Anton he relaxed in elaborate schoolboy pranks with masquerades, disguises, and guffaws. He also became more intimate with the writer: he conversed a great deal with him, explained his ideas on art, and told him of the spring that he had just spent in the Crimea, whose too-beautiful, too-"prim" natural assets had quickly wearied him. Nevertheless the drawings and paintings he had done there enchanted Chekhov. "His talent," he wrote, "is growing not day by day but hour by hour."

Was it in order to entertain his friends better that when he went back to Moscow in the autumn, Chekhov rented an entire house instead of an apartment? No doubt, but it was principally in order to establish his family in it with him. In a respectable street in "a clean, quiet neighborhood," Sadovaya-Kudrinskaya Street, near the center of the city, his sister had found him a rather

---

[2] Evdosya Efros (1861–1943) later married a Moscow lawyer, E. Konovitser, but this did not prevent her from remaining on very good terms with Chekhov and his family. She emigrated after the Revolution, lived in Paris, and died in a German transport camp in February, 1943.

strangely shaped three-story house. It was painted red and afflicted with a double bulge, so that Chekhov described it as being "bountifully colored" and looking like a "chest of drawers." In order to pay a deposit on the rent, which, at six hundred fifty rubles a year, was huge for him, he had to pawn his watch and borrow money from Leikin.

This time the family set itself up somewhat more permanently and comfortably: Anton had his bedroom and his office on the ground floor. He brightened them by hanging photographs everywhere—this was the current fashion, as witness Sofia Tolstoy's room at Yasnaya-Polyana, the walls of which were literally papered with photographs—and lining them with bookshelves, which were rapidly filled with a rather miscellaneous collection of Russian literature, travel narratives, and bound volumes of magazines. The other "drawers" in the chest were divided among his parents, Masha, Mikhail, the maid, the cook, the piano, the aquarium, and a dog named Raven.

The "red chest" was soon to become a literary headquarters, a meeting place for all Moscow's intellectuals and artists. Evenings brought to the warm and somewhat bohemian atmosphere that the Chekhovs knew how to create around their samovar a collection of young painters, friends of Levitan and Nikolai, authors famous and obscure, young men carrying manuscripts, and also, of course, Masha's friends, the "bouquet of pretty girls." In spite of his modest behavior and his "maidenly" air Chekhov was the center of all conversation—"fascinating, full of talent, always looking at life in such diverting fashion," in the words of Vladimir Korolenko, a frequent guest at the "chest."

These evenings at Chekhov's were often very lively, gay, even noisy. There was music, singing, excited discussion. One evening the guests included an old gentleman with dapper gray sidewhiskers, whom Anton introduced to everyone at once: the famous writer Dmitri Grigorovich. Impressed for a moment, the younger guests soon went back to their jokes and their flirtations, and then Grigorovich too unbent, enjoyed himself, and flirted outrageously with all the girls. The delightful old man was something of a hypocrite, however, because later he was to say to Suvorin's wife:

"Anna Ivanovna, my dear, if you only knew what goes on at the Chekhovs'!" Recalling his evening, he threw up his hands: "A bacchanal, my dear, a real bacchanal!"

Korolenko has described more restful evenings. In the little red drawing room, where the sister and the brothers sat in a smiling circle around their mother, who presided over the samovar, the atmosphere was warm with family unity. Korolenko and Chekhov often talked shop, and one evening Chekhov explained that for him writing was not only a means of existence but a diversion, a genuine pleasure. It was almost a sport.

"Do you know how I write my little stories?" he said to Korolenko. "Look. . . ." He gazed at the table and picked up the first thing he saw—an ashtray—then set it before Korolenko. "Tomorrow," he went on, his eyes sparkling with fun, "this will be a story. Title: 'The Ashtray.'"

Chekhov—still and always "Father Antosha" to his family—had comfortably established part of his family in the "chest of drawers" in Sadovaya-Kudrinksaya Street. His mother, Masha, and Mikhail had their own rooms, and the house was always open to the others. Often enough Anton fetched home Nikolai, whom he had found dead drunk in one dive or another. This brother had become a thorough alcoholic and Anton did his best to cure him both of this disease and of a tuberculosis that was becoming worse with every year.

Though Chekhov had thought a few years earlier that he could bring his prodigal brother to his senses and back to his art, in which he was extremely talented, he had virtually no illusions left. Poor Nikolai led a drunkard's life, dissipated his talent, went from one prostitute to another. Nevertheless, untiringly, Anton continued to lavish advice on him, to try, though kindly, to reform him, to encourage him: "I assure you," he said, "that as a brother I understand you and sympathize with you with all my heart. I know all your virtues." Remembering Grigorovich's letter, he wrote to Nikolai that he had "received from heaven a gift that others do not have: talent," and that he had no right to throw it away but must rather sacrifice "women, wine, and useless excitement" to it. A real artist—and he was one—did not wallow in a dirty bohemia of bare rooms with alcohol stoves and bedbugs and stale air, floors covered with spittle, and beds where people slept in their clothes, and what he wanted from women was not "the bed and animal sweat" but cleanliness, elegance, humanity. But to his brother's exhortations to work "day and night," read the great writers, and "break your vodka decanter," Nikolai replied with shrugs.

With his elder brother, on the other hand, Anton's relations had improved. Alexander seemed to have matured and to have understood what his younger brother meant when he declared that above all an artist must be "well educated." Anton had obtained a job for him as a reporter for *New Times*, and Alexander was now living in Petersburg. He had a tremendous admiration and a great affection for his younger brother, but these were mingled with envy and with regret that he was not Anton's peer as a writer. Nevertheless this did not prevent him from being completely devoted to Anton's needs: he ran his errands, acted as his intermediary with publishers and colleagues, attended to the sale of his books. He even took with quite good grace—though without doing anything about them—the counsels his brother offered with respect to the trade of writing. "You write too much and too fast," Anton told him: he should try to spend five to seven days on a story of a few hundred lines and he would see the difference. And he added without smugness: "Right now I am all the fashion in Petersburg and I don't want you to lag behind me" (April 6, 1886).

Chekhov had every right to offer the counsels that he lavished on his brothers, because for months he had been giving himself the same advice—and putting it into practice. It seemed as if his sudden fame and Grigorovich's letter of certification, after a period of soothing bliss, had stimulated him to give a great deal of thought to his profession as a writer and to its responsibilities. Even though he wrote to his eldest brother, who had turned thirty: "A man of thirty ought to be positive and have character. In my own case, I am still a greenhorn and so I can be forgiven for wasting my time on nonsense," in actuality he considered himself much less pardonable than he intended to admit, and now he was trying to evolve an ethic for himself as an artist.

This ethic was precise, strict, stoic, and wholly within the framework of what might have been expected from him. Like a heraldic device, it could be summed up in three words: work, self-mastery, reserve. While the days of pot-boilers were not yet altogether behind him—for he was still compelled to keep his family alive—the period of superficiality was definitely past: by now Chekhov was laboring fiercely over his manuscripts. He was soon to write to Leikin: "I have spent three weeks pulling a Christmas story out of myself for *New Times*. I began it five times, I threw it away as many times, I have spat and ripped apart, I scold myself and insult myself." And even though he was sure that the product of so much effort was no more than "a bad soft caramel," he was nonetheless convinced of the absolute necessity of work.

He was untiringly preaching "good breeding" to the bohemian Nikolai. What Anton meant by the term he explained at some length: more than to anyone else the artist owed it to himself to be polite, accommodating, kind—and not merely to beggars and cats —and honest. What in addition he considered to be indispensable to the artist, as we have seen, was renunication of everything that did not serve his art, renunciation of passions and of "reckless" living. But perhaps it should be added that if he subscribed so wholly and so easily to this rigorous code, it was because it dovetailed with his own ideas. This period of cogitation on his art and his obligations as an artist, then, was not, as some have contended, a sudden turning point in Chekhov's life but rather an advance and a further determination along the road he had followed since he was twenty.

Having had a taste of the first delights of fame, Chekhov also believed in the necessity of modesty for the artist. "Real talents," he wrote, "are always in obscurity, lost in the crowd, far from display." He had a strong distaste for poseurs, hoodwinkers, and boasters.

It was not that he completely despised the pleasures of a growing celebrity and the small change of fame. While his family unreservedly enjoyed his success, he himself savored it with more modesty. Nevertheless he was not displeased that he could tell his friend Kisselyev, for example, that in September he had eaten oysters for the first time in his life. He added in jest: "They are not so wonderful, and in fact, without the Chablis and the lemon, they are quite revolting" (September 20, 1886).

Undoubtedly, too, it was in a way because he wanted to inhale the incense of glory and impress Masha, who accompanied him, that he went back to Petersburg in January, 1887. According to his own account, he was handsomely treated there and produced a "colossal effect." It was true that almost all the magazines had just had articles about him in their New Year issues and that in Tolstoy's review *The Treasure* the well-known critic Obolensky had compared him in a long article with Korolenko and indeed found Chekhov superior. "There must be some mistake," Chekhov commented, but he still admitted that he was rather proud to be the first writer who, "having produced nothing but knickknacks for the papers," had succeeded in capturing the attention of the "long-eared critics." So he was still in fashion: his stories were read aloud in public and he was assailed with requests to contribute to publications. He was invited everywhere, he was considered delightful, and in addition he aroused surprise, as when he made nonconformist but Tolstoyan observations on "nonresistance to evil." And of course his dear Uncle Mitrofanos in his far-off province was immediately brought up to date on Antosha's latest successes.

In March Chekhov went to Petersburg again, but this time out of family feeling and in haste: he had just learned that Alexander had been stricken by typhus. Preoccupied with "dear, good Anna" (*Anna Karenina,* which he had just read on the train), he was shocked by the capital's appearance as soon as he arrived: it had been transformed into "a city of death." Typhoid fever was ravaging it appallingly; the streets were filled with funeral processions. Everyone whom one met was in mourning. Leikin said that his *concierge* had been carried off in a matter of hours. Chekhov found Alexander's wife even more seriously ill than her husband. He took care of both of them and did not return to Moscow until he was certain of their recovery. But he was much less certain of the health of "that dear old good fellow," Grigorovich, whom he had found suffering from angina pectoris.[3]

Chekhov spent only a few days in Moscow—just time enough to get rid of a bad cold—and then left again, but this time he headed south, for Taganrog. Finding after eight years of absence that his native city was exactly as he had left it, he was shocked. He had become accustomed to the animation of Moscow and Petersburg, and Taganrog's sleepiness stunned him. "It's completely Asia!" he declared. "It is so completely Asia all around me that I can't believe my eyes. All that interests the seventy thousand inhabitants is eating, drinking, and multiplying; no other interests exist for them" (April 7, 1887). Walking through the empty, dirty streets, he encountered nothing but "the bloated faces of complacent idleness and rogues satisfied with a few kopecks"; he did not see a single sign without an error in it (there was even a café called "Rassia"); every reality that he touched was, in a word, sordid.

Undoubtedly he found it all the more sordid because it drained the poetry out of all the memories that were rising within him. On every corner he encountered someone whom he had once known, and since it was Easter, he went to church with the secret hope of experiencing again the emotions of his childhood. But the spell was broken. While his delightful Uncle Mitrofanos still seemed as kind as ever and truly touching in his piety, the sight of the old family home, still occupied by Selivanov but looking empty and abandoned, depressed Chekhov: "How could I have lived there?" he wondered. It was with a bitterness that was unusual for him that he wrote to a friend that, if he, like his friend, were an architect of talent, he would "tear down Taganrog." But he added facetiously: "Now I have to go visit a little lady. . . . Farewell. Wine and women should be shunned."

He did not want to go back to Moscow without having seen again the steppes where he had spent his vacations. And this time, to his joy, he found all the memories of his childhood unimpaired and still as moving: the endless naked steppe broken by rare little

---

[3] According to Chekhov's diagnosis, the author could live ten years or die the next day. In fact Grigorovich lived on for twelve years, until 1899, when he died at the age of seventy-seven.

knolls, the soaring sparrow hawks, the darting swallows, "the deep blue horizon." For two days he stayed with the Kravtsovs, with whom he had once lived as their son's tutor. No, nothing had altered in Cossack life: Anton rediscovered hospitality as generous as ever, walls hung with carbines, whips, and powder horns, delicious garlic soups, and in the evenings in the moonlight "the steppe stretching out of sight, with its barrows, the wilderness, a gravelike silence" (April 25, 1887).

He broke his journey at Novocherkask and attended a "real" Cossack wedding. The celebration lasted two days, with musical accompaniment, "charming feminine voices and increasing, terrifying drinking." The bridal couple kissed without restraint, the *tsymlyunskoye** flowed in torrents, and Chekhov, with his borrowed formal clothes and his city ways, was a great success with the rich young marriageable girls. "But," he confessed to Misha, "I was so drunk the whole time that I mistook the bottles for the girls and the girls for the bottles."

After these orgies, like a true hero of Russian fiction, he went to recuperate for two days in the famous Monastery of the Holy Mountains on the shore of the Donets; then, by way of Taganrog and in a third-class carriage, since he had not a kopeck left, he went back to Moscow. But it was May and the city people were already leaving town for their dachas; a few days later Chekhov followed their example and moved to Babkino. The weather there was bad and gloomy, and the house was so cold that he spent the first few days in his autumn overcoat.

This summer vacation was quiet and uneventful, at least on the surface. Too quiet, indeed, and no doubt rather wearisome, for apparently Chekhov did not derive his usual satisfaction from it. He returned to Moscow at the beginning of September, rather tense and suffering from a kind of psychic malady, which, in spite of his habitual reserve, was to reveal itself frequently in his letters during the autumn. For the first time they contained, and frequently repeated, the word *boredom*—"depressing boredom," he wrote to Mrs. Kisselyeva—a word that in the years to come was to be a kind of leitmotif in his correspondence.

Was he longing for "someone" or had he suddenly been afflicted

* A sparkling wine.—Translator.

by the profound melancholy that was infecting and paralyzing so
many Russian intellectuals at the time? He gave no clue and did
not go beyond merely blaming his "nerves." He wrote to Leikin:
"These last three weeks I have contemptibly surrendered myself
to melancholy" (September 11, 1887), and a month later, he confided to Alexander that he no longer went to the theater or visited
friends and had become so solitary that his mother, shocked by
this sudden misanthropy, had nicknamed him "Grandpa." It was
now October, and he actually ended his letter in the manner of an
old man who is getting ready to hibernate: "I am waiting for summer" (October 17, 1887).

He was to free himself suddenly of this anguish, or at least unconsciously to try to free himself of it, by writing a play of which
it would be the theme. Besides, he had long been drawn to the
theater and he had often tried before to write for it. As early as
the beginning of the year, under the impulse of an amusing idea,
he had written in one spurt—in an hour and five minutes, he
noted—a pleasant curtain-raiser, *Swan Song*, subtitled *Kalkhaz*.
But, although Korsch, the director of a theater bearing his name,
had twice asked him almost importunately during the spring to
write a play for him, Chekhov had thus far not acted on the invitations.

The desire to write a major work had tormented him since the
day when Grigorovich had virtually ordered him to dedicate himself to it. But though he dreamed about it, he did not envisage it
in the form of theatrical writing. On his return from his vacation,
in fact, he seemed to have decided to refuse Korsch. "Obviously I
am not going to write a play," he told Mrs. Kisselyeva. "I don't
want to have anything at all to do with theaters and the public.
. . . They can all go to the Devil!" (September 13, 1887). But
writers propose and inspiration disposes: three weeks later he
wrote to a friend: "My play is finished!"

He explained to Alexander how the change had come about.
After a fresh talk with Korsch, "I went to bed, thought of a subject, and began to write." At the end of two weeks—"or, rather,
ten days," he specified—his play was finished. And the author was
satisfied with his work: his play seemed to him to be well constructed, light "as a feather," and without any dead spots. He had

handled each act like a story, using a gentle tempo, but ending it "with a slap or two at the audience." As for the theme, he considered it quite new and original. There was only one sore point: his "ladies," his heroines, with perhaps one exception, were not sufficiently developed.

It is true that the theme of his play had rarely been touched at that time, but it is equally undebatable that the story that was supposed to illustrate it was too turgid and not very theatrical. Ivanov, an intellectual who has become a gentleman-farmer out of idealism, is afflicted with what today would be called a "nervous depression" when he reaches the age of forty. He takes no interest in his estate, which begins to decline, in his wife, who is seriously ill, or even in the gossip about him that begins to circulate in the district. Sasha, a very young girl, the excitable daughter of his neighbor and friend, is so in love with him that she is ready to risk scandal, and he allows himself to be loved by her. When the family physician accuses him of hastening his wife's death by his behavior so that he can marry the rich heiress, Sasha, he does not reply. All that interests him, all that excites him, is his growing melancholy, his *toska*. His wife dies, and soon his wedding to the little romantic is announced. But on the very morning of the wedding day, attacked in front of everyone by the physician, Ivanov tells Sasha that he is not going to marry her; then, abruptly hurled out of his torpor, he kills himself in the presence of the wedding guests.

The innovation in *Ivanov*—and the "slaps" to the educated audience—consisted in its demonstration of the futility of the contemporary Russian intellectual, caught between his dreams and harsh reality. Since the assassination of Alexander II, the only reality was the measure of social and political repression that had ensued; the dream that the intelligentsia had cherished for twenty years, and with increased ardor since Tolstoy had made it fashionable again, was an ideal of humanitarian reforms that owed almost everything, however, to Rousseau and nothing to Karl Marx. Discouraged by the reactionary program of Alexander III, the upper-class intellectuals, symbolized by Ivanov, had fallen into apathy and despair and gradually had become almost trapped in them.

With that sense of reality and even business that he had so keenly—what he called having "the American soul"—Chekhov, his play completed, immediately launched a campaign to have it produced. The play was read to a group of friends, and then offered to Korsch and accepted. Much excited by this first success, the author sat down to calculate and concluded that *Ivanov* could bring him six hundred to a thousand rubles. He thought of everything, and therefore of publicity too, and wrote to his fraternal factotum, the obliging Alexander, to ask him to get an item inserted in *New Times:* "A. P. Chekhov has just written a four-act play, *Ivanov*. Read to a literary group in Moscow (or something of that kind), it made a very strong impression. The theme is new, the characters are well drawn, etc." (October 17, 1887). In fact he was busy with virtually nothing other than his play throughout October and November, and already his own *toska* seemed in large measure to have disappeared.

Chekhov was full of hope when, after long conversations with Davydov, the actor who was to play the title part, he began to attend the rehearsals. Very quickly, however, he was compelled to face the facts, and with each day his hope of seeing *Ivanov* succeed dwindled. He was outraged—without once suspecting that this was the fate of every author whose first play is being produced—to find that now it was no longer he but the director who was the master of *Ivanov*. He was refused when he requested assurance that his play would be staged in the spirit in which he had written it; the director wanted "the author's participation reduced to zero."

Chekhov's relations with Korsch, whose only goal was a full house, soon grew strained. And he was disappointed in the actors as well: he found that they were capricious, too sure of themselves, whereas their lack of education made them incapable of understanding their parts; they were puffed up with vanity and ridden by jealousies. As a result of all this, in addition to the lack of sufficient rehearsals, Chekhov was almost in dread of catastrophe by opening night.

The first performance was given on November 19. Highly nervous and almost mad with anxiety until then, Chekhov was amazed, when the day came, by his own composure; he was not at all disturbed. Such was not the case with his family, which went in a trembling body to conceal its apprehensions in a box, while the author, preferring to be alone, hid in another, as small as a monk's cell, that was very close to the stage. He had gone to visit the actors before retreating into it, and he had found them nervous, lacking in confidence, crossing themselves to avert bad luck. And then the curtain rose on that *Ivanov* that had so little resemblance to what he had imagined.

During the first act he had a first disappointment. Kisselyevsky, an actor on whom Chekhov had placed great hopes, did not know his part: he improvised and stammered. Nevertheless, when the first-act curtain fell and Chekhov heard the applause and the curtains calls, he felt entitled to think that he had succeeded. The second act, in spite of the actors' blunders—they "thrust a knife into the author's back"—confirmed the triumph, and the audience called for the author: this was repeated after the third act, which was also better done.

It was during the fourth act that things turned worse. The actors, who had been drinking, began to clown. Kisselyevsky, still floundering but by now drunk as a trooper, said appalling things, and the audience, bewildered at first, soon began to react. From the orchestra to the top gallery there were shouts, hoots, catcalls, whistles, angry remarks; the tumult became general: there were near-brawls at the bar; when students in the gallery tried to evict some rowdy, the police came and threw out two of the students. A frightened friend of the author fled the theater, and Masha almost fainted. The play finally ended; the audience understood nothing of Ivanov's suicide, and the theater was loud with applause, shouts, police whistles, and foot-stamping. Only Chekhov had retained his poise, and, writing to Alexander three days later, he finished his letter thus: "In the last analysis, weariness and a feeling of boredom. Even though the play had a real success, it's disgusting . . ." (November 20, 1887).

There were two further and more peaceable performances, and *Ivanov* was taken off the program. "Everything has finally settled down, dissolved, dissipated," Chekhov wrote, and "with a light heart" he sat down again at his desk and went back to writing stories. "With a light heart"? Was this a bit of boasting? Actually it was not, and apparently, once the ordeal had ended and his nerves, strained to breaking for weeks, had snapped suddenly back to normal; he had regained his serenity. He was no longer angry at Korsch or the actors, and he carried his good nature to the point of asking Alexander to make it a point with *New Times* not to attack them. He had so thoroughly recovered his composure and his sense for the practical that he again asked his brother to insert a favorable comment on his play in the same paper, so that it might thus get another performance and bring him fifty or a hundred rubles more.

It was an ironic tranquility with which Chekhov read the reviews, which were often savage, harsh, and totally devoid of understanding: "Nothing good has ever been expected from Mr. Chekhov," *The Moscow Gazette* observed coldly, "but nevertheless no one would have dreamed that a young man with a university education would have the gall to offer the public anything so insolently cynical. . . . What an immoral play!"

Cynical it was, since Chekhov had used it to tell the intellectuals—audience and critics—quite brutally what he thought of them. There was added insolence in the fact that he had named his sorrowful hero Ivanov—for a time he had thought of calling him Ivan Ivanovitch Ivanov—which amounted to calling him Jones: in other words, Mr. Everyman. "Ivanovs you can find by the thousands, you know," he told Korolenko. And in all good faith he said: "I have accused no one and I have absolved no one"; and this was true; but he had "shown" someone, the Russian intelligentsia, as it really was—discouraged and impotent—and that was enough to make it denounce both the portrait and the artist.

V

"I LACK PASSION"

It is still too soon to complain, but it is never too soon to ask one-self: "Am I devoting myself to worthwhile things or to trash? The critics say nothing, the public lies, but my intuition tells me I am dedicating myself to nonsense. . . ."

CHEKHOV in a letter to
SUVORIN, December 26, 1888

There is still a dispute between literary historians in Russia: depending whether they live in the one or the other capital, they argue that Chekhov preferred Moscow to Petersburg, or the contrary. This question, which is of only tangential interest, need not concern us or even delay us. It is enough to recall that Chekhov wrote that he could not "picture himself in any place but Moscow" and that he never thought of moving to Petersburg. Nothing, however, prevented his doing so; on the contrary, as the real intellectual center of Russia, the northern capital should have attracted him more strongly than Moscow. What he did enjoy, on the other hand, at least during the years between 1885 and 1890, was making short visits to Petersburg. He liked its baroque atmosphere, the wit that was everywhere in the capital, the drawing rooms, where people talked of literature—in a word, he went to Petersburg rather as a provincial goes to the theater.

That winter he went to Petersburg at the end of November, immediately after the fiasco of *Ivanov*. After a year of absence, he was enchanted—"in seventh heaven"—to return to his splendid city with the soft greens, reds, and ochres of its Italian façades, dazzling and contrasting with the snow, its lively streets, its rough-spoken coachmen, its luxurious restaurants, and its open-air *salon,* the Nevsky Prospekt. As for Petersburg, it seemed equally delighted to see him again and to play host to him. He had invitations every evening, and women of fashion fought for him: he met so many intelligent people that his only difficulty was in choosing his companions.

He had brought a manuscript copy of *Ivanov* with him, and it began to circulate from hand to hand; soon everyone showed so much enthusiasm about it that he was quite encouraged. "But of course your play could not have been a success," he was told: "the Moscow theater and audience are incapable of understanding it. The pieces in the Moscow papers just made us laugh." Everyone, and especially Suvorin, advised him to have *Ivanov* produced in Petersburg. Delighted, Chekhov at once told his brother Mikhail to notify the clan not only that his reputation as a writer was undamaged but also that in the December issue of *The European Messenger* Dmitri Merezhkovsky would devote a long and very laudatory article to him. There was even talk of awarding him the big annual literary honor, the Pushkin Prize.

"How I regret that I cannot always live here," he wrote, rather forgetting that it depended entirely on himself whether he did so. What pleased him most in Petersburg, perhaps, was the easy amiability with which new acquaintances could be made and how quickly they ripened into extremely cordial relations. With Suvorin, whom he barely knew, he was already discussing everything "with complete frankness," and he was immediately placed on equal footing by celebrities whom he was meeting for the first time, such as Repin, the painter, or Pleschev, the old poet who had been arrested with Dostoevsky thirty-eight years earlier as a member of the Petrashesky revolutionary group; they had faced the firing squad together before they were granted clemency and sent to forced labor in Siberia.[1]

---

[1] The cruel, gruesome comedy to which Dostoevsky and his companions were subjected is well known. Sentenced to death, they were taken before a firing squad in Semonov Square and it was not until the very last minute that they were informed that Tsar Nicholas I, "in his infinite goodness," had commuted their sentences to forced labor for life.

But what impression did Chekhov make on these rather skeptical Petersburgers? Korolenko, who saw him again at this time, considered him both profound and ingenuous. His bright eyes, his radiant face conveyed the impression of an intensely curious man who thoroughly enjoyed living. His speech was that of a man of independent mind, without any political ties. But though his face was that of an intellectual, it had a roundness and a candor that made one think of an unsophisticated young peasant freshly arrived from his village.

There was only one gloomy aspect to this visit to Petersburg, and that was the condition in which Anton found Alexander. He was very fond of his insufferable elder and grateful for what Alexander did for him; a few weeks before going to Petersburg, Anton had written to him, in that tone of banter he used to conceal his emotions: "My future historian will write of you too in my biography: 'He had a brother, Alexander, who took care of his business and made no small contribution to the development of his talent.'" Alas! staying with Alexander during his visit to Petersburg, Anton was disillusioned: his brother was incorrigible—the sight of the shabby, filthy, nauseating furnished rooms in which he lived with his wife was enough to make Anton despair of his ever changing his ways. Alexander's wife was ill and he himself was discouraged: their lives were made up of quarrels, lies, and self-pity. "Living with him for a week," Chekhov wrote to his family, "would be enough to drive one crazy and leave one as dirty as a mop" (November 30, 1887).

Chekhov himself was more determined than ever not to fall into the trap of facility. Only a few days after his return to Moscow he began work for the first time on a long story. Korolenko had asked him for a contribution to *The Northern Messenger*, a major magazine at that time, and as Chekhov attacked his story he felt the more anxious and excited because he wanted to make a good appearance in the publication and he suspected that his dear colleagues were lying in ambush for him "round the corner." He began a story about the steppe, but he found the initial pages badly done because "one can't smell the hay in it."

He persevered, however, and by an amusing coincidence, when he had been working barely a week on his "steppe," he received a letter from Grigorovich in which his mentor urged him once again to devote himself to a major undertaking; he even suggested a subject: the pathetic story of a seventeen-year-old boy whose poverty had driven him to suicide. With the deference he felt for his eminent elder, Chekhov immediately replied that he had already got to work on a very different thing: a new theme, something like "an encyclopedia of the steppe." But that summer, he promised, he would begin work on a novel.

He worked without a break, allowing himself to be distracted neither by the drinking bouts of the Feast of St. Tatiana, the patron of the University of Moscow, which he found "boring and vulgar," nor by his own birthday, celebrated with Levitan and other friends; not even by the few days that he spent with the Kisselyevs in Babkino. He even found time, in order to meet some bills, to write a little story on the run for *The Petersburg Gazette*, and it was a masterpiece: "The Wish to Sleep." He worked on his long story with pleasure and appetite, "like a gourmet eating quail: with feeling, understanding, and care."

But he was not accustomed to writing long stories, and what problems he encountered! His manuscript, which told of a child's journey across the steppe and was basically without plot or romance, would certainly be dull. "A story without a woman," he had written to a friend, "is like a steam engine without steam." And here was his engine without any steam at all—in other words, without love except for the love of the steppe. Would his readers understand what he had tried to do? Certainly there were fine "verses in prose" here and there in the manuscript, and it did indeed smell of summer and hay, but in spite of everything he had the feeling that he was "swelling up," turning stupid as he progressed, and dragging out his descriptive passages. He was no better after all than his young colleagues: "Fine birds, perhaps, and good singers, but no eagles" (January 22, 1888).

In a month his manuscript was finished. To the surprise of the author himself it amounted to almost eighty printed pages. But was he satisfied with himself? He actually did not know what to think of what he had written because this time it was too close to him, composed of his own recollections of childhood—"those images and scenes that were dear to me and that, God knows why, I preserved and concealed with care"—and he had not taken any perspective on them. Naturally he said that it was his masterpiece and that he could not surpass it, but in truth he suffered horrible self-doubts.

On February 3 he sent his manuscript, its ink barely dry, to Pleshchev with a request for his frank opinion of it: in advance he asked for indulgence. "For the love of God, my dear fellow, don't stand on ceremony, and, if that is what you think, tell me my story is bad and dull. I have a terrible desire to know the absolute truth" (February 3, 1888).

The "beginner"—that was how he had signed his letter—did not have long to wait; five days later he had the reply. Pleshchev said that once he had begun to read the manuscript, he had been unable to put it down. He had found in it a tremendous magnetism, "a well of poetry." "It is a gripping work," he wrote, "and I predict a great, a very great future for you." In addition, Korolenko and the entire staff of *The Northern Messenger* shared his enthusiasm.

This letter did more than reassure Chekhov: it enchanted him. So there was to be recognition for this story into which he had put "much sap, energy, and phosphorus," and he was going to receive a thousand rubles for it—the highest fee that he had ever had. He bragged of it to everyone, adding that for the first time he was going to be published in what the Russian intelligentsia called a "big" magazine—in other words, a quality publication.

"The Steppe" appeared in the March issue of *The Northern Messenger*. The critics reacted at once, and most favorably. Leskov called the author a genius, Saltykhov-Shchedrin and Ostrovsky praised him to the skies, and even Buryenin, the dreaded critic of *New Times,* joined the choir of laudation: he did not hesitate to compare Chekhov with Gogol and Tolstoy. And Pleshchev wrote to Chekhov that he heard nothing but praise everywhere and that their colleague Garshin had read "The Steppe" twice in succession and was "mad about it."

Glory called Chekhov to Petersburg: on March 13 he obeyed the summons. Pleshchev had not exaggerated: Garshin was reading "The Steppe" aloud every evening in friends' houses, and if anyone dared to criticize its author, he replied with tears in his voice that Chekhov was a unique phenomenon in Russian literature.

Chekhov stayed in Suvorin's home during his week in Petersburg. This publisher, who had made up his mind to acquire the successful young author, omitted no effort to dazzle him. He gave Chekhov an opulent suite in his house with a piano, a fireplace, a splendid desk, and a "revolving chaise longue." A carriage was put at his disposal and a servant, Vassily, was assigned to his needs and even helped him to dress. Actually Chekhov did not quite know what to do with Vassily. "It seems so odd to me," he wrote, "that he follows me everywhere with deference, on tiptoe, and tries to guess what I want." So he led a rather luxurious life, with carriage rides, visits to elegant shops with Mrs. Suvorina—he bought fabrics for Masha—and social evenings with champagne. In reality he allowed himself to be carried along, half awed and half mocking, delighted to be able to describe all these things to his family and at the same time a little ashamed. "I had the feeling," he was to write to Mrs. Kisselyeva, "that I was quite a swine."

With that inexhaustible butterfly, the mistress of the house, he talked about trivia, but with Suvorin he had serious conversations as well. They agreed on a reissue of *In the Twilight* and on the publication of a new volume of stories. Suvorin, a hard-working yet casual man of wealth, confused Chekhov: the publisher took him to visit his printing shop, talked intelligently about philosophy, then, with complete seriousness, advised him to take a wife and to marry none other than the publisher's daughter, "who at the moment," Anton wrote to Alexander, "crawls about under the table on all fours." Chekhov had heard much that was unflattering about Suvorin but basically he found the publisher congenial, and a real bond of friendship was established between them.

Alexis Suvorin was an extremely colorful man, one of those picturesque, powerful, and not overscrupulous individuals whom nascent capitalism had enabled to raise themselves swiftly to the top rank. Twenty-six years older than Chekhov, he too had come from the people: his grandfather had been a serf, his father had fought at Borodino as an ordinary private. He himself was extremely talented and greedy for success. At first he had thought that he could achieve it with intelligence alone: he had got his start as a schoolteacher in a little village in central Russia, then he had tested his strength in journalism in Moscow. There he had initially been a failure, but he had refused to allow himself to be discouraged and had moved to Petersburg. Once in the capital he had soon managed to attract attention and admiration—from men as knowledgeable as Pleshchev—for his brilliant, acute, and very liberal reporting for various publications.

But respect was not enough for a man like Suvorin. He had to have power, and in those days, for men who were not born to it, power was available only through money. Hence his real rise had begun in 1876, when he had bought a small daily paper, *New Times*, at auction. His success had been dazzling, but he had paid for it with the betrayal of his youthful ideals: in order to make his paper succeed, he had aligned it with the government and become the defender of the established order maintained by the iron fist of reaction. Thereafter his success was assured: in ten years *New Times* had become the largest daily newspaper in Russia. Suvorin had acquired a large publishing house of his own and he had obtained from the government the exclusive concession for all the Russian railway system newsstands. By now a multimillionnaire, he led a sumptuous life: he had come a long way from the time when his wife walked barefoot through the village where he taught in order to economize on shoes.

The avant-garde among the intelligentsia, who had nothing but contempt for Suvorin, insisted that he was really nothing but an opportunist, a cynical go-getter overawed by his own metamorphosis into a power in business. His private diary shows us that the man was considerably more complex: while he served a despotism, in reality he despised it for its stupidity and its brutality. Reactionary in his newspaper and often liberal in his speech, full of duplicity and inner contradictions, in that nineteenth-century Russian intelligentsia that in so many ways resembled a certain "Rousseauist" French élite of the previous century he was the kind of skeptic who had little faith in man but who loved the arts, especially literature. It was his vast experience, his originality as a self-educated man, his passion for letters—he was himself a writer and a playwright—that attracted Chekhov, who was to remain under his spell for more than ten years.

On his return to Moscow, Chekhov bade his "archimandrite," Alexander, to convey his thanks to the Suvorins. The week spent in their home seemed to him to have slipped by in a moment, of which, he said, "I can say through Pushkin's mouth: 'I remember that miraculous moment' . . ." (March 24, 1888).

Chekhov had assigned his brother Mikhail to find him a new dacha for the summer. Mikhail had discovered one in the Ukraine, on the shore of the Psyol, but it seemed abandoned—"a poetic ruin"—and Chekhov, who had lost no time in inviting the Suvorins and Pleshchev to visit it before he had even seen it, was rather uneasy. But he was highly pleased when early in May he found for himself that this little country cottage in Luka was actually very inviting with its bright, pretty, well-furnished rooms. Its park was an "old, old abandoned garden," rich in exquisite scents; in the evening there was "nothing but the rustles of the night, enough to weave a spell." And, by a miracle, there was not only the nearby river but also a lake a verst long. What gudgeon and perch fries to look forward to!

Always very sociable, Chekhov was soon on terms of friendship with the owners, a family called Lintvaryev. The Lintvaryevs were one of those families of the minor nobility, so common at that time in Russia, that were half bankrupt and doomed to disappear before the triumph of capitalism—on the Suvorin model— but that were still upholding a certain art of living composed of real and unostentatious culture, detachment, charming manners, and individuality without exhibitionism.

The Lintvaryev family was composed of a widow, three daughters, and two sons. The mother was a delightful old eccentric who read Schopenhauer in the original, loved hymns, and devoured the fashionable magazines. The eldest daughter, Zenaida, had studied physics, but stricken with a brain tumor and blind, she was now merely waiting for death with remarkable serenity. The second daughter, Yelena, was a gentle, timid, quiet girl who, having completed her medical studies, had gone back to her home: she loved family life, but she was ugly, and in her obscure country nook she had little hope of attracting a husband. The youngest daughter, Natasha, young, muscular, sunburned, gay, was full of

enthusiasms: she read Karl Marx and at her own expense she had
built a school on the estate where the village children learned to
read Krylov's fables in a Ukrainian translation. The Luka dacha
might have been called the house of the "three sisters," for there
was not much to say of the two brothers, except that one managed
the estate and the other was very much a disciple of Tolstoy.

In this somewhat old-fashioned and almost threatened atmosphere the writer found much pleasure. Everything that he saw
and heard—the old servants who had once been serfs, the abandoned house, the girls hoping for love, the sound of the water mill,
the barking of distant dogs—seemed known to him already
through old tales read long ago. He was impressed by old Mrs.
Lintvaryeva's culture, by her blind daughter's smiling courage—
the muzhiki called her "The Saint"—by Natasha's high spirits and
Ukrainian nationalism. Nor did he need much time to become
fond of the Ukrainian peasants with whom he stopped to talk during his walks. He found them "superb types" of gaiety, subtlety,
and wit.

He was so comfortable in Luka that he stayed there two months
without once leaving. He wrote, though not much—"coupling
with the muse is good only in winter"—went swimming in the
river, visited all the neighboring fairs, and organized carriage
trips to friends' houses. Everything gave him pleasure: catching
perch and crayfish in the Psyol, flirting with the girls, observing
nature, listening to the strange cry of the bittern, watching nightingales come out of their eggs "looking like little naked Jews."
Pleshchev, old, warm, and genuine, was one of the friends who came
to visit him, and the one who was best liked by the Lintvaryeva
girls. They went out of their way to cater to the sleepy, gentle old
man, gathered flowers for him, took him for boat rides, and sang
to him. "He is exactly the same here as in Petersburg," Chekhov
wrote, "an ikon before which one prays because it is old."

Did he enjoy himself, then, in his Ukrainian countryside? Well,
yes and no; for while he boasted of its charms, he also wrote: "It is
boring to be alone in a dacha, especially if there are no congenial
friends about." In fact he never felt quite at ease where he was,
and like many tuberculars, he possessed that inner drive that compelled him to go away, convinced that he would be better off

"elsewhere" and eager too to see everything during what he somehow guessed would have to be a short life.

On July 10, at "General" Suvorin's invitation, he left for Theodosia in the Crimea, where the publisher owned a luxurious villa beside the sea. Chekhov spent two weeks there, entertained like a prince. He rose at eleven in the morning, went to bed at three the next morning, enjoyed meals consisting of a dozen Tartar dishes, all "very tasty and very rich." His hostess amused him: she changed her clothes on the hour, began the day with laughter and gypsy songs, and ended it in tears on the empty beach. He swam often and long in "the splendid, deep blue sea, as soft as a virgin's hair" (July 18, 1888). To the gentle, regular beat of the waves the time slipped and slipped away. . . . Only the stifling heat and the dry, harsh wind—"enough to make one cry for help"—prevented him from thinking he was in paradise.

As the idle hours passed, the writer and his host talked incessantly and endlessly, until Chekhov had the feeling that he had turned into "a talking machine." He himself made fun of this orgy of Russian-style talk that touched on every imaginable subject. Not satisfied to resolve all existing problems in words, he wrote, Suvorin and he "discovered a quantity of new ones that no one has yet raised. We talk, talk, and talk."

Chekhov came out of these conversations with Suvorin lightheaded and yet as if reinvigorated. The fact that his host was an inexhaustible talker did not diminish Chekhov's liking for him; quite to the contrary, it converted the liking into friendship, honest and undisguised. He discovered a new Suvorin; he admired him as a self-educated man with original ideas, with "wholly animal" integrity and freshness. In the field of art Chekhov was impressed by Suvorin's extreme sensitivity untainted by any theory: when art was involved, Chekhov wrote to his brother, Suvorin "behaves exactly like a setter chasing a woodcock: he is filled with diabolic frenzy and literally burns with enthusiasm" (July 18, 1888). He even learned that once he had become accustomed to Suvorin's dense, sincere, but churlish manner of expression, conversation with him became "almost a delight."

In Petersburg he had quite often been repelled by Mrs. Suvorina's blue-stocking side. In Theodosia he discovered that while she was indeed a chatterbox, she uttered her trivialities with a remarkable talent. He forgave her for being, like all the fashionable women of her time, "wrapped to the ears in Tolstoy" and for understanding nothing of contemporary literature, since she also exhibited wit, imagination, and originality, so that "one could listen to her all day without being bored, as to a canary." He wrote to Masha: "One is never bored with her." From him, who was so easily wearied by people, this was the finest of compliments.

Before he went back to Luka, he made a rather extensive tour of the Crimea and the Caucasus with Suvorin's son Alexis; they visited New Athos, Sukhum, Batum, Tiflis, and Baku. Returning to the Lintvaryevs at the beginning of August, Chekhov was once more captivated by the charms of the Ukrainian countryside. How he would have liked to buy a farm there and establish a little colony of writers—for really he could not long endure without them —who would live there communally, far from noisy Moscow, "its bad plays, its restaurants, and its Russian ideas. . . ." He insisted that he would gladly spend the winter in Luka, but three weeks later, of course, he went back to Moscow. The truth was that without the literary life, its meetings and its gossip, he was soon lost.

Did he at least return to the red "chest of drawers" in Sadovkaya-Kudrinskaya Street with improved health, prepared to confront the rigors of winter? Unfortunately, not at all. He had had a number of hemorrhages since the beginning of the year, and only a few weeks after his return to Moscow they reappeared. He mentioned them to no one except Suvorin, and then he minimized them, declaring that they had been going on for three years, and if they had indicated genuine tuberculosis, he would long since have been "in the other world." He argued that spitting blood was only one of the symptoms of the disease and that he had none of the others. Besides, a man could lose half his blood supply without danger.

Was he deliberately deceiving himself out of fear of the truth, or was he giving in to a certain fatalism? It is more likely, despite his being a doctor, that he was living in that kind of blind optimism so often found in tuberculosis patients. He did not think about his illness and never really worried about it except when he saw blood. "In blood that comes out of the mouth," he confided to Suvorin, "there is something ominous, as there is in red flame" (October 14, 1888).

Nevertheless it was essential that he get back to work, and seriously. He needed money, not so much for himself as for his family, the demanding family that, he had told Shcheglov a few months earlier, "comes down on me if I don't earn a certain number of rubles every month—comes down on me and weighs on me like a millstone round my neck" (April 18, 1888). No, he had not really escaped from that world into which he had been born, "in which money plays a vast, horrible part," and furthermore he did not intend to escape from it alone: he would take his entire little world of family with him. And that resolve held even though his family was often a burden to him and at such times seemed much less charming than selfish, pretentious, excessively garrulous, impatient, and always demanding.

If at least that family had had some tact; but no, it took advantage. Ivan came to the house every day, and their father spent all his evenings there. Nikolai had come back to live there at the beginning of the year, and although he often created a scandal by wandering through the house half naked and dead drunk, Anton did not have the heart to throw him out. Besides, whenever he took a hand in family matters, it was always in order to ease things. Thus, during the autumn he had to occupy himself with Alexander, who had just had a dangerously serious quarrel with Suvorin in Petersburg.

Under the signature of Al. Chekhov, Alexander had published a poorly written story, and the publisher, who had seen this as a deliberate attempt at confusion between the two brothers' names, since Anton was already famous, had refused to have anything to do with him. Anton, the real victim of the ambiguity, could have been angry too; he preferred to undertake his brother's defense with Suvorin: who could have thought that so bad a piece was his? a likely chance. And to Alexander he wrote calmly: "I attach very little importance to my own writings, my reputation, my literary droppings." He urged Alexander to forgive Suvorin for a letter that was certainly unjust but that had been written in an access of nerves caused by his son's illness.

Chekhov had just completed "a rather tendentious" story, "Holiday," and he was revising *Ivanov*, when on October 7 he received news that simultaneously bowled him over and elated him: the Literary Section of the Petersburg Academy of Sciences had awarded him the most coveted of literary honors, the Pushkin Prize, for his volume of stories called *In the Twilight*. There was an explosion of joy in the red "chest of drawers": in their delight his father and mother babbled "enormous inanities" and Masha flew off to "carillon" the news to all their friends. Chekhov himself was swamped with dinner invitations and felt like an ecstatic "lover." He wrote to a friend: "My luck is so good that I am beginning to cast a suspicious eye up toward the heavens. I'm going to run and hide under the table and keep quiet." He set aside the five hundred rubles that the prize included; this money would go toward the purchase of the farm that had been his dream since the summer.

But again he had a realistic, practical, and rather surprising reaction. At once he wrote to Suvorin to say that as soon as the award had been officially announced, Suvorin must run advertisements for both his books in his newspaper "in at least three successive issues." At the same time he retained his clarity of view and an almost deliberate detachment. This was because he was afraid of being caught, "as in the tentacle of an octopus," by literary excitement, the emptiness of which he had already plumbed. "Everything that I have written and that has got me this prize," he told Suvorin, "will last less than ten years in people's memories." He had no vanity, no feeling of having become a great writer. "What I write is not literature," he said, "but something like Trishka's caftan"—the shapeless, patched garment of Krylov's fable—and he added: "I have not yet begun my literary career. . . . "

He wrote also to Grigorovich, a member of the Academy, to whom he was certain that he owed his prize in part, in order to thank him. "I still have no clear views, whether in politics, in religion, or in philosophy," he added modestly. "I change my ideas every month, and in fact that is what compels me to limit myself to describing how my heroes love, marry, raise families, and die, and how they talk" (October 9, 1888).

Reading his correspondence of this period—especially the letters exchanged with Suvorin—is enough to show that in actuality
Chekhov was constantly examining himself on his profession as a
writer. He was still asking himself—in spite of the praises of Grigorovich and the award of the Pushkin Prize—whether he was a
real writer; he was hoping for criticism that would enable him to
discover and profit by the secret common to all masterpieces; and
to himself he put the crucial question: "Why write, and for
whom?" He was shocked by other young writers because they
were so sure of themselves and their vocation; he felt that he was
a very ordinary person without distinction.

The first question that he put to himself—What was he: a physician or a writer?—had been insinuated by Suvorin, who was urging him to give up the practice of medicine. Chekhov replied that
he did not see why he "could not course both these hares at the
same time." As he told his brother Alexander, "It is a bore to concern oneself with nothing but literature." And, besides, medicine
kept him to a salutary discipline. In a word, he was not going to
give up either. "Medicine is my lawful wife," he wrote, "and literature is my mistress. When I get tired of one, I sleep with the
other. It may be disorderly, but it is not monotonous" (September
11, 1888).

But although his "wife" was not creating any problems for him
—even if for the moment he was neglecting her to a degree—this
was not true of his "mistress." With a pretense of ingenuousness
he confessed that he did not know what literature was—at least,
good literature. Was it the Tolstoy of yesterday or of today, the
delicately sensual description of Turgenev, the hallucinated psychology of Dostoevsky, or the irony-masked violence of Gogol?
Certainly it was not his own writings, which were only "unpreten-
tious minor stories and other little pieces." Without too much
hope of seeing it come into being, he dreamed of a scientific criticism, a kind of "philosophy of creativity" that would analyze the
masterpieces produced by artists over the centuries and arrive at
their common characteristics, at "what constitutes their similarity
and their worth." In this way the canons of an esthetic could be
established. But how far that was from the journeyman moralizing criticism of men like Buryenin and Merezhkovsky!

How perilous it was, however, to start questioning oneself on one's art! Would he not be better advised to do as he did when he received letters from unknown women readers who questioned him as to the meaning of his work? At such times he confined himself to "stealing" the stamps on the return envelopes and not answering at all. Otherwise one would soon reach that frightening question: "Why write, and for whom?" But to him it seemed futile to concern oneself with a vulgar, ignorant public; his relations with his readers, in any case, were always disillusioning.

Then why write? For fame? But praise irritated him. For money? Yes, obviously, he needed it—and all the more because he treated the majority of his patients without charge—but, as soon as he got his hands on it, the money vanished. "Besides, accustomed to not having any, I am almost indifferent to it," he wrote to Suvorin. In the end he found only one answer—a halting one—to the question he put to himself: he was simply a maniac who wrote books for his own amusement, and that was all.

Those who regarded him as a remarkable man because he was a writer and who liked him on this account were mistaken: he himself esteemed only ordinary men, and he was convinced that he was one of them. Why should the mere fact of wielding a pen make him think of himself as "a man apart," endowed with a kind of universal genius? "Only imbeciles and charlatans," he wrote "understand everything." The haste with which young writers divorced themselves from the commonalty and divided themselves into schools, their clannishness, their vehemence in defending their literary ideas—and their own interests—their mutual admiration: all these were things of which he disapproved. Moreover, he felt no solidarity with his colleagues, and he condemned their systematized defeatism, their mania for high-handed solutions of all social and political problems. Their mechanically "advanced" literary periodicals annoyed him, bored him, and stirred him up. He was in no hurry to "arrive," he had no specific goal, no desire to feel that he had the support of a literary group. With complete rationality he wrote to Suvorin that in order to be wholly himself, he needed only "solitude and time."

Nevertheless he had exaggerated somewhat when he confessed to Grigorovich that he still had no "philosophic and literary convictions." First of all, he was profoundly convinced of the artist's absolute necessity to be—and to remain—above all a fiercely independent individual, completely free of all ties to any political party or religious sect. And it was this concern with total independence that made him flee any literary school. Ordinarily so restrained in his words, he explained his views with passion to his colleague Pleshchev: "I am not a liberal or a conservative or an evolutionist or a monk or a person uninterested in the world. I should like to be free artist, and no more, and I regret that God did not give me the strength to be one" (October 4, 1888).

What use did he intend to make of this total independence that he demanded for the writer? A very precise but also a very modest use. In the course of his reading he had been impressed by the fact that the greatest writers—the Pushkin of *Yevgen Onyegin* or the pre-"conversion" Tolstoy—had been satisfied to state problems and not resolve them. Chekhov thought that they were right. For him the artist's work consisted in his observation, in the choice that he exercised among the things that he remembered, and, finally, in the composition of his production. He showed his characters and explained their problems, but he was very careful neither to judge the people nor to resolve the problems.

He wished to be neither judge nor moralist, but witness. "The writer's function," he had written to Suvorin a few months earlier, "is only to report how and in what circumstances his character spoke of God or pessimism. It is not for the artist to sit in judgment on his characters or on their words, but merely to be an impartial witness." Besides, shouldn't writers agree with Socrates and Voltaire that "one can understand nothing in this world" (May 30, 1888)?

The writer as impartial witness: what does that mean? It was on this point that Chekhov was no longer too certain what was required of him by his insistence on objectivity. The witness that he strove to be would want to tell everything of what he had seen and guessed—"the poetry and the anatomy"—but he knew that this was impossible; hence he must choose, not between the one and the other, but rather what seemed to him most significant in both. Nevertheless, as the years went on, he doubted more and more whether this objectivity in artistic creation was possible.

Was it even, in the last analysis, desirable? He confessed his doubts to Suvorin: "If one rejects problems and objectives in creative work, then one must concede that the artist creates without purpose, under the influence of some aberration" (October 27, 1888).

He thought of himself and spoke of himself as a realist, but when one rereads the advice he gave to his colleagues, one recognizes that unconsciously he was turned toward something quite different: a new art that was impressionistic, all shadings, deliberate choices, suggestions, filigree. In order to focus a story better, for example, he recommended that only one character be brought into the foreground. "One draws only him," he wrote; "one sculpts him, and one disperses the others in the background. . . . This creates something that resembles the vault of heaven: a great moon and, around it, any number of little stars." In order to explain that one must suggest rather than describe in detail, and flee the conventional, he offered this sly observation for the benefit of a colleague: "Women must be described in such a way that the reader feels that you have taken off your necktie and unbuttoned your shirt. The same applies to nature. Give yourself freedom" (October 20, 1888).

Give oneself freedom—in short, take every liberty: for Chekhov it all came down to this.

Oh, those counsels that writers barter one to another! In January, 1889, Chekhov said to Suvorin: "Never write a play in winter! Never write a line for the theater unless you are a thousand versts away from it." But that was precisely what he had been doing for three months. In spite of all his vows he had gone back to *Ivanov*, and little by little he had been led to make drastic alterations in the play.

This return to the theater was the more unexpected because Chekhov was constantly vituperating it at the same time. The theater seemed to him to have fallen so low, into the hands of such "greengrocers," that he wondered whether it was even still possible to reform it. "The contemporary theater," he said, "is like measles: a bad disease of cities. This disease must be eliminated." All that he could see in it was stupidity and chatter. But even though he told a colleague, "I do not like the theater," he could hardly do without it. Ever since his return to Moscow he had been a regular customer of the Maly and Korsch Theaters, and he often spent his evenings in the company of actors. Hence, as soon as there was talk of staging his play in Petersburg, he hastened to go back to work on the manuscript of *Ivanov*.

It was an arduous, vexing task to which he dedicated himself. The public had not liked his play, insisting that it was not a play —and perhaps the public was right—but was it not precisely this that constituted the play's originality? Besides, whatever anyone said, the theme was new. His play had also been accused of lack of realism. But he swore—in a letter to Suvorin—that his *Ivanov* was composed only of observations, of sketches drawn from life. "I know," he added, "that I have not lied about them by a line or adulterated them by an iota." But since no one had understood him, well, he would try to make things clearer, even though . . .

For three months he groped for new touches, varied a word or a phrase, suffered when he had to drop this line or that, went back again to the beginning. After these long weeks of dogged work he felt drained: he "detested" his play, but nonetheless he felt that he had labored successfully. He had thoroughly changed the second act, completely torn apart the fourth, and made his little Sasha into a totally new character. There was something even more important: "Now," he told Suvorin, "my Ivanov is much more understandable." It should now be plain to everyone that if Ivanov commited suicide, it was not because of slanders and insults but because he had in truth "come to the end of his road," and even Sasha's love, far from inspiring him to improve, had only further diminished him in his own eyes. "If the audience goes out of the theater," Chekhov wrote, "with the conviction that an Ivanov is a scoundrel and a Dr. Lvov is a great man, I shall have to give up the theater and toss my pen to the Devil" (December 30, 1888).

In his revising of *Ivanov*, Chekhov had been so recaptured by the demon of the theater that at the same time, for his own amusement, he had dashed off a one-act farce, *The Marriage Proposal*. This curtain-raiser, written with a sharp and rather broadly comic pen, placed face to face, and soon in each other's arms, a tearful widow and an "enemy of women," both of whom at bottom had only one wish, to be married. Chekhov had also given much thought to a plan for a play of which Suvorin had spoken to him during the previous summer—*The Wood Demon*—and that they had decided to write together. But despite frequent postal summonses to the task, Suvorin had backed out, and Chekhov had deferred the project indefinitely. He was to go to work on it during the next summer.

It was the Alexandrinsky Theater in Petersburg that had put *Ivanov* on its program. Rehearsals began in January, 1889, and Chekhov, who was determined to keep a close watch on them, returned to the capital and the Suvorins' home. His relations with the Suvorins had grown extremely friendly, so much so that on his return from his first visit to them in December, he had declared himself enchanted by the vast experience of Suvorin and the self-indulgences—"reproaches and retirement"—of Anna Ivanovna, his wife. But the rehearsals quickly discouraged him: the actors played badly, and this was true especially of the pompous Davydov, who, as Ivanov, had no understanding of the character. He and Chekhov quarreled and reconciled a dozen times a day. Just before the first performance Chekhov wrote to Misha that no good must be expected of it.

Although—as he was to acknowledge later—he was extremely upset the next day, he put up a bold front in front of Mrs. Suvorina and insisted that what happened to the play was of no interest to him. "I'm stuffed to my ears with vanity," he was to tell Suvorin one day, but he was adept at concealing the fact behind an appearance of invulnerability. Fortunately, instead of the anticipated disaster, *Ivanov* was a huge success, and the author, who appeared on the stage hand in hand with the actors to thank the audience, was given a great ovation.

The next evening there was a dinner in his honor, and then Chekhov returned to Moscow. For all his vanity, or what he thought was vanity, it was difficult for him to tolerate the success of his "fireworks." It was still his desire to "hide under the table" that made him write: "Ovations and success are so noisy and so little satisfying that in sum they fill one with nothing but weariness and the desire to flee, flee."

After he had returned home Chekhov read the newspapers. In

general they had liked *Ivanov*. But the "leftist" papers—for which Korolenko, Uspensky, and Mikhailovsky wrote—had rather strong reservations and objected to its lack of any social message. Chekhov took this with a smile: were they talking about Ivanov, he inquired, or General Boulanger? On the other hand he was delighted with an extravagant article by Suvorin: he talked of having it framed. Letters from the audience poured in, and for one, anonymous, that attacked his play, ten were intelligent and perceptive and demonstrated to the author, who was gratified by the fact, that his *Ivanov* had been understood. As for Leskov, he had written in his diary: "An intelligent play. A great dramatic talent."

Meanwhile the play was still running successfully in Petersburg. It had even become the "thing to see," as Chekhov took pleasure in telling his Babkino fishing companion, Mrs. Kisselyeva. "My *Ivanov*," he wrote to her on February 17, "is still enjoying its colossal, phenomenal success! In Petersburg these days there are two important things: Semiradsky's 'Nude Courtesan' and me, clothed." Still touched with melancholy, he added: "For all that, I am bored."

Chekhov was not one of those authors who delight in glossing their own works. But though he normally avoided talking of them —and jokingly discouraged people who questioned him about them—he made an exception in the case of *Ivanov*. He had barely finished rewriting it when he embarked, in letters to Suvorin, on lengthy explanations of its intent, its spirit, and its characters. He adopted a completely serious tone that was most unusual with him—"I tell you this honestly, in all conscience"—to assure Suvorin that this time he had sought to stick to realism and to realism alone: he had invented nothing, his characters were not the spawn of any preconceived ideas or philosophy or chance; they were "the fruit of observations and studies of life."

Naturally he had avoided platitude, and the stage would have no placards announcing that "this is a melon and not a plum," but otherwise he had taken great care not to "play tricks" of any kind with truth. Whereas the contemporary Russian playwrights simplified to the extreme and made their characters either saints or devils, he, on the contrary, had endeavored to portray them objectively, in their full complexity. His sole originality, he said, consisted in his reaction against the contemporary theater's "utter falsehood, slander of life, and rigid unsophistication" that allowed only truth to speak.

This concentration on absolute realism—even though it appears that at times, as he revised his play, the author unconsciously neglected it—nevertheless gives *Ivanov* a very special place in the body of Chekhov's dramatic work. It is in fact the only one of his plays that sets out to be realistic and nothing else. His *Platonov* is loaded with savage humor that distorts reality and turns its characters into targets for a shooting-gallery. As for the plays that were to come later, they were all to be impregnated with a subtle lyricism that would transmute their realism into a kind of psychological impressionism.

There is another aspect of *Ivanov* that makes it unique among Chekhov's work: he had intended to write a play in traditional, almost classic style. In contrast to *Uncle Vanya* or *The Three Sisters*, for example, in which "nothing happens," *Ivanov* focuses on action that, even though it is rather slow, nonetheless has its vicissitudes and its climax in the romance between Ivanov and Sasha. Furthermore, *Ivanov* is not yet one of those plays—as its successors were to be—in which the atmosphere is more important than the characters; it is, rather, a character play. Here, indeed, as in the traditional theater, there is one character who completely dominates the others and who, by resolutely opposing them, stands out remarkably. So we are still a long way from the real Chekhovian play, which, if it is to be well acted, must have a homogeneous company and cannot have a star, for all its characters, even the least important, have almost equal rank in it, like the singers in a choir.

To his brother Alexander—who was once more following in his footsteps and was now trying to write for the theater—Chekhov wrote that he should allow himself more intellectual freedom, be brief, and, above all, choose a "new subject." He was convinced—and he was completely right—that in *Ivanov* he had used an altogether virgin theme: that *toska*, that sickness of the age, that profound disillusionment peculiar to a certain contemporary European élite, and especially to the Russian intelligentsia, was essen-

tially a belated, almost breathless romanticism. This theme—
"complicated," as Chekhov said, "and not stupid"—had never
been dealt with on the Russian stage, even if it had already been
exploited by other European playwrights, particularly by Ibsen.

But even more than this special melancholy it was the character
in whom it was embodied that was the innovation. With Ivanov,
that wholly disenchanted intellectual, not only did a new hero
make his appearance on the Russian stage; for the first time this
hero was the opposite of a hero: an "anti-hero." In actuality there
was no resemblance between Ivanov and the character of the traditional theater, sustained by a great passion and brought by it
into conflict with those around him. What animates Ivanov—or,
rather, immobilizes him, like Hamlet, in an endless reverie—is
almost the opposite of a passion, or at least a lack of passion, and
it is his unsure behavior, his passivity broken by minor ineffectual
exaltations, that plunge him, and others with him, into drama.

Some critics have thought that in the disturbing character of
Ivanov they could find many elements borrowed from Chekhov's
elder brothers, Alexander and Nikolai. This "family resemblance"
is too obvious to require emphasis, and this undoubtedly explains
why Chekhov seems to have nurtured a special affection for his
Ivanov and why, replying to those who, like Suvorin, regarded
Ivanov as a swine, Chekhov defended him with a fire that was
most unusual. In order to gain understanding for his Ivanov, to
win him absolution and even love, he wrote a long commentary
that he intended to be impartial but that was nonetheless a piece
of special pleading. "If in my play," he wrote, "Ivanov is a scoundrel and an interloper, if no one understands why Sarah and Sasha
love him, it is obvious that the play is a failure."

Far from being a swine in Chekhov's eyes, Ivanov was an honorable man, sincere and moral, but given to emotions and weak
and mediocre in spirit. In his youth he wanted to play the hero, to
stand alone against the world and live to the utmost of his capacity; in a word, he had had, "like the majority of Russian intellectuals, a very admirable past." But after a few years of struggle,
when he was barely thirty-five—and it was true, as Irina Nemirovskaya has pointed out, that in nineteenth-century Russia one

was already "almost an old man" at forty—he gave up and threw the handle after the hammer head: life had already worn him out, discouraged him, broken him. He accepted his defeat, and abandoning the ideals of his youth, he counseled his juniors to "organize their lives in the most commonplace fashion. The grayer and more monotonous the setting, the better."

For this total surrender by Ivanov in his confrontation with life Chekhov found a number of explanations, which were as many excuses. He spoke first of the tremendous weariness that was like "a sort of void" and that condemned his hero to inaction. In addition, and by reason of this very inaction, Ivanov was crushed beneath an endless feeling of boredom, the effect of which was to make it impossible for him to be comfortable anywhere or with anyone. And he felt frighteningly, irreparably alone in that little provincial world whose mediocrity and pettiness he had plumbed to the point of nausea, among those idle gamblers and clumsy drinkers who surrounded him and from whom he wanted to flee— but where would he go?—undoubtedly in fear lest he soon come to be like them. Love too had abandoned him, and when he learned that his wife was going to die, he felt "neither love nor pity." He did not understand what was happening within him, Chekhov tells us, and throughout the play he shows us his hero doing his utmost, straining fiercely to gain a clear insight into himself. For basically the only thing that still interested Ivanov, that Narcissus in love with his own disorder, was endless self-interrogation and wonder over what he was going to do with himself.

Even when he spoke to others—to whose replies, however, he did not listen—Ivanov pursued a kind of monologue and continued explaining himself to himself. Even when he was alone with little Sasha, who, since she was in love with him, expected something quite different, he was still questioning himself: "Day and night my conscience makes me uneasy and I feel that I am dreadfully guilty, but I cannot arrive at any understanding of what I have done wrong." Hence he also felt a guilt, but this base of bad conscience was shifting and obscure, and it was in vain that he probed it; he could not explain it to himself. "I am guilty":

these words were constantly on his lips until soon there was no doubt that feeling this guilt and hearing himself voice it afforded him a kind of bitter pleasure.

If Chekhov insisted—even rather heavily—on this feeling of guilt, it was not only because he regarded it as one of his hero's characteristics but also because for him this was a "purely Russian" character trait. Now, as he told Suvorin, he was essentially concerned with making Ivanov a "typically Russian" character. And that was also why, in addition to a "guilt complex," as it would be called today, he endowed his Ivanov with another trait of character that, in his view, was also one of the dominant elements of the Russian soul: the rapid transition from the ardor of youth—what he called its excitement—to a strange apathy that struck in the thirties. Ivanov did not emerge at all from this apathy except in brief flashes of exaltation followed by immediate relapses.[2] When Sasha told him of her love, he broke out enraptured: "Then that means starting life again from the beginning? Yes, Sashenka? Oh, my joy!" But a day later he refused to see her, he looked on the beginning of their love as "a commonplace, a nothing," and he went back to his dreary meditation on himself and his failure. And the extreme Russianness of all this is confirmed for us by Berdyaev, if confirmation be needed, when he asserts that Chekhov was in fact "the singer of the melancholy of the best minds of the Russian intelligentsia."

In the play Ivanov the helpless was opposed by a man of extreme self-confidence, Dr. Lvov. Chekhov was amazed that many spectators could regard Lvov as a "great man," and we share his amazement, for the character is almost loathsome, and in any case he irritates us by the constant and tasteless flaunting of his good conscience. Chekhov denied that he had made Lvov into a caricature—"a dishonest business that leads nowhere," he wrote—but we are only half persuaded. Lvov was certainly an honest, virtuous man, but is a man of honor who constantly waves his purity in other people's faces and finds it his warrant to sit in judgment on the world really a just man? Against Ivanov's burden of muted guilt Lvov continually raised his own "honesty complex," but his

---

[2] In his letter to Suvorin, Chekhov, remembering that he was also a physician, illustrated this character trait with an extremely uneven fever chart.

narrowness of mind and his right-thinking prejudices, while they
provided the play with its great moments through their confronta-
tions, also prevented these in the end from being anything more
than pathetic dialogues of the deaf.

"There are . . . five women in my play," the author wrote to
Alexander. "I feel that, except for one of them, these ladies are not
sufficiently developed." The exception is Sasha, the young romantic, at once very pure, very headstrong, and governed by the desire to dedicate herself; she has read and thought too much about
love, and she is drawn by that gray-at-the-temples Hamlet,
Ivanov. "To her," Chekhov wrote, "it is so noble, so holy a task: to
restore a fallen man to life, to put him back on his feet, to give him
happiness. It is not Ivanov she loves: it is this mission." But in
spite of her fierce determination, her imperious way of launching
and guiding their love, Sasha will not succeed in "reviving"
Ivanov, and in her desire to redeem him she will only precipitate
his doom.

For Ivanov was incurably infected with the "disgust of living."
Walled within himself, moreover, fascinated by his own disease,
he did not wish to be healed. So there was nothing left for him but
to kill himself—which is a way of sealing oneself forever into one's
problem—and it is in fact on the hero's suicide shot that the play
ends.

More often than ever Chekhov himself felt depressed, disenchanted, without appetite for life. Constantly writing, writing,
writing, he confided to a woman friend, sometimes made him
want to go and bury himself in the country "and sleep there until
May, like a mole." To Suvorin he wrote in greater detail: he had
had his fill of endless banal conversations with people asking for
favors, of medical consultations at two or three rubles each, of
housecalls on patients who did not pay a kopeck. "In short," he
concluded, "such a feeling of upheaval that it makes one want to
run away." At times he was beginning to hate this sorry life—
"something that in the past never happened with me," he wrote.
The only misery really lacking was an unrequited love. He signed
his letter, almost as Ivanov might have done: "Your bored Chekhov."

Such a crisis of disillusion in a young writer already recognized and honored, who had just enjoyed a triumph in the theater, might be surprising if it were not already to be guessed that Chekhov was essentially a melancholy man. The humor of his conversation, the comic touches that livened his letters, might create some initial illusion, but when one reads his letters consecutively, one cannot help being struck by the incessant recurrence of certain phrases. "I'm bored" and "Life is gray, as usual" and "No news."

Nothing new: no doubt that was the clue to his melancholy. A man without passions—without love, even unrequited—Chekhov at the age of twenty-eight found himself face to face with an empty life, a life that had not yet begun and that at the same time was leading nowhere. For the life that the writer led in his "chest of drawers" in Sadovaya-Kudrinskaya Street was anything but exciting: it was the life of a tidy bachelor working from morning until night whose only diversions were the occasional evenings spent with actors and actresses. Occasionally, too, he sought out the group of young liberal Moscow writers that gathered round Mikhailovsky, though most often to play only a passive part; when he did happen to enter a discussion—automatically brushing back his long wavy hair with his hand—he made only brief comments without any sign of feeling.

Was he becoming an old bachelor? Undoubtedly the question occurred to his sister, Masha, who was completely devoted to him and, in her pride in him, dedicated herself entirely to his growing renown. A teacher in a private school, she often brought her friends to spend an evening in her home. Anton was always charming to them—simultaneously playful and teasing—but he fell in love with none of them.

Masha had introduced him, for example, to a fellow teacher at the Ryevsky Institute, Lydia Stakhievna Mizinova, and on their first meeting Anton seemed much taken with her. In fact the eighteen-year-old girl had everything that should have attracted him: a glowing complexion, fine lively gray eyes, "sable eyebrows," magnificent long blond hair, gaiety and at the same time reserve. But, although subsequently, like the rest of the family, he began to call her "the beautiful Lika," and he seemed to enjoy her company particularly, his relations with her were never anything but light, friendly, occasionally flirtatious, with nothing of the emotional.

Another schoolmate of Masha, Olga Kundassova, who was less beautiful than Lika but intelligent and lively, evinced a growing liking for Anton that needed no encouragement to become something more. But while he was very cordial with her and used to call her "the little astronomer" because of her passion for the sciences, he pretended not to be aware that she would have preferred more tender appelations.

He had no passions, then, and no deep griefs either; but cares in profusion, and, as always, these were occasioned principally by his family. As a rule there was no limit to his patience, but on occasion the burden would be too vexing and he would complain to Suvorin: "One of them is ill, another is in love, the third talks too much, and so it goes. What bother I have with the lot of them!" (April 22, 1889).

What irritated him more—the price of a fame that was too sudden not to have given rise to jealousy—were the malicious rumors about him that began to circulate through the literary circles of both Petersburg and Moscow. His vulnerable point was the open and affectionate protection that he enjoyed from Suvorin, whom the liberals hated: so it was on this score that he was attacked, and with fury. There was talk that he was trying to marry Suvorin's daughter—who was not yet ten years old!—and that he was going to join the editorial board of New Times, whereas actually, in order better to preserve his independence, he had just refused an offer to become a regular contributor to it. But this latter attack gained some credence: even his good friend Pleshchev believed it and thought it his duty to warn Chekhov that any collaboration with this newspaper—"this shameless slop"—would automatically place him in the reactionaries' camp. "Gossip irritates me," Chekhov grumbled. "Every student says I'm about to marry a millionnaire. What depravity" (March 18, 1889).

Alexander too annoyed him, and deeply: when would his elder, who was now thirty-three, finally make up his mind to lead a stable, decent life? A visit to his brother in Petersburg in December had left Anton thoroughly angry. Alexander never stopped complaining of his "galley-slave life," in Anton's presence—and that of their children as well—he continually assailed his wife with vulgar insults and harsh reproaches and half-drunk and in his underwear he paraded before the maid. How could a man let himself go in such fashion? Anton had written to him bitterly. And now Alexander was talking of a divorce and a new marriage!

No doubt envious of the success of *Ivanov*, he had also just announced to his brother that he too was about to begin writing for the theater. What did Anton think of this? And what did he think of Alexander's idea of buying a farm? His irritation dissipated, "Father Antosha" replied cordially with a liberal supply of good advice. As for the play, he would himself recommend it to Suvorin. And he offered an amusing addendum: "Incidentally, remember that declarations of love, mutual infidelities, and the tears of widows, orphans, and others have had a great deal of wear. The subject should be new, but there may not be a play. . . ."

Chekhov also kept Alexander regularly informed of Nikolai's health, which, already dubious, suddenly worsened at the end of March. "Our affectionate beagle"—their nickname for Nikolai—had been infected with a benign form of typhoid fever, but there were pulmonary complications, Anton wrote. "There is a suspicion of dullness on the right side and there are rales." He had the patient moved to his own house, where he took care of him. But once the typhoid had disappeared, he could see that the tuberculosis had extended its ravages, and Nikolai, who was now coughing constantly, was still very weak and running a very high temperature. As soon as possible, Anton promised himself, he would take his brother to rest in the country, with the Lintvaryevs in Luka.

He and "the painter" left Moscow at the end of April. Chekhov was pleased to be with his friends again, to see the gentle, majestic Psyol, "spring with all its honors," the apple and cherry trees in blossom, to hear the song of lark and oriole. But the passage of time made no improvement in the state of his brother's health; quite the contrary. As a physician he could have no further illusions. "The question," he wrote to Alexander, "comes down to this: not when will he be well but how long can he last?"

Nikolai was inordinately demanding, difficult, and irascible, and Anton, who was still trying to smile, treated him like a "real general." That incessant cough that he could not help hearing also reminded him of his own case. Nervous and unable to keep himself working consistently, he spent his time reading a great deal. He went from Goncharov, the rereading of whom was so disappointing that he struck the name from his "list of demigods," to Gogol, over whose spontaneity and strength he was in "ecstasy," and Bourget, whose rejection of materialism shocked him. As Nikolai lay dying in the same house, Anton wrote in connection with *Le Disciple*: "It would seem to me that even the most fanatical spiritualist, when he dissects a corpse, must necessarily ask himself: 'Where is the soul in all this?'" (May 7, 1889).

Days and weeks went by. As he grew weaker, Nikolai became quieter and more resigned. Anton went from a kind of almost indifferent acceptance to a painful resentment and a desire to flee. On May 14 he wrote to Pleshchev: "If it were not for the painter's coughing, I should be perfectly happy"; two weeks later he wrote: "Alas, I am tied down hand and foot here and I have no right to move even a step." He felt a terrible need for a change of scene, for escape from the deathbed. He thought of going to Odessa, to Paris. And how alone he felt, too, without his family and without visitors.

In mid-June, Alexander arrived in Luka, and Anton, now that there was someone to relieve him, went at once to the government of Poltava, where he was expected by friends, the Smagins. He knew that Nikolai's inevitable end was near, but he could not bear any more: "I wanted to rest for five days and breathe other air," he wrote later.

Unfortunately this was to be impossible. He had barely arrived at his friends' house—in inhospitable weather—when he received a terribly terse telegram: "Kolya dead." He decided to return at once; the journey was long and painful. In the little junction station of Romny he had to wait from seven o'clock at night until two in the morning for a train connection, sitting in bitter cold against a wall behind which actors were rehearsing a melodrama. When he rejoined his family in Luka, he found everyone in such depths of confusion and grief—it was the first death in the family—that, as usual, he took pity on them all and, exhausted as he was, assumed all the responsibilities of the funeral.

In death Nikolai's face had returned to its finest expression, and Chekhov, when he had contemplated its serenity, wrote in an almost Christian tone: "If he committed faults in the past, he has expiated them with his sufferings. . . ." Nikolai's coffin was borne by mourners on foot to the little village cemetery of Luka and buried beneath the trees. "He seems to be comfortable there," Chekhov wrote (July 27, 1889).

He himself was more than ever uncomfortable where he was. The many warm letters of condolence that his brother's death evoked were not enough to "distract" him. "I felt so sick at heart," he soon wrote to Leikin, "that everything revolted me: the summer, the dacha, the Psyol." Therefore, as soon as the rest of the family had returned somewhat to normality, he set out again. He left Luka on July 28. It was a kind of blind escape, and he did not know where to go: to the Caucasus, somewhere abroad, or Vienna, where Suvorin wanted him to meet him? Finally, "by chance," he ended in Odessa.

Again by chance, he met the Maly Theater's company there; it was on tour. Feeling that this high-spirited and carefree companionship might be good for him, he embraced it. The actors were staying in the Northern Hotel: he too took a room there and spent ten days with them. They went swimming and devoured innumerable ices together, and in the evenings he attended their performances and then joined everyone in a room where Karatinga, one of the actresses, kept the samovar going, and the conversations continued until early morning. The actress found it strange that this withdrawn man in his severe gray suit chewed sunflower seeds like any peasant, and he was at times annoyed by the jealousies that erupted among the various women in the company. Nevertheless Checkhov was able to relax in this society of actors, and they enjoyed his company so much that when he left, they presented him with two beautiful neckties.

After Odessa it was Yalta, to which Chekhov went "without any reason" and where he remained more than three weeks. The only things that pleased him there were the brilliant sea, the lulling pace of the cab horses, and the low cost of living. On the other hand the heat was unbearable, the vegetation was miserable, the wine was vile, the girls were numerous but ugly, and the writers were equally numerous but mediocre. He was alone again with his grief, and he felt too that he had abandoned a stricken, sorrowful family; he reproached himself for his "sybaritic" selfishness. Each day he prepared to rejoin his family, and yet he could not make the move. "I swim in the morning," he wrote, "I die of heat the rest of the day, I drink wine in the evening, and I sleep at night. . . ."

But he was also writing. It was in the stifling atmosphere of Yalta that he wrote one of his most astonishing works, "A Dreary Story."

Immediately after the award of the Pushkin Prize, Chekhov had written to Grigorovich that he had a "marvelous" subject in mind for a novel and that he had already begun to write it. His pride spurred by the receipt of the prize—as it had been two years earlier by his elder's magnanimous letter—he seemed quite determined this time to present, not so much to others as to himself, that proof of mastery, that great work by the idea of which he was haunted.

It was not, however, until the beginning of March, 1889, when he no longer had to concern himself with *Ivanov*, that he began serious work. Firmly resolved to complete his novel, he had started by revising all that he had previously done on it. Suvorin was the first to get the news: "Do you know what?" Chekhov wrote to him on March 11. "I am writing a novel! I write and write and I see no end to my work. . . . What a plot!"

Now, to be precise, his novel had no plot at all. The working title that he had given it was *Stories Drawn From the Lives of My Friends*, and he conceived it as "separate, complete stories" arranged in sequence but, since the same characters appeared in all of them, forming nonetheless a coherent whole. He had sketched out these characters—there were nine of them—but he said no more about them except that they would be radically different from conventional types: "Unfaithful wives, suicides, kulaki, virtuous peasants, devoted slaves, moralizing old ladies, sweet old nannies, provincial great minds, red-nosed captains, and the 'new' men. . . ."

On these exiguous foundations he had labored without rest for several weeks. Highly optimistic at the start, he talked of having his novel finished in November, and by the beginning of April he was able to send the first three chapters to Pleshchev and ask him for an evaluation.[3]

His friend replied that he liked these early chapters very much, but was the novel "focused"? Chekhov's response to this was that what mattered, the very skeleton of his novel, was "man's absolute freedom" with respect to preconceptions, violence, ignorance, and passions. He persevered: early in May he was to write again that his novel was still preoccupying him and that he was continuing to work on it. Then, rather suddenly, came discouragement and the admission that it would take him two or three years to write it. There was a final reference to the novel, to the effect that he spent more time meditating on it than writing it, and then silence.

So for the second time the great venture had ended in failure. Was the reason to be found in the emotional effect of Nikolai's death? Or was it to be ascribed, as it has been by many, to Chekhov's lack of any *Weltanschauung*, which alone could have given his novel unity and coherence? Nikolai's death had not made Chekhov stop writing, and the best evidence of that is that "Dreary Story" written in a few days in Yalta at the height of his grief. As for the coherent conception of the world that was supposed to be indispensable to the microcosm that is a novel, Chekhov himself did not regard it as necessary. In his view the novelist wrote not in order to provide answers but only to state the questions properly.

To be accurate, Chekhov was not—at least in the traditional meaning of the word—a novelist. An admirable storyteller, of stories without subjects, a magnificent playwright, though his plays had no plots, he lacked the seething imagination and the creative energy (which, it may be argued, is rather naïve, since it believes in what it does) that are characteristic of true novelists. A man without passions, a kindly ironic observer of the passions of

---

[3] These fragments, unfortunately, have never been discovered.

others, he was incapable of living the passions of imagined characters—by proxy, one might say—and this is the novelist's secret. He admitted this when he wrote: "There is a kind of stagnation in my soul. I explain it by the stagnation of my private life" (May 4, 1889).

What a painter he could be, on the other hand, when it came to portraying a disenchanted spirit! That is the whole theme of "A Dreary Story." He admitted to the editor of *The Northern Echo*, for which the story was written, that his manuscript was the reflection of "that abominable state of mind" of which he had been unable to rid himself during the summer. But while this story may seem to us actually the most subjective of all that he had thus far written, he was no less insistent on its "objectivity": his hero's ideas were not his. He wrote to Suvorin that one must not look for beer where there was nothing but coffee. "If I show you a professor's ideas, believe me, there is no use looking for Chekhov's ideas in them. . . . In the whole story there is only one idea that I share, and that one lives in the head of a teacher, the scoundrel, Gnekker. What is it? 'The old man's gone mad.' All the rest is imagined" (October 17, 1889).

The theme is indeed imagined. At the end of a brilliant career as a university professor, Nikolai Stepanovich reviews his life. He is very rational, mercilessly incisive, detached from everything, and because death is not distant, he suddenly recognizes that his life has had no "meaning," that he is a "spiritual bankrupt." He judges himself coldly, without pity, and he does the same with those round him: his old, prating wife, his sickly, romantic daughter, and even his student, Katya, whose presence he enjoys but whose distress he is incapable of understanding. He runs away from all of them to die alone, without having been able to reply to Katya's tragic "What is to be done?"; he is totally apathetic, convinced of the world's absurdity and even of death's.

Whatever Chekhov may have said about it, it seems obvious that at this time he bore striking resemblances to his old professor. The lack of any ideal and the anguish that ensued, the conviction that ostensible success is not real were characteristics that they shared. Old Stepanovich was directly confronted with death;

Chekhov had just faced it indirectly in the person of his brother, the victim of the same disease that was ravaging him. Both looked death in the face without real anguish—since to them it led only to nothingness—and with a sterile skepticism. Though he did not completely admit it to himself, Stepanovich, as he drew the balance sheet of his life, suffered by reason of what had been marked by "a lack of ideals"; and this is echoed in Chekhov's avowal to Suvorin: "A conscious life without a clearly defined conception of the world is not a life but a burden, a horror." Mikhailovsky, the critic, who knew Chekhov well through their frequent meetings in the literary groups of Moscow, was right, then, when he wrote: "If this story comes off and reflects life, it is because the author has put his own suffering into it."

In this story he had once more been very much influenced by Tolstoy. It is difficult not to be struck by the parallelism between it and "The Death of Ivan Ilyich" a parallelism of situation—confrontation of death—and of thinking. But if in Tolstoy's story the terror of death is more intense, more agitated, more dramatic, it ends in acceptance, it is dissipated in the last pages by the illumination of love. There is nothing of the sort in "A Dreary Story," in which death resolves nothing, in which no illumination glows between the dusk of life and the night of death.

During this same year, 1889, encouraged by the success of *Ivanov*, Chekhov had also gone back to the theater. The play that a year earlier he had suggested that he and Suvorin write together —*The Wood Demon*—had been begun by him alone in the spring. He wanted to avoid the dramatic effects that he himself had exploited in *Ivanov* and to show life as it was—in other words, another "sad story." All the action would be inner. But after he had written two acts, he abandoned the project. "It was becoming a bore," he wrote, "and there is nothing duller than dull plays" (May 31, 1889).

On his return to Moscow on September 4, Chekhov began again to think about the play. Everyone, furthermore, was urging him to write it, and he himself remembered that he had promised the actors of the Maly Theater that he would write a play for them. So he went back to what he now called his "romantic comedy" and attempted to endow it with a "completely lyrical general tone." He rewrote all that he had thus far done. This time he worked with spirit and enjoyment. Work having begun on September 20, the play was completed on October 5. Eagerly copied by his family and an actor named Svobodin—to whom Chekhov had promised the leading part—it was submitted to the censor on October 9, and certain cuts were made by him in the first act.

The reaction of the reading committee of the Alexandrinsky Theater, to which Svobodin read the play, was harsher: pure and simple refusal. Lensky, the director, said that the public would not like it, and Svobodin himself wrote that no one could find in it any interesting effects or characters or situations, only "stupid platitudes without talent." Questioned by Chekhov, Lensky told him rudely: "Write stories. You are too contemptuous both of the stage and of the rules of drama." And Vasily Nemirovich-Danchenko, who had become a friend of Chekhov, confirmed the verdict: "Lensky is right; you are ignorant of too many of the laws of the theater." Only an actor, N. Solovtsov, wrote to Chekhov after he had read the play: "I am delighted and enchanted."

On the surface Chekhov accepted the blow philosophically. He admitted that he was not a playwright and he announced that he would no longer write for the theater, except little curtain-raisers like *The Wedding*, which, in fact, he had just completed, and in a matter of hours. But in his innermost self he was bitterly hurt by the refusal. In a letter to Suvorin he likened the reading committee's decision to that of an "army court-martial" (October 13, 1889).

But he refused, even so, to allow himself to be discouraged; as he had done with *Ivanov*, he revised his script; on the advice of Nemirovich-Danchenko, he reconstructed the fourth act almost in its entirety. Thus recast, the play was taken by the Abramov Theater in Moscow. After rehearsals attended by the author, it was performed for the first time on December 27. It was a failure.

There was no exception to the cruelty of the press. The author was accused of a mechanical duplication of life and of total ignorance of the laws of drama. Chekhov showed no reaction, but he was more responsive to the rumor that was already coursing through Petersburg to the effect that his hero, Serebryakov, was nothing but a malicious satire on Suvorin. He asked his friend to believe nothing of the kind, adding, in connection with one of his colleagues: "How delighted they would all have been if I had put arsenic into your tea or denounced you as a spy working for the secret police!" (October 17, 1889).

Meanwhile life, like the theater, went on for Chekhov with its entrances and exits of friends and strangers. Natasha Lintvaryeva came to stay with the Chekhovs for three weeks, and her good humor was infectious: her shouts of laughter shook the walls of the old "chest of drawers." Peter Tchaikovsky spent an entire evening with them, and Chekhov, who—rather surprisingly—passionately loved his romantic compositions, was flattered to see how well the composer knew and liked his stories; they talked of writing an opera together. Chekhov had also acquired another new friend recently: Ivan Leontyev, a former captain with waxed mustaches and a tragic laugh, who hoped—in vain—to become a great dramatist under the pseudonym of Shcheglov; in spite of Leontyev's atrocious handwriting, Chekhov enjoyed corresponding with him. But there were also irritations: the increasing jealousy of other writers and, at the end of November, an attack of influenza with "desperate coughing and dullness in the right lung."

The summer's crisis of pessimism and misanthropy, far from having diminished, had become a permanent condition, a kind of black "indolence." It seemed that Chekhov, apparently so self-controlled, no longer had any self-confidence. In December, making a kind of inventory of his life for Suvorin, he allowed himself to enlarge on this. "I have a passionate desire," he wrote, "to bury myself somewhere for four or five years and devote myself to difficult, serious work. I must learn, learn everything from the very beginning, because as a writer I am absolutely ignorant. I ought to write with a good conscience . . ." (December 15, 1889). A few days later he went back to the same theme: "In January, I shall be thirty years old. Hail the old bachelor; a useless life wasted to the core!"

It was then, at the end of December, 1889, that Chekhov abruptly and without visible reason decided to set out for the other side of the world, for Sakhalin. And four months later he did indeed begin the journey.

What kind of man was this who, at the age of thirty, examined his brief past, found it "useless" and "wasted," and resolved on a brutal turnabout? He who was so rational when he was dealing with others—did he really take this view of his life, or was this merely a caprice? It was no caprice: as "A Dreary Story" had implied, as he never stopped repeating in his letters, Chekhov in spite of his reserve was now profoundly disillusioned and coldly despairing. He did not want to recognize that as much from the family as from the literary point of view, the four years just past had been the happiest of his life: he had discovered that existence was absurd and, like others after him, beneath his phlegmatic mask he was fascinated and devoured by the discovery.

By now he was already a well-known writer, but fame and even literature seemed to him as empty as everything else. "For two years," he wrote to Suvorin, "and without any valid reason, I have had enough of seeing my books in print, I have become indifferent to the critics, to talk about literature, to insults, successes, failures, big money. . ." (December 15, 1889). The critics' adverse reactions to "A Dreary Story" and the failure of *The Wood Demon* only partly explain this attitude. In actuality, no critic treated Chekhov so roughly as he himself treated his work: he said that everything he had written thus far was nothing but "twaddle" and that he still had to learn everything about the craft of writing. Furthermore, it was literature itself, in the form in which until now he had envisaged it, that he was now questioning: he had thought, he still thought that it consisted indeed in putting "questions" rather than in seeking to answer them, but how could one put them properly unless one had a "general point of view" on life and the world?

In "A Dreary Story" the old professor ended by saying: ". . . In my general way of looking at things there is no common factor that unites them into a complete, harmonious organism. . . . If that doesn't exist, then nothing exists." Such was exactly Chekhov's own case: he too had no dominant desire that anchored him to life, he too suffered from not having a "general point of view" that would make it possible for him to orient and dominate his life and his work. As he had written to Suvorin on November 28, 1888: "A conscious life without a clearly defined conception of the world is not a life but a burden, a horror. . . ."

During these recent years, however, Tolstoyism had to a certain extent taken the place of a "general point of view" for Chekhov, as indeed for many of his contemporaries. He was to speak later of the "hypnosis" in which for years he was held by Tolstoy's thought. But it seems likely that Chekhov—and especially his commentators—exaggerated Tolstoyism's influence on him. In October, 1888, he himself had acknowledged to Grigorovich: "I have never held firm views in politics, religion, or philosophy. I change them every month . . . ," and at that time he never made the slightest allusion to Tolstoyism in his letters.

Although Chekhov was to recognize, in a letter to Suvorin in 1892, that he had experienced the influence of Tolstoyism, he would take pains to specify: "What influenced me was not his basic principles . . . but the Tolstoyan manner of expressing himself, his common sense, and also, no doubt, a kind of hypnosis." Hence, if Chekhov was for a while "subjugated," it was not so much by Tolstoy's theories as by the violent way in which Tolstoy expressed sentiments that Chekhov himself felt: the hatred of all injustice, of all constraint, of all falsehood. He also liked Tolstoy's good sense and his Rousseau-like rationalism, which cast doubt on the imperatives of traditional faith and morality. And it seemed to him that the point of departure of the new morality proposed by Tolstoy, who preached individual and inner perfectionism, vindicated him who had always striven to surpass himself and to find his only basis in his own dignity.

At one time the "Tolstoyan manner of expressing himself" had even impressed him so much that he wanted to make it his own. In 1886 in a story called "The Good People" and in the following year with four briefer stories—"The Meeting," "The Beggar," "The Cossack," and "The Letter"—he had written moral tales, stories with a message, in the style of the master. Furthermore he admitted in a letter to Pleshchev that "The Meeting" had "something Tolstoyan." But he soon recognized that writing "in the manner of Tolstoy" was the diametrical opposite of his own genius, that it cost him his sincerity, his limpidity, his poetry, and his lucidity. And it is true that his "Tolstoyan" stories are weak and rather artificial and clumsy. Chekhov himself was later to drop the least successful of all, "The Meeting," from his "complete works."

After 1889 and "A Dreary Story," as we have seen, Chekhov went into opposition to Tolstoyism, and, moreover, by so doing he regained all his genius. This time, while the question—the meaning of life—posed by a man brought face to face by old age with the imminence of death was still Tolstoyan, the answer, to the extent to which there was one, was not. Tolstoy would have equipped the story with an edifying moral; Chekhov left his hero to struggle with his own doubts, and his long meditation ended only in unbelief and despair.

A few weeks before he left for Sakhalin, Chekhov had a last encounter with Tolstoy by way of "The Kreutzer Sonata," which had just been published and was creating a scandal. His reaction to the story was intense. He considered it brilliantly written and "a stimulant to thought"; but the author's dogmatic judgments, he confessed, often made him want to shout: "This stinks!" He, as a man of scientific training, found it difficult to forgive Tolstoy for his arrogant handling of problems of which he knew nothing, such as syphilis, reform schools, and feminine sexuality. For Chekhov the spell was broken, and Tolstoy became alien to him.

Did Chekhov, perhaps, abandon Tolstoyism in order to embrace the liberalism professed by that part of the Russian intelligentsia that did not follow the master of Yasnaya-Polyana? No; for while he admired intelligence, he distrusted intellectuals "who complicate the simplest problems." When Pleshchev accused him of doing nothing to help the cause of liberalism, he replied with a shrug: he denounced lies—was that not enough? He himself was a defeatist, and he shared the perplexity of the Russian intellectual élite, but that did not prevent him from speaking contemptuously of the "dreamy, apathetic, lazy, philosophizing, frigid intelligentsia."

To Chekhov, indeed, all labels and all ideological or political allegiances were "preconceptions." He often repeated that he was neither a liberal nor a conservative. For the moment he was still a fierce libertarian individualist, an atheist, and a materialist. At the same time it was only materialism on behalf of which he could be roused to action. Thus he wrote to Suvorin in connection with Bourget's *Le Disciple:* "To forbid man's materialistic tendencies is to forbid him to seek the truth. Outside matter there is neither experience nor knowledge, and hence no truth" (May 7, 1889).

This unbeliever, this skeptic had a kind of credo nonetheless. One day when his aging friend Pleshchev expressed his shock at so much indifference, Chekhov came out of his shell and explained his position with moving sincerity: "My holy of holies," he wrote, "is the human body, health, intelligence, talent, inspiration, love, and the utmost freedom—freedom from violence and falsehood in whatever form these may be expressed. That is the program to which I would adhere if I were a great artist. . ." (August 4, 1888).

A great artist he was. That his "program" should have included intelligence, talent, and inspiration is therefore no surprise: he had only to look into himself to discuss them better than anyone and defend them against stupidity and conformism. It is more moving to observe this man, already eroded by disease, making himself the champion of the human body and of health: the reason was that as a physician he understood that both were put into jeopardy by the falsely spiritual civilization of the time. As for love, the fact that he had not yet experienced it did not prevent his knowing that it was the beginning and the end of all things for man.

"And the utmost freedom. . . ." On this point Chekhov was adamant: the writer ought to be able to say *everything.* And above all to protest: "This year I want to write stories in a tone of protest," he said in November, 1888, against the blatant social injustices and "the monstrous established order." To Suvorin he wrote in connection with an article in the publisher's newspaper: "It is revolting to talk of servant girls as if they were felons." It was not because he was going through a phase of depression that he accepted, as he was accused of doing, "life as it is." At the top of his voice he demanded the right to battle "violence and falsehood" in all their aspects. In the end he summed up his "program" in a sentence: "I want to be a free artist, and that's all."

VI

A SEASON IN HELL

> I have learned a great deal and I come home revolted. As long as
> I was living there I felt nothing but a certain bitterness. Now, in
> my recollections, Sakhalin represents hell. . . .
> CHEKHOV in a letter to
> SUVORIN, December 9, 1890

At the end of 1889, then, Chekhov suddenly decided to go to the
Island of Sakhalin, Russia's contemporary Devil's Island. This
meant a very long journey that would require robust health and
consume months. Hence one cannot help immediately asking—
and all his biographers have done so—what precipitately impelled this ailing man, this physician who knew how seriously ill
he was, this realist little given to acting on impulse, this writer
more and more persuaded that art was his reason for living, to
attempt such an adventure.

Chekhov offered explanations to his friends, taken by surprise by
so strange and abrupt a decision, but the reasons he gave were
hardly persuasive. Presented, furthermore, as they almost always
were, several weeks after the decision had been made, they
seemed rather to be rationalizations. One thing was clear, however, and Chekhov insisted on this to Suvorin: it was not as a writer
looking for material for a book that he was going to Sakhalin.

To one person—Suvorin again—he said that all that made him
undertake this long journey was a desire for a change, "simply to
spend six months," he wrote, "living as I have not lived until now."

His ink mixed with a bit of acid, he added that, feeling that he was turning lazy, he was embarking on this arduous journey as a matter of self-discipline. His argument to others was the usefulness of learning and, as a result of his journey, conveying to his compatriots the darkest of Russian realities. "As the Turks go to Mecca," he wrote, "we ought to make pilgrimages to Siberia." He adduced as well—but always after the fact—scientific motives: he wanted to make a scholarly study of prison life on Sakhalin. And very much later, when his descent into hell had become only a memory, he was to insist on this last explanation. Questioned about the journey by Diaghilev in 1901, he replied: *"The Island of Sakhalin* was written in 1893 to take the place of a thesis that I had decided to write after I had completed my medical studies in 1884" (December 20, 1901).

Investigators have naturally looked for—and found—other explanations for this unforeseen journey. Some have interpreted it as a political act, a way of protesting against the tsarist government; others have taken it to be a kind of random flight, an act of despair, a "journey to the end of the night." A woman, Lydia Avilova, in a book published more than forty years after Chekhov's death, contended that it was the despair of unrequited love—for her, of course—that drove the writer to set out for Sakhalin.[1]

But simply because an old woman dreamed—and wrote—that Chekhov had been in love with her, must she be believed? And, what is more, she would have to be believed on her word alone when she assures us that Chekhov, desperate with a love for her that he knew could never come to fruition, fled to the end of the world in order to try to forget her; for she offers no other evidence.

In those years Lydia Alexeyevna Avilova was a reasonably beautiful woman of twenty-six, very slender, and generally known as "the young Flora" because of her long golden hair combed into two thick plaits. She had married "practically"; disappointed in an earlier love affair, she had become the wife of an official, and with him and their child—later joined by two more—she led a rather

---

[1] L. Avilova's memoirs, *A. P. Tchekhov in My Life*, were first published in 1947 in an anthology issued in Moscow by A. Kotov, *A. P. Tchekhov in the Recollections of His Contemporaries*. The full text, however, appeared only in the fourth edition of this collection, published in 1960.

dull existence in Petersburg. Romantic, imaginative, she consoled herself for her monotonous life by scribbling—short stories—and meeting writers in the home of her brother-in-law, Sergei Khudekov, Editor of *The Petersburg Gazette*.

In fact it was in her brother-in-law's drawing room on January 24, 1889 that she had first met Chekhov. We should like to believe her when she tells us that for her, who had long admired him, this one and only meeting was enough to make her fall in love— "something exploded in my soul," she was to write in all simplicity —but there is no evidence that the same thunderbolt struck Chekhov. Not only did he not mention her to anyone; far from declaring that he was in love, he wrote to Suvorin that while he had a sufficiency of worries, he was nevertheless still lacking one, "an unrequited love." In reality he was so little in love with Lydia Avilova that when he went back to Petersburg for several weeks at the beginning of 1890 in order to make preparations for his journey, he did not even try to see her again, although this would have been quite simple because of their many mutual friends.

His younger brother, Mikhail—with a certain innocence— offered his own version of the sudden origin of Chekhov's notion of going to Sakhalin. It was a time when the prison island was the subject of much discussion, in the newspapers and in intellectual circles. One evening, supposedly, Chekhov was in Mikhail's room while Mikhail was studying for his law course. Anton began to leaf through his brother's notes on penal legislation and came on those dealing with forced labor. "All our attention," he said, "is focused on the criminal at the time when sentence is pronounced, but he is hardly on his way to prison when we have forgot all about him. But what goes on in prison? I can imagine!" Then he spoke of going to Sakhalin, but Mikhail said that it was difficult to know whether he was serious or joking.

He did not always jest, however: for instance, when he wrote to his colleague and friend Shcheglov: "If we knew exactly what art requires of us, we should not find life so boring and insipid as we do at present. You would not be attracted by the theater or I by Sakhalin . . ." (March 22, 1890).

It would seem probable then that it was essentially in order to escape from a deep dissatisfaction, because he was also tired "of making books and money while old age comes closer and closer," that Chekhov decided on his journey.

He had had enough of the futile discussions of art that reminded him of the worst of the scholastic debates of the Middle Ages, enough of the intellectual environment in which he had bogged himself down, enough perhaps of his family too and of what he himself was so busy becoming—in other words, a man of letters. In addition, like all tuberculars, he was deviled by the desire to be "elsewhere"; when he was in the country, he dreamed of being in Moscow, in Moscow he yearned for Petersburg, in the Ukraine he had longed for the Crimea, and in Yalta he had been hungry for Moscow. This time he would go to the end of the world, to Sakhalin.

Chekhov, in whom there was nothing of the dreamer, did all things seriously: once his decision had been made, he spent three months preparing for his journey. Assisted by his sister, Masha, who enlisted her friends to help her copy passages out of certain books in the Rumyantsev Library, and by his brother Alexander, who carried out researches for him in the files of the Petersburg newspapers, he assembled a vast documentation on Sakhalin. Everything that concerned the island interested him: he read works of geography, ethnology, and geology as well as studies by experts in criminal law and penal colonies.

This documentary labor was not always diverting: how much "humbug" had to be read, and how badly the "scientifics" wrote! "They write so rugged a language," Chekhov said, "that not only is it sometimes difficult to read them but there are even times when their sentences have to be recast before they can be understood." Nevertheless he learned a great deal, and he "stole" ideas and information from other men's books that he would lightheartedly and naturally present as his own. "It is impossible to do otherwise in our time," he joked. In the end he was so conquered by his project that he diagnosed himself as a victim of *mania sakhalinosa*.

Suvorin too was helping him to prepare for his journey, and in order to facilitate it, had promised him a press card as a representative of *New Times,* but Suvorin did not at all share Chekhov's enthusiasm. He insisted that basically Sakhalin would interest no one. "Do you think so?" Chekhov said sharply. "Sakhalin is interesting not only because of the society that deports thousands of people there and spends millions, but also for anyone who is interested in studying penal colonies. . . . The books that I've been reading and am now reading show that we have sent thousands of men to die in prisons to no purpose. . . . All civilized Europe knows now that the guilt belongs not to the guards but to all of us. But we don't care. It isn't interesting . . ." (March 9, 1890).

He went to Petersburg for the whole of January, still documenting himself and consulting magazine files *in situ.* He also wanted to meet M. Galkin-Vrasky, the head of the prison administration. The official received him cordially, promised his support, and was amiable enough to let Chekhov read reports prepared by his subordinates which he found extremely mediocre. What Chekhov did not know—although we know it today—was that the exceedingly helpful high official at once wrote to his deputy on Sakhalin that steps must be taken in order to make sure that Chekhov be prevented from talking to certain categories of political prisoners.

Since he was in Petersburg, Chekhov also permitted himself a bit of diversion. Undoubtedly he was exaggerating later when he mentioned his "sins" committed there, but it was true that he spent frequent evenings feasting, drinking, and talking. At the same time his writer friends had the feeling that he was running away from them, and the story went around that it was because he "was very busy with a lady." But what did it matter to him! Anyway, he had had more than enough of gossip.

He was back in Moscow when serious student disorders broke out there in March. The students demanded complete autonomy for the university, the admission of Jews and women, and the abolition of police surveillance. There were violent demonstrations and arrests; the population attacked the Cossacks, who were carrying the students off to jail by night. Chekhov followed the events with keen interest. Without openly manifesting his sympathy with the students, he nonetheless wrote: "I consider the young generation healthy when it battles established ideas, even stupidly, and not when it accepts them without question. This is the will of nature, and progress depends on it" (March 29, 1890).

In the last letters that he wrote before his departure there is, rather strangely, a kind of moral balance sheet of his life and his work. On the problem of the relations between art and morality, which as a result of Tolstoy's influence was so prominent a concern of contemporary intellectual circles, he stated his position for the last time, with a certain irritation, in a letter to Suvorin. His view had not altered: it was not the writer's business to moralize to his reader. "You criticize me for my objectivity," he wrote, "and you call it indifference to good and evil; you criticize my lack of an ideal, of ideas. You want me, when I portray horse thieves, to say: 'Stealing horses is an evil action,' but everyone knew that long ago without my help; let juries decide on these offenses. My business is to show these thieves as they are" (April 1, 1890).

He did not look on himself as a hero: he was just like other men, neither better nor worse. In his view there was only one moral code, "the one that was once given to us by Christ." When his friend Shcheglov also reproached him for his "amorality," he wrote back: "As far as I am concerned, my conscience is easy. In all my life, in words, in thoughts, in my stories, in my sketches, I have never done harm to my neighbor's wife, nor his servant, nor his ox, nor any of his animals. I have neither stolen nor lied. I have not abased myself before the powerful. I have never blackmailed anyone and I have never lived at anyone's expense. I admit that I have often loafed in my life. There have been times when I have laughed like a fool, gorged myself, got drunk, wenched, but none of these things concerns anyone but me or implies that I am any different from the rest. Neither heroic deeds nor base ones. . . . I am like most people, full of faults . . ." (March 22, 1890).

He had just delivered himself of this honest confession when, on the eve of his departure, he saw in *Russian Thought* an article about him by V. Lavrov. This critic fell back on the argument so often raised against Chekhov: he was nothing but a "positive" writer "without principles." Outraged, Chekhov decided to break his own rule and defend himself. "I would not reply to this slander," he wrote to Lavrov, "if I were not soon leaving Russia for some time and might never return." He defended his honesty: he had never been a writer "without principles." He added: "I have never written a single sentence of which I should be ashamed today" (April 10, 1890).

Meanwhile the day of departure was approaching, and the writer, who felt as if he were "going off to war," was making his final arrangements. If as a result of drowning or other accident, he confided to Suvorin, he did not return, his sister, Masha, must be regarded as his heir. He packed his trunk—a heavy leather trunk, a gift from his brother Mikhail—with all the equipment that he had just purchased: a *tulup*—an officer's long leather greatcoat— big boots, a revolver, and a large knife "for cutting sausages and hunting tigers," he joked, adding: "See, I'm armed to the teeth." He was also equipped with a press card from *New Times*, and Suvorin had given him fifteen hundred rubles by way of advance on the travel notes—they would be called "Saturdays"—that he expected to send back.

The departure was set for April 21. At eight o'clock that evening, in one of Moscow's nine railway stations, the Yaroslavl, relatives and friends were gathered round Chekhov to make their last farewells. They chattered, they made an effort to be amusing—a physician friend hung a flask filled with cognac around Chekhov's neck and made him swear not to open it until he had reached the Pacific—but Mrs. Chekhova and Masha were in tears. Lovely Lika Mizinova choked back hers: that very morning Anton had given her a photograph of himself, inscribed: "To the wonderful creature who is making me flee to Sakhalin."

At the last moment Ivan, Levitan, and Olga Kundassova, the delightful *astronomka* who was still secretly in love with Chekhov, decided to accompany him as far as the Troitza station. His itinerary called for an initial leg of rail travel as far as Yaroslavl, then several days aboard ship on the Volga and the Kama as far as Perm, from where he would go by train again to Yekaterinenburg and Tyumen. After that would come the great voyage into the unknown.

Boarding the *Alexander Nevsky* in Yaroslavl, Chekhov had a surprise: Olga Kundassova was also aboard. Since she offered no explanation, he did not insist on any; moreover, he wrote to Masha, he was delighted to have her company, which she withdrew at

Kineshino. Chekhov the traveler relaxed: he was sleeping much and well, he had a good appetite, he was observing the passengers and, leaning on the rail, watching the river banks go by. "The Volga is not bad," he wrote. "Flooded meadows, convents in the sun, white churches. An amazing vastness. Wherever one looks there are beautiful places that would be just right for fishing." In another letter he drew a less pleased sketch: "The birches have not opened their leaves yet; here and there there are patches of snow. Ice is floating in the river. In a word, all the esthetic has gone to the Devil."

Was he gay? Was he sad? Neither; his heart was caught in "a kind of gelatin," and he mused all day long, motionless and silent. One day, for example, he had spoken barely "five words." As always, he was slightly bored, and when the ship called at river ports, the sound of accordions seemed sad to him. "When the cold wind blows, ruffling the water, which, since the ice broke, has kept the color of weak coffee, one feels the cold, boredom, and anxiety. . . ." But he had a smile when he noticed that a passenger—and a deputy prosecutor at that!—was reading his book of stories *In the Twilight*.

At Perm he took the train to Yekaterinenburg, where he was welcomed by rain and sleet. He established himself for two days in the Hotel America in order to heal his "coughing and hemorrhoidal person." As he had promised his mother, he went to visit one of their relatives, a "serious" man who urged him to see the museums, the factories, and the mines, all of which, of course, he avoided. What did he think of the city? "All towns look alike in Russia," he wrote. "Yekaterinenburg is exactly the same as Perm or Tula or Sumy or Gadyach. The belfries make a splendid soft music." But the natives—that "Asianry"—with their high cheekbones, their wide foreheads, their tiny eyes, their tremendous shoulders, and their huge paws frightened him.

The Siberian plain begins at Yekaterinenburg. But it was only after he had left Tyumin, which he reached on May 3, that Chekhov really discovered it. The Transsiberian Railway had not yet been built, and the local line did not go very far. He had to continue his journey to Tomsk in a hired *kibitka*, "an old bone-shaking basket attached to two horses." The first leg of what lay before him amounted to almost a thousand miles. It took him twelve days in abominable weather; the glacial wind cut his cheeks; he wore one pair of trousers on top of another, and the collar of his *tulup* was turned up. "I go on and on," he wrote, "and the road markers, the marshes, and the little birch woods appear and disappear" (May 14, 1890).

For the first three days he was so bruised by the jolting of the *kibitka* that when it stopped, he found it impossible to walk or to stretch out. Then he grew accustomed to it, and he was amazed that he felt no pain in his chest or his head and had a voracious appetite. Incidents now and then broke the monontony of the road: hang-dog groups of tramps, river fords, infrequent villages, huge flights of ducks, floods that covered the roads and turned them into "Venetian canals." One morning, just at dawn, where the road joined a trail, there was a sharp collision with a *troika* that threw Chekhov into the snow and broke the traces of his wagon.

Whenever he stopped, Chekhov was astounded at the mixture of races that populated the villages: there were Russians, deported Poles, Jews who had become peasants, Ukrainians, Tartars. Amid them all Chekhov sat and talked, ate pancakes and duck soup—"pure filth"—drank and drank tea made from cubes, "real mattress juice." He found his chance companions pleasant, clean, and well behaved, better educated, in fact, than many Russians. "No one belches in company," he wrote, "or picks his lice in public. If you ask for milk or water, no one shoves his fingers into the glass." In sum, without the functionaries Siberia would have been a happy, perfect place.

Arriving in Tomsk on May 15, Chekhov spent five days resting there. He sent off a few letters, wrote five brief "Saturdays" of "things observed" for *New Times*—"not for glory but for the money"—and did a great deal of sleeping and smoking. He found the town the dullest he had ever seen, without a single pretty woman, and steeped in "wholly Asiatic immorality." "I went to the public bath," he wrote to his sister, "and out of sheer boredom I bought some chocolate." He avoided the local intellectuals, but he could not escape the deputy chief of police, who of course asked him to read a manuscript and then took him on a tour of the local brothels. "I have just come back from these houses," Chekhov wrote to Suvorin. "They are revolting."

He resumed his journey in some splendor: he had bought new luggage (Misha's trunk having fallen apart) and, for a hundred thirty rubles, an open carriage, for he had had enough of rented *kibitkas* for the rest of his life. But the next stage of his journey, the five hundred versts that would take him to Krasnoyarsk, proved to be equally insufferable. The roads were mere mud tracks into which Chekhov and his vehicle sank "like flies in thick dough." Often he had to get out of the carriage and walk for versts, or else endure long delays while damage to the vehicle was being repaired. When he reached a relay point, he would be plastered with mud from head to foot, and he would fall asleep like an animal after ten or fifteen hours of unbroken travel.

After Krasnoyarsk—which Chekhov found delightful in its mountain setting—and the crossing of the Yenissei, he discovered a new world: this was the beginning of the Siberian taiga, a kind of virgin forest, not lush but dense and endless. When his carriage, which he was now sharing with three officers whom he had met, reached the top of a hill, all that Chekhov, like a man shipwrecked, could see as far as the horizon were the successive waves of the forest. The cold and the biting wind had been replaced by a heavy sultriness and by dust, dust that penetrated everything, "the mouth, the nose, and the pockets." It went on like this for 1566 versts, which the carriage covered in a week. Arriving at last in Irkutsk, Chekhov had only one thought: a bath as soon as possible, then sleep and more sleep. "It is only now," he wrote, "that I am learning what fatigue is" (June 5, 1890).

What occupied his mind during these endless days of traveling? Chiefly he thought of the persons whom he had thought he was fleeing. At every stop he wrote to his "magnificent mother, his perfect Masha, the good Misha, and all his near and dear." He remembered to ask Alexander to send Masha money advanced from *New Times*. From Irkutsk he wrote to his mother to remind her to take good care of her bad leg and to ask about Aunt Fyodosia and her son, and Misha's love affairs. He also requested that on June 17, the anniversary of Nikolai's death, a Mass be said for the repose of his soul. He thought too of his friends, of Suvorin and Pleshchev and Mrs. Kisselyeva. Undoubtedly he found his journey interesting, but, he wrote, when he went home again, he would not make another journey for a long time: instead he would try to buy a farm and establish himself on it. "I will rest there for five years," he wrote, "which means that I will stay in one place and twiddle my thumbs" (June 7, 1890).

Irkutsk, he thought, was splendid, "completely civilized with its theater, its museum, its public parks. Wooden sidewalks, but none of those gloomy fences, or vacant lots with 'No Dumping' signs." He spent five days in Irkutsk, amusing himself in the company of his three officers. But they were beginning to bore him: their only subject of conversation was women. And when it came to women, he wrote, "the girls and women of Siberia are frozen fish. Only a walrus or a seal could flirt with them" (June 7, 1890).

His tedious officers, unfortunately, stayed with him from Irkutsk to Lake Baikal, this time in the same troika with him. He had really had more than enough of these companions who never stopped singing and talking about everything while knowing nothing about anything. "It is absolutely essential to be alone when traveling," he wrote to Masha. "It is far more interesting, on the road or in a hotel room, to be alone with one's thoughts than to be with others." Fortunately the landscape was extremely beautiful and kept his mind off the empty chatter: they were following the course of the Angara, flanked by wooded mountains, and the weather was warm and sunny. Soon they would reach the shore of Lake Baikal—the sea, in Siberian—a vast immobile mirror ninety versts wide. The lake, which reminded Chekhov of the Crimean coast, amazed him: "Its soft turquoise color is pleasant to the eye. The shores are mountainous, covered with forests, a wild, profoundly primitive country" (June 20, 1890). But at Listvenichnaya he was somewhat disappointed, because he had to wait three days for the boat, living on nothing but buckwheat groats [kasha] washed down with quantities of vodka and offering his company not only to the three officers but also to "an overpopulation of cockroaches and bedbugs" (June 13, 1890).

Chekhov crossed Lake Baikal on the deck of a vessel loaded

with horses that snorted furiously and constantly while the paddle-wheeler slid through green-blue water so transparent that one could see its farthest depths, "which made the skin tingle." Then came the last highway stage of the journey, across Transbaikalia. The carriage moved along steadily, with relay stops for changes of horses, where already the mind was beginning to dwell on the next overnight halt. "By day we were galloping over the Caucasus, by night we were in the Don steppe, and next morning, coming out of a dream, we were already in the region of Poltava." In such fashion Chekhov reached Sryetensk, on the Shilka, on June 20, an hour before the departure of the ship that he was to take. The most wearing part of the journey—the "equine" part—was over, and Chekhov was more than a little proud that he had come through it without ill effects. "I have not been ill," he wrote. "All I lost was a pocket knife, a luggage strap, and a jar of carbolic ointment. My money is intact . . ." (June 20, 1890).

What began now was a kind of river cruise; it was to take him to the Pacific. Aboard the *Ermak* he took a first-class cabin in order to assure himself of some privacy. He hoped to be able to write a few things for *New Times*, but the ship shuddered "as if she were running a fever," and he had to give up. Having nothing to do, he chatted with the other passengers, went ashore at the river ports, and with his binoculars spent many hours examining the shore and observing flocks of geese, grebes, and herons, whose flights gave life to the magnificent landscape. When the ship arrived at the Amur, along which it would have to sail more than a thousand versts, he saw China on the farther shore—a country, a Chinese passenger told him, where for the slightest trifle "they cut off your head."

Splendid in its "savagery," the region was to afford him a few surprises. Its prevailing atmosphere reminded him of certain accounts of the American West: gold had just been discovered, and all the inhabitants, including the priests, the exiles, and the peasants, were afflicted to the root with prospecting fever. Utterly indifferent to anything that happened in Russia, they talked of nothing but gold, made fantastic amounts of money—which they as quickly lost again in gambling—and drank only champagne. But to a certain extent this gold fever was compensated for by a very considerable liberalism, so fully accepted by everyone that even a ship captain would never have thought of letting the police know if an escaped exile had got aboard his ship. Chekhov was delighted: "I have an *amour* for the Amur," he wrote, "and I would gladly spend two years here. It is beautiful, big, hot; there is freedom here. . . . The poorest exile breathes more freely here than the highest general does in Russia" (June 27, 1890).

Nevertheless, even though his "head was spinning with enthusiasm," although he was keenly interested in the Chinese, whom he found to be the most easy-going and amusing people in the world and whose "frightening politeness" he admired, although his visit to the Chinese city of Aigam made him feel that he was entering a world of fantasy, he still continued to give a great deal of thought to his family. He was uneasy at having no news from home and asked for a telegram. He himself sent many: to Masha for her birthday, to his mother, and even to his father on his birthday, and in spite of the exciting experiences of the journey, his letters and even his telegrams echoed with the leitmotif of these recent months: "I am bored. . . ."

On July 9 his ship entered the Bay of Castries, on the shore of Sakhalin Island, which it then followed. Chekhov's first sight of the island was quite dramatic, even Dantesque: there were five separate fires in the taiga. "The strange picture brutally emerging from the gloom, the profiles of the mountains, the smoke, the flames, the burning sparks, all seemed fantasy." Two days later he went ashore and traveled to Alexandrovsk, the administrative capital. He was to remain three months on the island of the damned.

In Alexandrovsk, Chekhov found lodgings with a medical colleague. At first sight the little town struck him as dreary, but clean enough and well kept. Nevertheless he was immediately impressed by the sound of an utterly new noise that broke the silence of the streets: the clanking of the chains riveted to the feet of the convicts who walked through them.

The day after his arrival he was received by the island's military governor, General Kononovich. The general was a pleasant man who seemed animated by genuine humanitarian feelings and who was the subject of a quite cordial portrait in the book that an American journalist, George Kennan, had just written about Sakhalin.[2] Kononovich received Chekhov very courteously and promised him what ever help he might need. This attitude was duplicated a few days later by Baron Korff, governor-general of the Amur region, who authorized Chekhov to go wherever he liked, promised him a general pass for the prisons and penal colonies, and also allowed him to consult the administrative records and interview the prisoners. Only political prisoners were made unavailable to him. "We have nothing to hide," the governor-general declared. Furthermore, he assured Chekhov that the life of the exiles—whom the Baron called "those poor devils"—was not so grim as it was painted. "There are no real life sentences," he explained. "Life imprisonment comes down to twenty years, in practice, and the forced labor is not cruel. There are no chains, no sentries, no shaved heads." [3]

Chekhov, however, was not a man to take these fine humanitarian statements at face value. Since he had permission to do so, he was firmly determined to make his investigation thorough, and also methodical. He had his plan of work: he wanted to make a complete census of all the exiles. This was a clever plan, for it would allow him, on the pretext of establishing his statistics, to meet and question all the prisoners on the island. His next step was to have the prison's own print shop prepare very detailed file cards for him, containing thirteen questions. Then, at once and alone, he got down to work.

For all the ardor with which he attacked his tremendous task, he never lost his physician's detachment. Sleeping only five hours a night, fully resolved to see everything, he traversed the island in all directions for weeks. He toured all the prisons and settlements, visited the *izbas* made of dried mud, went down into the mines, and walked through the penal colonies. Inexhaustibly he ques-

---

[2] George Kennan (1845–1924) had written articles on the Siberian prisons in 1885–1886 for *The Century Illustrated Monthly Magazine*. The Russian translation of the book based on these articles, however, was under a ban in Russia at this time and was not allowed to be published until 1906. Tolstoy, an admirer of the American journalist, did not wait until then to begin a correspondence with him.

[3] Chekhov, *The Island of Sakhalin,* chapter II.

tioned, consulted, filled out and filed his cards. In this way he collected almost ten thousand file cards in three months.[4]

He found, in contrast to what the General and the Baron had
told him, that Sakhalin was a terrifying, abominable Inferno. In
Chekhov's presence General Kononovich had declared his unalterable opposition to corporal punishment, but Chekhov himself
saw in the city prison, "two or three hundred yards from the General's office," daily punishment with the lash. Could it be possible
that the General was ignorant of this?

The convicts lived in appalling conditions: their feet were
weighted and chained to their wheelbarrows, the miners worked
lying flat, all these "poor devils" endured an inhuman existence.
Their hospitals, like the churches and schools that were prescribed for them, existed only on paper. In actuality they were
completely at the mercy of the tyranny, the brutality, and the injustice of their guards, themselves debased and unscrupulous.

So these prisoners—some of whom had even forgot for what
crimes they had been sentenced—wallowed in the blackest despair and in vice. They stole from one another, they countered the
insolence and unscrupulousness of their guards with lies, cheating, cowardice, and spying. They steeped themselves in alcohol
and played cards all night long by candlelight like madmen. "The
passion for gambling has spread through all the prisons like an
epidemic," Chekhov was to write. "The prisons have become huge
gambling houses and the penal colonies and military posts are
their branches and sub-branches." [5]

He wanted to see everything, and except for an execution,
which he was not allowed to watch, he did see everything. Thus
he was the horrified witness of a formal whipping. He saw the
doctor examine the convict in order to make certain that he was in
fit condition to endure the ninety strokes of the rod to which he
had been sentenced; then he watched the exasperatingly slow preparations for the torture session. He saw how the prisoner was tied
to the post under the sadistic eyes of the man who would lash him.
The victim's companions in constantly increasing number asked
permission to watch the revolting spectacle. When the whipping

[4] These cards are preserved in the Lenin Library in Moscow.
[5] *The Island of Sakhalin*, chapter XXI.

began, a methodical official counted each stroke of the rod, to the accompaniment of the victim's cries and calls for help as his naked body was swiftly turned into a bloody mass of raw flesh. Long before the end Chekhov could endure no more of the horrible sight and fled, but even far away he could still hear in his mind the hammerlike voice of the official at his counting: "twenty-two . . . twenty-three. . . ." "For three or four nights afterward," he was to write, "I dreamed of the torturer and the terrifying whipping post" (September 11, 1890).

In this "little concentration-camp universe"—the phrase was Chekhov's—there was also a large number of women. First of all there were the women criminals, the female galley slaves who accounted for something more than 10 per cent of the convict population. In order to survive they were virtually compelled to become prostitutes: the officials and guards chose the youngest, and the rest were left for the prisoners. The same thing was true of the "free women" who had gone to the island in order to be with their husbands and who, most frequently, had no other means of subsistence. The sale of very young girls by their mothers to rich colonists or guards was standard practice. "A free woman," Chekhov was to point out in his book "manages an 'establishment' in the outskirts of Alexandrovsk in which the entire 'staff' consists of her own daughters." [6]

Children who had been taken to Sakhalin with their parents or born there were the principal victims of this abominable state of affairs. "Pale, thin, listless, dressed in rags, and always hungry," many of them died very young. Those who survived, left to themselves in an utterly perverted world, were little criminals at the age of ten. Girls of thirteen were already prostitutes, and Chekhov met one who had been a prostitute since she was nine. He would long be haunted by the memory of another poor little girl who spent her days crouched beside the chains that bound her father to his wheelbarrow and who at night slept, rolled in a ball, under that same barrow.

And how could he ever forget the conversation he had in an *izba* with a boy of ten, blond and barefoot, already bent over as

[6] *Ibid.*

if he feared the whip, whose red-flecked face was frozen shut throughout their talk?

"What is your father's name?" Chekhov asked him.

"I don't know."

"But that's not possible. You live with your father and you don't know his name? You ought to be ashamed."

"He isn't my real father."

"What do you mean, not your real father?"

"No, he's my mother's lover."

"Is your mother married or widowed?"

"Widowed; she came here because of her husband."

"What does that mean, because of her husband?"

"She killed him."

"Do you remember your father?"

"No, I'm a bastard. I was born when my mother was in prison in Kara." [7]

On September 11 Chekhov made a final tour of the southern part of the island hell and thus put the final touch to his study. He wrote to Suvorin that he had seen everything on Sakhalin and that there was "not a single convict or exile" on the island to whom he had not talked. What was important now was to write the book that filled his thoughts.

Otherwise he had had enough of the damned island. "For three months," he wrote to his mother on October 6, "I have seen no one but convicts and people whose only subjects of conversation are penal servitude, whippings, gallows meat. It is a gloomy life. . . ." His nerves were "deranged" and he had promised himself that he would leave Sakhalin as quickly as possible and never go back. He was bringing presents for everyone.

On October 13 he boarded the *Petersburg*, which was to sail around the whole continent of Asia before it deposited him in Odessa.

Although it consumed two months, the return voyage was a comfortable tour in comparison to the exhausting crossing of Siberia. Chekhov had originally intended to go home by way of the

[7] *Ibid.*, chapter XVII.

United States, but his plans had been changed by the high cost and the monotony of the voyage, and he also avoided Japan because of the cholera that was aiming "its green eyes" at that country. His first port of call was Vladivostok, and what he saw there was not calculated to dissipate the disquieting impressions that he had accumulated on Sakhalin. "On the subject of our maritime province," he wrote, "and in general of our whole eastern coast, with its fleet, its problems, and its pretensions with respect to the Pacific Ocean, I have only one thing to say: what outrageous misery! Misery, ignorance, and nullity, enough to drive one to desperation. There is one honest man here for every ninety-nine robbers who disgrace the name of Russia" (December 9, 1890).

So he was indignant when, during a stop at Hong Kong, he heard his Russian traveling companions criticize the British colonial system. "Yes, I thought to myself," he confided to Suvorin, "the Englishman does exploit the Chinese, the Sepoys, and the Hindus, but in exchange he gives them roads, aqueducts, museums, and Christianity. We exploit them too, but what do we give them?" Hong Kong itself delighted him with its incomparable bay, its swarming ships, and its beautiful English-style lawns. He went for rickshaw rides and bought a large number of Chinese curios.

The voyage from Hong Kong to Singapore was notable for a violent typhoon that damaged the *Petersburg*, which was sailing in ballast, and gave her a thirty-eight-degree list. Disaster seemed at hand, and the captain advised Chekhov to keep his revolver near so that he could hasten his end if the ship sank, because those waters were alive with sharks. But the *Petersburg* rode out the storm and Chekhov observed with considerable satisfaction that he had fought the good fight against seasickness. His heart was wrung, however, a few days later when he attended the funerals of two passengers. "When one sees how a dead man wrapped in canvas is slid into the sea and rebounds," he wrote, "and when one reflects that it is several miles to the bottom, one is gripped by fear; unreasonably one imagines that oneself too is going to die and be thrown into the sea" (December 9, 1890).

While the only impression made on him by Singapore was one of sadness, Ceylon, in contrast, seemed to be the discovery of par-

adise. In Colombo, still under the influence of the strange funerals
that he had recently witnessed, he hastened to write a story,
"Gusev," the hero of which also dies at sea. Then he traveled
through part of the island by train. He was enchanted at being
surrounded everywhere by palm trees and beautiful bronze-
skinned women. "When I have children," he told Suvorin, "I shall
tell them, not without pride: Son of a bitch, in my day I had relations with a black-eyed Hindu woman, and where? in a coconut-
palm forest on a moonlit night!" He must have countinued to boast
of this exotic adventure after his return to Russia, because there is
an echo of it in a sarcastic letter to him from his brother Alexander: "Salutations to your anonymous wife and the children you
sired during your trip round the world. . . . So now suddenly
somewhere in Ceylon there's a Chekhov."

In spite of the beautful Ceylonese, however, his only impulsion
was one of haste, haste to be back at home as soon as he could.
The thirteen days of unbroken voyage after Ceylon seemed interminable to him. He was not affected by the heat, but he felt
"bored to imbecility." One day, in mid-ocean, he decided that he
wanted to swim, and he jumped off the deck into the waves and
swam alongside the ship, then got back on board by climbing a
rope ladder that was flung out. All that he remembered of the very
dreary journey through the Red Sea was the sight of Mount Sinai,
which moved him. After a short stop at Constantinople, which he
liked, he set foot again on Russian soil at Odessa on December 1.

Alerted to his arrival by telegram, his mother and Mikhail went
to Tula to meet him. They found him seated at a table in the station restaurant with his traveling companions; the table was surrounded by a curious crowd watching the mongooses—Chekhov
had bought three of them in Ceylon—that were cating with them.
After much embracing the Chekhovs set off for the brief remaining trip to Moscow. When they reached the capital and took a cab
from the station, it was not the old address in Sadovaya-Kudrinskaya Street that Misha gave the driver: the family had moved in
the autumn to Malaya-Dmitrovka Street.

Back at home after an eight-month absence, Chekhov was not
sorry that his great adventure was over. The next day he wrote to
Suvorin: "Hurrah! Here I am at home at last, back at my desk and

praying to my old *Lares.* . . . I now have the pleasant feeling that I never left the house. I feel well to the very marrow of my bones" (December 9, 1890).

During the return voyage he had had time to cast up the balance of his journey. Yes, in spite of Suvorin's opinion, he had done well to go to Sakhalin: that feeling of uselessness and unease that had so long burdened his conscience was gone. He had come back to his own country with a message to convey and a job to undertake. He had to explain that "the world is beautiful: it is only we, its people, who are bad." He wanted too to make absolutely clear to his compatriots that the other end of the Russian empire was prey to ignorance, shamelessness, idleness, debauchery, and injustice, and that honor there did not go farther than "the honor of the uniform." To Suvorin, after a description of the ferment in his spirit, he concluded: "The important thing is to be upright, and all the rest will follow" (December 9, 1890).

He had come home filled with "a diabolical number of projects." One suitcase contained nothing but notes and files, and before he did anything else he was going to write his book on Sakhalin, a book that he believed to be necessary and that would be at once a scientific work and a collection of "things observed." Afraid that his impressions might become blurred, he wanted to get to work on it at once. Furthermore, still under the influence of the appalling living conditions of the convicts' children, he wanted to interest influential persons in them and find means of obtaining schools, teachers, and books for them.

It was also his intention to write, in the form of a play to be called *General Flirt,* a biting satire on a high official at Sakhalin who had acquired this nickname. Subsequently he did write this as a three-act comedy, which he read to a few friends. It would appear too that some years later he had some thought of rewriting it with a view to publication. But he did nothing about it, and no doubt he destroyed the manuscript, which has never been discovered.

What could the theater, "literature," and even Tolstoy's moralizing works still matter when one had seen what he had seen? "Before my journey," he wrote, "I thought 'The Kreutzer Sonata' was an event, but now I find it absurd and ridiculous." And mocking himself as always, he added: "Either I have matured as a result of my travels or I have gone mad—the Devil knows which!"

That was what he wrote to Suvorin shortly after his return. But he was immediately snatched up again by the "torrent of living," battened on by his family, his friends, and the curious who wanted to hear him talk about his journey, and he did not have the time to put his plans into immediate execution. Subsequently he was to put off writing his book on Sakhalin from month to month, nor did he succeed in inspiring any current of opinion on behalf of the wretched convict children: he was to have to be content to send them a few cases of books.

"Papa and Mama must eat" was still true, and since the family till was empty, Anton had to busy himself, virtually as soon as he had got back, with filling it again. He quickly set about revising the story written in Ceylon, "Gusev," sent it to *New Times,* and began another and longer story, "The Duel." "The business of earning my daily bread," he wrote to Suvorin, "prevents me from getting to work on Sakhalin."

In addition Chekhov was finding that the new family residence in Malaya-Dmitrovka Street, which was small and noisy, was not conducive to work. It was as private as a railway station: there was an endless procession of friends, acquaintances, and journalists. And his mongooses added to the confusion. Delightful but excitable, unable to find the cobras that they preferred, the animals assaulted whatever came within reach, overturning inkwells, breaking dishes, and shredding the gloves and hats of visitors. Chekhov soon tired of having them cling to his trousers and go through his pockets: he kept only one, in the hope of educating it, and gave the two others to the Moscow zoo.

His boast of having returned from Sakhalin in perfect health was premature. While it was true that throughout the journey he had felt quite well, as soon as he was back in Moscow he began to have violent headaches and a sudden general lassitude. His bad cough came back, and he observed, not without some anxiety, that he was also having heart palpitations. "The Devil knows what is fermenting inside me," he wrote. "Every minute my heart stops for a few seconds and becomes inaudible" (December 24, 1890).

Hence, within less than a month of his return, his disillusion had reasserted its mastery. After Sakhalin and the tropics, he found life in Moscow so dull and middle-class that he wanted to "throw himself on people." His friends wearied him, his family irritated him with its raptures over Mikhail's glittering new sixth-class-official's uniform. Already he wanted to get away again, and indeed on January 7 he went to Petersburg, where for a month he would be Suvorin's guest and they would prepare for a journey to Western Europe.

VII

ESTRANGEMENT FROM TOLSTOY

I value stories for this reason: one can work with pen in hand for days on end without being aware of the passage of time while at the same time experiencing a sensation that resembles living.

CHEKHOV in a letter to
SUVORIN, November 13, 1891

During the month of January, 1891, almost all of which he spent in Petersburg, Chekhov was the man of the moment there. He was fought over by hostesses who wanted to have him tell of his journey to Sakhalin, and he was pursued even into his rooms at Suvorin's. He had taken along the unfinished manuscript of "The Duel," but he never had time for serious work on it. He would barely have sat down at his desk when there would be a visit by some stranger who wanted to "talk about Sakhalin." He soon confessed to being "as weary as a ballerina after five acts and eight *tableaux*" from this unbroken succession of dinners and receptions.

Nevertheless Chekhov kept a cool head and a skeptical posture. He had immediately sensed what lay beneath the dithyrambs of praise poured out by those "dear colleagues" who gave a banquet in his honor: what envy and resentment so sudden and intense a celebrity must have aroused among even those who held themselves out as his admirers. He felt surrounded by a climate of "undefinable ill will." To Masha, who was his only confidante other than Suvorin, he wrote: "If I shot myself, I would give the greatest of pleasure to nine-tenths of my friends and admirers."

The "undefinable" ill will was not long in becoming identifiable. First, there was a bile-charged article in *New Times*, written by V. Buryenin: on the pretext of assaying the younger writers, the critic listed Chekhov with Korolenko and Uspensky among the new men who, instead of progressing, had already begun to "wither." Then there were malicious stories: if Chekhov had gone to Sakhalin, it was because he had had nothing more to say and was looking for something to write about, and anyway it was not difficult to achieve a reputation like his when one had the backing of an obscenely rich publisher like Suvorin to take care of the publicity.

In actuality it was friendship that kept Chekhov and Suvorin together in spite of the pressures already put on the writer before his journey to the Far East, and it was this friendship that gave rise to the jealousies, the criticisms, and the ill will. The extremely powerful publisher was enthusiastically hated by the liberal intelligentsia—some writers even refused his invitations—and some of that hate overflowed onto Chekhov. While he was really genuinely fond of Suvorin, he never in any way made use of him. When Chekhov did ask for Suvorin's help, it was never on his own behalf but rather for the advancement of young colleagues who had sent manuscripts to Chekhov: when he thought that they were good, as he did in that year in the cases of Ivan Bunin and E. M. Shavrova, he recommended them to Suvorin.

The friendship between Chekhov and Suvorin, moreover, was so genuine and so invulnerable to gossip that at the beginning of March they decided to embark with Suvorin's son, Alexis, on a tour of Western Europe. When Suvorin first suggested it, Chekhov had hesitated at first, because his money was low and he was "ashamed" to leave his family again, but very soon his taste for adventure got the better of him. On March 11 he joined Suvorin in Petersburg. But before they left Russia, he insisted on seeing what all Petersburg was talking about, Eleonora Duse's performance in *Antony and Cleopatra*, and he was not sorry. "I don't understand Italian," he wrote, "but she acted so well that it seemed as if I understood every word. She is a remarkable actress."

The next day he left the capital for Vienna, Italy, and France. It was his first venture into Western Europe.

He was entering Europe—in a sleeping car, itself a marvelous luxury—by the best gate: Vienna, that great, inviting capital open to every current, including those coming from the east, and gay, elegant, sensual, sophisticated to boot. So the Muscovite was quickly captivated by the Austrian capital: he saw nothing but "beautiful and elegant" women and spruce carriages, the restaurants were excellent, courtesy and attentiveness reigned everywhere. The day after his arrival he wrote his family a long letter that was a pure chorus of enthusiasm and, at the same time, one of the most delightful evocations of Franz Josef's Vienna that has ever been written.

"Ah, my Tunguz[1] friends," he wrote ironically, "if only you knew how beautiful Vienna is! It cannot be compared with any of the cities I know. The streets are broad and splendidly paved, and there are many boulevards and squares. All the houses are seven or eight stories high, and the shops would make your heads spin. It's a dream! Neckties alone are on display by the thousands! And what marvels in bronze and porcelain and leather! The churches are huge but they don't overwhelm you with their size: they delight the eye because they seem to have been woven of lace. St. Stephen's Cathedral and the Votivkirche are the most beautiful. . . . Parliament, the city hall, and the university are magnificent! Everything is very beautiful, and yesterday for the first time I realized that architecture is indeed an art. And this art is not, as it is at home, isolated in little fragments; it constitutes a whole that extends for many versts. What monuments! And invariably a bookshop in every street. . . . What is amazing is that here one can read and discuss everything freely" (March 20, 1891).

After he had bought presents for his family, and, of course, neckties for himself, Chekhov left for Venice, where he stayed at the Hotel Bauer. Here again he was enchanted and dazzled in "a continuous joy of living." He spent his days strolling through the Piazza San Marco and in the little streets or gliding over the canals in gondolas. These fragile black craft with their birds' heads, which barely skimmed the water and rocked at the slightest swell,

---

[1] This nomadic Siberian tribe, the Tunguzi, which was still very primitive, lived by hunting and breeding reindeer. This way of life continued until 1930, when the Soviet government abolished Tunguz tribal government. Now the tribe is being absorbed.

seemed to him to be the very symbol of the city and its graceful, airy architecture. He was so completely won by its charm that he wrote to his brother that if he could stay in Venice, he would gladly become not only a Venetian but also a Roman Catholic. "One would like to spend centuries here, and listening to the organs in the churches makes one want to become a convert" (March 24, 1891).

He did not conduct himself, however, like a "good tourist," greedy to see everything, and still less like an esthetic tourist. As his traveling companion, Suvorin, was to report, "Art—statues, cathedrals, churches—interested him very little. . . . Venice charmed him by its individuality, but even more by its life and its serenades than by its ducal palace." Dmitri Merezhkovsky, who was also visiting Italy and Venice for the first time and met Chekhov there, was in fact shocked by his offhand behavior. Whereas Merezhkovsky was "insanely ecstatic," as Chekhov put it, and no doubt wanted to trade fine esthetic ideas with his colleague, Chekhov, with his usual smile, was interested only in trivialities: a guide's bald head, the voice of a woman selling violets, the endless bell-ringing in Italian railway stations. . . .

For Chekhov in Italy was anything but the traveling intellectual in search of new depths for his culture and of rare esthetic emotions—to be written down, of course, without delay. He was a poet on vacation—in absolute freedom—who was taking his pleasure where he liked, at once humble and ridiculously arrogant, since he made no effort to show that he understood the art of the past better than others and at the same time refused to allow his inner world to be intruded on even by works of genius. He wrote: "It is easy to suppose that a poor, oppressed Russian would lose his mind in this world of beauty, richness, and freedom." But he, enthralled as he was by "charming blue-eyed Venice," wholly ready as he was virtually to renounce Russia at the first opportunity—"compared to Venice, the Crimea is a mollusk, a whale"—nevertheless refused to lose his head.

It is easy to picture him standing in front of the Medici "Venus" a few days later in the Uffizi in Florence. Like everyone else, he could have rattled off what he had read about the "divine Greek proportions." He preferred to make a trivial remark worthy of a shopgirl or a surrealist poet: dressed in the current fashion, this so highly prized Venus would be "hideous, especially at the waist."

But it was not because the "Tunguz" tourist was being difficult. He proved that in Rome, where, under the guidance of a learned professor, he duly visited everything that he was "bidden" to see. But it was too much for him: the museums wearied him, the monuments bored him. While the guide displayed his knowledge, the writer dreamed of "eating cabbage soup with kasha." By way of summing up his impressions of the Eternal City he found an extraordinary sentence: "Rome, all things considered, is like Kharkov."

Were the women of Rome like the women of Kharkov? Not the Romans, but certainly two charming Dutch women at his table in the *penzione*, and later the recollection of them would mean much more to him than that of the Colosseum. "Just imagine," he wrote enthusiastically to Mrs. Kisselyeva, "I sit across from two little Dutch girls, one of whom looks like Pushkin's Tatiana while the other looks like her sister, Olga. I watch them both all through the meal, and I picture a spotless white house with a little turret, rich butter, first-rate Dutch cheese, Dutch herring, a venerable pastor, a solemn professor. . . . And I should like to marry a little Dutch girl and have our portrait done together, on a moor, in front of our spick-and-span little house. . . " (April 1, 1891). And this time it did not matter that the Dutch damsels undoubtedly had the waist measurements of the Medici "Venus."

After a sojourn in Naples—for which Chekhov had one word: "dirty"—he and the Suvorins turned north again, toward France. In Monte Carlo the writer immediately smelled something in the air that offended him, that made "nature, the sound of the sea, the moon itself vulgar." He was shocked by the falsity of the life that was led there and that had the reek of the brothel: "Monte Carlo is full of tarts, it's a tart's world," he wrote in his *Notebooks*. "One has the feeling that even the palm trees and the food on the table are whorish." Nonetheless, by his own admission, he enjoyed luxury and wealth, and he liked going regularly to restaurants where every dish was "a veritable artistic composition before which one goes to one's knees in veneration." But the ostentation of wealth revolted him, and the casino gave him the impression—again the surrealist was not far off—"of a sumptuous water closet."

He was not going on that account to snub the city, however; he played the game, and in Monte Carlo the only game was roulette. Although he was short of money—actually he was living on advances from Suvorin—he lost no time in risking five hundred francs in the casino, and he did not win. All the same he was delighted, and he immediately bragged about it to his brother Mikhail: "Surely you will say: How despicable! We're so poor, and he goes and plays roulette! You're quite right, and I authorize you to castigate me. But, as far as I'm concerned, I'm highly pleased with myself!"

As much as Monte Carlo "the tart" had displeased him, Paris "the civilized" won his love at first sight. He began by following the well-behaved tourist's itinerary of the Eiffel Tower, the Bourbon Palace, and the Grévin Museum, but what interested him much more was the swarming streets and, on the sidewalk, cheek-by-jowl with the crowds, "those drinkers sitting at little tables and feeling absolutely at home there." The French were really a charming people! Then, taken over by members of the Russian colony, he discovered nighttime Paris: "men who wind boa constrictors round themselves, ladies who kick their heels up to the ceiling, trapeze artists, lions, *cafés chantants*,[2] dinners, lunches." And it very quickly disgusted him: vulgarity was in truth not his pleasure. He also went through the *Salon des Peintures* and found that the Russian painters were far superior to the French: not one landscape artist, for example, came up to Levitan's ankle. True, he was acutely myopic, and since he had broken his glasses, he only half-saw the pictures.

Besides, he was beginning to be homesick for Russia. For the first time in his life he was spending the Easter holidays away from his family, and he was sorry that he could not be with them to hear the bells of the Kremlin and repeat the roundabout greeting, "Christ is risen." His friends tried to make him stay, but suddenly he had had enough of travel: he wanted to work, to get back to "The Duel," which he had abandoned, and finish it, and

2 Chekhov used the French term.

this he could do only at home. He had arrived in Paris on April 17; he left exactly a week later, directly for Moscow. He had left home with an empty suitcase that was now filled with presents for his family.

Immediately on his return to Russia, Chekhov and his family went to establish themselves for the summer in Alexin, a little village on the Oka River not far from Moscow. The choice of the dacha, which had been made by Mikhail before Anton's return, was not of the wisest: true, there was a fine view of the river and of the railway bridge that straddled it, and one could hear the nightingales sing, but the country house itself was really too small and uncomfortable. So as soon as he had the opportunity—after only a few days—Chekhov hastened to move. He had discovered something suitable to his needs in Bogimovo, only a few versts distant—"the second story of a stone house in a romantic, abandoned property," which he had immediately rented. The park was huge, with paths that ran out of sight, a pond, and a river full of fish, and close by there was a church "for the old people": in a word, it was ideal for anyone who wanted to work in tranquility.

That was precisely what Chekhov intended to do. He was badly in need of money—on his return he had once more found the family till empty, and besides he wanted to pay his travel debts to Suvorin as fast as possible—and, beyond this, he felt a kind of guilt at not yet having begun his book on Sakhalin. Hence he resolved to devote himself to both literary and scientific work: the first three days of each week would be devoted to his book on Sakhalin, the next three days he would work on "The Duel"—which he called his "novel"—and on Sundays, by way of relaxation, well, he would write brief stories.

In order to carry out his plan, he subjected himself to a bookkeeper's timetable, and we know from his brother Mikhail that he adhered to it. He rose at dawn—four or five o'clock—made his own coffee, then sat down to work, not at a desk but at a window-sill so that he might better enjoy the view of the park, and did not stop until eleven o'clock. Then he would go out to gather mushrooms or fish for perch, coming back to lunch at one and following this with a brief nap. The entire afternoon was again devoted to writing, and it was only after dinner that he would allow himself to relax, spending a few hours chatting and philosophizing in the Russian fashion with his guests in the vast drawing room, imposingly solemn with its colonnades and musicians' platform.

On Thursdays, Fridays, and Saturdays, when he worked on "The Duel," he had only to let his pen go. But for his book on Sakhalin he proceeded quite differently: here the least line, which compelled him to "leaf through a whole documentation and re-read his notes," required a great effort. He had never attempted a work of this nature, and since he wanted it to be simultaneously complete, scientific, and beyond reproach, he was constantly impeded by his scruples. Feeling that the documentation he had gathered was not adequate, he ordered books and more books from Moscow and Petersburg.

Sometimes, certainly, he did derive some reward from the work itself. For instance, after a whole day given to a description of the island's climate, he exulted: "I've given such a picture of that weather that one will shiver just reading it." But for the most part he labored, progressing only inch by inch . . . and more and more often he "cheated" on his daily routine and worked on "The Duel" instead *The Island of Sakhalin*.

He had given Suvorin his "word of honor" that the Sakhalin book would be completed and printed in the autumn, but on the last day of his vacation—if that is the word—he had to confess to the publisher that he had broken his promise. "There are times," he apologized, "when I am seized by the desire to devote three to five years to it, to work on it furiously, but in periods of discouragement I'm ready to drop it altogether." On the other hand, his long story, "The Duel," had easily been finished in a few weeks and sent to *New Times* on August 16.

"You are right, Excellency," he was to write to Suvorin with satisfaction at the end of the month, "I have produced a great deal this summer." And in spite of that he had found the time to give considerable attention to his guests, who had been numerous. They had included Suvorin and his wife; Natasha Lintvaryeva, who had filled the house with her trumpeting laughter from morning to night; Wagner, a zoölogist, with whom there was much discussion of that year's fashionable subject, degeneration; the Kisselyev family; and Levitan, the painter. Chekhov and his sisters organized picnics, swimming parties, and tarantass* rides for them. There was also furious gambling at roulette, for Chekhov, who served as banker, had constructed his own wheel.

The visitor most welcomed by all and most handsomely entertained was "the beautiful Lika" Mizinova. A close friend of Masha for more than two years, she had become the intimate of the entire family. Her relations with Anton were less simple: Lika would have liked nothing better than for the friendship to be transformed into a warmer emotion, but Chekhov, who of course had sensed this, invariably treated her in a manner compounded of gentle humor, jokes, and teasing, intended at the same time to keep her friendship yet discourage an affection that was only too obvious. He did occasionally say that he was in love, but he said it with great bursts of laughter, which was a way of taking the initiative and preventing any serious question of love between them.

There can be hardly any doubt as to Lika's sentiments. Her letters to Chekhov have not yet been published,[3] but what is known of them confirms what has been reported by "eyewitnesses" to her friendship with Chekhov: Masha, Mikhail, and others are unanimous in their agreement that she concealed—quite unskillfully— a much deeper and more ardent emotion. Masha, however, insisted that it seemed to her that "the stronger feeling was on her brother's side" but that he forced himself to suppress it.

Undoubtedly it was in order better to combat the attraction that Lika had for him that Chekhov was constantly calling her attention to her deficencies: her laziness, her lack of character, her disorderliness. And if he was in love, he was not enough in love to give up his independence and that inner solitude that was at once his torment and his secret joy.

Nevertheless he was extremely fond of the charming Lika, who pleased him by her youth—she was ten years younger than he— her gaiety, her comic sense, and also, perhaps, the hidden love that he sensed in her. Although he had not written to her once during his journey to Sakhalin, on his return he had immediately

---

* A four-wheeled carriage mounted on bars that serve as springs.—TRANSLATOR.
[3] Ninety-eight unpublished letters from Lydia Mizinova to Chekhov are preserved in the Lenin Library in Moscow.

resumed his friendly teasing manner with her. "Greetings to Lydia," he wrote on January 14 to Masha. "Nowhere will she find a greater adorer than I." Sometimes he played big brother to her, sometimes inane wooer. He gave her preposterous nicknames— "Never Cantaloup"—and sage advice: she should avoid Levitan (who was chasing her as he did every woman), never eat anything made with flour, take care of her figure, and further her singing career. There were times too, when, making a parody of being in love, he sent her jesting, affectionate letters signed with transparent pseudonyms or, occasionally, with his own name. On May 12 he drew a heart pierced by an arrow on a letter in these terms: "Charming, wonderful Lika . . . We often go for walks here, and then I make it a practice to close my eyes and offer you my right arm, imagining that you're beside me." He called her "my Lika of gold and mother-of-pearl and cotton," and he often invited her to spend a few days at Bogimovo with him. In July he told her: "I love you with passion, like a tiger, and I offer you my hand."

But he was completely determined to give that hand to no one. He often discussed this in his correspondence with Suvorin. He had barely returned from the Far East when he wrote to his friend: "I don't want to marry." An on May 10, 1891—when Lika was his house guest!—he confided again that his ideal was to remain a bachelor. "I am not at all inclined toward marrying," he wrote. "My ambition is to be a little bald old man sitting at a desk in a luxurious study."

Besides, if he had been in love, would he have been so extremely bored that summer? For in spite of his uninterrupted work, his medical attentions to the neighboring peasants, and the stream of his visitors, he still found time to be appallingly bored, as irremediably as during the months before his journey to Sakhalin. "Life is a burden to me in the highest degree," he confided to Suvorin, and he compared himself to a prisoner locked up in a fortress.

In his case, this disgust with everything manifested itself not in the Russian style, in apathy, but in a kind of perpetual anxiety, a poorly controlled unrest, a fundamental disharmony with his own self. He mocked at himself: "I always feel that my trousers don't fit, that I don't write what I ought to write, and that I give my patients the wrong treatments. It's probably a psychosis" (August 30, 1891).

As soon as autumn betrayed its imminence, as soon as he saw the departure of the first storks, he too wanted to leave Bogimovo. The desire to be "elsewhere" that was growing more intense with the years—it had become a kind of psychic need—had taken hold of him again and held him in a vise. He was making travel plans, talking to friends of going to the Crimea, Norway, the United States. Early in September he hastily went back to Moscow, but he had not been there a week when again he was sighing: "I am so terribly bored. . . ."

He was back in Malaya-Dmitrovka Street, in the family "lair," with his mongoose. He worked, corrected proofs, carefully read the manuscripts that young writers submitted to him. Nonetheless he could not shake himself free of his "anxiety." He was not comfortable anywhere, the presence of his family and his friends weighed him down, and he felt constantly at odds with himself. The doctor in him wanted patients and a hospital within reach, the artist dreamed once more of the country: "As a writer," he said, "I need to live among the people." Life in Moscow seemed to him to be a hermitage within four walls, far from nature, people, the joy of living, health. . . . Now he was talking of soon going to Java.

He was brought out of himself, however, by the famine that struck several regions of Russia after a year of exceptional drought. The peasants' situation was soon desperate, and Chekhov, who had seen the disaster coming in the summer, tried immediately to help them. It was not easy, because the government prohibited the organization of relief efforts through any means other than the Red Cross and the Church. In addition the press was filled with articles, undoubtedly inspired from high places, that tended to accuse the famine victims of having brought it on through their own negligence, and this outraged Chekhov. Suvorin had just published a courageous article about the famine in *New Times*, and it was to him that Chekhov cried out his indignation at "that impudence [that] is manifested above all in the very fact that the man with the full belly dares to give moral lessons to the man who is hungry" (October 19, 1891).

The example to be followed was set by Tolstoy. With the courage and the readiness for action that were characteristic of him, the master of Yasnaya Polyana, easily repudiating his own ideas on the futility of charity, had gone to the aid of the starving as soon as the famine struck. Fortified by his great prestige, he defied the authorities, published articles, collected funds, himself traveled through the disaster areas and, with the help of his daughters and his friends, set up hundreds of canteens in them. This magnificent generosity evoked Chekhov's admiration: "Tolstoy! that Tolstoy! In these days he is not a man but a superman, a Jupiter" (December 11, 1891).

Chekhov had decided to devote himself too, as a physician, to the rescue of the famine victims, and to this end he had already established communication with the head of the zemstvo of Nizhni-Novgorod, E. Yegorov—whom he had known fifteen years earlier as a young artillery officer in Vosskressensk—but then he fell seriously ill. From October to December a very heavy grippe with pulmonary complications compelled him to keep to his room for weeks.

His already bleak mood—"everything's going badly, as in the past," he wrote—was further deepened by a series of deaths. In succession he lost his beloved Aunt Fyodosia—a victim of the family illness, tuberculosis—his poet friend Palmin, and Zenaida Lintvaryeva. Miss Lintvaryeva, when he had known her in Luka, had amazed him with her serenity in the face of certain death, and now he wrote: "I have buried a number of friends this autumn. I have become indifferent to other people's deaths. . . . Let us not chant 'De Profundis,' because we too shall die. . . ."

Nevertheless he had not resigned himself to his own illness and, he admitted, he was afraid to look it in the face; he refused, too, to get the care he required. He wrote to Suvorin that medical treatment and the anxiety caused by the state of his health filled him with a kind of revulsion: "I don't want to be treated," he repeated. "I'm perfectly willing to take water and quinine, but I won't allow anyone to auscultate me" (November 18, 1891).

As soon as his own condition permitted, and even though, as he himself put it, he still had "the face of a drowned man" he tried to put into execution the proposal that had come to him from Yegorov and that, with his usual good sense, he had at once approved: it consisted of buying the famine victims' horses, which they could no longer feed, and giving them back in the spring, thus assuring the next crop. This required money, and Chekhov set about finding it by any and every means: appeals in the press, personal letters to friends, solicitations in homes. "I'm playing the lady of good works who is a bore to everyone," he wrote by way of excuse. He kept strict accounts of all gifts received—unfortunately they were very small—and sent them to his friend in Nizhni-Novgorod.

He went to Petersburg for the year-end holidays in order to see Suvorin and also in the hope of collecting more donations there. Without trying to do so, he found himself plunged at once into the capital's literary life, went to writers' lunches, and several times visited his friends Leikin and Shcheglov. On New Year's Day at a dinner in the home of the Khudekovs, he encountered Lydia Avilova again.

According to her, and even though their only previous meeting had taken place three years before, their conversation quickly took a quite romantic turn: they discussed—most unlike Chekhov —their having known each other in earlier incarnations, long since forgot, and having "waited for" each other ever since. During the evening Mrs. Avilova introduced Chekhov to her husband and, again according to her, the two men were icily polite to each other. Finally when she confessed that she too was a writer, Chekhov promised to read with care any manuscripts that she sent him.

In the preface to the book that she was to write a half century later, *A. P. Chekhov in My Life,* Mrs. Avilova declared: "This is a love story that no one ever knew, even though it lasted ten years. It was our love story. . . . I have not invented a single word." [4] Perhaps, perhaps; but then what a strange lover he was, finally finding her again after three years and being satisfied with this one meeting, never trying to see her again during the next ten days of

[4] This preface, discovered in the Chekhov archives in Moscow, was published for the first time in 1960 in *The Literary Heritage,* Volume LXVIII.

his stay in Petersburg. He seemed, however, to have taken considerably more interest during this visit in a delightful actress whom he had met through Suvorin, Marya Zankovyetskaya. He saw her on a number of occasions, called her "the Queen of the Ukraine," and promised to write a play for her. He spent one night drinking champagne with her until four in the morning, and he took her tobogganing on the hills outside the city.

But none of this had made Chekhov forget the famine and its anguished victims. He had barely returned from Petersburg when he went to join his friend Yegorov in Nizhni-Novgorod. In spite of the foul weather and the piercing cold, he toured the stricken villages by sleigh, and one evening, like Pushkin's hero, he was caught in a snowstorm and lost his way. He was indignant at what he found: misery everywhere and a total lack of assistance. "There would be no famine in Nizhni-Novgorod," he wrote on his return from a week-long tour, "if people in Petersburg and Moscow devoted as much action as talk to the matter" (January 22, 1892). After this first week in the field, however, a serious chill accompanied by back pains forced him to return to Moscow to recuperate.

As soon as he was back on his feet he set out again. This time, accompanied by Suvorin, he went to the Voronezh district. He found relief efforts better organized there, and there were canteens in the villages, but the "official" side of this inspection tour annoyed him. Because Suvorin was an influential person, they were received everywhere as important guests; Chekhov bitterly ridiculed all these receptions and gala dinners presided over by provincial governors and held in areas ruined by famine. After ten days, irritated at his friend, who seemed to him grotesque when he played the part of a busybody inspector, Chekhov went back to Moscow.

He had tried to emulate the example of "Jupiter" Tolstoy, but in spite of the sincerity of his efforts, they had ended in a semifailure. He, the practical man, the physician, had been completely vanquished in the realm of action by the old prophet, the Utopian of Yasnaya Polyana.

In October, Chekhov had confided to Suvorin: "When I live in the country, as I dream day and night of doing . . ." and since then he had not stopped dreaming of it. It seemed to him that if he lived in the country, all his problems would be solved at one stroke and he would finally be able to bring a certain order into his life. Financial order first of all: living in the country on land of his own would cost him much less, finally settle the problem of summer vacations, and assure him of greater independence of his publishers. Then, order in his way of living: in Moscow he no longer quite knew whether he was a physician or a writer, whereas in the country he would divide his time between his patients and his books. And finally, intellectual order: in the country he would have time not only to read but also to devote himself to really long works. Against all this what could Moscow or Petersburg offer him? The company of his friends, the theater, concerts, but also waste of time, diffusion of energy, and useless excitement. Besides, if he decided on the country, there was nothing to prevent him from going to spend two or three months in Petersburg in the dead of winter.

Methodical and practical as always, Chekhov had explained his plan to Suvorin. He had pointed out that he and his family could live on the income from his books and other writing alone, provided that they were in the country. "Ah, freedom, freedom! If I could live with a maximum of two thousand rubles a year, which is possible only in the country, I should be completely rid of all worries as to how much money was coming in or going out. Then I would work, and read, read! In word, it would be bread and jam, not just bread and butter" (November 22, 1891).

Because he had the happiest memories of the summers spent in the Ukraine with the Lintvaryevs, he asked his friend Alexander Smagin to find him a property in the area of the Psyol. Smagin's first suggestion was a farm costing five thousand rubles, and then, when the owner decided not to sell, he proposed another property, but this time someone else bought it, even though in the meantime Chekhov had written to him to expedite the matter. Chekhov said that since his health required him to live in the country, it was absolutely essential that he get out of Moscow soon.

His impatience mounted and he began to read the newspaper advertisements of real estate for sale. One of them caused him, in the midst of winter, to send Masha and Mikhail to look at a property situated not in the Ukraine but in the province of Moscow. On the basis of their report, which was rather favorable but emphasized the fact that the snow had made it impossible for them thoroughly to examine the condition of the place, Chekhov decided nevertheless to enter into negotiations at once.

It was not until two weeks later that he himself could get to look at the property, which was in Melikhovo, a little village some fifty miles south of Moscow. This was no mere farm but a reasonably large estate of almost seven hundred acres, half of it in poor woods, which also included a large park, an orchard, and two lakes. The house was relatively new and solid, but much work would be required in order to make it livable. The outbuildings were in good condition. Chekhov listened distractedly as the estate manager catalogued everything that would come with the property: three horses, one cow, one piano, two dogs, four geese, various carts and sleighs; and he was amazed to be told that under proper management, the estate could bring in a thousand to two thousand rubles a year. What particularly impressed him was the fact that on the ground floor of the house there was a beautiful room illuminated by three Italian-style windows that he immediately dreamt of as his study, and that one of the lakes was so close to the house that he could fish in it from his window. As soon as the deal had been made, one of his first steps would be to order tench and carp.

There was a major problem to be resolved, however: the price amounted to thirteen thousand rubles! Where was he to find them? With the help of the bank with which *New Times* did business, Suvorin helped him to pay the first four thousand rubles in cash; Chekhov signed mortgages for the rest, to be paid off within five years. These negotiations required him to spend long days in discussion with lawyers, bankers, insurance companies, and "other similar parasitical institutions." He was astounded and shocked at having to pay, over and above the purchase price, more than a thousand rubles in various fees, and he felt extremely incompetent and idiotic in the midst of all these bureaucrats. And so, when everything had been concluded and the title deed had been duly stamped and initialed—in other words, at the end of

February—he sighed happily: "This is a relief I dared not imagine" (March 3, 1892).

Now that he owned his house in the country, only one desire drove him: to move into Melikhovo. He set out on March 5 with part of the tribe—his parents, his sister, and his younger brother, Mikhail—plus a mountain of luggage and packing cases and an ample supply of pharmaceuticals. The park and the field were still covered with snow, and there was a tremendous amount of work to be done in order to make the "apparently simple and stupid" house comfortable and pleasant, but the entire family decided to set to work at once. The writer provided the example, and on the very evening of his arrival he wrote to his brother Ivan to send him "a broom, a horse brush, twenty-two pounds of nails, twenty-two pounds of rye bread, five loaves of French bread." The next day he wrote to Suvorin: "Sitting in my study with its three big windows, I am completely comfortable. I go out five times a day, I amuse myself by throwing snow into the pond. The roofs are dripping and everything smells of spring. . . . So far I'm in an excellent mood" (March 6, 1892).

He was still pounding nails when he received a rather surprising letter from Lydia Avilova. Since their meeting in Petersburg, she had sent him short stories in manuscript, and in his habitually light tone he had twice written to her about them with much good advice and sharp and direct criticism—letters like all those many others he sent to young writers who asked for his counsels. Now, after these first exchanges, here was Lydia Avilova writing to him on a very different note: she complained that all Petersburg was saying that on the very evening of their meeting, now more than two months behind them, Chekhov had got drunk and bragged to a friend—no doubt Leikin—that he intended to take her away from her husband, make her get a divorce, and then marry her.

Chekhov's reply was undoubtedly not what the young lady expected. Refusing to be drawn in, he rather coldly rejected the accusation of having "dragged her name in the mud." He wrote: "What is the meaning of all these excogitations in which you are indulging? . . . Dignity forbids me to justify myself; besides, your accusations are too vague to enable me to determine on what arguments I would base a defense." This was all the cheapest gossip, so common in Petersburg, the kind of nasty rumor that had already had him marrying a multimillionnaire, seducing his friends' wives, and so on. If she did not believe him, then let her ask Yassensky, who had been present at the famous night of debauchery. "Whatever the situation," he concluded, "God be with you. Defending myself against cheap slander would be like asking a Jew for a loan: useless. . . . Think anything you like of me" (March 19, 1892).[5]

What in any event did he care about the gossip and the hysterical women of Petersburg? Seen from Melikhovo, where spring had just suddenly burst out in clumps of green that surged up through the melting snow, in the sound of running water, and in flights of starlings, how ridiculous it all was! The important thing to Chekhov was the fact that his dearest dream had been realized and that now, the owner of an estate, he felt purged of the last drop of "slave's blood."

His happiness and pride shone in a letter addressed to Alexander, who was in a better position than anyone else to understand him: "We are living on our own property! Like a modern Cincinnatus, I toil and I eat my bread dipped in the sweat of my brow! Mother fasted all day today and has gone to church in her own carriage. . . ." The signature was half boastful, half mocking: "Landed proprietor A. Chekhov" (March 21, 1892).

Although Chekhov had in fact worked industriously since his return from Sakhalin, he had published little. In spite of the "Mondays, Tuesdays, and Wednesdays" given over throughout the summer to his book on the island of the damned, it was still far from ready for publication. Because of a need for money—and although it was "boring to write about the peasantry," he told Suvorin—he had quickly done a story that did deal with the subject, "The Busybodies," which was published in New Times in June,

---

[5] This letter, which Mrs. Avilova mistakenly presented as the first she had received from Chekhov—true, the first two, which were harmless enough, would hardly support her thesis of a "love story"—was published by her for the first time in her A. P. Chekhov in My Life. But though she gives no indication of the fact, she had in fact made deep cuts in it. The full text was not published until after her death.

1891. At the end of that year "The Duel" appeared first as a serial in the same paper and then as a book, published by Suvorin.

With "The Duel" Chekhov had finally succeeded in that "novel" he had so long dreamed of writing: it has a more full-bodied plot and more action than his other long stories. The narrative, laid in the pleasant setting of a little resort town in the Caucasus, deals with the lifelong, implacable duel—which, furthermore, ends in actual combat—between men who are opposites in everything: the weak, inane Layevsky and the energetic von Koren. Layevsky, a wasted intellectual who placidly resigns himself to his lot while ascribing it to society and fate, arouses the disgust of von Koren, who, at the peak of his contempt, finally provokes him into a duel. But neither's shot hits the other, and with the help of an army medical officer of broad views, they understand in the end that they are allied in spite of everything by a mutual drive of good will. They become reconciled. Is it because they have both come close to death? Both men have changed, and if Layevsky is now determined to lead a more virile life, von Koren has lost much of his rigidity.

While the story ends "happily," it is far from sweetness and light. The author uses it as the vehicle for a ruthless criticism—by way of the character of that "Moscow Hamlet," Layevsky—of a certain element in the intelligentsia of the time that hypocritically denounced the society and the world in which it lived as a means of justifying its own worthlessness. In this story, however, there is no longer the utter, rational despair of "A Dreary Story": the last pages of "The Duel" are brightened by a certain glimmer of hope. Both Layevsky and von Koren discover that all is not lost as long as men's hearts still hold a little love and a little faith in the future. This in fact is what von Koren thinks at the end of the story, when, as he leaves town, he goes to say farewell to his adversary: "In their search for truth, men take two steps forward and one backward. Suffering, mistakes, and weariness make them fall back, but the thirst for truth and their own stubborn good will always drive them onward. And, who knows? perhaps in the end they will reach the whole truth. . . ."

Chekhov too, since his return from Sakhalin and his tour of

Western Europe, had taken two steps forward and one backward in search of a certain truth. It was not that, as some have thought, the trek across Siberia was his road to Damascus, but unquestionably the man had changed, his personality had become stronger, his ideas about the world and the way in which man ought to conduct himself in it were beginning to become more focused. And this emerged clearly now in the fashion in which he established his reservations toward both the intelligentsia and Tolstoy.

It was not chance that in "The Duel," by way of the character of Layevsky, he had made so vehement an attack on a certain intelligentsia. Indeed, the story had enabled him to void an impatience, a disgust, that he could no longer retain: the cowardice of that class of intellectuals, its empty philosophy, its pharisaism revolted him. Having seen the horrors of Sakhalin—this was his own way of rubbing elbows with death—he had come back to these Moscow and Petersburg vaunters of their own nihilism who traded verbal violences and were far more concerned with their little selves and their tawdry rivalries than with what happened to the children of Sakhalin. If, like himself, they had indeed recognized that life in Russia was intolerable as much from the social as from the political point of view, why then did they make no effort to change it, to overthrow it, instead of allowing themselves to drift in a kind of comfortable Nirvana?

His indignation against these Pharisees was so acute that he had also written a violent article against them. He had sent it to Suvorin in December, asking that it be printed in the newspaper; at the same time he wished to preserve his anonymity and so he signed his tirade "The Grumbler." It was a savage mockery of the intellectuals, whose spokesman described himself thus: "I dress in the latest fashion, I have my hair cut at Theodore's, my house is luxuriously furnished, and yet I am an Asiatic and a countryman. . . ." His article was more than an attack, it was a veritable bill of indictment of these forever disillusioned "intelligent men," posturing, egocentric, negative, incapable of taking a real interest in others and trying to improve the lot of all. He confessed his desire to repeat to these drones, whose only talent lay in their complacent discussions of their boredom, what he had one day heard a stranger say: "Oh, go get a length of telephone wire and hang yourself from the nearest pole!"

In addition, while he had never been a true Tolstoyan, Chekhov until now, like almost all the Russian elite of the period, had been deeply influenced by the precepts and the examples of the reformer of Yasnaya Polyana. On his return from the hell of Sakhalin and the semi-paradise of the West, he had the honesty and the courage—it required both—to say, though with regret, that he rejected Tolstoy's doctrines. On August 30, 1891, he wrote to Suvorin, thus confirming that he had never been a complete Tolstoyan: "Alas, I shall never belong to Tolstoy's sect."

What did he criticize in Tolstoy? First of all, his renunciation of his vocation as a writer: Chekhov said he would trade all Tolstoy's philosophy for the wonderful story of a horse, "Kholstomir," that he had written when he still believed in literature. What Tolstoy was now publishing—for example, his *Postscript to "The Kreutzer Sonata"*—was sheer nonsense. His philosophy was clouded and futile: the return to the people, to the muzhiki, would not accomplish one single step of progress and indeed it was the surest way of turning away from the future. As for trying to make men give up tobacco, alcohol, and "Kreutzer sonatas," to Chekhov this was no more than a kind of infantile moralism. The future of mankind lay in science, and this Tolstoy stubbornly refused to concede or even to conceive. Chekhov was angry that Tolstoy treated the men and the work of science with such disdain. "Tolstoy," he wrote, "looks on doctors as scoundrels and considers himself competent to deal with all major problems . . ." (September 8, 1891).

What also exasperated him in the prophet of Yasnaya Polyana was his *grand seigneur* aspect, safe as he was from being taken to the police station or vilified in the press. "The Devil take the philosophies of the great ones of this world," Chekhov wrote. "They are impolite, indelicate, and as despotic as generals, because they are confident of their impunity."

But it is not through outbursts of ill humor that one frees oneself of a Tolstoy when one is a writer. In fact Chekhov continued to feel a tremendous admiration, mingled with a certain affection, for the old master, and thus he could not be indifferent to anything Tolstoy did. Chekhov had hailed Tolstoy's work on behalf of the famine victims, and he still insisted that "Tolstoy is my favorite author. . . ." He had reread *War and Peace* that autumn, and in spite of the few flaws he found in the novel—the exaggerated portrayal of Napoleon, in particular—he had been so taken by it that he had written: "If I had been with Prince Andrey, I would have saved him." He had also admitted his pleasure: "My curiosity is as great and my astonishment is as untainted as the first time I read it. It is wonderfully done" (October 25, 1891).

He also admired Tolstoy for having a "faith": Chekhov himself still had none. Nonetheless, during recent months, a small ray of hope had insinuated itself into his skepticism; certainly he clung to no doctrine, but it seemed to him now that the discoveries of science, especially those of medicine, could contribute some improvement to man's fate. He kept himself abreast of progress in the medical sciences, hailed their discoveries—"I believe in Koch and specificity and I glorify the Lord"—and was amazed at the advances of the preceding twenty years. But that did not turn him into a worshiper of science, because to him there were other values too: "beauty, cultures, refinement of thought."

He made harsh game of pseudo-intellectuals because they proclaimed an idealism of thought that was contradicted by the not infrequently shabby realism of their acts. As for himself—and not wholly without bravado—he proclaimed only one thing: his liking for a certain luxury, and to hell with those who considered this a "shopkeeper's" ideal. "I want carpeting, fireplaces, bronzes, and intelligent conversation," he wrote (August 30, 1891).

Thirty years behind Proudhon, Tolstoy was asserting that "property is theft," and, himself the victim of ownership of many hundreds of acres, he had just turned them over to his wife and children for lack of any better way out. It was just this moment that—without shame and indeed with a certain frank pride—Chekhov chose for the acquisition of an estate at Melikhovo.

VIII

MELIKHOVO,
"MY DUCHY"

Something is lacking in us, that is obvious, and if you lift the skirts
of our muses, you will find only skin and bone. . . .
CHEKHOV in a letter to
SUVORIN, November 25, 1892

At Melikhovo, Chekhov felt that he was the happiest of men, a
real "lord." How much better off he was, far from Moscow and its
bustle, far from its citizens whose never relaxed self-concern made
them such a burden. In the country there was peace, solitude,
"beatitude"; a day seemed as long as eternity, there were no regrets, one need not fear strangers knocking at the door. Seen from
a distance, mankind already seemed better to him. "One has the
feeling of being in Australia or somewhere else at the end of the
world" (March 17, 1892).

His estate, his "duchy," required substantial improvements, for
he had bought it blind and was now learning in just how pitiable a
state it was. He went to work at once and with enthusiasm. He
sent for carpenters, painters, and masons, who devoted their
efforts to the roof and the floors, painted and papered the house,
and repaired the faïence stoves. Various conveniences had also to
be installed, a new well had to be dug, fences had to be set upright again, and the barns and hothouses needed repairs. In the
large room with the three Venetian windows that he had chosen
as his study, Chekhov had a revolving door installed in order to
protect himself against drafts, as well as a fireplace and the enor-

mous couch essential to all Russian conversations. He was appalled to learn how poorly workers were paid in the country, and he wrote sarcastically to Suvorin: "I'm beginning to understand the charms of capitalism" (March 11, 1892).

The entire family cooperated in the work of rehabilitating the estate. Each one had his chore: the mother took care of the housekeeping, the father handled snow removal—and when spring came, laid out paths through the abandoned garden—Misha busied himself with the farm, Masha tended the vegetable garden. As for Anton, he kept an eye on everything, and as he had always done kept strict ledgers. He also assumed the task of evicting the mice that infested the house. He caught a great many of them in traps every day, but being soft of heart and not wanting to kill them, he carried them to nearby woods and released them, accepting the risk of renewing acquaintance with them in the house next day.

The abrupt arrival of spring with its thousand runnels of water was a marvel to Chekhov. "Something staggering and overwhelming," he wrote to Suvorin, "happens in nature, and the pleasure and the novelty of it compensate for all the inconveniences of living in the country. Every day brings a better surprise than the day before. . . . When I see spring, I have a terrible longing that there be a paradise in the next world" (March 17, 1892).

Since he would not delegate the care of the flowers and the orchard to anyone, he became a gardener. In this first spring he planted eighty apple trees, sixty cherry trees, and various kinds of rosebushes; subsequently he was to add further varieties of roses, and lilacs and hundreds of trees. He was not unlike Dr. Astrov in his own *Uncle Vanya* who loved trees and felt that he had made a contribution to human happiness when he heard the murmur of the growing forest that he had planted with his own hands.

The acquisition of Melikhovo was the realization of one of his most cherished dreams: at last to have a center, a "nest," for his family. In his country house his sister and all his brothers felt at home. In spite of the nightmare of his still vivid childhood memories—in a letter written at this time he had again recalled his days as a "little galley slave"—Chekhov was a devoted and attentive son; it gave him pleasure to see how his parents bloomed now that they had become respectable landowners. Now a true housewife, his mother did not attempt to conceal her great delight: she went to church in a carriage and she had hired a servant. But she was completely devoted to her dear Antosha—who had provided so handsomely for her declining years—and she herself still cooked his favorite dishes.

Though Chekhov treated his mother with solicitous affection, he could not bring himself to do as much for his father. He could not wholly forget the "despotism" that had tainted his childhood, and his relations with his father were marked by a singular diffidence. As for the father himself, he usually behaved discreetly, at once submissive to "Father Antosha" and secretly angry that this was so. But now and then he still reminded everyone of his own importance, lectured the family, pontificated ridiculously on all subjects. He kept a "ship's log" for the household and solemnly filled it, in his ornate handwriting, with reports of the weather, the temperature, the arrivals and departures of guests. Age had made him even more religious. He never missed Mass, and when he was not gardening, he spent most of his time in his room, which was arranged like a monk's cell, where he read bulky Lives of the saints.

Chekhov had no qualms about making gentle fun of him to his brothers. "Our little father," he wrote to Alexander, "is philosophizing as usual and raising such questions as, 'Why is there snow in that particular spot?' and 'Why put a tree here and not there?' He is constantly reading the newspapers and then telling Mother that an organization has been set up in Petersburg for the classification of milk. Like a real Taganrogger, he is incapable of any work except lighting the lamps" (March 21, 1892).

His brothers, fortunately, were less Taganrogger than their father. It pleased Anton to observe that all of them were now working: Ivan was moving ahead in teaching, Mikhail was an official and, in his spare time, a journalist, and Alexander, who was also a journalist, was even beginning to become respectable and talk about buying a little estate of his own. Anton got on well with all of them, especially with Misha, who delighted him as much by his keen, gay wit as by his talents in the kitchen.

But it was the "perfect" Masha with whom his bonds grew

closer and more intimate from year to year. On his side there was complete confidence, as well as a very great, if somewhat domineering, affection; on her side there were unlimited admiration, a jealous love, and absolute, undivided devotion. This mutual love was so complete and at times so excessive that it annoyed the others. After a visit to Melikhovo in 1893 Alexander wrote to his brother: "Your relations with our sister are not right. One kind word from you in a warm voice and she's your slave."

Was it this uncharacteristic affection that explained Chekhov's firmly entrenched desire to remain a bachelor and that caused him to write to Suvorin in that year: "Now let's talk about me. I don't want to marry and I have my eye on no one"? Certainly not, even though Masha herself seemed confident that he would never marry, and the confidence made her happy. There is no doubt that her love for her brother dominated her entire emotional life and had given her a kind of inhibition that prevented her from marrying—or at any rate from doing so without her brother's express consent.

This became apparent when there appeared, among the guests who inundated Melikhovo that summer, a young man whom the Chekhovs had met some time earlier in the home of his relatives, the Lintvaryevs, and who had since remained on close terms with them. Alexander Smagin, who was quite good-looking, very gay, and congenial, soon began to pay more and more pressing court to Masha; finally he asked her to marry him. What did the wise Electra do? After much hesitation, she was to relate later, she decided to tell Anton that she was planning to marry. "He did not say a word," she wrote, "and then I saw that this news did not please him, for he remained silent. In reality what could he have said? I saw that he did not want to admit that it would be difficult for him if I went away to set up my own home and family." Chekhov's strange silence continued for several days. But it was so transparent and so eloquent for Masha—who did not wish to do anything that might displease her brother and alter the established course of his existence—that in the end she decided to dismiss the charming Smagin.

It would be difficult to believe that Chekhov was not aware of the fact that with his sullen silence he had compelled his sister, who at the age of twenty-seven was not likely to have many more offers of marriage, to say No. But it made him feel easier to think that, like himself, she was born to be single. A few weeks later, his conscience already eased, he wrote: "I don't understand it at all. . . . There are not many girls like her who genuinely don't want to marry" (October 18, 1892).

Other guests as well as Smagin flowed into and out of the Chekhovian "duchy" during that year. It was like an endless procession: the Chekhov brothers' and Masha's friends, the friends' friends, neighbors, and the curious. Always eager to have people around him—even though he had said that he was leaving Moscow in order to get away from them—Chekhov himself had insisted that Suvorin come to visit his "stupid, simple" house and that A. Kisselyev bring his fishing rods even though the river was barren of fish. "The beautiful Lika" came and went; the young poet Tatiana Shchepkina-Kupernika spent several weeks; and Natasha Lintvaryeva came from Luka and filled the house with her great laugh as soon as she entered it.

In the spring Levitan had been one of the first to take advantage of the guest room. With its unpicturesque but typically Russian charm, its untouched woods, its birches against a background of firs, its endless fields, its black earth, and its red sunsets, Melikhovo delighted him, and he put it into nostalgia-filled paintings. He also went hunting and fishing with Chekhov.

While the two artists normally perpetrated their massacres of hare and partridge without a second thought, there were times when they were like two adolescents torn between cruelty and mercy. Thus one day Levitan's shot wounded a quail but did not kill it; he asked Chekhov, who had picked up the bird, to put it out of its misery. "The bird's great black eyes looked at me in astonishment," Chekhov wrote to Suvorin. "What to do? Levitan made a face, closed his eyes, and said to me in a shaky voice: 'Crush its head with your gun butt.' I refused. He insisted, shrugging with nervousness. The bird was still watching us in amazement. I had to obey Levitan and kill it. So there was one less loving being in the world, and two idiots who went back to the house and sat down to eat" (April 8, 1892).[1]

This was one of the last suppers the "two idiots" had together. A few days later a scandal over Chekhov's story "The Grasshopper" broke out in the artistic world of Moscow, and it was to keep them in a state of hostility for several years. Chekhov acted as if he did not understand what was happening, and in an innocent tone he wrote to Lydia Avilova after a brief visit to the capital: "Can you imagine? A lady I know, who is forty-two years old and has no children, has recognized herself in the heroine—who is twenty— of my 'Grasshopper.' Now all Moscow is accusing me of having written a lampoon. The chief evidence offered is the completely superficial identity of situations: the lady is also a painter, her husband is a physician, and her lover is a painter." All Moscow was not mistaken, and Chekhov, who protested a little too much, knew it very well. "The Grasshopper" was clearly inspired by the affair that his friend Levitan was having with Sofia Petrovna Kuvshinnikova, the wife of a Moscow doctor. Naturally the ages and physical appearances of the real models had been changed, but otherwise "The Grasshopper" was indeed the story of this fashionable woman, who, bored by her exceedingly studious husband, had gravitated to the artistic world—including Chekhov—where she found that she had a talent for painting; subsequently she had gone away with Levitan to spend several weeks somewhere on the Volga. "Completely superficial identity of situations"? No, total identity, even down to the settings, the psychology of the characters, and the relations between them.[2]

The real "grasshopper" was angry; a mutual friend, Lensky, who recognized himself in the "big actor" of the story, broke with Chekhov, and Levitan was furious and wanted no more to do with him. Chekhov tried to explain things in letters, friends attempted to effect reconciliations, but nothing could be done, and at a certain moment, it seemed indeed, the painter tried to provoke Chekhov into a duel. For almost three years they had nothing to do with each other.

[1] Chekhov was to recall this little "hunting drama" when he wrote *The Sea Gull*.
[2] Chekhov's manuscript corrections are also revealing in this respect. They clearly betray the efforts made by the author to eliminate the more glaring resemblances between his fictional characters and their originals.

One friendship was collapsing, but another, more subtle, more emotional, and also more equivocal, continued to play a large part in the writer's life: his connections with "the beautiful Lika." He seemed really to need her, writing her letter after letter to invite her to Melikhovo—where, for that matter, she frequently stayed during that summer—and always making it a point to see her on his numerous visits to Moscow. His letters, dosed with irony as always, were nonetheless often quite pressing. "I'm waiting for you," he wrote, "and dreaming of your arrival, as the Bedouin in the desert dreams of water"; or again: "Don't fail to come. You know how I need you. Don't disappoint me, Likusya, for God's sake, come!"

Masha, always closely observant, was deceived and thought that her brother was really in love; but what was Lika's view? Early in the spring Anton had written frankly to her: "Unfortunately I am already an old young man, my love is not a sun, and it creates no spring either for me or for the bird I love. Lika, I don't love you so passionately. What I love in you are my past sufferings and my lost youth" (March 27, 1892). Did that mean, then, that all hope was vain for her, who made no secret of her love? While Chekhov tried to discourage her by talking of his age and his "lost youth," he was nevertheless extremely careful not to break with her, and in fact he never resisted the temptation to see her. The alternating play of seduction scenes and flight which had begun a year earlier went on, and there were long passages of tender-reproachful discussion between them that clarified nothing and led to new ambiguities.

One letter from Chekhov, dated June 28, 1892, was an admirable summation of the strange permanent vacillation—"we are in no way committed to each other, but let's keep up our little journey into tenderness"—that he maintained toward the girl. "Brave, noble Lika," he wrote to her, "ever since you wrote that my letters don't bind me to anything, I've breathed more freely, and now here I am writing you a long epistle without any dread that some unknown aunt may read it and make me marry a minister like you. As for myself, I hasten to assure you that to me your letters are only scented flowers and not official documents. . . . Well, good-bye for now, ear of corn of my soul! I envy your old shoes that see you every day!" He admitted, too, that his heart "bore her marks," but that he was guided only by his mind. Was it not natural, however, that Lika should hope in spite of everything that in the end the heart's voice should triumph?

Nevertheless, the flirtation with Lika, the constant visits of friends, the work in the garden did not prevent Chekhov, who seemed oblivious to the very notion of a vacation, from still giving a great deal of time to his "mistress," literature, and his "lawful wife," medicine. He wrote every day, in the morning and the afternoon, and that summer he put the finishing touches to several stories: "My Wife," "The Chorister," "Neighbors," and "Ward Six." As for medicine, which perhaps he had somewhat neglected in recent years, he had been constrained to go back to it now that he was living in the country, and he did so with good grace.

There were very few doctors in the Sherpukhov area, and since word had quickly spread that the new owner of Melikhovo was one, Chekhov was attacked from all sides. Almost every day patients, some of whom came from as much as fifteen miles away—peasants, workers, *babas* with little children—went to see him, and the cases of pharmaceutical products that he had brought from Moscow—he gave away medications without charge—were barely enough to meet the needs of so many kinds of suffering. He never refused to help, even when he was summoned in the middle of the night and when, because of the foul weather, his mother urged him not to leave the house. "Dysentery won't wait, Mother," he would tell her. And it mattered little to him that his patients were seldom in a position to pay.

Such great devotion soon won the blind confidence of the *muzhiki*, almost to the point of veneration. It impressed Tatiana Shchepkina-Kupernika, who at that time had not yet met Chekhov, when she was visiting her old nurse in a village in the neighborhood. The nurse was ill but unworried. "There's nothing to fret about, little one," she said. "We have a doctor here who doesn't have his like in Moscow. He lives six versts away: his name is Anton Pavlovich. He's in everybody's heart—yes, in everybody's heart. He gives me all my medicine for nothing."

In July, when the district was threatened by cholera, Chekhov's reputation as a physician was already so firmly founded that it was he to whom the Regional Health Council turned to organize the necessary preventive measures. He accepted at once, made a study of the disease, and ordered the construction of reception buildings in the twenty-five villages for which he was responsible. Since he did not have enough money, he did not hesitate to appeal, "with a beggar's eloquence," to his friends and his rich neighbors.

For weeks, from July until October, he gave of himself without stint. He jolted over the roads in a wretched tarantass that bruised his body, visited the relief centers set up in villages and factories, and taught the peasants how to take the basic hygienic measures. He cared for the ill and treated diphtheria, typhus, and scarlet fever. He trembled constantly at the possibility that the abominable cholera, which had reached and ravaged the neighboring districts, might spread into his own, but his efforts were rewarded: in October he was able to announce that victory had been won. In those few weeks his records had grown by the names of five hundred patients, and his examinations had actually included a thousand.

Was he gratified by the task accomplished, by his triumph over the epidemic? Yes and no, for as a result of the expenditure of himself, his body was exhausted and his spirit was weary and sorrowful. "It is awful not to be one's own man any more," he wrote with his usual fine honesty, "to think only of diarrheas, to leap out of bed at night as soon as the dogs bark and there's a knock at the door. . . ." For weeks he had had no time for writing or reading —apart from medical papers—or even for dreaming: "Oh, gentle tones of poetry, where are you?" And basically what was the reason for all this? He gave his best effort to doing what he considered it his duty to do, but it was without enthusiasm and with skepticism that he performed his humanitarian obligation. He confided to his friend Suvorin that to concern oneself with nothing but cholera "and at the same time to be utterly indifferent to that disease and to the people one is helping—that, my friend, represents a plague that no one can stand up to" (August 16, 1892).

His work, however, had also given him much to think about. His collaboration with the authorities of the zemstvo and the local intelligentsia resulted in certain conclusions: there were many

men of good will among them, men who were capable of dedication and of giving of themselves and their money without
reserve, who knew how to work effectively. Inevitably, he had encountered some rich men who were despicable, like Count Orlov-
Davidov and his wife—she was a millionnaire who, for all the
huge diamonds at her ears, behaved like a fishwife—who had fled
at the threat of the cholera; and there was also the police, which
was abominable. But now Chekhov respected the intelligentsia,
which he regarded as "kind, interesting, and, what is most important, honest." Tolstoy, in his view, was as wrong in ridiculing the
part played by the provincial élite in the fight against suffering as
he was in branding all physicians "knaves."

Chekhov was also harsh in his judgment of those who were ex-
ploiting the situation for political ends. "If our Socialists were really using the cholera for their private purposes," he wrote to Suvorin, "then I would condemn them. Using despicable means to
fulfill good purposes makes those purposes themselves despicable.
. . . Why lie to the people? If I were a politician, I could never
bring myself to cast discredit on the present in order to serve the
future, even if I were promised a hundred *poods* of happiness for
every crumb of falsehood" (August 1, 1892).

He hated falsehood enough to unmask it in himself. He had
thought that he would find happiness in his "duchy," but after
those first months of country life, he was recognizing that he had
not found it there. Of course it was delightful to hear nightingales
sing under one's windows, to plant rosebushes, and in splendid
solitude to "receive packages of newspapers and weeklies from the
whole world," but he had soon exhausted these small joys. "Everything is as it was before," he observed, "neither gay nor sad." He
was only thirty-two years old, but already he was feeling "the approach of the forties." He wondered whether he was not a victim
of that new disease that the press called "overwork." What else
could explain the fact that he began and ended every day in
apathy, with the feeling of having grown old, and devoid of all
joy in living?

In October he drew up the balance sheet of these first eight
months spent in the country. He had accomplished good work,
true—his help to the zemstvo, his assistance to the ill, his numer-

ous tree-plantings—but the charms of country life had not got the better of his disenchantment. Oh, if only he could be someone else, he wrote, "take a bath in black acid, shed the skin, and then put on a new one. . . ." To Shcheglov he wrote: "Is it growing old or just boredom with living? I don't know, but I have no very great desire to live. Or to die, either; but really I have had about enough of living. In short, my spirit is as if frozen in an icy dream" (October 24, 1892).

Autumn came; the leaves turned and fell, the fields blackened with cold and then whitened with the first snow, and then it was the complete isolation of the start of winter. For a city man like Chekhov, the real test for country living was beginning, and it must be admitted that for him it was difficult to endure. He found the snowdrifts and the empty fields monotonous, the spectacle of the naked trees appallingly depressing; the chickens huddled one against another in defense against the cold, and the old muzhiki wrapped themselves in rags. "The hermit's life," he wrote, "is for the arrogant and the neurasthenic," but in his case it was chiefly neurasthenia, a kind of apathy blended with indifference and sadness, that was dominant. He began to understand an intellectual young neighbor who, for all his love of reading, admitted to him that he had become incapable of reading any book to the end.

Fortunately this was not yet entirely true for Chekhov. Unquestionably he found the mornings "extremely long," and having started smoking since his removal to the country, he was now consuming four cigars a day instead of three, but he was reading a great deal, and for him it was still possible to finish a book. He had gone back to Turgenev's works and found them "charming." He had to admit that in comparison with Tolstoy's they were rather thin, and he wrote that, "compared to Tolstoy's Anna Karenina, all these Turgenev ladies with their lovely shoulders have no body," but nevertheless what pleasure there was, for example, in Fathers and Sons. "It goes right into you," he wrote to Suvorin. "Brezarov's illness is described with such authenticity that I felt I had caught the disease myself" (February 24, 1893). From Dr. Chekhov this was no faint praise.

The fact remained that he fled from his "duchy" as soon as he could. In October and November he found various pretexts for frequent trips to Moscow, where he plunged himself with joy into artistic and literary circles. At the end of December he left for Petersburg, where he remained for five weeks. As usual, he stayed with the Suvorins: the fact that he was about to terminate his connections with *New Times* in order to write for *Russian Thought,* which was of a much more liberal cast, in no way influenced their friendship.

When, for instance, Suvorin became ill at the end of the autumn, Chekhov had at once rushed to Petersburg to take care of him. Briefly he had feared that Suvorin would die, and he wrote to Shcheglov: "To me this would be so great a loss that I think it would add ten years to my age" (October 30, 1892). A few months later he was to tell the publisher himself: "In those moments of depression when one needs to unburden oneself, you are the only person I can talk to" (August 7, 1893).

On his return to Melikhovo on January 29 he faced the long wait for spring. That year the winter hung on, and Melikhovo was enveloped in snow until April. He had to see to his father's health and then to Masha's: she had a kind of typhoid infection. The bad weather, which was unremitting, made him quite irritable, as always. He admitted that his mood was "shrewish" and he wrote to Alexander that if the sun did not make up its mind to appear, he would wind up a drunkard. And he was up to his ears in all those guests who, in spite of the weather, never stopped invading his house. "Every intellectual who takes this road," he wrote, "feels it his duty to pay me a visit, warm himself at the fire, and sometimes even stay on and on" (December 8, 1892).

He dreamed of travel like a boy shut up in a boarding school. In his letters—and this was to be the case in the following winter as well—he spoke only of going back to Sakhalin or visiting Japan, India, South Africa, or Madeira. In Petersburg he had met Tolstoy's son Lev Lvovich, and they had planned to go together to Chicago in the spring for the opening of the World's Fair. But this had to be abandoned for lack of money.

There was another reason for Chekhov's suppressed irritation: "a vile, shameful" affliction of which he dared not speak to anyone except Alexander and Suvorin. "It isn't syphilis," he wrote to the publisher, "but something even worse: hemorrhoids." He had had them for years, but now they were causing him intolerable pain. There were days when he could neither sit nor walk, and his whole body was filled with such discomfort "that it made me want to lie down and die." He was aware, too, that his affliction was making him misanthropic and irascible, so that he spoke stupidly to those around him, whom he too often regarded as unjust and inane. Nonetheless, physician though he was, he never thought of having surgery.

It was a fact that often—regardless whether he was in physical pain—his family was a burden to him. He found evenings with them very long, and he was immeasurably bored by conversations that endlessly repeated the same anecdotes and the same petty household problems. He lived in a world of thoughts so different, so remote from theirs! His father pontificated, solemnly pronouncing imbecilities; his mother talked on and on about Ivan, the teacher, the serious son of the family, who was about to make a "splendid" marriage—indeed, the wedding was to be held at Melikhovo in July—with some minor aristocrat, "a sweet girl with a long nose. . . ." Oh, how Chekhov longed to run away from that monotonous life, that "quiet pious life. . . ." "My ambition is freedom and money," he wrote forthrightly. "To sit on a ship's deck, open bottles of champagne, talk about books, and, at night, women . . ." (July 28, 1893).

He confessed this thirst for escape to Alexander, who went to Melikhovo for a few days in June. His elder brother understood him so well that subsequently he wrote urging Anton to go away. "No matter what it costs, you must keep your soul alive," Alexander said. "Give up all of it: your dreams of living in the country, your love for Melikhovo, and all the emotion and the work that you have invested in it. Melikhovo is not unique in the world. What sense does it make if Altimantran[3] eats your soul away like rats gnawing a candle? And it's not difficult to eat it away. . . ."

[3] In their letters to one another the Chekhov brothers sometimes still used nicknames, absurd allusions, and symbols that had been part of their "gang" language when they were children. Altimantran and Vissarion were among the many terms that they used for their father.

Had not Anton done enough for that despotic father and all the rest of the family, whereas they treated him with "complete incomprehension"?

In Chekhov, however, family feeling was stronger than all his revulsions and all his dreams of flight. In addition to his deep affection for his mother and Masha, his sense of duty kept him bound to the home that he had established for this family of gypsies that he had taken it on himself at the age of eighteen to support and that he had ever since maintained and protected. Furthermore, as he wrote to Suvorin, he was content now that, thanks to Melikhovo, he had been able to resolve his financial problems in large measure: food, shelter, and transport were now directly provided for him by the estate.

When at last, early in May, the sun returned, Chekhov regained some of his good humor. He began planting new trees and rosebushes and supervising "his crops," which promised to be good. Once more seized by a rage to write, he was in a hurry to finish that *Sakhalin* on which he had been laboring for three years. Work went well in the country: how could his colleagues not understand that? "Send the poets and novelists to the country!" he wrote to Suvorin. ". . . City living cannot offer rich poetic or artistic material to the poor man. He lives within four walls and meets his fellow man only in newspaper editorial offices and porters' lodges" (April 26, 1893).

As a physician he himself, in fact, saw somewhat too much of his fellow man and at too close quarters. It was not only the "stupid, stubborn" *babas* with their eternally ailing children who took up his time. There was a fresh threat of cholera and, as in the previous year, he had again to spend the summer coursing through the villages, organizing relief and discussing requisite action with the authorities. "There are times," he sighed, "when I am sent for at home four or five times in a single day. I've just come back from Kryukov and already there's someone outside from Vaskma waiting for me." His literary work suffered by this, but could he abandon all those sufferers? Nevertheless there were days when he cursed his "lawful wife."

Summer had also brought an army of friends to Melikhovo—charming people no doubt, but often extremely burdensome as well. Chekhov gave then a great deal of attention: he organized mushroom-gathering parties for them, croquet games, and walks with his two new bassets, Bromide and Quinine. At dinner in the evening, over delicious dishes prepared by his mother, the laughter and conversation of which Chekhov was always the center went on for hours. Then everyone would go into the drawing room, and Anton would pass out cigars to the men, put on some skit or other, or call on Lika, who was studying at the Moscow Conservatory, to sing while she accompanied herself at the piano. Among the newer guests there was a writer named Ignatyi Potapenko, whom Chekhov initially baptized a "god of boredom," but whom he now found quite pleasant and amusing; Potapenko played the violin well and sang Tchaikovsky and Glinka ballads in a rich, pleasing voice.

Chekhov was a delightful host. Nevertheless he did not always deceive his friends; in spite of his cordiality, he was isolated from others by a kind of inability to communicate, an impenetrability. He avoided confidences, giving the impression of repressing his own emotions, to such a degree that Potapenko, for example, wondered whether it was possible to have an intimate friendship with him.

He always seemed somewhat distracted from his surroundings. Was it because he was incessantly preoccupied with what he was writing? One might think so, because often he would leave the table in the middle of a meal, or slip out of the evening of *Kammermusik*, to go and write down an idea or a phrase that had just come to him. Then he would go back to where he had been sitting among his friends and apologize by saying that he had "just earned fifty kopecks." Tatiana Shchepkina-Kupernika, who knew him well by now, observed that in company his laughter and his jokes never prevented him from being elsewhere, from seeming "an older person playing with children." She sensed a strange "disinterest" in him.

In spite of this troop of laughing friends that he liked to have around him, Chekhov was in actuality a solitary man and, furthermore, one who clung to his solitude and defended it. More than ever he was the spectator that he had already been in his youth, a very interested spectator, to be sure, of everything in his vision, so that sometimes it seemed almost as if he were about to join in the spectacle but could never quite make up his mind to do so. He said very little about himself to all those friends who trooped round him, so little, in fact, that no one knew what he thought, for example, of God or love. In the last analysis he had only one passion: his art, writing.

He also much enjoyed the company of women, provided that they were pretty and charming, but he took care to make no ties of passion with any of them. As he himself conceded in a letter to Suvorin, he had "carved out a life apart" for himself, and behind a pretense of good nature, this life was monotonous, colorless, and sad, but it was what he had chosen. "It would bore me to concern myself with a woman," he admitted, "even though I know that a great love can be a distraction." Precisely because he wished to have no distractions, he continued to avoid great loves.

This finally became clear during the summer of 1893 to "the beautiful Lika." Chekhov continued sending her charming letters full of ambiguities: "Dear Lika: I haven't written to you because there has been nothing to write. My life is so empty that I am unaware of living until the flies tickle me, and that's all. Do come, my blonde darling, and we will talk and argue and make up. . . . I sleep seventeen hours out of the twenty-four. If you've fallen in love with someone and already forgot me, Lika, at least don't make game of me." But the girl was aware now that Chekhov did not love her, or at least had no intention of marrying her or, for that matter, anyone else. She was all the more convinced of this because out of an almost desperate coquettishness she had begun to flaunt a flirtation with the handsome Potapenko in front of Chekhov, who had shown not the slightest jealousy. Indeed, he had only compliments for Potapenko, and even wrote to Lika that Potapenko had made a good impression on him. When Potapenko sang while Lika played the piano, Chekhov smiled.

At the end of the summer Lika sent him a kind of final letter that was completely frank. "You know very well *what* I feel for you," she wrote, "and that's why I'm not at all ashamed to write it. I know too that your attitude toward me is condescending and indifferent. My greatest desire is to be cured of this hopeless condition that I am in, but it is very difficult to do it alone. I'm asking you to help me. Please don't ask me to visit you any more, and don't try to see me. . . ." It was undoubtedly out of chagrin, or defiance, that she threw herself into Potapenko's arms at this time and became his mistress.

That autumn, moreover, another woman came into Chekhov's life—as a visitor. In Moscow he had met a young actress, Lydia Borisovna Yavorskaya, and he had been captivated by her exotic beauty, her spirit, her elegance, her husky, seductive voice. He thought that she was slightly affected, but she sustained his interest with her coquetries and her subtle manner of admiring him. All literary Moscow was soon talking about their romance, and there seemed to be fact behind the talk, to judge by the letters that the actress sent to Chekhov with the signature: "I embrace you and love you. Your Lydia." [4]

Poor Lika knew from the start that she had a rival, and one who was luckier than herself. Ambitious and eager for marriage, Lydia Yavorskaya had insinuated herself into the "squadron" of young women who surrounded Chekhov every time he went to Moscow. All these women saw one another frequently, went out of their way to be gracious to one another, and detested one another. "Mrs. Yavorskaya spent the evening with us," Lika wrote perfidiously to Chekhov in November. "She said that Chekhov was delightful and she wanted to marry him at all costs. . . . She asked me for my help, and I promised to do my best for your joint happiness. . . . Write me a line to let me know whether you love Lydia Borisovna Yavorskaya. Write to me, of course, and not to her. Good-bye, torturer of my soul" (November 7, 1893).

Chekhov did not fall into the trap: poor Lika's ruse was only too transparent. He was content to thank his "dear go-between" without, of course, saying whether he expected to marry Lydia Yavorskaya. The situation amused him. He enjoyed the laughing company of his "squadron," with whom he would talk and drink until morning in his room in the Grand Hotel in Moscow—a man of strong habits, he always reserved Room 5. "I have never before

---

[4] Lydia Yavorskaya's letters are preserved in the Lenin Library in Moscow. It is difficult to understand why these letters, like Lydia Mizinova's, have not yet been published. Those that are quoted here are taken from L. Grossman's book *The Romance of Nina Zarechnaya* (Moscow, 1960).

felt so free," he confided to Suvorin. ". . . And girls, girls, girls!" He allowed his photograph to be taken with the actress and Tatiana Shchepkina-Kupernika, and when he saw it—he with his face turned away and austere, the girls eager, simpering, looking at him—he titled it "The Temptation of St. Anthony." When Christmas came, he invited Lika and Potapenko back to Melikhovo as if nothing had happened.

In Chekhov's view, too, there was too often talk of love when what was involved was merely sexual instinct. For instance in Zola's *Dr. Pascal*, he pointed out to Suvorin, the author was wrong to call ordinary coupling "love." But even sexuality's importance must not be exaggerated. "Is the sexual function in itself the expression of health and life?" he wrote. "Is that the characteristic of man?" This did not mean, however, that he was taking it on himself to preach morals: let people sleep with whom they pleased; it was their own business. "In my old age I probably won't give up 'drawing my bow,' as Apuleius puts it in his *Golden Ass*." Incidentally he remarked that "the majority of thinkers are impotent by the age of forty" (November 11, 1893).

"Not writing is living on debt and boredom," he told Suvorin in December, and indeed it was for writing that he lived. Everything was subordinated to it: he would hesitate to set out for Moscow or Petersburg, where friends were waiting for him, lest he "lose all his ideas on the way." And, as always, he was haunted by the thought of not writing enough. He complained, for instance, that for two years cholera had taken up all his time and thus prevented him from working.

Since 1892, however, Chekhov had completed a number of manuscripts. Thus his big undertaking, *The Island of Sakhalin*, was finished in 1893, and it began to appear serially at the end of the year in the magazine *Russian Thought*. He was reasonably satisfied with this book, which had required enormous effort: he felt that he had written a good study, well documented without being pedantic, and too that he had at last paid his debt to science. "It is an academic work and I shall have the Metropolitan Makarios Prize," he wrote in jest to Suvorin. "I'm glad that rough convict cloak is hanging in my literary closet. Let's leave it hanging there" (January 2, 1894).

That literary closet was now the object of universal admiration, and Chekhov was recognized as the best prose writer of his generation. The "big magazines"—the literary reviews—clamored for contributions from him, and his stories were also beginning to appear abroad in English, French, Czech, and German translations. But *The Island of Sakhalin* was a great disappointment to the public. Chekhov's admirers had been expecting a very personal, dramatic, and accusing book, along the lines of Dostoevsky's *Recollections From the House of the Dead*, and finding that it was only a piece of very honest but rather dry reporting that made no concessions to romanticism, they did not conceal their disillusionment. And when *Sakhalin* appeared in book form in 1895, it made little stir and went almost unnoticed by the critics.[5]

Chekhov sent a copy of his book to the Prison Administration and he was quite shocked—"stunned"—to receive in return only a curt acknowledgment of receipt: "In response to your dispatch of . . ." Filed by the administration without any action, neglected by the public, the book did not win "the Metropolitan's Prize" or any scientific honors. On the other hand it was very much read and discussed, in Russia and elsewhere, by experts in penal law and prison management. It also had a practical result that must have given the author pleasure: it attracted the Russian government's attention to the island concentration camp, to which an official investigating mission was sent. As a consequence the corporal punishments denounced by Chekhov were abolished, the exiles' living conditions were improved, and schools and hospitals were built.

A year earlier the short story "Ward Six" had been published and had aroused sharp reactions in the public. It told the story of the filthy, neglected ward reserved for mental patients in a provincial hospital. The author described the lives of these wretches, utterly abandoned to the whims of their male nurse, the tyrannical and alcoholic Nikita, and their doctor, Andrey Efi-

[5] This is still true even today. That is why, for example, though there are two so-called "complete" editions of Chekhov's works in French, neither includes *The Island of Sakhalin;* no doubt it is considered insufficiently "Chekhovian." Moreover, the book has never been translated into French. [The *Encyclopaedia Britannica's* bibliography—1968 edition—does not mention any English translation.—TRANSLATOR.]

mich, an uncaring dreamer who let things drift. He had tried at
first to combat the disorder, the extortion, and the alcoholism that
were the dominant influences in the hospital; then he allowed
himself to give way to the terrifying "What's the use?" that paralyzed so many of Chekhov's heroes. In order to justify himself he
began even to preach a semblance of a philosophy of resignation
—a kind of ridiculous Tolstoyism—to his miserable patients. Subsequently, however, gradually, he came to take an interest in
them, and infused once more with a certain energy, he decided to
improve their conditions. But he reckoned without the spirit of
routine, which was not slow in taking its vengeance: the poor
physician was certified as insane and locked up in his turn in the
sinister "Ward Six."

This gloomy story—naturalistic? philosophical?—inspired impassioned discussion in Russia. As was natural in a country where
censorship was tantamount to an invitation to read between the
lines, each reader found a different philosophical thesis in it that
he interpreted according to his own lights. For some, who were
beginning to turn away from the master of Yasnaya Polyana, it
was a merciless criticism of Tolstoyism. "Without theories, without wasted words," Sophie Lafitte was to write in our own time,
"in his own sober, concrete, and irrefutable fashion, Chekhov
proved the unawareness, the artificiality, the falsity of Tolstoyan
preaching face to face with the brutal realities of life." [6] For
others—and even today for certain "orthodox" Soviet critics such
as Ermilov—the story was a political attack on the goverment:
Ward Six was the "mental prison" of the empire, the narrow-
minded, tyrannical nurse was the tsarist system or the Tsar himself, the disillusioned doctor was the intelligentsia. Lenin was impressed above all by the story's remarkable power to weave a
spell: "When I finished reading this story last night," he noted, "I
was literally frightened. I could not stay in my room; I got up and
went out. I had the feeling that I was locked into Ward Six."

Chekhov's own fear was that the story might prove boring; it
seemed to him to smell of "the hospital and the morgue." He
admitted that it lacked what Suvorin called "alcoholic stimula-

[6] Sophie Lafitte, *Léon Tolstoï et ses contemporains* (*Lev Tolstoy and His Contemporaries*).

tion." He was pleasantly surprised by the censor's indulgence toward it and by the many letters that came from enthusiastic readers. But as was to be expected, he never offered any clue to the meaning that should be given to "Ward Six."

He had also just finished another story, quite without parallel and very different from everything that he had thus far published, "The Black Monk." It was written as the result of a dream. According to Chekhov's brother Mikhail, during the afternoon-nap period one summer afternoon in Melikhovo, Chekhov burst out of his room and said to him in great agitation: "I've just had a terrible dream. I saw a black monk." The impression of the dream was so strong that it took Chekhov, normally so completely self-controlled, a long time to regain his composure. A few days later he wrote the story.

Later he explained to Suvorin—who, like most of the critics, for that matter, was disturbed by this story—that he had wanted it to be a study of a neurosis: the case of a young man suffering from delusions of grandeur. The specter of a black monk flying across the fields appears to Kovrin, a strange young philosopher distraught from overwork, and persuades him that he is one of the elect of God who need account only to Eternal Truth. The monk explains to the philosopher that geniuses are above the level of ordinary mortals and need not concern themselves with logic or common sense. For a while the influence of the "black monk" over the young man is successfully contested by his new bride and her father, both of whom admire him. Kovrin accepts medical care and returns to normality. Deprived of his dream, however, he suffers from being now only an ordinary person, and he is angry with his wife for having thus reduced him to the everyday. He leaves her in the hope of recapturing his ecstatic hallucinations, but soon dies of tuberculosis.

This half-surrealist, half-Freudian story was certain to arouse the critics. Some called it one of Chekhov's best works; others called it a complete failure. A friend told Chekhov that Tolstoy, when he had read it, exclaimed with an enthusiasm that was rare for him: "It's delightful! Oh, how delightful it is!" This was certainly a compliment, but a strange one. Still others said that the story was a new satire on the intelligentsia, too many of whose members, despising the ordinary, pretended to the possession of the secret of universal happiness, which they intended to keep for themselves. As for Mrs. Suvorina's suspicion that "The Black Monk" was a description of the author's own mental disorder, it merely amused Chekhov. "Tell Anna Ivanovna," he wrote to her husband, "that poor Anton Pavlovich isn't mad yet, thank God. But he is an abundant drinker and that's why he is haunted by monks in his sleep" (January 25, 1894).

What still often haunted him, or at least preoccupied him, in his waking hours were the eternal problems posed by his trade as a writer. He was constantly questioning himself on the form and the direction that should be given to his stories. During the preceding two years he had thoroughly read and reread the great masters, Tolstoy, Turgenev, Zola, and the novelists of the new generation, Potapenko, Korolenko, Garshin, and he had reached the conclusion that realism, restricted to the task of "reproducing" as exactly as possible the unaltered image of life, was really rather inadequate and flat. "Tell me in all good conscience," he wrote to Suvorin, "who among contemporary writers has given the world even one drop of alcohol." His reaction to the Realist painters was the same: "Do Repin's or Shishkin's paintings make your head spin? They are pretty and full of talent, but they won't keep you from wanting a smoke" (April 25, 1892).

It was not that he was giving way to moralism or that be conceived it to be his duty to teach the reader—as Tolstoy was doing —that he could not and should not smoke. In fact, Chekhov so detested preachers at this time that he advised Suvorin to write a coldly clinical account of "the rape of a chambermaid" simply to irritate them. Besides, he was convinced that moralism was the easy way in literature. "It's easier to write about Socrates," he said, "than about a girl or a cook" (January 2, 1894). He was equally irritated by sentimentalism: even when one was writing sad stories that made the author suffer with his characters, he wrote to Lydia Avilova, the tone should retain its objectivity because "it is essential to remain aloof."

The break with Tolstoy had been made once and for all. Chekhov was no longer "under the spell" of the master of Yasnaya Polyana, whose style of writing was so enthralling that for years, without giving the matter much thought, his younger colleague had accepted part of his moral teaching. Chekhov had muzhik blood in his veins and he had done everything in his power to emancipate himself from it; henceforth it was forbidden to tell him anything more about the "holy" Russian peasant and his virtues. While he agreed with Tolstoy's denouncing of war and slander, he did not see why he must therefore conclude, he said, "that I should wear sandals made of linden bark and sleep on the oven with my hired man and his wife." He considered electricity and steam more important to human happiness than chastity and vegetarianism. "Tolstoy has drawn away from me," he confessed sorrowfully; "he has gone out of my heart saying: 'I am leaving the house empty, there's no further need to lodge anyone there'" (March 27, 1894).

Nevertheless Chekhov now felt, so keenly that it was almost painful, that literature ought to be more than literature: it ought to have meaning. He wrote to Suvorin that the writers of his generation, though they were full of talent, intelligence, and guts, were nonetheless infected with an illness more serious for an artist than syphilis or sexual impotence. "We are lacking something, that's apparent," he wrote. But what was it? Simply that something that all great writers had in common: a goal toward which they directed their readers. It made little difference whether this goal was material—the abolition of serfdom, the liberation of the nation, beauty—or a loftier ideal—God, the afterlife, universal happiness; what was important was that there be a goal, that the reader sense, beneath life described as it is, "life as it ought to be."

As for himself, Chekhov frankly admitted that he had no such goal, either immediate or distant, and that therefore there was "a great empty space" in his work. He did not believe in the efficacy of politics, he had no faith in either God or revolution, and he was not even afraid of ghosts or death. But, he added, "he who is without desire, without hope, and without fear cannot be an artist." Incapable of playing out a comedy decked with the ideas of others, unable to reach a conclusion, he ended with a question that to him was full of significance: "Are we sick men?" (November 25, 1892).

Physically ill Chekhov certainly was, growing worse and worse, and he gave more attention to his health than he had done in the past. His severe cough attacked him more frequently than before, became more intense, and now compelled his notice. But on the subject of his illness he had a kind of shame that soon masked itself in bravado, and it was in an abstract tone that he mentioned —as seldom as possible, however—"bronchitis" and "pulmonary consumption." He even resorted to paradox in order to explain to Suvorin that in general a serious illness of which one was aware was less to be dreaded than a minor but unrecognized disease. "What seems trivial is to be feared," he wrote; "what frightens us presents no danger. I am not making myself clear: nature gulls us by making us disappear like a child that the nurse takes out of the drawing room at bedtime" (August 24, 1893).

Was he gulling himself? Not only did he have no doubt as to the nature and the seriousness of his illness; he knew very well what he ought to do in order to try to extirpate it. Potapenko recounted an astonishing incident: traveling with him, Chekhov encountered a passenger on the train whom he immediately identified as a tubercular, and in a manner as unexpected as it was urgent he advised the stranger to leave Russia without delay and live in a warm, dry climate for two or three years if he wanted to try to get well. When the stranger showed hesitancy about abandoning everything, Chekhov insisted and even commanded: "Leave your family, sell your property, and go away! Otherwise you'll come to a bad end." But he took no care of himself, and while he knew what treatment to employ, he categorically refused to separate himself from Melikhovo and his family. There was moreover a kind of fatalism in him that was a logical parallel to his "lack of passions." Besides, had he not survived more than ten years since his first hemorrhage? So he did nothing to battle his disease except—and that for only a limited time—to give up cigars and alcohol.

Out of modesty and a horror of being pitied he always avoided discussion of his illness. He even concealed its attacks from those close to him. When his brother Mikhail observed him spitting blood at Melikhovo, Chekhov forbade him to mention it to anyone. "It's nothing," he said; "you must not say anything about it to Mother or Masha."

In the garrulous, petty republic of letters, however, the best-guarded secrets quickly furnish the grist for everyone's gossip. In November, 1893, some of Chekhov's "dear colleagues" in Petersburg spread the story that he was suffering from frequent tubercular crises and that he was not going to live much longer. When he learned of this—through Alexander—he was angry; he assured Suvorin that he did not have tuberculosis and that he had not spat blood for years. As for his friend Leikin—who was the source of the talk—Chekhov charged his brother with telling him what Chekhov thought of him: "Thank Leikin for his sympathies," he wrote sarcastically. "When he has an attack of apoplexy, I'll send a telegram" (November 29, 1893).

During the winter, however, he himself began to be anxious, even though he continued to insist on the opposite and admitted only to "physical weariness." His cough grew worse and at dawn he would be afflicted with painful and prolonged spasms. In mid-February he suddenly decided to spend a month in the sun, in the Crimea, and he left for Yalta on March 2. When he arrived there, it was spring: the weather was mild, the sky was bright, and the sea was a gay blue among the black cypresses. He settled into the Hotel Russia with the intention of resting and also, impenitently the eternal writer, composing a play.

But soon he was writing of the "idiocy" that he had committed in going to spend a month on the Black Sea Coast. He had been recognized at once in Yalta and had had to pay his tribute to his own reputation: he spent hours talking with L. E. Obolensky, the critic, and other hours helping the local aristocracy to rehearse *Faust*, posing for a sculptor, and "eating lamb fried in grease with onions and chops in the company of a teacher at the girls' school." Nevertheless he found the time to write a story, "Evening," if not a play. But how "unpleasant, insipid, and colorless" these "natives" were, and the highly touted natural beauty was like a "cemetery." If at least his health were benefiting . . . but for a week he had uninterrupted heart palpitations. When he started homeward after a stay of a month, he was still coughing.

At Yalta he had received an unexpected and rather hysterical letter from Lika, whom he now addressed as "the fat blonde." She wrote from Berlin to announce that she was going to Paris, ostensibly to pursue her vocal studies but really to meet Potapenko there. Her letter clearly indicated that she was highly disturbed, for it dealt with nothing but charges that Chekhov had rejected her and threats that she was going to "die soon." Chekhov pretended not to understand and answered in his usual joking manner: no one had refused her and he was convinced that she was not going to die. He advised her to make Potapenko buy her a return ticket to Russia, because of course he was expecting her at Melikhovo in June.

He returned to Melikhovo in April in time for the real Russian springtime that he loved so much, and once more he fell under the spell of the place. He could lie in the grass again, sit on the bench near the gate, go outdoors in his dressing gown, take horseback rides followed by Bromide and Quinine yapping behind him: "paradise, in a word." He cut down dead trees, planted flowers, laid out new roads. The scent of freshly mown grass intoxicated him. He wrote to Shcheglov that sitting a few hours beside a haystack was enough "to imagine oneself in the arms of a naked woman" (July 5, 1894).

He had had a little wooden summer house built in the park, at some distance from the main house, and when it was finished, he was delighted with it and christened it his "doll's house." It was indeed a real toy, a little cottage composed of two rooms and an attic, and it had cost him 125 rubles. He soon acquired the habit of going there to work when he wanted to get away from his guests, who, now that it was summer, had turned up again in considerable force at Melikhovo. It was in this cabin, this "spiritual bakery," that he was to write *The Sea Gull*.

And yet the summer had barely begun when once more he was swept up in the desire, which soon became irresistible, to be "elsewhere." He urged Suvorin to go away with him, no matter where: it was up to Suvorin to choose—the Volga, the Don, Switzerland, or Suvorin's own country place in Theodosia. On July 7 Chekhov wrote to the publisher: "Some mysterious force, like a premonition, forces me to make haste. Perhaps it is not a premonition but simply regret at seeing life slip by so monotonously and familiarly." And eleven days later he returned to the same theme: "I want to live; a mysterious force is pulling me I don't know where —to Spain or Africa." He had just begun a play, but what of it? He had had enough of writing, and, he said, when he sat down at his desk to work, he was seized by an attack of nausea "as if I had eaten cabbage soup into which a cockroach had fallen. Excuse the simile" (July, 1894).

When Suvorin refused to be enticed, Chekhov went away in July—with Potapenko. As if nothing had happened, the seducer of "the beautiful Lika" had come back to Melikhovo, and Chekhov seemed to have no rancor against him at all. The two writers made a rather frenetic zigzag journey through Russia with abrupt changes of itinerary. Starting down the Volga at first for Tsarytsin, they went no farther than Nizhni-Novgorod. For Chekhov the turmoil of the summer fair and, in particular, the coincidental presence of a colleague, Sergeyenko, a pompous, verbose Tolstoyan, was enough to give him "nausea" and send him elsewhere. Still accompanied by Potapenko, he went to Luka, in the Ukraine, to visit his friends the Lintvaryevs: he was delighted to see the Psyol again and he spent a week "eating, drinking, and loafing."

When Chekhov returned to Melikhovo it was a little kingdom of rain and mud, darkened further by a sad letter from Taganrog. His beloved Uncle Mitrofanos was in most grave condition. Chekhov's reaction was immediate and affectionate: "I must go and take care of him, console him and his family," he insisted. Almost happy at having a new pretext for going away again, he immediately set out for his native city.

His intentions were of the best, but the first sight of Taganrog depressed him mortally. It was cold and rainy, and in addition he was annoyed by a story in the local newspaper that the presence in town of "the famous writer, A. P. Chekhov" had been announced. Nevertheless it is rather astonishing that having found his uncle at the point of death, Chekhov did not wait for the end but left six days later, this time for Theodosia. He spent a week there in Suvorin's luxurious villa. But the wind was cold, the sea was stormy, and at night three blankets piled on his bed were not enough to keep him from shivering. He was still coughing, and he dreamed of hot places—Egypt or Lake Como—and fell victim again to boredom. No question, he was not at ease anywhere: he took ship for Yalta. There he learned that his uncle had died. "I loved my late uncle with all my heart, and I respected him," he wrote to his cousin. Three days later he went to Odessa, which he left immediately, this time to go abroad: his destination, selected almost at random, was Abbazia on the Dalmatian coast.

He left "like a thief," without a word to his family or even to his confidante, Masha. In fact he had made so little preparation for this departure that he had just written to a friend that in a few days he would be back in Moscow. This time Suvorin was with him. From Vienna he wrote to Lika: "I beg you, don't tell anyone in Russia that I've gone abroad. . . . I don't feel at all well. I cough virtually without letup. Obviously I've let my health get away from me as I let you get away" (September 18, 1894).

IX

THE SEA GULLS

I write incessantly, as if I were pursued by time, and I cannot
do otherwise. . . . Oh, what a stupid life! I am with you, I am
moved, and yet not for one second do I forget that an unfinished
story is lying on my desk waiting for me. . . . I catch every word
of yours and every word of mine on the wing . . . and immediately store them away in my literary cupboard. Who knows, they
may be useful one day! . . . And it is always like this, always,
and I never have a moment's respite, I know that I am murdering
my life, I feel that I gather the pollen of my most beautiful flowers for the honey that I give to others, indeed I tear out those
flowers themselves and I trample their roots. Am I not insane?
                      TRIGORIN in *The Sea Gull*

It was only two weeks after his hasty departure, when he was in
Milan, that Chekhov at last made up his mind to write to Masha.
He was worried: did she have enough money for the house?
He had just received royalties from the book division of *New
Times* and he would send her some. He sketched his journey for
her: in Vienna he had bought a new inkwell, in Abbazia he had
found nothing but rain, and, still chasing the sun, he had gone on
by way of Trieste and Venice, where he had indulged himself in
the purchase of glass with all the colors of Paradise, three silk
neckties, and a scarfpin to hold them in place. In Milan, where he
had finally found better weather, he had gone to the circus, the
crematory in the cemetery, and the theater, where he had seen an

adaptation of *Crime and Punishment:* Italian actors were infinitely better than Russians. He was already preparing to leave for Genoa, where he would treat himself to another cemetery visit. His traveling companion, Suvorin, was to remark, moreover, that on journeys he cared only about circuses and cemeteries.

In Nice several letters from Lika were waiting for him. Now she was ready to tell him her whole story without sparing herself. Yes, she had fallen in love with Potapenko, become his mistress, and gone to Paris with him. But he had soon left her and gone back to his wife, with whom he then went to Italy. Meanwhile Lika was pregnant, and she had fled to Switzerland; she was desperately afraid of the future and felt utterly deserted and alone. She was quite certain that as a result of her idiotic affair everyone whom she loved would have nothing to do with her. . . . Would that be true of Chekhov too? He must tell her at once that he would go and see her in Switzerland, because her only wish was to see him again. . . . "I imagine none of this will surprise you," she wrote. "If you are not afraid of being disillusioned by your old Lika, please come. There is very little left of the old Lika. How these past six years have knocked my life to pieces!" (September 20, 1894).

Poor Lika also made it quite plain to him that what had happened to her was in large part his fault. "What else could I have done, little father?" she pleaded. "You always managed to get away from me and turn me over to someone else." Even while she was begging him to go to her, she openly accused him of indifference. "I don't think you'll cast stones at me. It seems to me that you have always been indifferent to people, to their faults as well as their weaknesses."

Outraged by Potapenko's behavior, Chekhov immediately wrote to Masha to tell her what he thought of that ———[1] that swine. But he also had to reply to Lika's plea for help. Undoubtedly hurt by what she had written, he wrote with a certain aloofness, as if he preferred not to be drawn into this painful business. "Unfortunately," he wrote to her, "I can't go to Switzerland because I am with Suvorin, who has to leave for Paris. I am staying in Nice for five days to a week, then two or three days in Paris,

[1] The word has been excised by the Soviet censor.

and after that I'm going back to Melikhovo." He was especially wounded by Lika's accusation of indifference: "You shouldn't have mentioned my indifference to people." But he sent her his "very best" wishes, and by way of postscript he added a consolation that was not only gratuitous but illogical, since Suvorin had been with him throughout his journey: "If only I had had your letter when I was in Abbazia, I'd have gone to Switzerland to see you on my way to Nice. But at this moment it would be impolitic to drag Suvorin with me" (October 2, 1894).

He spent only a few days in Paris and returned to Melikhovo on October 19. No doubt he and his sister had long talks about Lika's misfortune, but he did nothing to help the girl. Was she right in accusing him of indifference, or had he been profoundly offended by her charge that he was partly responsible for her woes? What is certain is that in the ensuing weeks he did not even write to her again and did not mention her. As for Masha, while she got Potapenko's version of the matter, she continued corresponding with Lika. Thus she learned, in due course, that Lika had given birth to a daughter, that she had seen Potapenko again in Paris, and that she hoped to return to Russia soon.

At the end of November, Lika made another approach to Chekhov. "I've been in Paris almost two months now," she wrote, "and I have not had a word from you. Is it possible that you've turned against me? . . . Without you I feel utterly lost and rejected! I'd give half my life to be at Melikhovo, sitting on your couch and talking to you for ten minutes. . . ." But it would seem that Chekhov did not reply. As for "that swine" Potapenko, there is every reason to believe that Chekhov quickly forgave him, for in December they had a friendly reunion in Moscow.

So the page of the half-in-love friendship with "the beautiful Lika" had now been turned. Much later Masha was to write that her brother had really been quite attracted to Lika but that it had always seemed to her that he resisted his emotions because Lika had certain characteristics—a lack of stamina and a preference for bohemian living—that he did not like. But how could Masha have known what was really in the heart of that secretive man who revealed nothing of his inmost feelings even to his wholly devoted sister? Nor did he confide any more fully in his friends, if one is to believe what Nemirovich-Danchenko was to report: "It seemed that he was very successful with women. I say *it seemed* because neither he nor I liked to talk about these things. I base my opinion on the rumors that were current."

That Chekhov should have been "successful with women" was in no way surprising. He was a very handsome man, charming and reserved, amusing, attentive, and full of compliments; in addition he was a successful author. It is well known that a whole court of young women had grown up round him and they racked their brains to tempt this "St. Anthony." But though this flattered him, though he flirted occasionally with one or another of them or even had a minor affair, he was always extremely careful not to commit himself too far. The truth was that he did not trust women: "These delightful creatures," he wrote, "give love and in exchange they strip a man of his youth."

He was always charming with the women who fluttered round him, but when it happened—seldom—that he talked of them to another man he was more realistic and more severe. Obviously, for example, pretty little Tatiana Shchepkina-Kupernika, who was so often his guest at Melikhovo, had no idea that he wrote to Suvorin about her: "Three days a week I can't stand her. Like the Devil, she's full of wiles. . . ." As for Lydia Yavorskaya, who, it will be recalled, was his mistress for a while, he found her—both as a woman and as an actress—very sympathetic and attractive, but he immediately added, repeating what seemed to be a very firmly established idea in his mind: "Fie! Women take your youth, but they won't take mine. In my life I've always been the overseer, not the owner" (January 21, 1895). Besides, he disliked her "shrill, affected voice."

He confided to Suvorin, however, that in spite of his reputation he had had "few affairs." In this respect he liked to say that he was to Catherine II—who had had innumerable lovers—what a nutshell was to a battleship. Doubt whether he was even particularly sensual is raised when one reads a remark in a letter of the same date: "To me, a woman's silk nightgown is merely something comfortable—that is, soft to the touch."

It was actually because he wanted to give himself wholly to his work that he defended himself against women "who take your

youth"—and also your creative genius. It is amusing to note that
the man who most accurately sensed this was his rival for Lika,
Ignatyi Potapenko. In his *Recollections* Potapenko observed that
Chekhov had a kind of caution that prevented him from living
fully because his art required all of him. "He restrained himself,"
Potapenko wrote, "from having a private life. He thought that it
robbed the creator of too much of his vigor and his concentration."

Chekhov, then, for all his attractiveness, seemed firmly resolved
to remain a bachelor. Nevertheless he had a wholly admirable
concept of love, and he wrote in his *Notebooks:* "When a man is
in love, he is the paradigm of what he ought always to be." But it
was undoubtedly precisely for this reason that love that becomes
reality, love in marriage, frightened him. When Suvorin was pressing him that winter to marry, he wrote: "I'll get married if you
like. But on one condition: everything must remain as is: in other
words, she will have to live in Moscow and I in the country, and
I'll go and visit her. Happiness that goes on from day to day, from
morning to night, is something that I could not endure. If someone talks to me every day about a single, identical thing, in an
unaltered tone, I become cruel. For example, Sergeyenko's presence makes me nasty because he is much like a woman (intelligent and sensitive) and seeing him makes me think that my wife
might be like him." And he added a sentence that clearly proved
once more that above all else he was a writer preoccupied with his
art: "And being married wouldn't make me write better" (March
23, 1895).

There was in Chekhov's life, however, one dedicated, loyal
woman who made no demands: his sister, Masha. When he returned to Melikhovo that autumn, he found that she had given
much thought to him. During his absence she had endeavored to
make the house more comfortable: she had had the bedrooms re-
papered and new stoves installed. Her brother gave her a ring, re-
established possession of his study, and went back to work. Most
of his time during this winter in Melikhovo was to be spent in continuous writing.

He began by correcting a collection of stories that was to be published by Sitin under the title of *Stories and Tales*. He did this with the care that he usually devoted to this kind of work and that in this instance extended to rewriting the pieces in large measure. But what particularly occupied him during the last weeks of 1894 was the planning of a new novel. He had been thinking about it for several months and he worked on it without interruption, but this time too the plan came to nothing. At the end of December he acknowledged that what he was producing, in spite of all his efforts, was "flaccid and dull." The projected novel, called *Three Years*, became a long short story that he dropped after he had written some eighty pages, which he sent just as they were to *Russian Thought*.

His disappointment at his inability to complete his novel—this was to prove his last such attempt—was soon turned to bitterness by the outrageous excisions made in it by the censor, who eliminated many passages dealing with religion. "This robs you of all desire to write spontaneously," he told Suvorin with rancor. "All the time you are writing you have the feeling that a bone is stuck in your throat" (January 19, 1895).

This man who reproached himself for laziness did much more besides abandon himself to his rage to write. He also found time to take care of the ill and to brave the bad roads in order to visit them in their homes. In addition, at the request of the local school board, he had agreed to sponsor the neighboring village's school. It was to be built in Talezh, a fact that meant further drains on his strength. And then in November he was called for jury duty in the court in Sherpukov; appointed foreman of the jury, he had to attend a number of court sessions.

These diverse activities helped him to gain a better knowledge of rural institutions, which were riddled with wretchedness, and of the provincial intelligentsia—minor nobility, factory owners, merchants—whose honesty could not be questioned but who at the same time were "superstitiously simple-minded and dreaded personal opinions like the plague." All this traveling resulted in tremendous fatigue, so that at times he was "ready to go out of his mind." And in addition there were all the favors that were constantly requested of him and that he was too kind to refuse: reading manuscripts, recommending writers to publishers, even giving reading lessons, with Masha's help, to Anyuka and Mashenka, two peasant girls who worked for him. He had also decided to become a patron of the public library in Taganrog—no doubt in memory of the hours of passionate reading that he had spent there in his adolescence—and he often sent it parcels of books that he purchased or took from his own library.

During this winter his visits to Moscow were few and short, and he went only once to Petersburg, in order to see his friends. But one evening when he was dining at Melikhovo, he was surprised by the barking of Bromide and Quinine. When Masha, with a lamp held high in her hand, opened the door, he saw a ghost: Levitan. Tatiana Shchepkina-Kupernika, the young poet, was with him. It was she who, at Chekhov's urging, had prevailed on the painter to see his friend again and who had virtually forced him to come with her. Until then Levitan had always refused to forgive Chekhov for having portrayed him in "The Grasshopper" in the person of a cynical painter, and the two men had not seen each other for more than two years.

The reconciliation was accomplished that evening with tact and without rhetoric; after a moment of silence, Chekhov and Levitan cordially shook hands and began to talk about the journey and the weather as if nothing had ever happened. But during dinner the young poet observed that Levitan's fine dark eyes were wet and that Chekhov's were glittering with gaiety. When he returned to Moscow the next day, the painter wrote to the writer: "I have got back what was so dear to me, what in fact never stopped being so dear" (January 3, 1895).

The men were to meet again a few days later, in the painter's studio in Moscow, and then at Melikhovo again. This joyfully recaptured friendship, however, did not stop Chekhov from saying frankly what he thought of Levitan's new paintings. He still regarded Levitan as Russia's best landscape artist, but it seemed to him that the painter had lost all his freshness and youth; now he was painting "stylishly." And it was women, with whom Levitan went to excesses, that in Chekhov's opinion were to be blamed. "Painting landscapes requires an enthusiasm of which a sated man is incapable," he wrote to Suvorin. "If I were a landscape painter, I should lead an almost ascetic life" (January 19, 1895).

Even without being a landscape painter Chekhov led such an ascetic life. In fact, a few months later, he admitted that a completely monastic existence suited him: "If cloisters would accept people without religion and allow them to abstain from prayer, I'd become a monk" (December 1, 1895). He further confided to Suvorin that "I am weary of mistresses and I am gradually getting rid of them."

But women went on being interested in him, and Lydia Avilova more than any. During the whole of 1894, however, Chekhov had not written her one letter. In fact he seemed so little concerned with her that he mislaid her address and had to ask Alexander, no doubt in order to return a manuscript to her, to get it from her brother-in-law's newspaper. According to her, she and Chekhov met in February in Petersburg, at a party at Leikin's, and Chekhov paid a great deal of attention to her and asked her to see him the next day. But Leikin's diary, which meticulously reported all his encounters with Chekhov, contained no allusion to this dinner.

It is a fact, however, that Chekhov went to visit Lydia Avilova on the evening of February 13. Her memoirs contain a very detailed account of this visit, in which the romantic and the comic were mingled. Since her husband was not to be present, she had prepared to receive Chekhov in a seductive intimacy, but just when he was supposed to arrive, a couple of her husband's friends appeared and delightedly consumed the special supper that she had lovingly prepared. When at last Anton Pavlovich rang, she could not even talk to him: one of the visitors, an insipid, chattering woman, immediately took him over and besieged him with questions and preposterous comments.

After this unwanted couple had gone—according to Mrs. Avilova, of course—the conversation took a romantic and indeed a pathetic turn. Chekhov talked to her about her writing and then suddenly, she reported, made her a kind of declaration of love *a posteriori*. "Do you remember our first meetings?" she said that he said. "Do you know I was truly in love with you? It was serious. I loved you. It seemed to me that there was not another woman in the world that I could have loved like that. You were beautiful and touching. But I knew that you were not like the many women

I had left or who had left me, that love for you ought to be pure and sacred, and endure a lifetime. . . . I was afraid to touch you, afraid of offending you. Did you know that?" Immediately after this confession, she said, he gathered together the manuscripts that she wanted him to read and left "seeming angry."

The letter that Chekhov wrote the next day to Mrs. Avilova made no allusion to these passionate avowals.[2] He limited himself to telling her: "You are wrong when you say that I seemed unpleasant and bored at your house"—rather a surprising "seeming" for a lover who has just declared his passion. But more was to come. Two days later he sent back the manuscript stories that she had asked him to criticize, accompanied by a very cold letter that showed no mercy. "You have talent," he told her, "but you lack lightness, or, to put it more coarsely, you're like someone drenched in a downpour. Your language is as elaborate as an old man's." This was signed: "Sincerely yours." He also sent her a copy of his new volume of stories, with an inscription: "To L. A. Avilova from the author." The language of a man who had just proclaimed his love?

The same day Chekhov went to Moscow without trying to see Mrs. Avilova again. She was to write that, tortured by doubt, not knowing whether to hope or despair—but still determined to go after Chekhov again—she went to a jeweler and ordered a watch fob for him. This jewel, shaped like a book, was inscribed on one side: "*Stories and Tales,* by A. Chekhov," and on the other: "Page 267, lines 6 and 7." The sentence thus alluded to appeared in the story called "Neighbors": "If ever you need my life, come and take it." The lady had her brother leave the gift, addressed to Chekhov but without a card, at the offices of *Russian Thought.* The invitation was direct enough, but Mrs. Avilova herself confessed in her book that she waited in vain for a response to this romantic message.

What she did not say, but what appears from Leikin's diary, is that three weeks later she went to Moscow and wrote to Chekhov

[2] After Chekhov's death Lydia Avilova asked Masha Chekhova, and for good reason, not to include this letter in *Chekhov's Correspondence,* which was published in 1913, and in which it would appear that Mrs. Avilova found the raw materials required for the fabrication of her "romance" with him, This letter was published for the first time in the 1949 edition of the *Complete Works* that appear in Moscow.

in Melikhovo, asking him to join her in the capital. This time too her invitation went unanswered.

Chekhov was always impatient for the return of spring, "which stirs up mad notions." Again this year, when he was working on the proofs of *The Island of Sakhalin,* the wait was a long one. He was glad to be in the country, "far from restaurants, cabs, and other temptations to time-wasting," but March had already become April and the snow was still in the process of melting while the cattle searched in vain for new grass. One day he saw a drunken muzhik jump naked into the icy water of his lake; when the man came out, his aged mother beat him with a stick and the man fled into the snow just as he was.

A week later it was suddenly spring: "The swallows are singing in the fields," Chekhov wrote on April 28, "and the blackbirds are calling in the woods. It is warm and gay." And suddenly the "mad notions" took him. He suggested that Suvorin put on a "monster party" in Moscow: "We'll shock no one but those old parrot hens who think writers are made of plaster."

Good weather brought all the members of the tribe back to Melikhovo. All of them were doing well, too, each having more or less found the happiness that suited him. Mikhail was stagnating somewhat in Yaroslavl, true, but as a result of his brother's influence, he had just been raised in grade in the hierarchy of officialdom. By hard work Ivan had earned a reputation as a teacher, and Masha was still teaching at the Ryevsky Institute and dividing her leisure between her friends and her painting studies. Even Alexander seemed at last to have achieved a certain balance: a journalist on the staff of *New Times,* he had a good reputation, wrote stories that were published, and was quite proud to be able to tell Anton that he had just opened a bank account and was renting a dacha of his own for the summer.

What about "Father Antosha"? He was leading a rather colorless life with his writing desk, his rosebushes, and his two bassets. He was completing the reading of proofs for his book on Sakhalin, treating the ailments of the muzhiki in the surrounding villages, and being a good host to his visiting friends. He still dreamed of distant journeys—to Australia or the valley of the Yenissei—but he stayed in Melikhovo all summer except for brief trips to Moscow and Petersburg.

As if nothing had happened Lika—who had returned to Russia with her child in May—made three separate visits to Melikhovo. She was happy to be back with the family that she loved so much and that returned her love. She had regained her composure, and her relationship with Anton was now one of easy comradeship. Though they often made the trip from Melikhovo to Moscow together, the time of delightful, equivocal letters was quite past, and Chekhov no longer wrote to her. As for Potapenko, the "swine," Chekhov seemed to have no anger against him at all. To Suvorin he spoke highly of Potapenko's vivacity and kindness, and when Chekhov was in Petersburg, the two writers were often together.

Levitan, who had left his forty-year-old "grasshopper," had new loves that were veering toward the tragic—as he preferred them to do, for that matter—and Chekhov had to take a hand in them during the summer. In July he received a cry for help from the painter's latest conquest, another lady of "Balzacian" age, Anna Turchaninova: he must come at once, because Levitan, who had tried to kill himself, had only wounded himself but was in a state of appalling depression. "A man's life," she wrote, "hangs on your arrival." What the good lady did not mention was the fact that she and her daughter were at swords' points for Levitan's affections and that this was the reason he had tried to end his life in sheer desperation.

Chekhov left at once for Gorka, in Novgorod province. He found Levitan in rather pathetic shape, with a bandage round his head; but fortunately the pistol bullet had made only a superficial wound. Chekhov stayed with Levitan for five days, and it must be assumed that he raised the painter's spirits, for soon after Chekhov's return to Melikhovo he had a pleasant note from Levitan— pleasant for Chekhov, at any rate, if not for the Turchaninova ladies: "I don't know why, but those few days that you spent here have been the calmest and the serenest of the summer for me" (July 27, 1895).

Not the most peaceful but certainly the most exciting days of that summer of 1895 for Chekhov were those he spent at Tolstoy's. Hitherto he had hesitated to emulate the example of his colleagues and make the pilgrimage to Yasnaya Polyana or to Tolstoy's winter residence in Moscow in order to meet the illustrious writer-prophet. On a number of occasions mutual friends had offered to introduce him to Tolstoy but he had always refused, saying that when the time came, he would arrange an appointment. Apparently—perhaps because Chekhov had definitely divorced himself from Tolstoyism—that time was now at hand, because when Tolstoy's disciple Garbunov suggested in August that Chekhov go with him to Yasnaya Polyana, he immediately accepted.

As Chekhov was walking up the avenue of birches that led from the entrance of Yasnaya Polyana to the manor, he met the old man, who, wearing a white linen blouse and carrying a towel over his shoulder, was on his way to swim in the river. After a few cordial words of welcome, Tolstoy asked Chekhov to swim with him. Stark naked in water up to their necks, the two men held their first conversation—a circumstance that delighted Chekhov. Thus put at his ease from the start, he spent two days with Tolstoy—in whom there was decidedly nothing of the pontificator and whom he liked very much—in extremely open and friendly talk.

In spite of his age Tolstoy was still interested in everything: walking with his guest on the road to Tula, he admiringly called Chekhov's attention to the young adepts of the bicycle, an instrument of sport very much in vogue in Russia at that time. The old man himself was an ardent cyclist, to the great scandal of his virtuous disciple Chertkov, who exclaimed in stupid shock: "Tolstoy rides a bicycle. Isn't that a contradiction of his Christian ideal?"

In the evening the family and friends would gather. Tolstoy having just finished the first draft of *Resurrection,* Chertkov or Garbunov would read passages of it aloud. Chekhov felt so much at home at Yasnaya Polyana that he did not hesitate to tell the old master that while he admired the courtroom scene, it seemed highly improbable to him, in the light of the Russian penal code, that the heroine of the novel, Katya Mosslava, would be sentenced to only two years at forced labor. Tolstoy, indeed, was later to correct the error.

This first encounter left old Tolstoy enchanted and at the same time, master thinker that he was, somewhat disappointed. A few days later he wrote to his son Lev about Chekhov: "I like him very much. . . . He is full of talent and he must have a very good heart, but so far he seems not to have a definite outlook on life" (September 4, 1895).

As for Chekhov, he was completely disarmed by his senior. Not long afterward he who was so chary of enthusiasm was to say: "When one talks with Lev Nikolaevich, one feels entirely in his power. I have never met anyone more captivating, more harmoniously conceived, so to speak. He is an almost perfect man." To Suvorin, who had uttered certain doubts on the sincerity of Tolstoy's message, Chekhov retorted sharply that he himself had been completely convinced by the attitude of Tolstoy's daughters. "They adore their father," he wrote, "and they believe in him fanatically. That shows that Tolstoy represents a great moral force, because if he were not sincere and above reproach, his daughters would be the first to be skeptical about him. . . . One can deceive a fiancée or a mistress at will, and to a woman in love even an ass can seem a philosopher, but with daughters it's another matter" (December 26, 1895).

Chekhov had no notion that he himself had enchanted Tolstoy's eldest daughter, Tatiana. Though she was not pretty, there was a great attraction in her liveliness and her generosity to everyone with whom she had any dealings; in spite of her age—twenty-eight—she still had the romantic impulses of an adolescent. She wrote in her diary: "Chekhov is a man to whom I could devote myself madly. At out first meeting he penetrated the very depth of my soul as no one has ever done." [3]

Having just bought a theater in Petersburg, Suvorin proposed in April that Chekhov write a play for him. Chekhov replied, ra-

---

[3] During the months that followed, Tatiana Tolstoy saw Chekhov again, and according to what has been related by her daughter, Tanya Albertini, she was so thoroughly infatuated with him that at one time she even thought of marrying him. She discussed it with her mother, who was appalled: "He's not a man for you! You're a countess and he's only of the lower classes, and poor. You wouldn't have even a pillow for your head, at best an ordinary red cotton cushion." Tatiana never mentioned Chekhov again, and a few years later, in 1899, she married Sukhotin.

ther evasively, that perhaps he would begin one in the autumn; thereafter he did not mention it again. Besides, since the failure of *The Wood Demon* five years earlier, he seemed to have almost totally lost interest in the theater. Then suddenly, on October 21, he told Suvorin in a kind of explosion of joy: "Imagine: I'm writing a play! It probably won't be finished before the end of November. I am enjoying writing it, even though I commit dreadful sins against stage conventions. It is a comedy with three women's and six men's parts, four acts, a landscape (a view over a lake), plenty of literature discussions, little action, five *poods* of love." A few weeks later he gave the play its title: *The Sea Gull.*

Within a month of having started it he would be able to say: "Well, my play is already finished." Meanwhile he was overloaded with work: he was preparing for the building of a school, himself supervising the plans and specifications, and in addition he was trying to rescue a medical periodical, *Annals of Surgery,* writing letters everywhere in the effort to assemble the necessary capital. At the same time he had been working steadily on *The Sea Gull,* allowing nothing to divert him. Suvorin invited him to spend a week in Petersburg: out of the question, he would not leave Melikhovo until the play was finished. He was having palpitations again and he could not sleep: never mind, the play was progressing and he wanted to complete it as quickly as possible. It seemed as if he feared he might lose the thread of it. "When I am writing a play," he said, "I am full of anxiety, as if someone were prodding me in the back."

As soon as his play was finished, he had two copies typed, sent one to Suvorin, and then, his nerves beginning to unwind, he was at once filled with doubt of what he had just written. "I began it forte," he told Suvorin, "and I finished it pianissimo, in violation of all the rules of drama. I am more unhappy than pleased with it, and when I read my newborn play, I realize once again that I am not a dramatist." He added: "Don't let anyone read it" (November 21, 1895).

It was not only because he was afraid of having failed of his purpose that he requested secrecy. Undoubtedly he was also afraid of his own indiscretions, because his *Sea Gull* was a little too similar to the romance between "the beautiful Lika" and

Potapenko. Its nostalgic, emotional heroine, Nina, seduced and then deserted by a writer, Trigorin, was certainly Lika and her unfortunate love, both in its betrayal by Potapenko and, perhaps secondarily, in its rejection by Chekhov. He had had the couple under observation before, during, and after their own drama, and once more, as in the case of Levitan's love affair, he had been unable to resist that too frequent temptation of the writer: taking the inspiration for his work from the lives of his intimates.

The interest of this new play, however, lay far less in its story line than in the profound upheaval in its author's dramatic tendencies that it so clearly indicated. Much more sharply than in *Ivanov*, Chekhov had broken with realism, with the objective depiction of life, in order to give free rein to his poetic genius. In *The Sea Gull*, as he had already done in his most recent stories, the author no longer described but dramatized, treating people and life not as they seemed to be but rather as they were in their deepest, inmost reality. Action, in sum, was supplanted by an emotional climate that endeavored not to keep the audience in suspense but to compel and spellbind it.

On the first reading of the play to his family and friends at Melikhovo the resemblance to the real drama lived by Lika was immediately apparent to everyone: some even found a resemblance between Potapenko's wife and the character of Arkadina in the play. When Chekhov read the play aloud not long afterward in the blue drawing room of his actress friend Mrs. Yavorskaya— that other "sea gull"—to a group made up of writers and theater people, Tatiana Shchepkina-Kupernika was the spokesman for everyone when she raised the same objections. Nemirovich-Danchenko, who read the play at Chekhov's request, was also struck and embarrassed by this similarity. Had Chekhov, with the blindness peculiar to writers, really been unaware that he was so closely replicating Lika's drama of unhappy love? One might almost think so, for when Suvorin too called the resemblance to his attention, Chekhov replied in all innocence: "If it's true that I've described Potapenko in it, then certainly it's impossible to publish it or perform it" (December 16, 1895).

His friends' opinions on the play's intrinsic qualities, unfortunately, were equally unanimous: the innovations and oddities of

The Sea Gull shocked them, and they believed that it could not be acted. Even before he had offered it to a theater, then, Chekhov saw his new play refused. But he made no attempt to defend it: when Chekhov, visiting Nemirovich-Danchenko, was given a lengthy criticism of it, he stood near the window, his back turned and his hands in his pockets, and did not say a word. The story of *The Wood Demon* was repeating itself, but he seemed almost indifferent to the fact. "I am not destined to become a dramatist," he wrote calmly to Suvorin. "I have no luck. But I am not unhappy about it because I can always go on writing stories" (December 13, 1895).

During the early months of 1896, however, he was to go back to his play and rewrite it completely.[4] The new version was completed at the end of March, and this time, in order to avoid any misunderstanding, Chekhov candidly sent it to Potapenko, who offered no objection.

In the beginning of January, Chekhov made what was now his traditional visit to Petersburg, and he and Potapenko saw a great deal of each other. Having repented and gone back to his wife and her luxurious apartment, Potapenko invited Chekhov there; they also went together to see the plays performed at the theater recently bought by Suvorin, particularly Rostand's *Faraway Princess*, translated by Tatiana Shchepkina-Kupernika. They also had their picture taken together. Chekhov, who, contrary to his usual custom, did not stay with Suvorin during this visit but took a room in the Hotel England, thoroughly enjoyed his two weeks in Petersburg in every way. He saw many friends, was the guest of honor at various dinners, and shone in literary gatherings. Perhaps he would have remained longer in the capital if he had not had to return to Melikhovo in order to be present at the wedding of his brother Mikhail and a "sweet woman, her heart in her eyes and an expert cook," on January 22.

Although Chekhov had given her no sign of life, Lydia Avilova had found out that he was in Petersburg and she had sent him a copy of her book of short stories, *The Happy Man and Other*

---

[4] The first version of *The Sea Gull* has never been found, and hence it is impossible to determine whether those who found it a shocking duplication of the "Lika-Potapenko" relation were right.

Tales. He had been unmoved by this new invitation, and he wrote his thanks for the book from Melikhovo, saying that he had not yet had time to read it but that he liked its appearance. He assured her, too, that he would not forget to let her hear from him when he next visited Petersburg on January 20 or 25. But it would seem that although he did in fact go back to the capital at the end of the month, he said nothing to her. Lydia Avilova assures us, however, that she met him there, although by chance, at a masked ball in Suvorin's theater on January 27.

Her intuition, she tells us, had suddenly impelled her to attend the ball, and she had barely arrived when she immediately recognized Chekhov, with whom she spent the entire evening. This time it was she, protected by her black velvet mask, who spoke of her love for him, she says. Although he had unquestionably recognized her, he pretended to mistake her for Lydia Yavorskaya. Asked "whether he knew who she was" and "whether he had received her gift," he supposedly replied that his new play, *The Sea Gull,* which would soon be performed, would give her his answer. "Listen to it very carefully," she says that he told her. "I will answer you from the stage. But you must listen well. Don't forget!" [5]

On his way home from this short visit to Petersburg, Chekhov stopped off in Moscow and, with Suvorin, went to visit Tolstoy. He found the old man in a vile humor, denouncing the new Russian poetic school of the Symbolists, whom he called "decadents." Countess Tolstoy was also out of temper, but her target was Gay, a painter of religious subjects who was also a friend and admirer of her husband. But in this stormy climate Chekhov found appeasement in the presence of two of the Tolstoy daughters, Tatiana and Masha, who went on quietly playing cards.

A vacationing author in Petersburg and Moscow, Chekhov on his return to Melikhovo was anything but a writer getting back to his desk. Although his health was bad—in April he had spat blood again—he was exhaustingly active. This poet had a remarkable taste for order, organization, and building. To expedite progress,

[5] Let us recall, however, that at the time of this alleged conversation Chekhov had not yet rewritten his play and therefore he could not have predicted that it would be staged "soon" or that it would be done in Petersburg. In reality it was ten months before the play went on. But in her memoirs Mrs. Avilova proceeds at once from this "scene" to the first performance of the play.

to bring the future closer . . . these were the things that haunted him. And he was not satisfied to beautify his estate, to have more beds of zinnias and asters and rosebushes. The road between the Lopasnya station and Melikhovo was unspeakable: he labored ceaselessly, in the face of all the inertia peculiar to bureaucracies and to Russians, until he had succeeded in having it repaired, a bridge rebuilt, and in addition a telegraph and post office established in the station. He also regularly attended the meetings of the Sherpukov Health Commission.

He was a believer in progress through education, and he had taken the leadership of the movement to have a new school built in Talezh. He was put off by none of the difficulties that he encountered. He even assumed the task of gathering the necessary funds, organized collections, concerts, and theatricals to this end, and in addition made substantial contributions from his own pocket. He himself drew the plans for the school, bought the building materials, and supervised the work of the masons and carpenters. In August the finished school was solemnly dedicated, and the grateful peasants presented Chekhov with the traditional gifts of an ikon, two silver saltshakers, and loaves of bread.

Other intellectuals preferred to confect acrid commentary on the accession of the new Tsar, Nicholas II, and the events that had accompanied the celebration of his coronation: brutal and incompetent police crowd-control in Kostinka Square had cost the lives of more than a thousand spectators. But Chekhov found it more useful to build schools.

A man of action and a builder, he was still no less a writer on that account. He was working on a very long story, "My Life," that was to occupy him for the entire summer. Laid in a little provincial town, it was the story of a middle-class young man, too rigidly brought up by his father, who breaks out in revolt. This rebellion by a son against his father was not in the Turgenev mode but inspired by the purest Tolstoyism: the young man makes a total break with the privileged class into which he was born in order to become an ordinary worker: a house painter. The story, which began appearing serially that year in a magazine called *Niva* (*The Field*), was construed as a condemnation of Tolstoyism. Nothing, however, could be less accurate, because while the hero of "My Life" ultimately fails in his effort to become one of the people, he still does not on that account renounce his Tolstoyan principles and he remains a workingman. True, his life is a failure, but nevertheless it is much more to be respected than those of his friends of both sexes who have clung to their middle-class world.

Chekhov had by no means lost interest in the fate of his *Sea Gull*. He had submitted it to the censor, and when some objections of detail were raised, he had turned to Potapenko to get them resolved and to use his own judgment in making the requested corrections. A few days later, when Chekhov was spending the week in Theodosia with Suvorin, Potapenko telegraphed him that the Alexandrinsky Theater in Petersburg wanted to stage the play. The best actors of the time would be engaged, and the first performance would be given on October 17. Delighted, Chekhov telegraphed his approval.

While he was impatient to see the play staged, he remained skeptical of the reception that *The Sea Gull* would meet from the audience. Even those who like Potapenko liked the play for its originality and its poetic atmosphere reproached him for not having taken into account the "dramatic exigencies." Chekhov retorted that he had tried to show life in its confusion, with its mixture of the tragic and the ridiculous, the trivial and the subtle; to express all that, he argued, one must resort to new dramatic forms. But would Karpov, the director of the Alexandrinsky Theater— who was a second-rate playwright as well—be able to grasp this and take it into consideration in his staging of the play? After an exchange of letters with him, Chekhov began to doubt it seriously. As soon as rehearsals began, therefore, he set out for Petersburg. "The thirst for glory drives me there," he wrote to Shcheglov, "and even more the fear of being betrayed."

He had not been mistaken. The day after his arrival in the capital he attended a rehearsal and came away from it beaten. The other rehearsals—five or six—that he attended in the following days merely confirmed his bewilderment and his disappointment: he had nightmares about them and dreamed "that he was being married to a woman whom he did not love and that he was being insulted in the newspapers." Under bad direction the actors, many of whom had not yet learned their parts, understood nothing of the characters they were playing or of the poetry of the play itself, and they performed with the bombast and grandiloquence that were mandatory on Russian stages in those days. They seemed not to understand what Chekhov meant when he often interrupted them to repeat: "The main thing, my children, is that it's absolutely unnecessary to make 'theater' of it. The characters are simple, ordinary people."

He was profoundly discouraged. Leaving the theater one evening with Potapenko, who had attended the rehearsal with him, he said: "It won't come off. It's boring and uninteresting, no one's going to be able to like it. The actors aren't interested and so the audience won't be interested either." He wrote to Masha that he was in a black humor, that he was bored in Petersburg, where the chilly sun alternated with fog, that his play "was going badly," and that therefore, contrary to the arrangments they had made, he advised her not to come for the first performance. Suvorin, with whom he was staying, observed that Chekhov had started spitting blood again.

On October 14, three days before the opening, after the replacement of one of the actresses—which ordinarily might have made things even worse—there was a miraculous change in the atmosphere. Marya Savina, playing the part of Nina—on which the entire play rested—had just announced that she could not act the part, and it had been necessary to replace her on the spot with a young actress, Vera Kommissaryevskaya. And this fragile little woman, with her great dark eyes in a childish yet pathetic face, her remarkably musical voice, stepped right into the very skin of the character with such passion that she communicated it to the rest of the company. Potapenko, who had again accompanied Chekhov to the rehearsal, thought that as soon as Vera Kommissaryevskaya came on, "the stage caught fire," and everyone present began to weep in the tragic moments. Chekhov himself was dumbstruck and immediately wrote a letter full of hope and of admiration for the actress to his brother Mikhail.

The miracle, alas, was only the flash of an evening. The two final rehearsals were crushingly bad. "It was all flat and gray," Potapenko said, and Chekhov, discouraged and miserable, talked to Suvorin about withdrawing the play. On the morning of the opening, October 17, he went to the station to meet his sister, who was arriving with Lika on the night train from Moscow. He was gloomy and depressed, and he was coughing constantly. "The actors don't know their parts," he told Masha. "They haven't understood anything and the acting is dreadful. Only Kommissaryevskaya's good. The play will be a flop. You came for nothing."

When on October 17, 1896, the curtain rose on the first act of *The Sea Gull*, the audience had no idea that the drama had certain projections on the other side of the footlights—that the play was being duplicated in a way in a second, silent, but very tense and very Chekhovian drama. A second Trigorin, excited much less by living than by writing, Chekhov was sitting in the darkness of Suvorin's box. Beside him sat another "sea gull"—or, rather, the real "sea gull," in any event the sea gull whose adventure in love had very intimately inspired his play: "the beautiful Lika." In another part of the theater sat another woman who would have been delighted to be Chekhov's "sea gull" and who, after his death, was to try to convince the world that she had been: Lydia Avilova.

The audience that filled the theater, paradoxically, was that least calculated to understand Chekhov's play. It was not even the usual first-night audience: it was made up of shopkeepers, office workers, soldiers, all of whom had come because this performance was a benefit for an actress named Levkeyeva, a successful, chubby, attractive comic actress who brought laughs as soon as she appeared on stage.[6] This audience was expecting broad comedy, and the play that it was about to see, and in which, moreover, its favorite actress had no part, could only be bewildered by it. And, of course, though there were friends of Chekhov in the theater, there were also a few curious and malicious colleagues who were hoping for a failure.

They were to be well provided for. At the first exchanges of dialogue between reserved, pensive characters quite different from what they were expecting, the spectators recoiled and froze. But suspicious like all stupid crowds, they soon began to wonder

[6] It was a tradition in contemporary Russian theaters that the first performance of a new play be a benefit for some actor favored by the public. Another custom was the frequent performance of two plays on the same evening. On this occasion Miss Levkeyeva was to appear only in the comedy that followed Chekhov's play.

whether they were not being deliberately made fools of. When Vera Kommissaryevskaya, in her fascinating voice, began Nina's famous monologue, "Men and animals, hares, eagles, and partridges . . . ," there was at first a hoarse laugh, almost immediately followed by jokes and noisy objections. The schism between stage and audience was total. So, as soon as the first-act curtain fell, there was some applause but it was immediately drowned out by whistling and angry shouts.

The disorder spread during the second act. The spectators engaged in loud conversation, made imbecilic comments, and burst into laughter at the most touching moments. The actors, completely devoid of composure, forgetting their characters and their lines, rambled in a vacuum without the slightest conviction. During the intermission, the lobby was filled with writers and journalists whose delight at an envied colleague's fiasco expressed itself in savage comments. They agreed unanimously that no such disaster had ever before been seen on a Russian stage. Chekhov remained in seclusion: at the end of the second act he had fled for refuge to Miss Levkeyeva's dressing room.

It was a total flop, and the last two acts simply confirmed the fact. As soon as the play had ended, Chekhov turned up his coat collar and disappeared into the night like a thief. As he made his way through the crowd, he heard one indignant man exclaim: "I don't know what theater directors are trying to do. It's revolting to put on a play like this." He went alone to dine in the Romanov Restaurant, and then, his nerves on edge and his thoughts overwhelmed by his black defeat, he walked the snowy streets of Petersburg for hours.

In spite of the jokes, the laughter, and the insults of the audience, Masha had stoically remained in her box until the final curtain. It had been agreed that she would meet her brother and Lika in the hotel room that she and Lika were sharing, but the women waited in vain for him. At one o'clock in the morning Masha, apprehensive—and the more so when she learned from her brother Alexander that Anton was not at the theater, at Potapenko's or at Miss Levkeyeva's, where the actors had gone to eat—went to Suvorin's house. Chekhov's rooms there were empty. Determined to wait for him, Masha had to listen to Mrs. Suvorina's social small talk and her husband's harsh criticism hurled at *The Sea Gull.* It was not until two o'clock that Chekhov appeared. When Suvorin questioned him, he said that he had simply walked the streets without a break as if he had been drunk. "I couldn't just forget that performance, could I?" he said. He did not want to see anyone. Disappointed by his withdrawal but reassured nevertheless, Masha went back to her hotel.

The next day, unaccompanied, Chekhov took the first train—a very slow passenger and freight train—to Moscow and then went straight to Melikhovo. He had seen no one: he was in flight. He left a note for Suvorin asking him to hold up publication of the book that was to include *The Sea Gull* as well as his other plays. "I'll never forget last night," he wrote, "even though I slept well and I'm leaving now in a reasonably bearable frame of mind. . . . *Never* will I write another play or allow one to be staged." He left a note for Masha too: to reassure her, he lied unscrupulously and insisted that the failure of his play had neither surprised nor upset him. "If you're coming to Melikhovo," he added, "bring Lika with you."

Potapenko, the only person whom Chekhov could bear seeing, because Potapenko had not been one of the "witnesses of his triumph" the night before, had gone to the station with him. Chekhov chatted with him on a note of pretended gaiety while they waited for the train: how glad he was to be going back to Melikhovo and seeing no more of actors or directors or audiences or newspapers! But in spite of his jests and his bursts of laughter, Potapenko was shocked by the depth of the distress in his eyes as he boarded the train. Chekhov, always so meticulous and orderly, was to forget his luggage aboard the train that day. And when Masha returned to Melikhovo the following night, the first thing that he said to her was: "Not another word about that performance!"

But what had the two "sea gulls" in the audience thought of the play? It would appear that "the beautiful Lika" had not taken the slightest umbrage at it. Chekhov had unquestionably taken her wretched adventure with Potapenko as his inspiration, but the magic of art had done its work and he had infused the story with such poetry that she had not clearly recognized either herself in

Nina or Potapenko in Trigorin, who, for that matter, sounded as often like Chekhov. There was even a kind of amazement in what she was to write a few weeks later to Chekhov himself: "Yes, everyone here says that *The Sea Gull* is also taken from my life, and, what's more, that you've given a certain person a good lesson!"

As for Lydia Avilova, she had followed the play's course with passion. Resolved to find the mysterious answer that Chekhov—supposedly—had promised her nine months earlier during the masked ball, she devoured every word. She had to wait for the third act, but then, when she saw Trigorin offer Nina a locket engraved with his initials, the title of one of his books, and a reference—page 121, lines 11 and 12—her heart, she reported, began to beat feverishly. The reference was not what she had had engraved on the watch fob. "There could be no doubt," she was to write, "that this was his answer. In reality it was to me that he was speaking from the stage, to me and to me alone, and not to Yavorskaya or anyone else."

When she had got home, she had to wait until her husband was in bed before she could look up this answer in Chekhov's works: alas! the reference made no sense. The she too went to bed, but she could not sleep. Suddenly the light dawned on her: it was her own collection of stories that Chekhov meant. She jumped up, ran to the library, took out her book, and read lines 11 and 12 on page 121: "It is not suitable for young women to go to masked balls." Since she was virtually devoid of a sense of humor, this reply, which was a plea in bar, with a smile and even something of a jab, was enough for her, and in fact it delighted her. "He had guessed everything," she would write, "he knew everything."

She, who guessed nothing, could not suspect that Chekhov actually attached not the slightest importance to that gift of a watch fob. What would she have said if she had known that he had indeed just got rid of it by giving it to another charming woman, Vera Kommissaryevskaya? Having encountered the actress in the wings, he had told her that she had played his Nina marvelously, that she had eyes like Nina's, and as a tribute to her talent he had given her the present bestowed on him by Lydia Avilova. It was a gracious gesture, which, it might incidentally be added, caused the actress to think that Chekhov was interested in her too and that finally it was perhaps herself who was his "sea gull."

Chekhov had not given a thought to the fob except as a source for pleasant levities. No doubt that was what gave him the idea, not long after the performance of *The Sea Gull*, of giving Lika a locket of the same kind. He told her what it would be like and what would be inscribed on it: "Catalogue of plays by members of the Society of Russian Dramatic Authors, page 73, line 1." The joke was somewhat heavy: indeed, when Lika consulted the catalogue as indicated, she found the title of a farce: *Ignaska the Madman, or An Unexpected Insanity*. This was a direct allusion to her sorry affair with Ignatyi Potapenko.

The Sea Gull could almost be staged in the same setting as *Ivanov* or *Uncle Vanya:* one of those country houses, with a veranda, a birch-lined path, and a croquet pitch, where everyone gathered in summer—relatives, friends, and neighbors—for pleasure and boredom, friendships and feuds. This time there was, however, one innovation in the landscape: at the back of the garden behind the dacha the shore of a lake was discernible. It was summer, and the owner of the dacha, Sorin, was host to a famous actress, Arkadina; her lover, Trigorin, a successful author; the actress' son, Treplev, a young writer; a pretty young neighbor, Nina; and another girl, Masha.

These six characters were in search of themselves or, rather, much more than themselves. The country leaves one only too much time for fantasy, and these people's fantasies were of impossible things: old Sorin wanted "at last to live," Arkadina never to grow old, and Trigorin, the man of letters, to learn other passions besides those of writing and catching gudgeon. But it was above all the young protagonists of the play, Treplev and Nina, who dreamed of a future beyond their capacities: the young unknown writer aspired to establish a new art and the girl wanted to become a great actress and thus attain to "glory, true glory, resounding glory."

Treplev, who had written a poetic play, decided to have it performed on an improvised stage set up in a corner of the garden. In this way he hoped to impress his mother, Trigorin, and above all Nina, whom he loved. But the play had hardly begun when it was broken into by his mother's fatuous remarks, and Treplev, outraged, decided to stop the performance. This defeat was soon duplicated by one in love: Nina was lured away from him by the fascination of the famous Trigorin, who could give her both love and fame. In desperation the young writer attempted, but failed, to kill himself. And before the end of summer, he would see his mother, who had "had enough of this charming rural sadness," and Trigorin, whom he envied and despised, go off to Moscow; but Trigorin was the victor, because Nina, finally won over, left with him.

Two years elapsed: enough for the total destruction of everyone's cherished dreams. Sorin, far from "escaping this fish life" and knowing a second youth, was nothing but an old invalid waiting for death. Masha, who secretly loved Treplev, had married an obscure schoolteacher and was drinking in order to forget. Trigorin had not succeeded in escaping from literature, and Nina, whom he had soon left, had borne and lost his child. She had not attained the theatrical glory of which she had dreamed. She had been a failure in Moscow and now she was a member of a shoddy little traveling repertory company. Treplev met her again and assured her that he still loved her, but when he could not persuade her to remain with him, he attempted suicide again, and this time he did not fail.

"Life is vulgar," Nina sighed. But for Chekhov it was even worse than vulgar; it was cruel, it was inexorably and implacably inhuman, because it forced each and every man into frustration. The author of *The Sea Gull*, even more than the author of *Ivanov* or "A Dreary Story," seemed fascinated by the absurdity of the human condition, and this time he wanted to make us share his conviction that every life is destined in advance to disillusion and defeat: between what man dreams of being and what he is capable of being there is an unbridgeable chasm. Hence it might be said that in contrast to the classical theater, in which the action consists almost invariably in an ambition that is fulfilled, *The Sea Gull* is the drama—or the comedy, according to its author's self-effacing and dishonest subtitle—of ambitions that will never be realized, of inevitably doomed ambitions.

In this play Chekhov goes farther than in his earlier dramas, and here he gives us the essence of his thought, even if he does so in a less brutal fashion, more insidious and, as it were, cloaked in symbols. This time it is not enough for him to show that every life disintegrates—inexorably, and quite soon, often long before death —in an inner shipwreck. He compels us to understand why this is so, why it cannot not end in defeat. It is because man lacks the stature of his dreams, because he is really drawn only to what is beyond his reach, because, constantly gulling himself about himself, he seeks a destiny that is not meant for him. All these failed lives, basically, have the same explanation: lack of will, the tendency to passivity—which increases with age—an inner fragility against which one can defend oneself only through resignation. The human soul—as Chekhov definitively conceives it—is, in the image of his own, a soul without the passion to live and hence without passions.

But though Chekhov finally reveals himself in *The Sea Gull*, he does so obliquely or, rather, by means of a continuing contradictory dialogue. He is constantly drawing parallels, duplicating, if the term may be used, his characters and their words, outer and inner reality; behind life as it seems to be he brings into focus life as it really is, in depth. Neither Treplev nor Nina explains—and indeed both would be quite unable to explain—why they fail in their aspirations. But in our presence they dream aloud, they rejoice, and they weep, and through their contradictions, their unfinished sentences, and even their silences we understand far better then we could through any explanation or ratiocination that their tragedy—the tragedy of man and the absurdity of his destiny—is duality, the wish to be other than what one is, and though never losing sight of them, premature resignation to the impossibility of realizing one's illusions.

The profound sickness that paralyzes the characters of *The Sea Gull*—that sickness of soul that Dr. Chekhov at last diagnoses here, though with discreet ambiguity—is revealed to us along the way by Masha. "One must not just drift," she says, "and wait for one does not know what. . . ." Only Arkadina, the headstrong, self-assured egotist, does not drift. "I'm always at my best," she says, and without expecting anything from the future, without "ever thinking of old age or death," she compels recognitions and triumphs in the present. All the other characters are triflers who lack the courage of their ambitions and who are rapidly worn out by life. At the end of the play old Sorin wants to offer Treplev a subject for a story, "The Man Who Wished," the lamentable story of a man who, because he did not wish enough, never got what he wanted out of life. As much as the incident of the sea gull brought down by a casual hunter—perhaps more—this suggested theme for a story is the real symbol of the play, because it reflects the central theme in a gripping synthesis.

Chekhov the writer also dropped the mask in *The Sea Gull:* profoundly the poet, but an "invisible" poet hitherto, he dared at last to write a poetic play. Not, however, because he makes us the audience for lyric evocations, or presents us—as, for example, Maeterlinck does in *Pélléas et Mélisande*—with rare and sublime scenes. Quite to the contrary, Chekhov forges ahead on the road of realism, but it is a realism that, surpassing itself, condemns its comfortable illusions and penetrates as well into the "second" reality, which is poetry. The poetry is allusive, and so private that often it is expressed only in a long silence, as is fitting, for it opens the door of man's most secret self, the self of his exquisite, unbearable inner contradictions, that star chamber of conscience, that secret core where he is endlessly in dialogue with himself, rebelling at being only what he is and dreaming of being "other." This Chekovian poetry plunges the spectator into a strange state of soul and anxiety, disquiets him to the point of apprehension, for he feels that he is the terrible accomplice of these characters who resemble him. This insidious poetry, indeed, revives our own thwarted ambitions within us for the space of an evening.

Chekhov wrote to Suvorin that there was a great deal of love in *The Sea Gull*—" five *poods* of love." [7] He exaggerated, for in fact love occupies no greater place in *The Sea Gull* than in his other

[7] The occasion is most appropriate to point out that translators often have a very personal way of weighing their words. In every French translation these "five *poods* (one *pood* = 16.38 kilograms, or 36.113 pounds) of love" become "five tons of love."

plays. His characters, who lack passion, especially lack it in love. True, they spend much time dreaming about love and they are always ready to talk about it, but how very quickly they resign themselves to not "living" love and to being unloved! Arkadina, afraid she is losing her lover, is the only one who cries out her love. Masha puts up no struggle and allows herself to be married to a man whom she does not love, and Nina makes no effort to capture or recapture the vacillating Trigorin. As for Treplev, he does not exceed himself in trying to hold Nina, and when he sees her again two years later, he kills himself rather than try finally to make her love him. All these characters comport themselves as if from the very outset they are convinced that love could be only unhappy, that it is unattainable. Love here—and this is true of almost the whole of Chekhov's work—is much less than love; it is merely the dream of love.

Chekhov was on more solid ground when he asserted, again to Suvorin, that his play contained "a great deal of chatter on the subject of literature." This is so true that one might say even that this "chatter," next to the problem of thwarted ambitions, represents the second theme of *The Sea Gull*. Trigorin, Treplev, Nina, Arkadina—all are artists who, as much by their way of living as by their words, never stop posing the problem of artistic creation, of its basic ambiguity, and of the artist's mission which is also ambiguous. It is not enough to proclaim, as Nina does (for in spite of her failure, she still believes in her vocation): "Art is a cross that God imposes, a mission with which he charges a chosen few." Like her, one must be profoundly steeped in that mission, and furthermore one must know in what it consists. It is precisely this double problem that, after many years, Chekhov was trying to resolve.

It has been said, and often repeated—so difficult is it for criticism to divorce itself from the idea that an author is necessarily incarnated in one of his characters—that Chekhov had given himself a spokesman in *The Sea Gull*. But some critics think it is Treplev while others opt for Trigorin. The truth is that here again Chekhov was satisfied to "state the problem," and in order to do so, in all its often contradictory aspects, he spoke sometimes through the one and sometimes through the other, sometimes even through Nina or the minor character of Dr. Dorn. It might almost be said that, schematically, Trigorin is the unexceptionable "man of letters" that Chekhov himself was, Treplev is the creator who wants to impose his "new ideas," Nina is the artist who wants to believe in her mission, and Dorn is Chekhov the physician, smiling and without illusions.

Trigorin may be a caricature of Chekhov by Chekhov, but if that is the case, what an affectionate and also painful, almost pathetic caricature! This writer who has "arrived" has all the idiosyncrasies of the man of letters, his ridiculous and even his repugnant aspects, but he also lives a deep and enduring drama, which is that of the sacrifice of his private life to his work. Like Chekhov, he turns everyone—even himself—and everything into grist for his literary mill. We know that Chekhov used the experience of "the beautiful Lika" for the writing of *The Sea Gull,* and we can guess that Trigorin, following his example, will turn the shabby business into which he drags Nina into the subject of a story. He lives only for literature, he always has a notebook in his hand and writes down furtively—almost with the furtiveness of a thief— whatever he hears, sees, thinks he senses; and if he enjoys fishing, it is because it helps him to chew over the sentences that he will write when he is back at his desk.

The character would be odious if he were self-satisfied and wrapped himself in his glory of a successful writer. But Trigorin suffers from being only a man of letters, a galley slave of literature, obsessed with the page to be written. One no longer feels any desire to rail at him when one hears him admit: "A single thought that I cannot get rid of pursues me day and night: I have to write, I have to write, I have to write. . . . And I feel that I am murdering my life, I feel that I gather the pollen of my loveliest flowers for the honey that I give to others, indeed I tear out those flowers themselves and I trample their roots. Am I not insane?" Perhaps not insane, but beyond a doubt possessed by the demon of literature. And if at least this "possession" were compensated for by the certainty, by the sure happiness of success in his work! But Trigorin acknowledges that while he enjoys writing, he is seized by doubt the moment the work is completed, the book is published. "I know," he says, "that that's not it at all, that I've gone wrong. . . . I'm bored and uneasy." He goes even as far as to admit that he "does not like himself as a writer" and that his work is not worth much. "At most," he says, "I'm good at painting landscapes. . . . "

Treplev—that other Chekhov—accuses his elder of never accomplishing anything new, of rigidly applying the "procedures" of a vulgar realism from which one can draw "a small moral that is very easy to digest and useful for a small existence." Like the Chekhov of these recent years, he too believes that realism has said everything it had to say—to the extent that it had anything to say at all—and that a new art must be created.

He would create something new, for he would show life "neither as it is nor as it ought to be, but as it appears to us in dream." Subsequently, however, he went farther, and when he had written his early works and considered them carefully, he came to reject all literary theory. Writing itself had taught him that it must be done without allowing himself to be fascinated—and hobbled—by the phantoms of forms, old or new. The less he thought about them, the better he would express himself. All art in the end came down to this: "Let the soul speak, freely."

But wasn't this untrammeled flowering of the soul equally a literary theory? For Treplev, with horror, soon discovers that, like Trigorin, he is slipping "little by little into routine." For to the writer the problem of the form to be given to his dreams can never be resolved. And no doubt this is how it has to be, and this permanent doubt is the necessary and even the essential goad of artistic creation. As he is about to kill himself, Treplev cries: "I am forever floundering in the chaos of dreams and images. Why, why this? I just don't know. . . . " And the audience is the more sorrowful that Treplev ends his life, because his last words prove that he is a genuine writer.

After the failure of *The Sea Gull* on the stage, it was disemboweled, as was to be expected, by the press. Only Suvorin spoke kindly of it, in *New Times*, as "an original play," and of its author's real talent; and there was a favorable comment in *The Petersburg Gazette*, signed with Lydia Avilova's initials. Otherwise the venom was universal: one critic found the play "utterly absurd," another—Yasinsky, a friend—considered it "confused and disordered," a third made jokes about that sea gull that was actually mere "sea game."

In spite of this bad press, the play was a success on its second performance. Some changes had been made in it on Suvorin's suggestion, and this time the audience, which was not made up of music-hall experts, reacted favorably, understood, and was moved. "Anton Pavlovich, my dear," Vera Kommissaryevskaya wrote, "we've won! The success is total and unanimous." Potapenko, enthusiastic and devoid of rancor, telegraphed: "Colossal success." The following performance confirmed the judgment of the second audience, and friends urged Chekhov to return to Petersburg. But he refused to be persuaded. "Nothing," he wrote to Bilibin, "can wipe the impression of the first performance out of my heart" (November 1, 1896).

Three days after his return to Melikhovo he had boasted to Suvorin, who had jokingly accused him of having fled "like an old woman," that he had regained all his composure. He had taken castor oil and shaved with cold water, and now he proclaimed himself ready even to write another play. It was not cowardice that had made him flee: he had behaved sensibly, like a dismissed suitor who has no choice but to remove himself. But these were the words of a proud, secretive writer who wanted no one to know that the failure of his play had really deeply and very gravely wounded him.

It was only two months later, in December, that he made up his mind to admit the truth, and once more to Suvorin alone. When Judge Kony, a highly cultivated lover of letters and a friend of Tolstoy, wrote to Chekhov in friendly praise of his play, the author replied that the judge's gesture had made it possible for him to contemplate his play's failure with serenity, but to Suvorin he confessed that the memory of it would continue to be as painful to him as that of "a slap full in the face."

To be accurate, however, it was not the failure of The Sea Gull —he had known hardly anything but lack of success—that had wounded him so deeply. "On October 17 it was not my play that failed," he wrote. "It was myself." He had been shocked that evening to see men whom he had regarded at his friends, to whom he had given proof of his devotion, wearing on their faces "a strange, a terribly strange expression. . . ." It was not his success, then, that displeased them, but himself, and it was not so much his own failure as the faces of his false friends, suddenly unmasked and alive with malevolent joy, that he had fled.

In revulsion he thought for a time of fleeing even farther than Melikhovo. In December, when there was talk of armed conflict with England over the Near East, he wrote to Suvorin: "If there's a war in the spring, I'll go into it. In the past eighteen to twenty months there have been so many events of every kind in my life . . . that, like Vronsky,[8] there is nothing left for me to do but enlist, though not to fight, of course, but to heal" (December 2, 1896). In any event he spent the end of the autumn and the winter in a kind of voluntary exile at Melikhovo. When Nemirovich-Danchenko—one of the future founders of the Moscow Art Theater—urged him to come back to the capital so that they could have serious talks like good Russians, he answered with a shrug. What would they talk about? Life in Petersburg was monotonous, vulgar, and uninteresting; it offered neither public life nor political life, and as for literary conversation, it was stupid. In his country house he had repose, at least, and he was making the most of it to read a great deal and to work on a new story: "Peasants."

The tone of this story was one that was quite new for Chekhov: it was hard and almost brutal. Here he depicted the Russian peasant in his true light, which was something quite other than the glow that aureoled the "holy muzhik" made fashionable by Tolstoy and part of the intelligentsia. But seeing the peasants exactly as they were did not prevent Chekhov from constantly concerning himself with them and curing their illnesses with an indefatigable dedication. He was no believer in fine philosophical dissertations; his credo was the necessity for action, for unremitting war against disease, misery, and ignorance. A poet in whom there was nothing of the abstracted dreamer, he wrote in his *Notebooks:* "It would be so wonderful if every one of us left behind him a school, a well, or something of the same character, so that our lives would not slip into eternity without having left a trace."

[8] Anna Karenina's lover, who, in despair over her suicide, enlisted and went to the Serbian-Turkish front.

In Chekhov's case it was not one but several schools that he wanted to leave behind. That winter he started the construction of a new one in a village near Melikhovo, and once again he was the architect, the contractor, and the collector of funds. Furthermore, not content merely to heal the ill and always ready to give of himself, he took part from January 10 to February 3 in the national census ordered by the government. As he had done on Sakhalin, he worked methodically: he toured every village in his district, went into every *izba*—invariably banging his head on the extremely low lintels, to which he could never accustom himself— and filled out thousands of cards. In addition he supervised the work of fifteen other census-takers. When his job was done and he had gone home in exhaustion, he limited himself to an ironic comment in his *Notebooks:* "I've been given a medal."

In February he went to Moscow for two weeks of rest. He visited his friend Levitan, whom he found quite ill but all the more enthusiastic about life; he made various social appearances; and he went to festive dinners that lasted until five o'clock in the morning. A year earlier friends had told him of their plan to build in Moscow a Palace of the People, which they intended to be a kind of cultural center, as it is called today, with a theater, a library, a museum, and reading and meeting rooms, and the project had excited him. He wanted now to know what had been done with it. He attended a meeting of the project's sponsors, offered some suggestions, and asked his architect friend Shektel to show the designs that he had prepared on Chekhov's request. But the undertaking required a half million rubles, and so nothing came of a splendid idea that was no doubt too revolutionary for its time.

To all appearances, then, Chekhov was caught up again in the social and intellectual current of Moscow, but he was no longer deceived by it. Hence, though he agreed to attend a tremendous dinner at the Continental to commemorate the anniversary of the liberation of the serfs, he took an acerb view of it in his *Notebooks:* "Dull and ridiculous. Eating, drinking champagne, jabbering, making speeches on the awakening of the people's conscience, the national conscience, national liberty—while liveried slaves, exactly the same serfs as before, wait on table and coachmen wait outside in the cold of the street. This is a sin against the Holy

Ghost." Exhausted at the end of two weeks of Moscow life and knowing no desire except the longing to sleep, he went back to Melikhovo. There he would put the final touches to "Peasants."

He could not get rid of his exhaustion, and he had begun coughing badly again.

On March 21, as he had promised Suvorin, Chekhov went back to Moscow. He had felt ill and spat blood the day before, but he took the train nevertheless, and booked a room in the Grand Hotel. At dinner the next evening with Suvorin in the Hermitage Restaurant he was just starting to eat when suddenly blood began to gush out of his mouth. Ice was immediately applied, but with little effect, and Suvorin, who was staying at a different hotel, had Chekhov moved there. Dr. N. V. Obolensky was immediately summoned. Chekhov returned to the Grand Hotel the next day, but the hemorrhages began again and after three days Obolensky ordered him into a hospital run by a specialist, Dr. Ostroümov.

Reproaching himself for having "made a scene" in the restaurant, Chekhov pretended to take the whole matter lightly. When Suvorin went to visit him in the hospital, he found Chekhov "joking" as usual while he spat blood into a big receptacle. But when Suvorin said that the ice was beginning to break up in the Moskva River, he saw Chekhov's face change. "Is the river really open?" Chekhov asked. With an almost physical pain Suvorin remembered that only a short time earlier Chekhov had told him: "When a peasant has consumption, he says: 'There's nothing to be done about it. I'll die in the spring, when the snow melts.'"

One of Chekhov's first visitors was Lydia Avilova. She was staying with her brother in Moscow and undoubtedly she had let Chekhov know, because after a silence of fourteen months he had written to her shortly before his departure from Melikhovo. "I very much want to see you," he said, "even though you are angry with me," and he had invited her to lunch or dinner with him. In reply, Lydia Avilova had made an appointment with him at his hotel for the evening of March 22, and she had been quite beside herself when she had not found him there; she was the more upset when she saw her unopened letter among the others that were awaiting him. Three days later Chekhov sent her a short message saying that he was ill, and Mrs. Avilova, having learned that he was in Dr. Ostroümov's hospital, went there at once.

She had difficulty getting permission to see him, but it was finally granted on condition that she refrain from speaking to him. According to her *Recollections,* however, she and Chekhov had a conversation, and another, longer one the next day. During this second visit she told him that she would not come again because her husband had sent her a telegram summoning her back to Petersburg. She had brought Chekhov roses and lilies of the valley, for which he thanked her later in a charming note like those that he sent to everyone who expressed sympathy. "Far from fading," he wrote, "your flowers grow more beautiful every day. My colleagues are allowing me to keep them on my table."

Did these conversations really take place and did the patient beg his guest, as she insists he did, to stay another day in Moscow and pay him another visit? It is difficult to believe this when one reads in Leikin's diary what Mrs. Avilova herself told him of her visit to Chekhov in Dr. Ostroümov's hospital. "She went there to see him," Leikin wrote, "but although the doctor allowed her to visit Chekhov, he forbade her to speak to him. All talk with him was prohibited; he lay stretched out on his back in the bed without moving." This was confirmed by Masha, who saw her brother on the day of Mrs. Avilova's second visit: "Anton Pavlovich was flat on his back," Masha wrote. "Talking was forbidden."

Two days later, when Chekhov was still extremely weak, an illustrious visitor was announced: Lev Tolstoy. The old writer settled himself in the big oilcloth-covered armchair between the bed and the wall, and not being a man to observe the protocol of hospital-visit conversations, he immediately launched into a serious discussion. He started with a subject that anyone else would have tactfully avoided: death and the immortality of the soul. "We had a very interesting conversation," Chekhov wrote later with a touch of irony, "interesting especially for me, who listened more than I talked. . . . He thinks that all beings—men and animals—will survive within a principle—reason or love—whose essence and purpose are a mystery to us." To Chekhov this kind of immortality was merely a "shapeless, gelatinous mass" of which he wanted no part and understood nothing, to Tolstoy's amazement. Beyond doubt, even in the face of death, his dear Chekhov was still lacking in a "general idea."

Tolstoy then switched to another subject that was the focus of all his interest at the time: his conception of art. He told Chekhov that he had dropped his work on *Resurrection* and already read more than sixty works on esthetics in order to ground himself for the writing of a treatise on art, the thesis of which he then explained.[9] According to him, art must necessarily have a moral or religious aspect—a view that was completely opposite to Chekhov's thinking. Utterly disregarding Chekhov's arguments, Tolstoy, excited, categorical, and peremptory, declared that contemporary art was completely decadent and must be denounced without mercy. "There is nothing new in his ideas," Chekhov later wrote to Suvorin. "All the sages of all the ages have sung the same tune. Old men are always inclined to see the end of the world at hand, and they have always proclaimed that morality has sunk *nec plus ultra,* that art has grown thin, impoverished, worn out, that men have become cowards, etc. Lev Nikolaevich wants to convince us through his book that art has entered into its final phase, reached a dead end from which it can escape only by retracing its steps . . ." (April 17, 1897).

When at last the "irascible old man" made up his mind to depart, he left Chekhov, who had been shocked by his aggressive manner, in a state of great agitation. Chekhov slept badly and at the end of the night he had a relapse accompanied by a new hemorrhage.

Since his arrival in the hospital Chekhov had lost—if indeed he still had any—his last illusions about his condition. The doctors had diagnosed extended pulmonary tuberculosis and, like Masha, he had been able to see, on the chart fastened to the foot of his bed which depicted his lungs, that the upper part of both organs was largely colored red. He had asked his sister and his brothers not to let their parents know how serious his condition was, but he himself was fully aware of it.

Moreover, his colleagues urgently prescribed a drastic change in his mode of living. He accepted their advice only in part: to live

---

[9] Tolstoy was then preparing to write his essay "What Is Art?" which aroused passionate controversy throughout intellectual Europe as soon as it appeared.

the whole year in the country seemed impossible to him, but on the other hand, he was quite willing to give up the practice of medicine completely. "This will be at once a relief and a great deprivation for me," he wrote to Suvorin. "I'm going to resign all my responsibilities in the district, buy a dressing gown, warm my bones in the sun, and eat heavily. They tell me to eat six times a day . . ." (April 1, 1897). To Alexander he made jokes: "I am under orders to eat a great deal. Which means that it is no longer Papa and Mama but I who have to eat" (April 2, 1897).

His colleagues had also prescribed rest and silence for him, but he paid no attention. His unfailing kindness made it impossible for him to dismiss his innumerable visitors, and it was only afterward that he was sometimes irritated by their lack of consideration; then he wrote to Suvorin that he almost wished that he had married a shrew who would be able to throw out a good half of these intruders. His table was loaded not only with the flowers, the wine, and the caviar that his friends sent but also with the manuscripts of young writers in search of counsel and help: he read them carefully without exception and then wrote his criticisms to their authors and his recommendations to publishers.

It is not easy to write when one is lying flat in bed, he told a young woman schoolteacher, but nevertheless he continued to be generous with his advice and encouragement. His suggestions were wonderfully simple and direct: "It is essential that writing give you pleasure. . . . One must not speak much of oneself. . . ."

When he received the letter announcing that Chekhov was going to give up the practice of medicine, Suvorin replied in jest that he seemed now to be making a cult of loafing. "No, it's not loafing," Chekhov wrote back. "I despise laziness as I despise weakness and the lack of mental and moral energy." Of course he enjoyed leisure—"one of the basic conditions of happiness"—but the future of a semi-invalid that he clearly envisaged for himself, in which there would be only too much leisure, and all of it enforced, was a horror to him. He wondered too how, if he were compelled to remain inactive, he would be able to keep himself and his family alive.

As soon as his health permitted, after ten days in bed, he began

walking around the hospital and its vicinity. This part of Moscow
—the Novodyevichy quarter—was quiet, and he enjoyed strolling
through it in the cool April sun. He had always liked cemeteries:
he visited that of the Novodyevichy Monastery, walked around it,
and paused at the grave of his friend, Pleshchev, who had died in
1893.[10] "Occasionally too," he wrote to Shcheglov, "I go into the
church, lean against the wall, and listen to the chanting of the
nuns. Then my soul grows strangely calm."

Did he remember the conversation about death that he had had
with Tolstoy a few days before? "Death fills me with something
larger than terror," he was soon to confide to Suvorin. " . . . It is
frightening to be reduced to nothingness. They take you to the
cemetery and then they go home and sit down and drink tea and
exchange hypocritical remarks. It revolts me just to think about
it." But how not think about it?

He would think about it less at Melikhovo, to which he was
now impatient to return. He was able to leave the hospital on
April 10, and the next day, with the help of his brother Ivan, he
arrived in Melikhovo. A day later the always affectionate Lika
came to visit him.

Back in his "duchy," Chekhov did not give much further
thought to the advice, pressing though it was, that his medical
colleagues had offered him. True, he did convey to the local peasants, by way of Masha, the news that he had given up practicing
medicine, but in other respects he made little or no change in his
way of living. In spite of his sister's vigilance he soon resumed all
his other activities. "I'm doing nothing," he wrote to Ertel; "I feed
the sparrows hemp seed and I trim one rosebush a day"; but in
fact he had lost no time in getting back to work. He wrote, he answered his numerous correspondents, he sent packages of books to
the library in Taganrog, he initiated work on the school in No-
voselky, he was host to many teachers, and he still found time to
go to Talezh to give examinations in the school there.

He also returned to his concerns as a writer. When "Peasants"
appeared in the April issue of *Russian Thought*, he was outraged

[10] It was in this same cemetery, in the "poets' row," that Chekhov himself was to
be buried in 1904.

to find that the censor had made deep inroads into it and cut out an entire page for which the official had substituted one of his own invention. But Chekhov should have been expecting such a reaction, because his story, which depicted the Russian peasantry in the unretouched light of its real misery and brutalization, could only irritate the tsarist government. And how deeply it must have offended the intelligentsia, too, which, slavishly following in Tolstoy's footsteps, had idealized the peasantry in the manner of the enlightened minds of eighteenth-century France hailing the virtues of the "noble savage."

As was also to be expected, "Peasants" created a great stir. There were violent disputes in the press over its meaning, even though the story's import was so obvious. But in general the critics were extremely favorable. The tone was set by *The Northern Messenger,* to which the public shock occasioned by "Peasants" recalled the effect produced, in their respective times, by the new books of Turgenev and Dostoevsky. Chekhov received many enthusiastic letters from friends and colleagues, including this from Leikin: "I've just read your 'Peasants.' What magic! I read it in a single night, in one sitting, and for a long time afterward I couldn't fall asleep."

Others criticized Chekhov for having generalized excessively by calling his story "Peasants." He would have been fully entitled to retort—but he never replied to his critics—that having associated with and treated the peasants of Melikhovo for five years, he was dealing with a subject that he knew only too well. In fact it was with his habitual objectivity that he had painted this picture of the appalling wretchedness of the peasantry. In the story it is seen by a city woman who, married to a peasant's son working as a waiter in a Moscow restaurant, takes him back to his native village when he becomes very ill. There she discovers the revolting truth, the "misery without a solution": these ignorant, superstitious, simple-minded, profoundly religious peasants accepted their lot in absolute passivity and drew a modicum of hope only from their faith and another modicum only from their "terrible vodka." She does not condemn them, however, and when she and her daughter go back to Moscow after the death of her husband, she leaves with her heart overwhelmed by a tremendous pity. "Yes," she says, "living with them was horrible, but after all they are people, they suffer and weep like everyone else, and there is nothing in their lives that doesn't have its justification."

This year Chekhov was forbidden to concern himself with the muzhiki of Melikhovo. In spite of that, however, he did not enjoy the solitude that he so badly needed. As soon as the good weather began, there was an unending flood of visitors. His married brothers descended on him for weeks with their wives and children, and his friends—Levitan, "the beautiful Lika," Ivanenko—came in successive invasions. He wrote wearily to Shcheglov: "Can you imagine? In recent days there have been at least a dozen guests here from Moscow. I might as well be running an inn." Shcheglov was the more outraged because he had been thoroughly alarmed by the condition in which he had seen Chekhov: he was coughing a great deal, his face was yellow and drawn, and even on very mild evenings he was wrapped snugly in a shawl.

He took refuge in his "doll's house" or in an isolated corner of the garden, where he sat on a bench, with Bromide at his feet, and mused as his eyes wandered over a bed of blooming tulips. He dreamed of running away from his family, of traveling in Sweden, Corfu, Malta. . . . He had come to the point, he said, at which he had found that it was impossible for anyone except a drunkard to live eternally in the country.

Neither his guests nor his own brief visits to neighbors or friends could have made him change his opinion. Levitan took him to spend two days with a millionnaire named Morozov, and Chekhov wrote to Suvorin that he had found a country house as big as the Vatican, lackeys in white piqué waistcoats, vulgar furniture, and on the master of all this a face devoid of all expression. "I fled."

To combat his boredom, he read a great deal. He liked Maupassant so much that he said he was going to translate him: he believed that he knew French well enough to be able to do it. But his great discovery that summer was Maeterlinck: Chekhov found his plays strange and wonderful. He told Suvorin that if he owned a theater—a word to the wise. . .—he would lose no time in producing *The Blind*. But recalling the murder of his own poor *Sea*

Gull, he would insure himself against a possible failure by inserting a summary of the play into the program for the "half-idiot" audience.

By way of breaking the monotony of his days, he made brief visits to Moscow, and at the end of July he went for a few days to Petersburg, where in spite of the touching scenes that, if Lydia Avilova is to be believed, had occurred in the hospital, he made no effort to see the lady. At the end of August he was at the end of his strength, and since in addition his doctors were insisting that he leave for a warm climate before the first chill of autumn, he seized the first opportunity.

Having learned that his friend Sobolevsky, the publisher of *Russian News,* was in Biarritz, Chekhov wrote to him that he would meet him there. He was afraid to travel alone in Europe, he joked, because he knew "all languages except foreign languages" and for him changing trains in Paris was like playing blind-man's buff, but he was going nonetheless: what was the best hotel and the most comfortable route? And indeed on August 31, in his beautiful flourished handwriting, Chekhov's old father wrote in the family log: "At eight o'clock this morning Antosha left Melikhovo for Biarritz."

X

TOO ILL TO LIVE

Living with the knowledge of eventual death is already not very pleasant, but living with the knowledge that one is going to die before one's time has come is absolutely absurd. . . .

CHEKHOV to GORKY

The Chekov who was being carried across Germany in these first days of September, 1897, almost suffocated by the smoke of his fellow passengers' cigars, was no longer the all-curious traveler who had set out for Sakhalin seven years before and who had then twice cut a wake through Western Europe. He was a seriously ill man who knew that he was doomed to a more or less early end and who, in order to put it off, was willing to reduce himself to half-living, to being a mere invalid. On his doctors' orders, and for the first time, he was doing what he ought long ago to have done: he was fleeing the Russian winter. Shortly before he left he had written to Shcheglov: "Do you know what I need now, Ivan? A year of rest, no more and no less. I should really rest, have a year of slack."

He interrupted his journey for a few days in Paris, where he behaved like an exemplary tourist. The Suvorins were there; with them he visited the city's showplaces, a number of popular cafés, and the notorious Moulin Rouge, where he saw a belly dance to the accompaniment of a piano and tambourines. With the Suvorins' daughter he shopped at the Magasins du Louvre—a sweater, a cane, neckties, shirts—and took long walks from which he came back tired but content. He would have remained longer if he had not already told Sobolevsky the date of his arrival on the Basque coast.

In Biarritz he stayed at the Hotel Victoria. The place pleased him: the weather was good, the view, with its beach ringed by jagged cliffs, was pleasant, the pier was quite lively. He spent two weeks in enjoyable dawdling: he had bought a silk hat and he went for walks or settled himself in one of the little wicker cabins on the beach, read the newspapers, and watched the parade of summering beauties, who protected their milk-white skins with huge straw hats, and the strolling guitar players. He felt absolutely well and, he wrote to Suvorin, he had no desire to return home.

Since he was rather ashamed at understanding nothing of the language—although he had thought that he knew it—he took some French lessons from a nineteen-year-old girl named Margot. But he avoided the rather numerous Russians in the resort—too numerous for his taste—and he saw only the Sobolevskys and an old friend encountered by chance, Leikin. When the weather turned cold and rainy after two weeks, Chekhov and Leikin went to Nice in quest of sunshine.

In Biarritz he had shunned his compatriots. In Nice he went to live in their staff headquarters, the Russian *pension,* rue Gounod, 9. This was the barracks of some forty of his compatriots, many of whom, like him, were ill; there were a number of women with nothing to do, provincial families, retired professors, and a baroness and her daughter. Chekhov selected a large room on the third floor with big bay windows facing south, a deep carpet, and a bed "the equal of Cleopatra's." The cook, the cooking, and the dinner conversation were all Russian.

Chekhov adapted without too much discomfort to the well-ordered little life of the place. At mealtimes he amused himself by watching his neighbors: the evil-tempered widow who was always afraid that someone would rob her of the morsel that she had already reserved for herself; the sad old maids; the talkative, gossipy, stupid matrons whom, he said, he feared he might one day be like. One afternoon he heard the people in the next room reading aloud in Russian; he put his ear to the wall and was surprised to recognize one of his own stories.

The doctors had urged him to rest: so for a few weeks he loafed. All that was required for that was to let himself yield to the atmosphere of the city, a veritable paradise for idlers. Everything invited him to do nothing: the sunny weather, the flowers and the palms in the parks, the animation of the streets, and the "calm, touching sea." He spent mornings in long walks along the Promenade des Anglais, and then he sat on a terrace and read the newspapers. "To sit on the promenade, warm oneself in the sun, and watch the sea is such a delight," he wrote to Suvorin, whom he asked to join him. In the afternoon he took a nap, went for another stroll, and read in his room. He went back to his French studies too, but in spite of the lessons he took, he made little progress. By the time he left Nice he had not yet learned to speak the language or to follow a conversation in French.

He had become friendly with a few Russians—Kovalevsky, a lawyer and a professor at the University of Moscow who had been dismissed from his post because of his political ideas and who had taken refuge in France; a painter, Yakobi; and the Vice-Consul Yurasov—and in the evenings he would play piquet with one of them or go to the Taverne Gothique for oysters. He also went to the Municipal Casino to hear Sarah Bernhardt and the famous singer Adelina Patti. In sum, it was a respectable old gentleman's vacation.

In mid-October he wrote: "I'm doing nothing, writing nothing, and have no desire to write. . . ." But within a few days this was untrue. His conscience stirred, as it were, by his inactivity, he went back to work and wrote a story. His friends were aware of this at once: for a week they hardly saw him, and during the rare walks he took with them he seemed distracted, preoccupied by something. When he had finished his story and he rejoined the group, his face seemed different.

He soon became aware that he was writing with difficulty and without any pleasure. Was this because of the rather enervating air of the Côte d'Azur or the overabundant meals—"it seems to me that I eat all day long without a break," he wrote—or the fact of writing in a strange room, or the good weather that constantly urged him outdoors? He also blamed his desk, that desk to which he was not accustomed and that made him feel as if he were "sewing with someone else's sewing machine." Nevertheless he made himself keep at it; even though he felt as if he were "hanging by one foot with his head down," he was not the man to follow his own sybaritic counsel: "This place is good for reading but not for writing." But although he wrote three stories before the end of the year—"Pechenyeg," "At Home," and "In the Cart"—it must be acknowledged that they are not among his best works and that they seem labored.

Undoubtedly it was because he himself was aware that this was not "it" that when he had sent one of these stories to a publisher, he insisted that the proofs be sent back to him. He was also aware that often he did not find the right "tone" until he began correcting proofs. "I don't read proofs solely in order to correct external errors," he wrote. "It is normally in proof that I really polish and correct the whole story with its musical quality in mind, if I may say so" (November 20, 1897).

His lack of energy could also undoubtedly be explained by the state of his health. During the first weeks it had apparently improved, but after the middle of October he began spitting blood again, though, it is true, in small amounts. Chekhov kept this from his family—"almost honestly," he admitted to a woman friend—because these minor hemorrhages did not prevent him from feeling that he was in "splendid" form or from "gamboling like a calf." His doctor, however, took the matter more seriously and ordered him to move into a ground-floor room in order to avoid having to climb stairs; in addition, he was to be indoors before sunset. But in spite of these precautions, Chekhov had new hemorrhages throughout November and December. "Because of the blood," he wrote to Suvorin on December 16, "I keep to the house as if I were under arrest. I find it boring and sad to live completely alone."

Although Chekhov's departure from Russia had also been to a degree a flight from his family and friends, he soon began to miss both. He complained that he received few letters, whereas in spite of the fact that it took his letters five days to reach their destinations, he wrote a great many. His two chief correspondents were Suvorin, through whom he maintained contact with the world of letters, and Masha, who supervised Melikhovo and the family in his stead. Disciplined and almost meticulous in his letters to his sister, he managed things from a distance, down to the smallest details: if she needed money, she could ask *Russian Thought* for an advance; as for the young poplars that he had ordered, they ought to be planted in such and such a spot. He thought of everything: at Christmas, Masha must not forget to give a ruble to the cowherd, little presents to the schoolchildren in Talezh, and three rubles to the village priest, and she must also thank their father for having sent him the Russian newspapers and the Melikhovo "log."

He also continued to correspond with his "sea gulls" in his usual half-teasing, half-serious manner. He wrote to "the beautiful Lika" to complain because a well-intentioned millionnaire—Levitan's friend Morozov, with whom Chekhov had spent a few days the summer before—thinking that he was in need, had sent him two thousand rubles, which he was going to return with a suitable letter of thanks but mainly in order to tell Morozov about her. Who was pursuing her at the moment? Still Sumbatov-Yushin the playwright? He himself would prefer to see her marry a man with a mustache and—given her bad character—an even temper. When Lika told him that in order to be able to continue her singing studies, she planned to open a lingerie shop, he applauded: "The work," he told her sententiously, ". . . will give you an independent position, peace of mind, and a guaranty for the future. I myself would be delighted to throw myself into an enterprise of the same kind." He promised to visit her in her shop and shower attentions on her pretty salesgirls.

As for Lydia Avilova, it was she—naturally—who tried to resume correspondence with Chekhov. "I felt that I was forcing myself on him by writing to him," she was to confess in her *Recollections,* "but I could no more have put an end to that correspondence than I could have killed myself. . . ." The pretext was admirably handy: she was sending him some stories and she wanted him to tell her what he thought of them. In his first reply Chekhov informed her that he was out of the country at present, and probably for the whole winter, and he apologized for having mislaid her address again: he was asking Potapenko to forward the letter to her.[1] In a second letter he discussed her stories: one of them was a "little thing" full of intelligence and talent, but the others still showed too much of the beginner who overdoes description and has not learned to polish sentences.

Lydia Avilova reproached him for having specialized in gloomy, mournful protagonists, and he did not deny it. "It is not my fault, alas," he wrote to her. "It happens involuntarily, and when I am writing it does not seem to me that I am mournful; in any case I am always in good humor when I am working. It has been observed that gloomy, melancholy people always write gaily and that lighthearted people's writing is often depressing. And I am a lighthearted man; at least I've lived the first thirty years of my life 'in clover,' as they say" (October 6, 1897).

Chekhov also was one of those rare writers who know themselves and do not believe that they are capable of working successfully in every form. He knew, for example—or thought he knew—that he was a bad reporter, that actual observed scenes did not inspire him directly, and that he required months, if not years, for his poetic alchemy to assimilate and decant the impressions received from new people and places. As long as he was incapable of identifying himself with them in depth, it was impossible for him to talk about them. He painted not from nature but from "memory," and the life of Nice, for instance, which he had before him, give him no inspiration.

Chekhov had to explain this to the editor of *Cosmopolis*, a new Russian magazine that was published simultaneously in a number of languages and that had asked him for something unpublished. "In one of your letters," Chekhov told the editor, "you ask me to send you an international story, choosing something in the life of this place for a subject. I could write such a story only in Russia, from memory. I can write only from memory, and I have never written directly from nature. I must allow the subject to filter

---

[1] Mrs. Avilova did not mention these two passages in Chekhov's letter, undoubtedly because they did not sit well with the "love story" in which she intended to make us believe.

through my memory until its important, typical components alone remain in the bottom of the filter" (December 15, 1897).

In Nice, however, a host of new impressions, some of which he had already dared to mention to his correspondents, was being deposited in his "filter." He was beginning to form his own notion of France and the French. He was hardly moved by Mediterranean landscapes, but on the other hand he was much impressed by the sophistication and the high level of culture that were apparent in even the most trivial things, such as shop windows. "Here," he wrote, "every dog stinks of civilization."

In contrast to his compatriots, the French amazed him with their feeling for equality, their urbanity, their delicacy in daily contacts. The maid in his *pension,* in spite of the fatigue that showed in her face, gave him the smiles of a "duchess," everyone exchanged greetings in shops and trains, even the policemen and the beggars, whose courtesy was exquisite. But it was not without effort and sacrifice that the French had reached such a degree of refinement. "How it suffers, how it pays for everyone," he wrote, "this people that marches in the van of the other nations and sets the tone for European culture!"

It was undoubtedly his reflections on the Dreyfus case that made Chekhov think of the sufferings of the French nation. He could actually watch as France lived through an astounding drama of conscience that as the result of recent disclosures and campaigns had just been renewed. Captain Alfred Dreyfus, sentenced by a military tribunal in 1894 to life imprisonment on a charge of having spied for Germany, was currently serving his sentence in the penal colony on Devil's Island. Was he really innocent, as he had unremittingly insisted? Almost every day there were new facts in the papers, and there was every reason to wonder whether the real criminal was not Major Esterhazy, whom Dreyfus' brother had just publicly accused. Was not Captain Dreyfus, in the last analysis, the victim of the racial and social prejudices of his army colleagues?

A great reader of newspapers, Chekhov began to follow "the case" with growing interest. His favorite papers were *L'Aurore* and Drumont's *La Libre Parole.* He was soon excited and overwhelmed by the Dreyfus case: it was the first time in his life that a political matter had forced him out of his indifference. On December 4 he wrote to Sobolevsky: "All day long I read the papers and study the Dreyfus case. In my opinion Dreyfus is not guilty."

A month later, on January 13, in *L'Aurore*, he read Zola's famous open letter to the President of France, in which the author accused the government and the Ministry of War of distorting truth and proclaimed his conviction that Dreyfus was innocent; Chekhov was delighted. "Zola is a noble spirit," he wrote to Suvorin, "and I am carried away by his action. France is a marvelous country and its writers are marvelous too."

Chekhov was now so excited by the case, Alexandra Khotyaintseva reported, that he could not conceal his agitation whenever he spoke of it. In February, when Zola's trial for defamation began— it was to end with a sentence of a year in prison—Chekhov followed it as closely as possible, reading the stenographic transcripts published in the newspapers. His admiration for Zola grew still greater. "You ask me whether I think Zola is right," he wrote to Mrs. Khotyaintseva. "And I ask you: do you really have so poor an opinion of me that you could doubt even for a second whether I was on Zola's side? I would not give one of his fingernails in exchange for all the men who are taking part today in his trial in the criminal court, all those wellborn generals and witnesses" (February 2, 1898).

When he thus unconditionally aligned himself with Zola and Dreyfus, Chekhov was moreover being logical with himself. He had long been a liberal, even though he rejected the label, which in Russia could lend itself to misunderstanding. Fiercely independent because of his firm belief that a writer owed it to himself to be so, owing no political allegiance, he had nevertheless shown on what side his personal convictions lay by his activity on behalf of schools and by his collaboration with such liberal publications as *Russian Thought* and *The Russian News*.

In all fairness he wanted to explain his position to Suvorin. The time had now come to know whether, as Chekhov had always believed, the reactionary views of *New Times* did not necessarily reflect those of its owner. It was Suvorin himself who had given Chekhov cause to believe that he could be dissociated from *New*

Times through his conversations, his actions, and even some of his articles, which were much more liberal than those in his newspaper. And a year earlier Suvorin had printed two quite courageous pieces in his newspaper: one was an attack on the reactionary *Moscow News* and the other was a defense of the students who had just brought on disorders. "I have an infinite admiration for you," Chekhov had said at that time, "when you are liberal—that is, when you write what you want to write" (January 4, 1897).

Chekhov had hoped to be able to have a face-to-face clarification with Suvorin on the "case." Early in January, in the same letter in which he expressed his admiration for Zola, he told Suvorin that he wanted him to come to Nice. But this hope was not fulfilled, and on February 6 Chekhov sent Suvorin a very long letter. Eager to preserve, but in completely open understanding, a friendship that meant a great deal to him, and still hoping that it was lack of information that had caused Suvorin to make his newspaper anti-Dreyfus, Chekhov set forth all the facts known about the matter, assumed the defense of Zola, and explained his own position. "I know the case from the stenographic transcripts," he said, "and these are completely different from what one reads in the papers." He summarized everything from the start: the Ministry of War's equivocal attitude during the trial, the exclusion of certain testimony, the obvious reluctance of the authorities to reopen the trial in spite of the existence of new evidence, the refusal to hold an inquiry into the conduct of Major Esterhazy, whom many believed to be the real culprit, and the wave of anti-Semitism that the right-wing press had inspired in the hope of further confusing matters. It was in order to force the government to review the trial of Dreyfus, whom he regarded as the victim of an abominable judicial error, that Zola had courageously thrown himself into the battle.

Chekhov's defense of Zola was fiery and unqualified. In a recent comment in *New Times*, Suvorin had remarked that Zola was jealous of the laurels of Voltaire—the defender of Calas[2]—but unfortunately, Zola was not Voltaire. "None of us is Voltaire,"

---

[2] Jean Calas, a Toulouse merchant, was falsely accused in 1762 of having murdered his son rather than allow him to abandon Protestantism. Voltaire was instrumental in his posthumous rehabilitation in 1765.—TRANSLATOR.

Chekhov retorted, but Zola had nevertheless been right in acting as he had. The important thing, Chekhov continued, was that Zola was sincere and based his judgment not on preconceived ideas but on what he saw. Sincerity, even when it was in error, inflicted less harm than calculated lies, prejudices, or political considerations. "Even if Dreyfus is guilty," Chekhov wrote, "Zola is still right, for the writer's duty is not to accuse or to persecute but to defend even the guilty as soon as they have been sentenced and subjected to punishment."

The Zola case thus gave Chekhov the opportunity to define once and for all, and quite clearly, what he conceived to be the writer's function in political life. In contrast to Tolstoy and the "committed" intellectuals, he believed that the writer must refuse to take sides but must be the "clerk" who, though he struggles to maintain a permanent "non-commitment," does so in order to safeguard his supreme possession, the freedom to think and write. According to Chekhov, it was not for the writer in society to play the part of the public accuser, the prosecutor, or the policeman, "all of whom are plentiful enough as things stand," but to defend the innocent and even the guilty. "The truth," he concluded, "is that great writers and artists should concern themselves with politics only to the extent to which they have to defend themselves against it."

Suvorin's reply to this moving letter from Chekhov is not known. If Kovalevsky's unpublished *Memoirs* are to be believed, Chekhov told Kovalevsky that Suvorin wrote back: "You have convinced me." Chekhov, however, was soon compelled to yield to facts: *New Times* was still behaving—in his own words—in a "simply vile fashion" with respect to Dreyfus. Chekhov attributed this to a lack of character in his friend, who could not resist the pressures of the authorities and his political friends. "I am very fond of Suvorin," Chekhov told Shcheglov, "really very fond of him, but, you see, . . . people who have no character are capable of behaving like the worst of criminals, and sometimes in the most critical moments of life."

Chekhov soon decided that it was useless to pursue his debate with Suvorin. He explained his views quite openly to his brother Alexander: "On the subject of *New Times* the old man and I have exchanged letters (though always in a very moderate tone) and now we have stopped. I don't want to write to him any more or have any letters from him in which he justifies his paper's lack of tact by saying that he likes the military. I don't want any more of it because for too long I've had it, up to my ears" (February 22, 1898).

Did this mean, as some students have said, a final, brutal rupture between Chekhov and Suvorin? No, because Chekhov was not a man given to outbursts or intransigent positions. Though less regularly than in the past, he was to go on seeing Suvorin—he would meet him in Paris, in April, on his way back to Russia—and writing to him quite regularly. But though Chekhov was the incarnation of indulgence and forgave many things, he had no further illusions about his friend, and though he did not say so, he had withdrawn his friendship and his trust. The very outspoken, unreserved conversations that he had enjoyed having with that "character," Suvorin, and their debates by correspondence were finished. Their intellectual friendship, like so many in France, had foundered on the Dreyfus case.

The winter in Nice was exceptionally mild that year. "The weather here is wonderful, like summer," Chekhov wrote on January 23. "Not once this winter have I worn my galoshes or my heavy overcoat." The state of his health was improving with every week. In February he sarcastically informed Alexander and his other "heirs" that they had occasion to rejoice, because as the result of a tooth infection that had made him howl with pain and that had required surgical treatment, he felt as bad as possible, but what was really important, he added, was that his hemorrhages had stopped. Furthermore, he was living like a sybarite: "I do nothing except sleep, eat, and sacrifice to the Goddess of Love." Even so, far from his home, with no friends other than those in the little Russian colony of Nice, fundamentally very much alone, he was beginning to be bored. And that monotonous life of a retired civil servant in a boarding house . . .

For weeks he had dreamed of going to North Africa with Kovalevsky. To visit Africa was an old wish to which he had often returned, and now, since there was only the Mediterranean to be crossed, he really hoped to be able to fulfill it; his program was

"Algiers, Tunis, et cetera." Hence it was a major disappointment to him when Kovalevsky announced to him in February in Paris that because of his own health he had to forgo the projected journey. "And already I was dreaming every night that I was eating figs!" Chekhov reproached him sorrowfully. There was nothing left for him but to immerse himself once more in reading newspapers.

He was working seldom and badly. He had promised stories to various magazines, and since he was unable to write them, he was compelled to send rather embarrassed excuses instead. He explained ironically to Suvorin that a real Russian writer can work only in bad weather. With this sunshine, this silken sky, these flowering trees it was impossible for him to spend two hours a day at his desk. "I've grown as lazy as an Arab and I do nothing, absolutely nothing." Oh, if only he were back in his little "doll's house" in Melikhovo with the black and white of the snow-covered woods for his only distraction, how he would work!

Potapenko's fortuitous arrival in Nice on March 2 provided Chekhov with a diversion as unexpected as it was pleasant. The former lover of "the beautiful Lika," gay and lively and talkative, moved into the Russian *pension* and shook it out of its bovine placidity. A great gambler, Potapenko insisted that he had come with a very specific purpose: to win a million at roulette in Monte Carlo and thus assure his independence of advances from publishers. Amused, overwhelmed, soon captivated, Chekhov, who thus far had gone to the casino perhaps three or four times, allowed himself to yield to infection by the gambling fever. But one must be certain of winning: the two friends therefore bought a little roulette wheel, locked themselves into a room for whole afternoons, and spun the wheel and noted down each result in long columns of data that they analyzed rigorously in their determined search for an infallible system. Since each of them reached different results, they fell into argument and then plunged again into their interminable and ingenuous calculations.

Almost every day they went to Monte Carlo to try their luck. Excited, impatient, impetuous, Potapenko played hunches; Anton Pavlovich, his eyes steady behind his glasses but his mind in equal turmoil, gambled more calculatingly and never placed large bets.

Fate, unfortunately, has no sense of humor: it stubbornly refused to make millionnaires of the two authors, and the cautious one lost as much as the hothead. After two weeks Chekhov decided that this excitement was of no use to him, and he stopped gambling. But Potapenko did not give up until he had lost everything; he had to borrow enough money from Chekhov to get him back to Russia. He left Nice on March 28.

"I'm bored without Potapenko," Chekhov soon wrote to Masha. Morozov, the millionnaire, was in Nice, but this individual was "the dullest of gentlemen" and Chekhov fled from him. Commissioned by Pavel Tretyakov, a patron of the arts and founder of a well-known gallery, Braz, the painter, came from Russia expressly to do a portrait of Chekhov, who spent more than two weeks of entire mornings posing. The finished portrait was not to Chekhov's liking: he saw in it "something that was not him, but on the other hand nothing of himself," and he found it depressing to look at the painting. "If I have become a pessimist and write boring stories," he said, "the fault lies with that portrait of me." [3]

In actuality Chekhov had only one thought now: to go back to Melikhovo. He wrote anxious questions to Masha: had the snow already gone from the woods? was the road from the Lopasnya station usable? All his thoughts were on Russia, and he imagined his garden and poured out suggestions: "Put up supports for the lilies and the peonies so that they don't collapse," he wrote. "We have two lilies, one in front of your window and the other near the white rosebush, on the path with the narcissi. . . . Don't cut the rosebushes until I am back. Just cut off the stems that were frozen or that are very unhealthy. But be careful: don't forget that sometimes the ill get well!" (April 1, 1898). He also asked about Lika: had she opened her shop?

Early in April, Masha told him that the weather in Russia was still too severe for him. No longer quite so insistent, he decided to go to Paris and wait there until Masha sent word that he could go home. After eight months of exile he had had enough of Nice and

---

[3] Of all the portraits of Chekhov this one is the most popular in the Soviet Union today. On display in the Tretyakov Gallery, there is always a crowd of admirers before it.

the "unpleasant, boring, idle gentry" of the Russian *pension;* and enough too of watching out for his health, which was "the most revolting of all selfishnesses."

Since Suvorin was scheduled to be in Paris, Chekhov had written to him from Nice: "Telegraph me the day and time of your arrival and I'll meet you at the station. I've accumulated a mountain of things—feelings and ideas—to discuss with you. . . . From Paris we'll go back to Russia together." Before Suvorin's arrival he spent a week going to theaters and exhibitions and seeing members of the Russian colony. He was also determined to meet Mathieu Dreyfus and Bernard Lazare, the latter of whom had dedicated his pamphlet on "the case" to Chekhov. He also went to Versailles. Even when he was traveling, he did not forget his native city: from Nice he had sent more than three hundred French classics to the municipal library of Taganrog and from Paris he sent it a large collection of documents on the Dreyfus case. In addition, he persuaded Antokolsky, a sculptor, to give the city a statue of its founder, Peter the Great. When Suvorin joined him, he abandoned the modest Hôtel de Dijon, in which he had been staying, to live with Suvorin in the Vendôme.

When the Paris weather had turned to rain and his head was spinning from having had to listen to so much idle talk, he finally received the news for which he was waiting: it was spring at Melikhovo. He immediately sent a note to his brother Alexander: "Shine your shoes, put on your Sunday suit, and come and meet me." He packed the umbrella that he had bought for his mother along with the other presents, and on May 2 Suvorin took him to the station to board the Nord-Express for Petersburg. Three days later he was at Melikhovo. "He arrived at five o'clock this afternoon," his father noted. "He has lost much weight."

Shortly before leaving Paris, Chekhov had had a letter from Nemirovich-Danchenko, who wanted permission to stage *The Sea Gull.* This old friend, a teacher of dramatic art and, in his spare time, a writer, had just joined Konstantin Stanislavsky, the actor and director, in founding a new theater, the People's Art Theater, which was soon to become the Moscow Art Theater. The new company, made up of Nemirovich-Danchenko's best students and the enthusiastic amateurs who admired Stanislavsky, wanted to do new things. It proposed to revolutionize the theater, to throttle the bombast prevalent on the Russian stage in those days, but at the moment it had neither physical premises nor money—only enthusiasm. It also wanted to rejuvenate the repertory, and that was why Nemirovich-Danchenko had turned to Chekhov.

The wound opened in the author of *The Sea Gull* by the failure of his play a year earlier, however, had not yet healed over. From Nice he had written to Suvorin on March 13: "It used to be that nothing gave me so much pleasure as going to the theater, but now I go with the feeling that someone is going to yell: 'Lunatic!' at me from the gallery. And I don't like actors. I've been demoralized by writing plays." So he refused Nemirovich-Danchenko's request. But the director insisted: Chekhov was the only contemporary dramatist who had anything new to contribute, and if he would approve a presentation of *The Sea Gull*, Nemirovich-Danchenko promised to have a thorough discussion of it with him before starting rehearsals. Unable to refuse anything for very long, Chekhov thereupon gave in. Overwhelmed, enthusiastic, Nemirovich-Danchenko replied: "I am continually rereading *The Sea Gull*. . . . The public does not yet know how (perhaps it never will) to let itself be carried away by the spiritual climate of a play, that spiritual climate that one must be capable of creating with intensity. But that's what we're going to try!" (May 31, 1898).

And he did really try, putting his whole heart into it. Stanislavsky, on his own admission, considered the play "unperformable," but his collaborator gradually succeeded in infecting him with his own enthusiasm, so much so that soon he was thinking only of evolving the staging and setting—this was his responsibility—that would reflect all the remarkable magic atmosphere of the drama. When the young actors of the company began reading *The Sea Gull* in a dacha outside Moscow, it was again Nemirovich-Danchenko who with his indomitable ardor succeeded in "working them up" for the play. "We love you beyond measure," he wrote to Chekhov without caring whether it sounded absurd, "for your talent, your subtlety, and the sensitivity of your soul" (August 24, 1898).

Chekhov, meanwhile, was spending a quiet, uneventful summer at Melikhovo. He had the illusion that he had regained his health, and with no further thought to his physicians' counsels, he had gone back to all his former activities. He was doctoring the peasants again, concerning himself with the district schools, and even planning the building of a new one, this time in Melikhovo itself. With Bromide and Quinine at his heels he was working in the garden. And as soon as he had got back he had resumed writing.

"My engine is already running again," he wrote jubilantly a few weeks after his return to Melikhovo. And in fact, in spite of the large number of friends who had learned of his return and descended on him, he worked a great deal during that summer. Using material that he had amassed in his *Notebooks,* he wrote four stories in succession, three of which—"The Man with the Case," "Gooseberries," and "On Love"—were connected by the fact that the same characters appeared in all of them. For years he had contemplated writing a series of stories joined to one another by rather flexible links, which would have been a way of taking his revenge on the novel that he had never been able to bring off, but this time too his project ended abruptly and he dropped it after having written only these three stories.

Besides, as the summer wore on, his zeal declined, and at the end of July he confessed to Lydia Avilova that he was weary of writing. "Now, when I write," he told her, "or when I think I ought to write something, I feel the same disgust as if I were eating cabbage soup from which a roach had just been extracted, if you will excuse the simile. . . . And it is not only the act of writing that repels me; it's that whole literary *entourage* [he used the French word] that I can't escape . . ." (July 27, 1898).

Did he really want to get away from it? It was very often he who insisted that his friends from the literary world come and stay at Melikhovo. And in the beginning of September, when Nemirovich-Danchenko informed him that rehearsals of *The Sea Gull* were about to start, he immediately went to Moscow.

He found the new group set up in the Hermitage Theater under less then perfect conditions: the building was cold and damp, and the naked, curtainless stage was lighted only by candles stuck into bottles. The young actors were quite excited at the thought of rehearsing in the author's presence, but Chekhov soon put them at their ease with his smiling simplicity. At the end of the first rehearsal, through which he had sat wrapped up in a heavy coat, playing silently with his glasses, he answered their questions with good humor and jokes. Kindly but still firmly he made several suggestions to Nemirovich-Danchenko for changes in the acting and the sets. At the second rehearsal he suggested that Stanislavsky take over from the actor who played—in Chekhov's opinion badly —the part of Trigorin.

Chekhov was also far from entirely approving the staging conceived by Stanislavsky. According to Meyerhold, who was a member of this company, Chekhov considered it too realistic, much too concerned with a colorless replication of reality. The thought that Stanislavsky wanted the croaking of frogs and the barking of dogs to be audible on stage made him laugh outright, and the idea of having a woman come on at the end of the third act with a weeping child seemed to him to be in abominable taste. "The theater," he said, "knows its own conventions. There is no fourth wall. Aside from that, theater is an art, it mirrors the quintessence of life, and therefore nothing superfluous must be injected into it."

Of all the actors the one most affected by Chekhov's presence at rehearsals was the woman who played Arkadina. She was then twenty-eight years old, extremely attractive if a bit overblown, and her rather broad face was very mobile and handsome beneath her jet-black hair; her eyes were vivacious, her voice was beautiful and warm. Just out of dramatic school, she had decided to spend her life in the theater. Of German ancestry, she was named Olga Leonardovna Knipper. Chekhov had noticed her and she undoubtedly would have been delighted to know that after he had seen her play Irina in Alexei Tolstoy's *Tsar Fyodor,* he had written to Suvorin: "In my opinion Irina was marvelous. Her voice, the nobility of her bearing, her sincerity were so perfect that I was deeply moved. . . . If I had stayed in Moscow I should have fallen in love with that Irina . . ." (October 8, 1898).

But on September 15 Chekhov left Moscow for the Crimea. The summer was over, and there was no question of his going back to Melikhovo and spending the autumn and winter there. In addition, he had lost the illusion of having regained his health: in August he had begun spitting blood again. So he had to resign himself to following the urgent orders of his colleagues and spending the long Russian winter in the south, in the sunshine. But although for so many years he had dreamed only of travels abroad, now, after the experience of Nice, he was revolted by them and regarded them merely as a kind of exile. Between one sun or another, he preferred the Russian sun of the Crimea.

Nevertheless there was no enthusiasm in his move to Yalta. This vacation city, with its glaring white hotels, dry palm trees, cactus, and rock gardens, seemed to him to be barren of spirit and life, exactly like its crowds of summer vacationers, in which he saw mainly "aged ladies dressed like girls" and "plenty of generals." On a friend's advice he had rented two rooms in a privately owned dacha: he very much liked the surroundings of the quiet garden, still in full flower, and its fine view of the sea. He quickly established new habits: after work he took long walks on the promenade, often concluding them with a brief stop in the combination tobacco shop and bookshop of Isaac Abramovich Sinani which was called The Little Russian Izba. This shop was in a way the resort's "intellectual center," where visiting poets, artists, and writers gathered. There Chekhov met, among others, Konstantin Balmont, the young poet; Fyodor Chaliapin, the singer; and Sergei Rachmaninov, the composer, who dedicated his Fantasy for Orchestra to Chekhov, whose story "On the Road" had inspired it.

Besides, since he was very well known, Chekhov quickly fell prey to the local lion hunters and aspiring writers. In order to elude them, he got into the habit of frequently taking refuge and meals in a girls' school whose headmistress, Varvara Kharkeyevna, he knew. Very soon he was appointed to the board of trustees of the institution and as such he was greeted with respectful little diving curtseys by the white-cloaked little girls when he walked through the corridors.

He had been in Yalta a month when one afternoon, as he was entering The Little Izba, Sinani handed him a telegram that Masha Chekhova had sent the day before: How would Anton Pavlovich take the news of their father's death? Thus informed, somewhat clumsily though with the laudable intention of easing the blow of his father's sudden death, Chekhov learned the details soon afterward. Lifting a heavy case of books at Melikhovo, Pavel Yegorovich had sustained a severe hernia; taken to a hospital in Moscow, he had undergone a long and painful operation that he had not survived. Subsequently Chekhov was more than once to express his regret, both as a son and as a physician, that he had not been at Melikhovo when the accident occurred.

Chekhov replied to Masha by telegram, saying that he was deeply affected by their father's death. Was this true? In any event he had long since forgiven the erstwhile family tyrant for his wretched childhood years. At the moment he was more concerned for those whom this unexpected loss had plunged in sorrow: his mother and Masha. He wrote to his sister: "I can't rid myself of the thought that all of you have to endure such grief in Moscow while I am taking my ease in Yalta. It haunts me" (October 14, 1898).

Their father's death, he wrote later to Masha, meant the end not only of his "log" but also of the lives of all of them at Melikhovo. He knew that his mother had grown attached to the "duchy" and that it would be difficult for her to leave it, but he could not see her continuing to spend the winter there with only Masha for company; as for himself, it was out of the question that he should go back there. It would be best, then, to sell Melikhovo and build a "new nest" for the family on the Crimean coast.

Another "poet" would have spent months pondering the problem. Chekhov was a man of decision, and within one month the matter was settled. Although he only half-liked Yalta—but the climate was good for him, and that was what counted now—he decided to set up the new family home there; even better, for this ailing man was afraid of nothing, he resolved to build it himself. Even before his father's death he had begun to think of buying property in Yalta, and with this in mind he had gone to look at a piece of land in Autka, a half-hour's walk from Yalta, as well as a delightful little four-room villa fifteen miles farther, but still on the coast, near the Tartar village of Kushukoy; perched amid the mountains, it had a magnificent view of the sea. Without much hesitation he decided on the site in Autka. There was still the matter of finding the money. He talked to Suvorin, who promised him a five-thousand-ruble advance against royalties, and a local bank was willing to lend him seven thousand more and take back a mortgage. Before October had ended he had bought his land, made his financial arrangements, and chosen a young architect, L. N. Shapovalov. Construction was scheduled to start in December.

Chekhov found it slower going to convince his mother and sister. Invited to come and admire the site in Autka, Masha showed little enthusiasm; at the moment, it was true, it was only an abandoned vineyard overrun by weeds and abutting on a Tartar cemetery. Yevgenya Yakovlevna had become set in her ways at Melikhovo and had no intention of being made to change them. But Chekhov, the strong-minded businessman, was also a skillful and persistent advocate: after Masha left Yalta, he devoted himself to praising, in every letter that he wrote, the charms of the "nest" that he was going to build. For Masha's benefit he described in detail the garden and the orchard he was going to plant. In order to convince his mother that life in Yalta would be a delight, he multiplied the allurements: the kitchen would be splendid, "with all American comforts and running water," and there would be a laundry, a cellar bin for wood, and a telephone. Besides, Yalta would remind her very much of Taganrog, coffee was extremely cheap there, and—the final argument—at ten o'clock, her favorite time, there was Mass said in the church quite close to Autka.

But even while he was thus vaunting the ideal house in Autka, Chekhov was still dreaming of the little dacha in Kushukoy on its isolated mountain perch. Masha must have been rather astonished on December 8 when he informed her that on an impulse he had bought it. Yes, he wrote, he was now the happy owner of "one of the prettiest and most curious properties in the Crimea." But she was not to mention it to anyone outside the family lest there be gossip about his mad extravagances.

Masha herself was very careful not to let her brother know of the request that she had just made to the management of the Art Theater: that the first performance of *The Sea Gull*, set for December 17, be postponed. She knew, better than anyone, how cruelly Chekhov had been wounded by the first failure of his play, and she was very much afraid that a second fiasco would be very

dangerous to his already shaky health. Her pleas and even her
tears, though they much affected the directors of the theater, did
not succeed, however, in persuading them to withdraw the play.
The Art Theater's season had got off to a poor start; its first five
plays had been semi-failures and only a success for *The Sea Gull*,
into which considerable money had already been sunk, could still
save the young venture.

The evening of December 17 arrived. The theater was only
three-quarters full, and the cast made a wholehearted all-out
effort, well aware that its own fate as well as that of a beloved
author was at stake. Although all the actors had dosed themselves
with valerian—a sedative much in vogue in Russia at that time—
their nerves were on edge, and Stanislavsky himself related that as
he played the part of Trigorin with his back to the audience, as
the new stage directions required, he could barely conceal the
trembling of his whole body. When the curtain fell on the first act,
Nemirovich-Danchenko was to write, "something happened that
happens in the theater perhaps once in decades: silence, utter silence in the audience and on the stage. Out there everyone
seemed frozen; on stage, no one understood yet. . . . This lasted
for some time. . . . And suddenly it was as if a dam had burst, as
if a bomb had exploded: a deafening roar of applause. Everyone,
friends and enemies, was applauding." With each successive act
the success was greater, until it became a triumph. At the end of
the final act the actors threw themselves into one another's arms
and Stanislavsky broke out in a triumphal dance while the audience shouted to him to send a telegram of praise to the author.

Chekhov received the telegram next day: "Just did *Sea Gull*,
colossal success. . . . Innumerable curtain calls. . . . We're
mad with joy." Extremely moved, Chekhov wired back: "To
everyone: infinite thanks from the bottom of my heart. I am exiled
in Yalta like Dreyfus on Devil's Island. I am miserable at not being with you. Thanks to your telegram, I am well and happy."

In the next few days he learned that the press had been unanimous in its enthusiasm. Letters and telegrams of congratulation
poured in. Performances had to be suspended for a few days because Olga Knipper was ill, but when they were resumed, the
house was full every night. The play was so successful that lines

formed every night outside the box office; most of the people waiting were young, and they spent the night reading by lantern light, dancing, lying on deck chairs until the box office should open in the morning. Maxim Gorky, who had recently begun corresponding with Chekhov, wrote to him that a friend had talked to him of *The Sea Gull* "with tears of emotion." Gorky added: "And you don't want to write for the theater any more? Good God, you must! . . . I wish you health, good heart for your work, faith in yourself. And long live life, no?"

With the triumph of *The Sea Gull* Chekhov had indeed got his revenge, both as an artist and as a man. He had found not only his public but also new friends, that Art Theater company whose enterprise was soon to become "his theater" and with which he was about to launch a dazzling career whose brilliance, as the years went on, would shine far beyond the borders of Russia. But for all his revenge, Chekhov was no less aware once more how adept life was—having compelled him to be present at the appalling failure of his play and prevented him from later seeing its triumph—at bitter irony.

Chekhov must have smiled in his unique fashion when he read the effervescent young Gorky's line: "And long live life, no?" He himself wrote: "As I grow older, the pulse of life beats faster and stronger in me . . ." but as a physician he knew quite well that this could also be translated into a single word: fever. During his stay in Yalta his health had not improved. At the end of November he had again begun to spit blood so badly that for five days he had had to stay in bed. Since he was keenly aware of his condition, he consented for the first time in his life to be the regular patient of one of his colleagues, Dr. Isaac Altschuler. Chekhov could talk the more frankly to Altschuler because the doctor was not only a specialist in tuberculosis but, like himself, its victim as well.

Nevertheless Chekhov did not wish to be regarded as a sick man, and he rejected the thorough treatment that Altschuler urged on him. He concealed his hemorrhages from his family and his friends, and when *The Petersburg News* devoted a front-page "dispatch" to them at the end of October, his reaction was angry, and he sent a formal denial to the press. Only Suvorin was in his confidence, but "say nothing to anyone," Chekhov wrote to him. "My blood frightens others more than it does me; that's why I try to hide it from my family." Moreover, he continued sending reassuring bulletins on his health to the north.

He had led the life of a semi-invalid the year before in Nice, but he wanted no more of such withdrawal. In Yalta, he wrote, he was building and, what was more, he was caught up again by his irrisistible need to make himself useful to the community in which he was living: he was at everyone's service. He had a few patients, he was active in school affairs, he was a member of the local Red Cross committee, and he was also busy with a relief fund for the children of Samara, which had been struck by famine.

But how lonely he felt in Yalta, and how far away from family and friends! In the whole of the winter he saw only his brother Ivan, who came to spend a few days with him at Christmas. Masha and their mother had taken an apartment in Moscow and said nothing about joining him in spite of his enthusiastic descriptions of the "ideal house" in Autka, the foundations for which had been laid in December. And he missed Moscow too, "terribly"— Moscow with its friendly conversations, its theaters, its restaurants. Constantly seeing the blue sea made him homesick for snow and the black and white of winter. "I'm bored here," he wrote to Tikhonov, "and I'm turning into a *petit bourgeois*, and no doubt the next step will be to set up housekeeping with some nice wrinkled woman who'll beat me on weekdays and feel sorry for me on Sundays and holidays" (January 5, 1899).

Only his letters gave him the feeling of still being a part of life, of living. So he wrote more of them than ever, to Masha and to his old friends. Since November he had also been exchanging letters more and more frequently with Gorky, whose name as a writer was just beginning to be known. Gorky had initiated the correspondence, writing a letter of unrestrained admiration for Chekhov's stories from Nizhni-Novgorod. Chekhov had sent a cordial reply, they had exchanged books, and though they had not met, they had quickly reached the stage of being able to say without reserve what they thought of each other.

On Gorky's side it was genuine, total, almost juvenile admiration. He declared that he spent "marvelous moments" in the company of Chekhov's stories and that when he saw a performance of *Uncle Vanya*, he wept like a girl. Chekhov's admiration for the younger man was equally genuine but much more qualified. "When you describe something," Chekhov wrote to Gorky, "you see it and touch it with your hands. That's real art." But he criticized Gorky for the lengthiness of his descriptive passages, a strong tendency toward rhetoric, and an excessiveness that frequently bogged his prose down in monotony. He told Gorky what he was always repeating to every young writer who asked his advice: one must learn to discipline oneself, to be brief. Thus the tone of their future friendship—frankness and plain speaking— was set in their very first letters.

And what had become of the "sea gulls" who had sought to attract Chekhov's attention over the past few years? One of them, "the beautiful Lika," whose company he had so much enjoyed, had almost completely vanished from his sight. Increasingly seldom he had some news of her through Masha. Then one day, after months of silence, he had a letter from Lika, half ironic, half jealous: was it true that he was about to marry? Gallantly he replied: "You know very well that I would never marry without your permission."

During recent months he had heard more often from Lydia Avilova. He answered her letters politely, but never in the tone of friendly teasing that he had so often used with Lika. At times, in fact, he was quite short with her: when Mrs. Avilova asked whether he ever visited the Shapin district, where she was spending her summer vacation, he forthrightly refused this tactful invitation. "I have never been in the Shapin district," he wrote, "and it is highly unlikely that I shall ever go there. I stay at home, writing a little, and hence am busy" (June 10, 1898).

But women like Mrs. Avilova, who take their dreams for facts, can find hidden meanings in the most ordinary words. In a letter in which he mentioned his lack of pleasure in writing, Chekhov added: "I have to send in something for the August issue of *Russian Thought*"; she at once took this as a personal allusion, an oblique way of directing her special attention to this story. Therefore, as soon as the August issue was off the press she hurried to buy it. Its table of contents did indeed list a story by Chekhov,

"About Love." The mere sight of the title, she was to write later, threw her into "violent agitation." She read the story feverishly, and inevitably reached the conclusion that this story of a love that had been incapable of fulfillment was hers, or rather, theirs, and that the protagonists of the story, Alekhin and Anna Alexeyevna, could only be Chekhov and herself. It was through Alekhin that Chekhov was at last explaining to her why he had not declared his love. "I did not weep much longer," she was to write, "but I sobbed like a hysteric. . . . He was not blaming me but vindicating me, he understood me and he suffered with me. . . ."

"Like a hysteric. . . ." These words, which came spontaneously from Lydia Avilova's pen, tell everything, for in actuality it was only in her imagination that there was any connection between the love story in the magazine and her few social encounters with Chekhov. But for her this was too good an opportunity for a new attack: she wrote to Chekhov at once. Determined to make him react, she composed a sarcastic, angry letter to "thank" him for having made her the heroine of one of his stories. "Which means," she added, "that the writer, like the bee, gathers his honey wherever he finds it. . . . The colder the writer, the more sensitive and touching the stories. So let the readers weep over them. That's what art amounts to."

Chekhov answered this provocative letter in his habitually measured tone, and with the caution of a physician dealing with a disturbed woman. "Your view on the bee is incorrect," he informed her. "First the bee must find bright and beautiful flowers, and only then does it gather its honey. As for all the rest—the indifference, the boredom, the idea that people of talent live and love only in a world made up of their own images and fantasies— all that I can say is this: another person's soul is only a mystery." Otherwise Mrs. Avilova's accusations were left unanswered.

Furious that Chekhov had apparently guessed where this little game of "imaginary love" might lead and had refused to be enticed, she wrote again, this time to accuse him of having tried to break relations with her and put an end to their correspondence. "I've read your letter," Chekhov replied, "and all I can do is throw up my hands in despair." If she saw things in his letters that were not there, he remarked ironically, the reason, no doubt, was that

"he did not know how to express himself." But he was still concili-
atory, and after some comments on his new life in Yalta, he concluded: "In any case, don't be angry with me and forgive me if
there was anything cruel and unpleasant in my last letter" (October 21, 1898).

Once again Chekhov resorted to irony tempered with kindness,
a discreet suggestion that she stop playing at being a "sea gull"
and restrict herself to a kind of comradeship tinged with affection.
But Mrs. Avilova had no better understanding of what he was asking than the other young women who had been drawn by the
writer's charm. It must be admitted, too, that the business was not
so simple: he had never said flatly either to Lika or to Mrs.
Avilova, nor for that matter to anyone else, what he expected from
a woman: she should be beautiful, gay, companionable, very female, and rather affectionate. He was not looking either for a
great love or an adventure without a sequel, but rather for a kind
of smiling, light, very subtly loving friendship.

He had written to Lika that he would not marry without her
permission; in actuality he still rejected marriage. When his
friends urged him to give it thought—as they had been doing for
fifteen years—he replied with a smile that marriage seemed too
complicated and wearing for him. "The very role of a husband
terrifies me," he wrote. But did he reject love too? It was his
brother Misha to whom for once he declared himself quite clearly
on the subject. "As to my marriage, on which you insist," he wrote
on October 26, "how can I explain myself? Marriage is interesting
only when one is in love: to marry a girl simply because she's
attractive is like buying something useless in a bazaar just because
it's pretty. The most important thing in family life is love, sexual
attraction, the fact is, they are one and the same thing; all the rest
is uncertain and dull, and the fact that we may have made the
most careful calculations changes none of this. The problem, then,
is not to find a congenial girl but to love her. . . ."

He was not—or no longer—systematically rejecting love, then.
But as weary and worn out as he so often felt now, was he still
capable of love? Perhaps he was, given the fact that though he
was ill and had already, so to speak, withdrawn to the margin of
life, he could not contain one admission: "As I grow older the

pulse of life beats faster and stronger in me." Within less than a
year he would at last have discovered, and quite suddenly, that he
was still able to fall passionately in love. But would that lead him
to the conclusion that it was "interesting to marry"?

For years Chekhov's books of short stories had been published
by Suvorin's firm in Petersburg. Nevertheless the author had often
complained to his friend about the way in which he and his books
were treated: proofs were not sent to him, publication was late,
the books were badly printed and even worse distributed, and
there were major errors in the calculations of his royalties. But
habit and friendship had led Chekhov to sign another contract
with Suvorin that autumn, this time granting Suvorin the right to
publish his "complete works."

He began correcting the proofs of the first volume in January.
Again he was exasperated by the more than careless fashion in
which Suvorin's subordinates treated him; the publisher himself,
busy with his other concerns, had not time to see to the management of his book division. Manuscripts were being lost, letters
were going unanswered. If things went on like this, Chekhov
wrote to Masha, his "complete works" would not be finished before
1948! This was the moment that A. F. Marx, another well-known
publisher—he had just had a tremendous success with Tolstoy's
Resurrection—chose to make an offer to Chekhov, through Sergeyenko, to buy the rights to all his works and bring out a complete
edition.

Chekhov immediately told Sergeyenko that he was willing to
start talks with Marx. The publisher's proposal was alluring: instead of paying royalties on sales, he offered a large lump-sum payment at once in return for all rights. Undoubtedly it was the prospect of laying hands on a large sum quickly and all at once that
induced Chekhov—who saw this as the means of liquidating his
debts, paying for the house in Autka, and assuring Masha's and
their mother's future—to enter into such an agreement. He made
it a point to let Suvorin know of Marx's offer, but he paid no attention either to Suvorin's advice that he think about it or to the publisher's offer of an immediate advance of twenty thousand rubles
against future royalties. Masha insisted that in view of his reputa-

tion, he was making a bad bargain by giving up all his rights; following the example set by Countess Tolstoy, she offered to publish his books herself, but he rejected this suggestion and declared his resolve to "drive a hard bargain" with Marx.

And indeed, as he also wrote to Ivan, he was "bargaining stubbornly." Between him and Sergeyenko the Tolstoyan, who was acting as Marx's representative, between these two writers the telegrams flew back and forth as if they were two hardheaded businessmen: Marx offered fifty thousand rubles; Chekhov demanded eighty-five thousand. In the end agreement was reached on seventy-five thousand. The contract was signed on January 26. It provided that in exchange for a consideration of seventy-five thousand rubles to be paid within two years, Chekhov conveyed to the publisher all his existing and future works except his writings for the theater. At the same time, the author reserved first-publication rights to his future works for himself; they would subsequently become Marx's property subject to payment based on the number of printed pages at a rate that was to increase as time went on.

Chekhov professed to be highly satisfied with the deal. Whatever disadvantages it might have, he wrote to Masha by way of reassuring her, his books would be very well produced physically and he himself would be rid of the business of accountings and printers. He told his friends: "I am now a 'Marxist.' "

He had kept Suvorin consistently informed of his negotiations with Marx. This did not prevent him, as soon as the contract had been signed, from feeling that he still owed his friend an explanation. It was solely the necessity of immediate access to a large sum that had made him conclude the agreement with Marx, and this gave him the uncomfortable feeling of "having married a woman for her money." On the other hand, he had taken good care of his own interests and—here a wink to Suvorin the businessman—he had sold only his rights as a short-story writer, keeping the best part for himself: that is, the rights to his plays. Besides, what mattered was that after thirteen years of working together without a disagreement, he and his friend had been able to end their collaboration amicably. "We leave each other harmoniously," he wrote, "just as we have always understood each other.

If I remember correctly, we have never had the slightest misunderstanding as long as you have been publishing my books" (January 27, 1899).

The contract with Marx obligated Chekhov to provide his new publisher with a complete bibliography and copies of all his published works within six months. The magnitude of the task, to which the writer set himself at once, was such that he was soon to talk of veritable "forced labor." He actually had to search out everything that he had published since his youth in all kinds of periodicals and reviews, many of them transitory and hence difficult to locate, and provide copies. But, meticulous as he was, Chekhov did not stop with this: as he found the material, he first exercised a rigorous selectivity and then corrected whatever he wanted to preserve, so carefully that at times the work was equivalent to completely rewriting them. With all that, he wrote to Gorky in all seriousness: "I'm . . . frightfully lazy. . . . I spend my time walking and whistling" (January 18, 1899).

In Yalta, Chekhov did not have access to the files and libraries necessary for the successful completion of his "forced labor," and he had to call on Masha, Alexander, and his old friends to consult the periodical collections in the Petersburg and Moscow libraries and to see to the copying of his contributions. He had also published stories in *The Petersburg Gazette*, whose editor was Lydia Avilova's brother-in-law; he wrote to her—and this was in fact the only time when it was he who took the initiative in renewing their correspondence—to ask her to find a girl who would search out and then copy those that he wanted to include in his complete works. But remembering the rather abrupt way in which their correspondence had terminated four months before, he asked whether she was still "angry with him."

On the contrary, as the perceptive Chekhov had undoubtedly guessed and as she herself was subsequently to acknowledge frankly in her *Recollections*, Mrs. Avilova was in transports of delight at the thought of being able to do this work for him. For her this was the long-awaited chance to "get close" to the beloved great man and maintain a sustained correspondence with him. So she promised that she herself would do the necessary research, and she performed the job with great care and to Chekhov's complete satisfaction. For some weeks they corresponded quite regularly. In a rather playful tone, addressing the young woman now as "*Matoushka*," * Chekhov wrote about their joint task and also about mutual friends and his day-to-day life. To her as to his other correspondents he sometimes spoke too of his weariness and his depression. "Why am I in Yalta?" he wrote to her. "Why is it so sad here? . . . I don't like the thought of writing and furthermore for the moment I'm not writing anything" (February 18, 1899).

He had developed an aversion to Yalta and its narrowly provincial little life, but in spite of this he had made up his mind to bow to the strict orders of his physicians and remain there. A winter that was unusually severe for the Crimea delayed the work on his house for a few weeks, but as soon as the weather improved, Chekhov spurred the resumption of work. He often went to see how it was progressing, and his eye was on everything. He called his house a "sardine tin," but in fact it was quite spacious, though nondescript and without style. It had a kind of tower and broad verandas. He did not forget that he had promised Masha that he would surround it with a fine garden; he was already laying it out and planting trees and rosebushes. After having spent two days at the latter task, he wrote to his sister: "It was really a protracted joy. I've planted twelve cherry trees, four tapering mulberries, two almond trees. . . . The trees are perfect and will soon be bearing fruit" (March 14, 1899).

He enjoyed building—he was also contemplating rebuilding his little Tartar house in Kushukoy—planting, doing. He also enjoyed being of service to others and to the community, and as soon as he had his hands on the first fifteen thousand rubles from Marx, he indulged himself in it. His response to the most trivial appeal was always generous; thus, having run across Gavryushka, who as a little boy had been a clerk in the family grocery store in Taganrog, Chekhov offered to pay for his daughter's education. He contributed money for the construction of a new school near Yalta, helped young writers in need of money, and lent without interest to his dear harebrained brother Alexander, who had also taken it into his head to build a small dacha near Petersburg. Gaily and

* "Little Mother"; an affectionate form of address to an older woman.—TRANSLATOR.

generously the rubles flowed through Chekhov's hands. Still a bit schoolboyish with his eldest brother, he signed his letters, in French: "The rich philanthropist."

Though Chekhov felt that he was in exile in his "southern Siberia," the people who thought of him and wrote to him were many, and not only friends or young authors in search of advice. In the Russia of those days, as so often happens in an authoritarian state, the writer was *nolens volens* a public figure whose views on current problems were often requested and carried weight; and so, when serious student disorders broke out in Petersburg in February, and soon afterward in other cities, many students appealed to him.

Faithful, however, to what he had always conceived as the artist's duty—"our business is to write, and only to write," he was to write to Mrs. Avilova in April—and as well because of a certain modesty and reserve that had always prevented him from taking a public stand on political, social, or moral problems, Chekhov again kept himself aloof from the controversy. Nevertheless, as his letters show, he still had his own opinion both on the students' demands and on the government's savage repressions, as well as on other political questions. For his position had changed in recent years, and now his political views placed him virtually in what today would be called the left center.

He contributed to the quasi-Marxist publication *Life*, always read Peter Struve's clandestine magazine *Liberation*, and undeniably sympathized with the students. But at the same time, in contrast to the Marxists, he did not believe that Russia's salvation would be assured by a revolutionary movement of the masses. "I believe in individuals," he wrote to his old friend Dr. Orlov. "In my opinion salvation will come from isolated persons scattered all through Russia, whether they be intellectuals or peasants. Even if they are not numerous, they have strength on their side" (February 22, 1899). But his hope was certainly not invested in that intelligentsia whose muddled thinking, weakness, and, often enough, insincerity and cowardice he had had ample opportunity to observe in the twenty years during which he had been a member of it. He even went to the extent of confiding to Orlov that in the serious crisis through which the country was living, it was not so much the government as "the whole intelligentsia that was at fault, in its collective entity, my good friend."

The question of the student disorders brought new conflicts with Suvorin. The publisher, not satisfied with putting *New Times* at the service of the government's defenders, had himself written articles that condemned the student strikes and congratulated the Tsar for having appointed an investigating commission. As a result the intellectuals boycotted the newspaper, Gorky wrote a vehement article in *Life*, and the rumor quickly spread that Suvorin had been paid ten thousand rubles by the government. He was thereupon summoned before a court of honor of the Russian Writers' Mutual Aid Society to give an account of himself, under threat of suspension. Thus attacked from all sides, and ill as well, Suvorin, who feared that his paper would be grievously damaged by the campaign launched against him, turned to Chekhov. He wanted quickly to justify himself, to have Chekhov's opinion, and perhaps to get his help.

Chekhov answered him at once, very honestly, and unreservedly denounced Suvorin's articles. He reproached the publisher for having treated serious matters lightly and for having dealt only with "the rights of the government," even though he well knew that the government would prevent the truth from being learned. Chekhov stated the question bluntly: if there were disorders, whose was the fault? "When people do not enjoy the right to free expression of their opinions," he wrote, "they express them with anger, with exaggeration, and often, from the government's point of view, in an ugly and shocking manner. But let freedom of the press and of conscience be granted, and then there will be the respite that everyone desires and that, though it cannot last long, will certainly last as long as we ourselves." But Chekhov did not approve of the idea of a court of honor, because in his view, while writers had the right to engage even in violent controversy, it was not for them to sit in judgment on one another. And, as to the rest, hadn't *New Times* done everything in its power to substantiate the story that it was being subsidized by the government and the French General Staff?

The controversy ended there, but though it was not bitter, it had nonetheless widened the breach that now separated the two old friends. Chekhov had no further illusions about Suvorin, who, he told young Leskov, was not a wicked man but who had been corrupted by money and by the "scandalous *camarilla*" in *New Times* that surrounded and dominated him. But when his old friend was going through a dark period, he could not entirely desert him. He continued to write fairly regularly to Suvorin and, as in the past, several times invited him, though without success, to make trips with him.

One friendship was slowly disintegrating while at the same time another was forming. Gorky, who for some months had been fervently corresponding with Chekhov, went to Yalta to spend some time with him at the end of March. The two writers had never met, but they liked each other immediately, and they spent whole days together, sometimes talking until dawn about literature or politics. Each as generous of mind as the other, they also had long discussions of the famine in Samara and of the frightful situation of the penniless, ailing teachers whom Chekhov had seen arriving in Yalta and for whom he wanted to build a sanitarium.

Chekhov liked Gorky for his enthusiasm, his vitality, his brusque frankness. "He looks like a drunkard," he wrote, "but inside he is a most elegant character. . . . I'd like him to meet some women, because that might be helpful to him, but he refuses." Gorky himself was completely under Chekhov's spell, and the respect that he had already acquired for the older writer was matched now by a real affection for the man. He wrote to his wife: "Chekhov is a remarkable man. Friendly, kind, attentive. . . . Nothing could be more enjoyable than talking with him, and I don't remember ever having conversed with anyone with so much pleasure."

What also aroused Gorky's admiration was the amazing simplicity of his famous colleague, who from their first meeting had been completely natural and unaffected with him. Gorky then saw that in spite of the troop of admirers that pursued him, Chekhov was a very lonely man whose "sad, gentle smile hid the subtle skepticism of a man who knows the worth of words and things." With Gorky he was indeed charming, but his observations on others were often tinged with a deep misanthropy, a great disenchantment, and sometimes even a certain bitterness. Besides, he was quite well aware of the seriousness of his illness, and one night, lying on a couch, he confided to Gorky that sentenced as he was to die before his time, he found life "completely absurd."

As soon as Gorky had gone, Chekhov fell back into his gloom. He had had enough, he wrote to Suvorin, of his "role" as a patient sent to Yalta to be rehabilitated. Patients too had a right to vacations: on April 10, without asking Altschuler's opinion, he left for Moscow. At first he stayed in the small apartment that his mother and Masha had taken in Malaya-Dmitrovka Street, and he spent a few days there in a whirlwind of visits from strangers and friends.

From morning to night it was a constant round of arrivals and departures, submissions of manuscripts by strangers, and chatter and long confidences around the constantly bubbling samovar. Chekhov did not have a moment to himself to work on the revision of the material that he had brought for Marx and it is doubtful whether in all the noise he could hear even the bells, close as they were, of the Strastnoy Monastery, which he loved. After four days of this, for the sake of peace he moved alone into a furnished room in the same street.

Even though Chekhov might have had some idea of the impression that he had made on Gorky, he must nevertheless have been touched by the letter the younger man wrote immediately on his return to Nizhni-Novgorod: "I am happy to have met you, immensely happy! I think you are the first free man I have ever seen, the first who has no reverence for anything. It is good that you can make literature the first, the biggest concern of your life" (April 22, 1899). This was certainly the first time that a member of the intelligentsia—and a Marxist at that!—had congratulated Chekhov on his insistence on rejecting all philosophic or political allegiance in order to devote himself solely to literature.

This was precisely what Tolstoy criticized in Chekhov: his "commitment" only to literature. Chekhov, meanwhile, had just received further proof that while he could not prevent himself from loving the old prophet—"in my entire life I have never respected any man so deeply, I might even say so totally, as Lev

Nikolaevich," he had recently written—Tolstoy too greatly liked Chekhov's work. Tolstoy's eldest daughter, Tatiana, had just written to Chekhov: "What a delightful thing your 'Darling' is! My father read it aloud on four successive evenings and he says it has given him a lesson in wisdom" (March 30, 1899).

Chekhov had barely arrived in Moscow when Tolstoy, in a fresh demonstration of his affection, went to visit him. But two actors had got there first, and their inane jabber prevented the two authors from having any real conversation. The next day, fortunately, they met again, this time in Tolstoy's house, and they were able to talk freely on everything that interested them. They spoke a great deal about Gorky, and Chekhov, always the good colleague, lost no time in reporting to Gorky that Tolstoy had called him "a remarkable writer." Gorky exclaimed in delight: "I feel as if I'd just swallowed a drop of honey!"

Chekhov also saw Lydia Avilova again. She was passing through Moscow with her three children, and no doubt it was she who suggested their meeting, which took place in a station, between trains. Chekhov wanted to thank her for the research work that she had done for him, but it would seem that in spite of this, and according to her own recollections, their brief talk was anything but pleasant and was indeed strained. Still plunged in her illusory dreams, she could think of nothing but the last conversation between the protagonists in "About Love," which she had interpreted as "their" story. This was to be her description of their farewell: ". . . the train slowly began to move. I saw the silhouette of Anton Pavlovich slip past the window, but he did not turn round. I did not know then, nor could I have imagined, that I was seeing him for the last time."

Meanwhile the Moscow of which he had dreamed so eagerly was already tiring Chekhov. He had been there only two weeks when he wrote to Altschuler at Easter: "An army of visitors, and endless conversations. . . . On the second day of the holiday weariness almost kept me from moving, and I felt as dead as a corpse." He decided to go to Melikhovo in May to rest. Before he left, he had his photograph taken with the company of the Art Theater in a remarkably stagey *"tableau vivant":* around him, as he pretended to be reading *The Sea Gull,* actors, actresses, and director, in extremely studied poses, pretended to be listening to him without a glance for the little sea gull that was about to come out of the camera. Next to Chekhov, in pensive profile, stood the young actress Olga Knipper.

XI

THE LAST PAGE
OF MY LIFE

Love is either the residue of something that is degenerating and
that was once tremendous or else a part of something that will become tremendous in the future. But in the present it cannot satisfy, it offers much less than is expected of it.

CHEKHOV, *Notebooks*

"I advise you," Masha had written to her brother during the winter, "to pay some attention to Knipper. In my opinion she is very
interesting." Chekhov's sister had in fact become infatuated with
the Art Theater, which was doing so much for her brother, and
since she spent much time there, she had come to know the young
actress, for whom she soon felt a friendship full of admiration.
During his stay in Moscow, Chekhov made a point of following
his sister's advice and even of paying considerable attention to
Olga Knipper. He went to see her perform, he met her at his sister's, and he was invited to tea with her in the home of what Gorky
called "the mad Knipper family." Together they went to see an
exhibition of Levitan's paintings.

Olga had been brought up as a highly respectable middle-class
girl. The daughter of an engineer of German origin, she had attended a private school before proceeding to the ultra-refined and
utterly useless tutoring then in vogue for rich young ladies: lessons in music, drawing, and foreign languages. When her father
died, leaving nothing but debts, the "young lady" was abruptly
transformed into an emancipated young woman who had to earn

her own livelihood. She had given music lessons and for three years she had also attended Nemirovich-Danchenko's dramatic school before joining the Art Theater company. With her "mad family"— her mother and her two uncles—she lived a rather frugal but still gay, careless, and very bohemian life in a small three-room apartment. While she was rehearsing in one room, her mother, who had become a singing teacher, would be giving lessons in the second; in the third room her physician uncle and her officer uncle would be arguing, getting drunk on vodka, or reading aloud from Tolstoy —or Chekhov.

There was nothing of the romantic "sea gull" in Olga, nor was she an intellectual. Unquestionably she liked her profession, at which she worked assiduously and to which she was completely dedicated, but at the same time she was a thoroughly natural person, full of energy, aggressiveness, and love of life. While there was still much of the "young lady" about her and she was quite capable, if the circumstances warranted, of singing a romance or discussing literature, she was also solidly estabished in her way of life and she would as soon talk about her colleagues, her clothes, and her favorite foods. Brought face to face with Chekhov and wanting to please him, she did not need much time to understand that for him it was much less essential to play the melancholy, dreaming Chekhovian "sea gull" than to be the happy canary: so she was amusing, pleasingly flirtatious, vivacious, spontaneous, in love with life. In addition to the beauty of her twenty-nine years she also had the appearance suitable to her profession: a glowing complexion, a wealth of hair, fine smiling eyes, and good clothes sense.

Chekhov was only eight years older than Olga but, burdened by illness, he was already graying, his smile was disillusioned, and he was almost never without his glasses on their black silk ribbon. He was attracted and held by the youth, the ruddy health, and the spirit of this young woman, all of which soon made him in his turn gayer and more vivacious. Perhaps after all he had been wrong in thinking that he was already an invalid, almost an old man, doomed for the rest of his life to loneliness and boredom. And it was spring, too, spring unfolding over Moscow and opening the lilacs and the new foliage above the fences and the gates, and that too might have been an element.

But he wanted to see spring in Melikhovo again, and so he went there in May and immediately invited Olga. She was to say later that her first visit there was "three days completely filled with a wonderful premonition, with you and sunshine." She was captivated by the atmosphere of spontaneous gaiety and affection that dominated the Chekhov family and by the kindness of the writer's mother, " gentle Russian woman endowed with a sense of humor." Chekhov paid a great deal of attention to Olga, taking her on a tour of his "duchy" and showing her his vegetable garden, his lake, his trees, his blossoming "cherry orchard." After he had shown her the "doll's house" in which he had written *The Sea Gull,* he gave her an inscribed photograph of it. "How enchanted I was by everything!" Olga told him later. "I was a little awed by you then. But that wonderful morning when we went walking together!"

When she went back to Moscow, they were enchanted with each other, eager to know each other better and hence to see each other soon again. In June, Olga went to spend her vacation with her brother in Georgia, near Mtskhet. When Chekhov wrote to her, he fell back—defensively—on the teasing tone that he had so often used with Lika: "Where are you? We're beginning to think you've forgotten us and perhaps got married in the Caucasus. . . . So you've forgot the writer? How horrible, how cruel, how perfidious!" (June 16, 1899). But next day, hastily scribbling a postscript to a letter that Masha had written to her friend, he let something more of his real feelings show through: "Hello, last page of my life, great actress of the land of Russia. I envy the Circassians who see you every day. . . . I wish you magnificent health and enchanting dreams."

Chekhov was packing all his belongings in Melikhovo and arranging his books in shipping cases. He had resolved to sell the estate, and he put advertisements into the newspapers, but without success. He had been very fond of Melikhovo, into which he had invested a large part of himself and where he had written some of his best-loved works, and yet it was without anguish that he was giving it up; he confessed, too, that since he had written "Peasants," the place had lost "all literary interest" for him. He was resolutely turning over that page of his life, and the more easily because the next—and last?—drew him much more strongly.

He wanted very much to see Olga again, and when at the end of June she offered to join him in the south, he accepted her "wonderful invitation" with enthusiasm. They agreed to meet on July 18, in Novorossisk, did so, and together boarded the boat that was to deposit them in Yalta two days later.

They spent ten days there, Chekhov in the Hotel Marino and Olga with mutual friends the Shredins. After his three-month absence Chekhov found the work on his house well advanced, and he divided his time between visits of inspection and outings with the young actress. Olga was appalled to see how badly he ate: rather than accept lunch invitations from friends, he preferred to gobble a bit of bread and cheese at Autka. Nevertheless he occasionally took her out for seafood dinners washed down with a little Crimean white wine in a Tartar restaurant in the harbor. He showed her the city and the country around it, surely without omitting the magnificent view from Oreanda (where he would soon place one of the love scenes of "The Lady With the Pet Dog").

Did Olga find that he paid too much attention to his housebuilding and not enough to herself? There were times when he seemed strange, spiritless, even somewhat sullen. Bewildered, Anton wrote to Masha—who must have been quite surprised to learn that they were staying in Yalta together: "She [Olga] is depressed. Yesterday she came to visit me and have tea: she just sat there in silence . . ." (August 21, 1899).

Called back to rehearsals by the Art Theater, Olga left for Moscow on August 2; Chekhov went with her. They covered the first stage of the journey in an open carriage as far as Bakhshisaray, where at that time the railway from Moscow ended. They crossed the Aï-Petri mountain range: the country had a wild romantic beauty and the weather was splendid. The road ran past fields of roses bordered by cypresses, then through Moslem cemeteries and Tartar villages; it dropped, shut off every view, then rose again over sparkling little gulfs. They crossed the beautiful Kokhaz valley, rocking in their aged carriage, battling the heat of the sun, half intoxicated by the strong scent of the pinelands; they chatted "in the style of the Chekhovs," with warmth and levity. Reaching Bakhshisaray in the evening, they took the night train for Moscow. The time of vacations and happy outings, unfortunately, was at an end, but it had brought them much closer to each other.

Although Chekhov spent three weeks in Moscow, they saw each other hardly at all. The Art Theater was preparing for its autumn season and Olga was very much involved in rehearsals. Chekhov, for his part, was busy with the publication of the first volume of his complete works. He approved the contract for the sale of Meli-khovo, which Masha had initiated in his absence: he sold the place to a wood merchant for twenty-three thousand rubles. He also attended some rehearsals of his new play, *Uncle Vanya*, at the Art Theater, and this gave him the opportunity to see Olga, who had a part in it.

At the end of August the weather turned cold and Chekhov became ill. "I seem to have reached the limit of my endurance," he wrote to Suvorin, with whom, in spite of all their disagreements, he was still corresponding, "and my head is always ready for the pillow." Although he had no desire to go away, he left Moscow for Yalta, where he arrived on August 27; on September 8 his mother and Masha joined him there. For all of them "the Melikhovo time" —which had certainly been the happiest in their lives—was a closed book and the Yalta time was beginning.

The Chekhovs established themselves immediately in the new house in Autka, even though the "family nest" was barely livable. In reality they were camping in a construction project. "The carpenters and floor layers hammer from morning until night," Chekhov wrote on September 15, "and keep me from working." It would be many weeks more before the inside of the house was finished. In spite of the discomfort, Anton's mother soon became fond of Yalta, and when Masha left for Moscow at the end of October, the old lady no longer mentioned going with her.

Chekhov was impatient to take possession of the plain but pleasant study that had been arranged for him. Papered in a *fleur-de-lis* pattern, the room was illuminated by a very large, rounded Venetian bay window that looked out over a beautiful tiered landscape: the garden, then the green hills and a view of Yalta, finally the soft blue triangle of the sea. Above the raw-brick fireplace a landscape by the well-loved Levitan was to be hung, and the walls, in the contemporary fashion, were covered with family photographs and watercolors surrounding portraits of Tolstoy, Turgenev, and Grigorovich. Above the big desk, covered with little figures carved of wood and stone, a shaded lamp, and a curious horseshoe-shaped inkwell, a peremptory notice greeted the visitor: "Please do not smoke." But Chekhov never reminded his visitors of it, even when the smoke of their *papirossy* made him cough violently.

During the autumn he was still deeply involved in the preparation of his "complete works," the first volume of which was to appear in December. At the same time he felt a kind of guilt at having created nothing new for months, and he again found the time to write two long stories. One, "In the Ravine," dealt with peasants and was in a way a farewell to his country life in Melikhovo. In the second, "The Lady With the Pet Dog," he was attempting a first— and masterly—sketch of Yalta's artificial atmosphere.

Out of the subject of this story—a commonplace vacation adultery that both parties want to prolong and that develops into a passionate but hopeless love—Turgenev would have made a long, static novel, Tolstoy, the Tolstoy of 1899, would have created a terrifying moral lesson, and Maupassant would have written a mercilessly cruel short story. Chekhov made it into a brief impressionist film done all in half tones: everything in it was suggested, the rather languid atmosphere of the resort with its dancing light, its brief encounters, its moonlight, and the gentle sound of the sea; the casual vacation flirtation that soon takes fire in the memory; the casual protagonists gradually transmuted and, as it were, given substance by passion. "Do you know what you're doing?" Gorky wrote to Chekhov when he had read the story. "You are killing realism. . . . It will soon be dead, and for a long time. . . . No one knows how to write so simply as you, and of simple things. . . . Your stories are exquisitely carved vials filled with all the perfumes of life. . ." (January, 1900).

The story, with its unrealizable love, was certainly not autobiographical. But like every work of the imagination "of which," to quote Julien Green, "all the details are true," it was woven of the thousand and one observations that Chekhov had been recording since his arrival in Yalta, all of which had by now had time to seep through his "filter." This time, however, there may have been something more. How is it possible, indeed, not to think of the author and almost visualize him when one reads: "His hair was already beginning to whiten. . . . Time was going on, he was meeting people, friendships were forming and dissolving, but he did not love. In these encounters there was everything except love. And it was only now, when his hair was white, that he really loved, for the first time in his life." [1]

But did he really love that Olga Knipper who had enchanted him with her youth and vitality, or was it again only a matter of "one of those encounters in which there is everything except love"? He himself did not yet know whether he loved her. Unquestionably he missed her, he longed for her, "his sweet and wonderful actress, a remarkable woman." He had barely returned to Yalta when he wrote to her: "I have grown accustomed to you. And I feel so alone without you that I cannot accept the idea that I shall not see you again until spring. I am in a foul mood. . . ." A month later, when Olga was rehearsing *Uncle Vanya* with the Art Theater company, he confessed to her: "I am bored, I rage and rage again, and I envy the rat that lives beneath the stage of your theater" (October 4, 1899).

But, though in the beginning a real emotional impatience seemed to thrust through the playful tone, as the weeks went by, his letters, which also became less frequent, began to be very like those that he used to write to "the beautiful Lika." And yet what letters he was getting from Masha in Moscow, where his sister was now completely under Olga's spell! "What a fine person she is!" Masha wrote. "I'm more and more convinced of that." Chekhov took the opportunity to ask her to insist that Olga promise to spend her summer vacation in Yalta, but still he did so in a joking, almost buffoonish manner: "I'll pay her a salary," he said. And to Olga herself he explained his long silences offhandedly: "Dear ac-

---

[1] In 1957 "The Lady With the Pet Dog" inspired the Soviet film director Josef Kheifels to make an impressionist film that is a model of cinematographic adaptation.

tress and delightful woman, I have not written to you because I've been plunged in work and don't allow myself to be diverted from it" (December 8, 1899).

In actuality he lacked everything in that Yalta to which he had returned against his will. He was longing for Olga Knipper, true, but he was longing as well for his friends, his Moscow literary conversations, the theaters, and even the restaurants. He explained to Olga, with a sigh immediately corrected by a smile: "I want so much to escape from Yalta, where loneliness is killing me. I'm a Johannes without a woman . . . but a Johannes without culture or courage" [2] (November 1, 1899).

But it was Masha, still the only person in whom he confided, to whom he wrote one evening when solitude was intolerably crushing: ". . . Actually, you can have no idea how boring and stupid it is to go to bed at nine o'clock and lie there, in a temper, knowing there is nowhere to go, no one to talk to, and no reason for working because what you do is unimportant if you don't see or hear your work. The piano and I are the two things in this house that are mute, constantly asking ourselves why we have been put here when there is no one to play on us . . ." (November 11, 1899).

Anyone else would have withdrawn into his desperation. But Chekhov, far from cloaking himself in his solitude, did not abandon himself even to the subtle kind of languor with which Yalta was imbued. In spite of his own condition, he was no less attentive than ever to the sufferings of others. He smiled gently when Gorky, in his letters, talked about "changing life" through his writing, but as far as what depended on him was concerned, Chekhov sought, as he had done for so long, to change it through direct action. Thus, shocked for months by the dangerous and often abominable conditions in which the poor tuberculars who had come to Yalta for their health were living—often in filthy tents— he decided to do something about them without further delay.

He intended to build a sanitarium for the needy, but that required him to find a great deal of money. He went to work at once: he set up a sponsoring committee in Yalta, collected money, prepared a public appeal that appeared in various newspapers in

---

[2] An allusion to the hero of Gerhart Hauptmann's play *Einsame Menschen*, which the Art Theater had just added to its program.

both capitals of the province, and called on his friends, including Gorky, who at once put himself at Chekhov's disposal. Many people refused to listen to his appeal—the self-styled progressives among the intelligentsia, for example, who argued that there was too much to be done and who therefore preferred to do nothing, an attitude that angered Chekhov. He managed nevertheless to amass some money, with which he was able to establish some thirty patients in a little boarding house converted into a rest home; it was called Yauglar. It was only two years later, after a second public appeal—for he was as tenacious in good works as in literary work—that he was finally able, with the forty thousand rubles thus raised, plus five thousand more from his own pocket, to establish the institution that is known today as the Anton Chekhov Sanitarium.

Chekhov's play *Uncle Vanya*—a recasting of *The Wood Demon*—had already been performed regularly and successfully in the provinces when at the beginning of 1899 the author had approved its presentation by the Maly Theater, which was the oldest and one of the most famous in Moscow. But after a first reading the director had asked for major changes in the text: the author must understand, for example, that it was indecent, if not impossible, to show an educated man like Uncle Vanya firing a revolver at a university professor, even if the title were merely honorary. Chekhov had burst out laughing and, of course, taken back his play. A short time later he had given it to the Art Theater, which had made such a success of *The Sea Gull*.

During his summer visit to Moscow he attended a number of rehearsals of *Uncle Vanya*. Anything but a passive author, he again did not hesitate to permit himself a number of observations, some of them quite cutting, when he was displeased with the way in which one or another actor played his part. He was an advocate of spontaneity, and as he was soon to write to Meyerhold, he urged above all the avoidance of straining for naturalism and over-stressing of effects. In spite of the outspoken manner of his criticisms, however, he was unfailingly polite to the actors and especially to the actresses—among whom, we must not forget, was

Olga Knipper—and as a result he was soon known to the whole company under the friendly designation "Actress Inspector."

On his return to Yalta he maintained contact by mail with his new friends in the Art Theater. "What sadness and bitterness it gives me," he wrote to Vishnyevsky, an old friend from his Taganrog youth whom he had been delighted to encounter again and who was playing the title character in *Uncle Vanya,* "not to be with all of you. As far as I'm concerned, the rehearsals and the performance are almost for nothing, since all I know about them is hearsay" (October 8, 1899). He was anxious about the progress of the rehearsals, and he sent his inquiries to Olga. She was playing the part of Yelena, for which she asked him for advice—"with a kiss on the right temple"—and he lost no time in supplying it. She was to take no notice of Stanislavsky's opinion, because he had not really understood the character of Dr. Astrov, which he was playing and who was not at all passionately in love with Yelena. It was only her beauty that had attracted Astrov, who in the last act finally became so aware of this "that he kissed her almost distractedly, to kill time."

The Art Theater was having a huge success with the start of the new season: when the box office opened for the first time, twenty-five hundred people were waiting. The first performance of *Uncle Vanya* was scheduled for October 26: an enthusiastic cast performed before a packed house. The next evening telegrams announcing a triumph began to pour into Yalta. Each one, as it arrived, was telephoned to Chekhov, who had already gone to bed. "I woke up every time," he wrote to Olga, "and ran barefoot in the dark to the telephone, shivering with cold. Then I would hardly have fallen asleep again when the telephone started ringing. It's the first time my own glory has prevented me from sleeping" (October 30, 1899).

This first performance, however, was not really the "brilliant success" that Olga called it, and Chekhov could see as much when he read the newspapers, all of which mingled their high praises with reservations about both the play itself and the actors' work. As the performances continued, however, the public, which was beginning to understand Chekhov, grew more and more enthusiastic over *Uncle Vanya.* When he had seen it twice, Gorky wrote in

January with a perfect candor rare among writers: "*Uncle Vanya* forever. And I'm going to see it a third time, I've already bought a ticket. I don't regard it as a pearl . . . but it is overflowing with thoughts and symbols, and its form makes it an original work—incomparable." With a touch of malice he added: "I saw your brother standing on his feet to applaud. I myself never applaud, because it offends the actors."

As for Stanislavsky and his colleagues, Gorky assured his friend that if he lived in Moscow, only he would be seen in their "wonderful theater." This was also the opinion of the public, which stormed the box office in numbers that increased daily. Chekhov himself in his far-off Yalta, even though he was not sparing in his criticisms of it, was beginning to recognize that this enthusiastic new theater group was rejuvenating the Russian theater by putting on his own plays in a new style. Hence, when one of its directors, his old friend Nemirovich-Danchenko, wrote that he was tired of his career and was thinking of giving it up, Chekhov adjured him to do nothing of the kind. "Don't let it get you down, don't lose your enthusiasm," he wrote. "The Art Theater will provide the finest pages in the book that will one day be written on the contemporary Russian theater" (November 19, 1899).

Tolstoy went very seldom to the theater, but he did go to see *Uncle Vanya.* He did not like his younger colleague's plays, and he had told Suvorin in connection with *The Sea Gull*—which, moreover, he had merely read, not seen—that all Chekhov's plays were high-flown nonsense written in imitation of Ibsen and he saw no value at all in them. *Uncle Vanya,* he noted in his diary, made him "angry." In conversation with A. Sanin, an actor, he demanded in an outraged tone: "Where's the drama? What does it consist of?" When Nemirovich-Danchenko attempted to defend his author and explain the play, Tolstoy retorted that there was no tragic situation in it and its place could not be taken by guitars and crickets.[3]

Wounded on Chekhov's behalf, Nemirovich-Danchenko nevertheless relayed Tolstoy's remarks but thought it necessary to add

[3] Did Tolstoy want to prove that he could do better than Chekhov? One is tempted to wonder, because it was on the evening when he went home from seeing this performance that he wrote the outline of *The Living Dead* in a single sitting.

that Tolstoy had not understood the play. But far from resenting the slashing criticisms of the old master, Chekhov was amused by them. In a subsequent conversation with his friend P. Gnedish, he admitted that Tolstoy did not like his plays and considered that he was not a playwright. "There's only one thing that consoles me," he added. "He once said to me: 'You know, I can't stand Shakespeare, but your plays are even worse than his.'" When he told this story, Gnedish said, "Anton Pavlovich, that quiet man filled with reserve," threw back his head and laughed so hard that the glasses fell off his nose.

Tolstoy's peremptory, emotional, and unjust judgments, however, did not affect the almost filial admiration that Chekhov felt for his work and himself. When *Resurrection* was published during that winter, Chekhov immediately hailed Tolstoy's new novel as a magnificent work of art. When he read certain passages, he said, "my heart pounded furiously, they were so good." For all that, he did not lose his critical sense, and he confided to Gorky: "I've just read *Resurrection*. With the exception of the rather confused and artificial relations between Nekhlyudov and Katya, everything in this novel impressed me: its power, its richness, its scope, and also the hypocrisy of a man who is afraid of dying, doesn't want to admit it, and clutches at texts out of Holy Writ" (February 15, 1900).

In January, when it was widely reported that Tolstoy was seriously ill, Chekhov quite spontaneously manifested the kind of filial affection that he felt toward the older man. As much for himself as for Russian literature Chekhov dreaded that death of which Tolstoy admitted to "being afraid." Chekhov wrote to Menshikov: "I fear Tolstoy's death. If he dies, it will make a terrible void in my life. In the first place, I've never liked any man as much as I like him. I am an unbeliever, but of all beliefs, I consider his the closest to my heart and the best suited to me. In the second place, as long as a Tolstoy exists in the world of letters, it is easy and pleasant to be a writer. And even if one is aware that one has done and is doing nothing, it is not really terrible because Tolstoy creates for all of us. His work is the justification of everything that one hopes and expects from literature. In the third place, Tolstoy's position is solid, his authority is tremendous, and as long as he lives bad taste in literature, everything that is vulgarity, insolence, or sentimentality, all the soured egos will be kept at a distance, wrapped in darkness. His influence alone can raise the various literary currents and tendencies to a certain level. Without him writers would be nothing but a flock without a shepherd" (January 28, 1900).

The old shepherd of Yasnaya Polyana felt a kind of tenderness toward his junior that matched Chekhov's in spite of everything that divided them. When Tolstoy had read Chekhov's story "In the Ravine," he wrote to Gorky: "What a fine story Chekhov wrote for *Life!* I am remarkably happy about it." And his affection was sometimes supplemented by a great critical acumen, as, for instance when he was to be the first to describe Chekhov as an "impressionist" writer. "Like the impressionists," he was to tell a reporter who interviewed him the day after Chekhov's death, "Chekhov has his own form. It seems as if he is splashing all the colors in his hand at random, and one feels that all these dabs of paint have nothing in common with one another. But as soon as one steps back and looks from a distance, the impression is extraordinary. The picture is magnificent and irresistible."

Chekhov's talent, moreover, was officially recognized and consecrated during that winter. The Russian government had just established a Literary Section in the Academy of Sciences, and the author of *The Sea Gull* was one of the first ten academicians appointed, along with Tolstoy and Korolenko, a fact that must have given him pleasure. He received many telegrams of congratulation, but it would seem that he himself was not unduly impressed by this honor. It rather amused him and, incorrigible schoolboy that he was, he signed some of his letters to his close friends "Honorary Hereditary Academician" or "Academicus." To make Masha laugh, he told her that their old servant, deferring to the traditional hierarchy of rank in Russia, which put academicians on the save level as generals, was now ordering all his visitors to address him as "Excellency." But he admitted that he was pleased with the privileges to which his new title admitted him: immunity and a special passport, which would exempt him from harassments at customs. As for the question of whether he would remain an academician, he seemed to have some doubts, and he made a kind of prophecy to his friend Menshikov: "I'll be happier still when some disagreement causes me to lose this title" (January 28, 1900). This was in fact to occur two years later.

Chekhov carried reserve to such an extent that he never told anyone at exactly what period in his life he had written *Uncle Vanya,* which is justly one of his most famous plays. According to some of his biographers, he wrote it in March and April of 1890—in other words, before his journey to Sakhalin; others, in greater number, believe that it was not until several years later, in 1896, that he wrote it. But this minor and still unsolved enigma of literary history can really excite only those biographers excessively concerned with marking off Chekhov's life with milestones of key dates, and one would almost like to be able to prove to them that the play dates from the beginning of 1890 and thus to show them how arbitrary it is to make the journey to Sakhalin the great dividing line in the author's work.

In actuality there were neither abrupt ruptures nor deep mutations in Chekhov's work, and this is as true for his stories as for his plays. Few writers have found themselves so quickly and remained so faithful to themselves. *Uncle Vanya* contains the themes already dealt with in *Ivanov* and even in *Platonov:* the erosion of the spirit by the everyday, the "horror" of country life, and in the final analysis the inescapable frustration of every human destiny. It contains also, barely altered, certain characteristics and, what is more, almost all the characters of *The Wood Demon:* the selfish old intellectual, the country doctor making a bad bargain with cynicism, the frigid beauty, the romantic young girl. But principally, in filigree, it contains Chekhov and his individual view of the world, a disenchanted but in its very disenchantment a strangely compelling view as well.

"In life," Chekhov told the young writer Goroditsky, "one does not shoot oneself in the head, hang oneself, or declare one's passion at every fencepost, and one does not pour out profound thoughts in a constant flow. No; mostly one eats, drinks, flirts, makes stupid remarks: that is what should be seen on the stage. One must write plays in which people come and go, have dinner, talk about the rain and the sunshine, play cards—not because this is the author's whim but because this is what happens in real life. . . . Nothing must be fitted into a pattern." This program of deliberate banality —except for Uncle Vanya's revolver shot at Serebryakov, but then the peaceful Chekhov had a weakness for gunfire and it is to be heard in all his plays except for *The Cherry Orchard*—was religiously followed by the author of *Uncle Vanya*. In this play nothing happens, except that life goes on and in this vacuum one hears it going on, inexorably, without any possibility of turning back, and leading dreams to defeat, freezing the momentary into a permanent gray. *Uncle Vanya* is, before our eyes—eyes to which tears come, as they came to Gorky's—not the search for time gone by but time itself going by.

Chekhov gave his play, exactly as he might have done for a book of stories, a subtitle: *Scenes of Country Life*. These scenes— tea in the garden followed by a game of croquet, a restless night of storm and sleeplessness, a family council on money problems, and then the farewells of those who are going back to town—are linked together by a rather weak plot. It creates, out of the mere fact of living together, a conflict between Uncle Vanya and his brother-in-law, the famous Professor Serebryakov, whose second wife is the young and beautiful Yelena Andreyevna.

Kind and devoted, Uncle Vanya has for years managed, with the help of his niece, Sonya, the estate she inherited from her mother, Serebryakov's first wife. Working conscientiously and sacrificing himself completely, he has always sent the entire income from the estate to the professor, whom the whole family, including himself, admires and regards as a great man. But since Serebryakov and his young wife have come to live on the estate, Uncle Vanya has begun to sense his brother-in-law's real character beneath his noble exterior and to wonder whether he himself has not been the dupe and the victim of "family feeling." Deprived of his own future, which he has sacrificed to others, he begins to drink because "that way in spite of everything it seems a little like living."

Serebryakov, whose selfishness is exaggerated by his real or imagined illness and who is tormented by old age, is bored in the country: he wants to leave it and travel. Since the income from the property will not permit this, he plans to sell the estate and, accustomed to being obeyed, he announces as much to the family. It is at this moment that gentle Uncle Vanya's terrible anger bursts forth: his repugnance for his brother-in-law has grown steadily as he has increasingly discovered that Serebryakov is only an imitation great man and as his affection has increased toward Serebryakov's young wife, the object of her husband's constant caprices and complaints; but she does not return Vanya's feeling. The scene is sharp and violent, and in his desperation Uncle Vanya fires at Serebryakov but misses.

Everything, however, falls back into normality, the lame, mediocre, unjust normality that is the rule of middle-class life. The grand dreams of love—Uncle Vanya's for the beautiful Yelena, ardent little Sonya's for a family friend, Dr. Astrov—are the first to vanish, and even the affair begun between Astrov and Yelena has no outcome. The professor and his wife return to the city after a makeshift reconciliation with Uncle Vanya, and everything goes back to what it was before, with perhaps the loss of a few illusions, compensated for by still more resignation. Uncle Vanya and Sonya will go on sacrificing themselves for the greater glory of Serebryakov, to whom, as before, they will send all the income from the estate.

When Gorky had seen the play, he wrote to Chekhov in all sincerity: "It seems to me, you know, that in this play you handle people with the coldness of the Devil. You are as indifferent as snow, as storm" (November, 1898). The point was well taken: it is true that here more than anywhere else, perhaps, we are indeed far from the "tender Chekhov" who has been dinned into our ears for the past fifty years. Never had the author gone—or would he again go—so far in almost clinical observation of wasted lives, to the point of showing in the end that they, we, are all "life's failures." This time—and this is the innovation—there is added the theme of frustration, a psychosis with which virtually every character in the play is afflicted. And from the rise of the first curtain there is a climate of disillusion—enveloping, insidious, and in effect perfidiously "enchanted," for no one can escape it, and the spectator least of all.

Speaking of the theater, Chekhov had written to Suvorin in 1891: "The public must be frightened, and that's all." One might say that in *Uncle Vanya* he completely succeeded in doing so, in making us see that every life, in its very progression, is wasted. A subtle dramamaker, he convinces us of this "without making a drama of it," without involving death or major misfortune, simply by showing us, as Astrov says, that, "in ten years or so, provincial life, this abominable life, has gripped us all, poisoned our blood, and we have become cynics like the rest." But it would perhaps be more accurate to say failures, malcontents, melancholics, resigned but seared by brief hot flames of revolt. Astrov is a clear-sighted man without illusion who no longer knows "what is his real vocation"; Uncle Vanya is a beaten man awakened at night by the chagrin and the rage of never having fulfilled himself; Yelena says of herself that she has never succeeded in being anything but a supernumerary. And Serebryakov himself, far from having been "saved" by his selfishness and his arrogance, will come to admit that "accursed, repulsive old age" is in itself a frustration that spares no one.

Abominably exploited by his brother-in-law, Uncle Vanya discovers in our presence that he has been frustrated. And his eyes are opened to one of the laws of the human jungle: on one side there are those who—oh, so kindly, so affectionately, and sometimes even so silently—extort every sacrifice from their intimates, and on the other side there are those who, like him, are sacrificed and thwarted. This feeling of frustration is exacerbated in Uncle Vanya because it makes him incapable of believing any longer in his famous brother-in-law. That is when he cries out: "Oh, how duped I have been! I adored that professor, that miserable goutweed, I worked like a horse for him! . . . I was proud of him and his work, I lived and breathed through him. . . . And . . . he's nothing. A soap bubble." So too Yelena, who has sacrificed her youth, her beauty, and her love to her old husband—she has learned too late that her love for him was "imaginary"—is exhausted in the end by the unceasing harassments. Even the open-hearted Sonya, exploited by her father, has flashes of rebellion.

But it is in the nature of the exploited, even when their eyes have been opened, to resign themselves to their frustration—out of generosity, out of acquired habit, and also out of a certain propensity to lassitude. This is explained in his own way by a minor character in the play, another self-made frustrate, Telegin: "My wife ran away with the man she loved the day after our wedding. . . . In spite of that . . . I still love her today and I'm faithful to her. I help her as much as I can, and I've sold off my property to educate the children she had by her lover. . . ." Yelena, similarly, is resigned to remaining faithful to her old, complaining husband, and young Sonya, doubly bled by her father, says meekly: "I endure it and I'll go on enduring it until life ends by itself." Even Uncle Vanya's furious revolt is to have no sequel. At the very moment of taking leave of his tyrannical brother-in-law he makes an act of submission to him: "You'll get everything regularly again, just as you did before. Everything will be as it was."

While Uncle Vanya gives his name to the play, is he on that account its major hero? To some, the leading part, and therefore the title of the play, should be, rather, *Astrov, Country Doctor*: this was especially true of the Russian physicians meeting in January, 1900, at the Pegorov Congress, all of whom the Art Theater graciously invited to a performance. To them it was a play about a doctor and by a doctor, and from this point of view they overwhelmed their honored colleague, the author, with their telegrams of congratulation. It is of course unquestionable that Dr. Astrov has a major part in the play and that he serves as a counterweight to Uncle Vanya. Against the latter's grumbling generosity he offers his lucid detachment.

He is a strange man in any case, this Astrov. He is an excellent example of the paradox of the physician: devoid of all illusion about men and yet, by vocation, devoting himself to them. In his lucidity, as in Chekhov's, there is something frightening—Gorky called it diabolical: to him life is "sad, idiotic, dirty"; he regards his friends as "petty, stupid, hysterical whiners"; and he expects nothing from people. He is successful with women and he exploits the circumstance, but it is long indeed since he last believed in love. His profession of faith, frequently reiterated in the play, is a profession of despair: "I no longer desire anything, I need nothing, I love no one." And yet not only does this skeptic devote himself to his patients; this man who has a horror of provincial life has not even a thought of abandoning it, but he too pursues a chimera. "The only thing that can still enchant me," he acknowledges, "is beauty," and he seeks out that beauty and labors to spread it over the earth.

Other doctors, in search of consolation for their excessive closeness to the "dirt" of life, also take refuge in a certain cult of beauty and collect paintings. Astrov, that eccentric, collects trees. To him the woods and the forests are earth's finest adornments, and, appalled by men's massacre of them, he dedicates himself to new planting, new forestation. When this cynic speaks of his beloved trees, he becomes lyrical, touching in his naked emotion. Nonsense! for all his sarcasms he loves mankind too, for he confesses: "When I hear the rustle of young trees that I have planted with my own hands, I have the feeling . . . that if in a thousand years man is happy, it will be to a degree because of me."

"Where's the drama?" Tolstoy grumbled when he came away from a performance of *Uncle Vanya*. François Mauriac, like many others, provided the answer to this question when he pointed out that there is indeed a drama hidden in the play and that this drama is social, the drama of "those last years before the revolution when people bogged down in the depths of remote countrysides made themselves suffer and weep over their wasted lives; the Promised Land was virtually within reach and they knew that they would not enter in." No doubt the same thing will be said one day of Mauriac's own somber provincial novels—since criticism tends more and more to explain works of art by their "historical and social context"—and one will make the same error of viewpoint as he, whose novels are placed essentially on the religious plane. If there is indeed a drama in *Uncle Vanya*, it lies elsewhere, because for these bemired, disenchanted provincials there is not now or ever a Promised Land. As for the concept that Chekhov's characters knew that it was near, this endows them with a prescience that even their author, who did not believe in revolution, lacked.

It is Uncle Vanya himself who makes the right answer to Tolstoy when he asserts: "Everything will be as it was." This is the drama, the real drama of the play: this certainty, which we of the audience feel from the start, that the game is rigged, that every attempt by the characters to pull themselves out of their bog will be futile. We know that what they still regard as transitory circumstances have grown denser from day to day and as it were solidified into their permanent lives. Moreover, there is something else besides resignation in Uncle Vanya's final surrender: it is accompanied by a sigh of relief. For him and his like, disenchantment has become virtually second nature, and if they resign themselves to being frustrated of everything else, it is undoubtedly in order not to be cheated of this pleasurable unease.

Early in January, Gorky wrote to Chekhov: "I hear that you're going to marry an actress with a foreign name. I don't believe it. But if it's true, then I'm glad." Tongues were indeed wagging about this marriage, as busily in Petersburg as in Moscow: Alexander, in fact, told Anton that he had heard it said that his brother was going to marry not one but two actresses. What gave these rumors a certain substance was the fact that Olga Knipper was never seen unaccompanied by Masha Chekhova. They were always visiting each other, and they went to meetings and parties together. Masha's letters to her brother were filled with praises for the actress, moreover, and Olga herself often added a few warm, unstudied phrases by way of postscript.

Chekhov did not answer Gorky's implied question: for fifteen years his plans for marriage had been a perpetual joke by which he was no longer amused. Besides, he had no idea of marrying Olga, and it seemed in fact that their long separation had not produced in him that crystallization of love so dear to Stendhal. By now he was writing to Olga only quite rarely, and the tone of these letters never went beyond that of a pleasant friendship. It was, rather, she who was pursuing him and who, without saying so outright, was asking for something different. When someone told her that Chekhov was going abroad, she asked him whether he had already forgot her. "No, no, that's impossible," she added, "I don't want that. For God's sake, write! I'm waiting, I'm waiting!"

Chekhov replied to such charming impatience in a tone that was almost angry and bitter. "Why are you in bad humor? You dream, you work, you hope . . . you laugh . . . what more do you need? With me it's different. I've been torn out of the ground. I don't live completely: I don't drink even though I like to drink. I like noise and I don't hear any. In short, I am now in the position of a transplanted tree that hesitates: is it going to acclimate itself or wither?" (February 10, 1900).

Now it was Olga's turn to be petulant. She reproached him for not understanding her and practicing a certain coquetry with her; his melancholy mood depressed her. Furthermore, he was making a fool of her, who was supposed (and who made herself supposed) to be so close to him. "All about me I hear talk of your new play," she wrote to him on March 22; "I'm the only one who knows nothing about anything that's going on. No one believes me when I'm asked about it and I just shrug in all honesty and say I know nothing."

Since January, on Chekhov's suggestion, plans had been under discussion for a spring tour in the Crimea by the Art Theater, and the "Actress Inspector" was much pleased by this. He mentioned it in almost every letter that he wrote—"I'm still dreaming that you'll all come to Yalta"—and when in February there was a momentary possibility that the project would be dropped, he made no secret of his very acute disappointment. He was vastly relieved when Stanislavsky, who was very eager for Chekhov to see his various versions of the plays, definitely scheduled the tour for the beginning of April, and he wrote to Vishnyevsky that he was greatly delighted at the thought of a reunion with everyone and the opportunity to admire the company in his own plays. Enthusiastic and indeed quite excited, he alerted all his friends and urged them to come to Yalta for the occasion.

Without the hope of this reunion with the Art Theater company —and Olga—it would have been difficult for him to endure this new winter in the Crimea, which was long, monotonous, and lonely. The "transplanted tree" was not successful in acclimating itself to Yalta: he was bored and he found time endless. He now had a study that suited his tastes, but he was discouraged and wrote hardly at all. Although he was visited by throngs of admirers, people who called themselves his friends, and young writers, he felt utterly alone. It was Gorky, who seemed to have taken Suvorin's place as his friend, to whom now he occasionally confided something of his infinite weariness of life. "Here in this damned Yalta, without letters, it's enough to make one fall apart.

. . . I'm tired, it seems to me that the winter has been dragging on for ten years," he wrote to Gorky on February 3. And a dozen days later he wrote: "I'm bored, not in the sense of *Weltschmerz*, not in the sense of disgust with existence, I'm simply bored without company, without music, which I love, without women, who don't exist in Yalta. I'm bored without caviar and without sauerkraut."

Fortunately he still had his gardening and his dogs. He had made up his mind to convert his pebbly empty land in Autka into a garden, and by sheer effort he was succeeding. "If I had not been a writer," he wrote to a friend, "I think I could have been a gardener." By this was a calumny against himself, for he was a gardener, and an excellent one. He had managed to blend the essences of north and south in his beloved "dabbler's garden," which was divided by a row of acacias: pale birches and rustling poplars were the neighbors of black cypresses, murmuring palms, and extravagant eucalyptuses. He had also planted fruit trees and above all rosebushes—these were his favorite flowers—whose soft or brilliant colors were everywhere.

The bassets he had had in Melikhovo had died and been replaced with two mongrels who followed him everywhere on his walks. When he sat on one of the many benches scattered about the garden, Chestnut, a fat, placid, dreamy dog, went to sleep in the sun at his feet, while Little Finger, more aggressive, stayed on his feet playing watchdog and barking whenever anyone came. Two gray storks with clipped wings had taken up residence in the garden. Curious but suspicious, they followed Chekhov at a distance when he trimmed his rosebushes. When Arseny, the handyman, came back from town with provisions, they would run to him, uttering hoarse cries and clacking their beaks, and offer for his delectation a kind of whirling-dervish dance.

Marx was sending Chekhov money and he was collecting large royalties on his plays. He deposited five thousand rubles in a bank account in Masha's name, and having taken a liking to another piece of land in Gurzuf, about a dozen miles east of Yalta, he bought it with its three-room cottage that overlooked the sea. In order to gain absolution from Masha for this rashness, he told her that all of them—she, their mother, and he—would spend their summer vacations there.

Early in April, a few days ahead of the Art Theater proper, which was not due to arrive in Sebastopol until April 7, Olga Knipper and Masha arrived in Yalta. Chekhov had written to Olga that he would be delighted to see her alone: "That way we'll have at least the time to talk, to take walks, and to see things," he wrote. But his hope was not fulfilled and he had little opportunity to be alone with her. Gorky too had just arrived in Yalta, and in addition Chekhov suffered a hemorrhage that compelled him to remain in his room. Although he had barely recovered, he insisted nonetheless on boarding a boat on April 9 for Sebastopol, where he arrived just in time for the Art Theater's first performance.

That night, concealed at the back of the director's box, he saw his *Uncle Vanya* for the first time, acted by a company that he had never before seen in public. It was a great success and in fact a triumph, and in spite of his shyness the author had to emerge from the obscurity of his box and acknowledge the numerous curtain calls of an enthusiastic audience. He also saw a performance of *Hedda Gabler*, which, he told Stanislavsky, corroborated his belief that "Ibsen was not a playwright." Then, without waiting for the final play, which was *The Sea Gull*, because he was again ill, he went back to Yalta on April 13.

The Art Theater company arrived there the following evening. This was a big event for the rather sleepy little resort, and in spite of a howling storm, quite a large crowd thronged the station to greet the actors with much noise, throwing of flowers, and jostling around the mountains of luggage as it was unloaded. On the next afternoon, the actors and actresses, augmented by a number of writers and artists who had come to Yalta expressly for the occasion—they included Ivan Bunin, Maxim Gorky, Alexander Kuprin, and Sergei Rachmaninov—flocked on foot and by carriage to a party in Autka given by Chekhov.

Cordial and smiling, he saw his house and garden filled with a peaceful but bustling invasion of their customary tranquility. Around tea tables, in the study, on the terrace, in the garden, groups gathered and talked: Gorky grew excited, Bunin made everyone laugh with his endless, typically Russian anecdotes, Masha and Olga went round with trays of pastry. Transformed, radiant, constantly taking his hands from behind his back to settle his glasses, Chekhov went from one cluster to another with a friendly remark for everyone.

It immediately became a habit to meet at Chekhov's, and during the ten days that the Art Theater spent in Yalta, actors and actresses thronged there every afternoon. They were attracted and conquered by what Olga Knipper called "the delightful warmth of the Chekhovs' home," that at once playful and affectionate atmosphere in which they could simultaneously enjoy the most serious conversations, schoolboy laughter, and the wildest dreams. They talked about art and literature, about the pleasure of being together, and, growing excited, about meeting in Yalta every year and even building a communal residence there. "Always eager to talk of what most interested him at the moment," Stanislavsky wrote later, "Anton Pavlovich went from one to another with the artlessness of a child with the same unvarying question: had this or that guest seen our productions yet? . . . Occasionally he withdrew into his study, apparently to get some rest."

On April 16 the company gave its first performance, Uncle Vanya, in the municipal theater before an audience of summer residents, teachers, officials, and local burghers. Chekhov's nerves were on edge—partly because of the presence of his mother, who had never seen any of his plays and had insisted on attending, especially dressed for the occasion in an old black silk dress discovered in a trunk, and partly because of the band playing in the nearby park and, seemingly, diabolically intent on sounding all its brasses fortissimo at the most moving moments of the play. Nevertheless it was a triumph and there was an ovation for the author. A week later, when the play was The Sea Gull, it was an even greater triumph, and after an ovation that seemed to have no end, Chekhov was solemnly presented with a scroll of congratulation containing almost two hundred signatures, including those of all his friends in the literary and art worlds.

Before they parted, Stanislavsky's group, Chekhov, and his friends were invited to a farewell dinner given by an enormously

wealthy admirer, Fanny Tatarina, on the roof garden of her sumptuous house. Then there were exchanges of farewell gifts: the actors gave the writer, as an ornament for his garden, the wooden
bench and the swing that had been used in the set for *Uncle
Vanya*, and Chekhov gave each of them a gold locket shaped like
a book and containing a miniature copy of the photograph that
showed him pretending to read *The Sea Gull* to them. On the
other side of Nemirovich-Danchenko's there was an inscription:
"You gave life to my *Sea Gull*. Thank you." After the actors had
gone Chekhov, happy and exhausted, wrote to a friend: "After a
long, boring winter, I have had to stay up every night until three
or four in the morning and dine in large groups, and all this for
two weeks. Now I am resting" (April 27, 1900).

He did not rest long. After the Art Theater's departure Yalta
seemed drearier and emptier than ever, and early in May he left
for Moscow, where he spent ten days. He visited Levitan, who
was dying, and he made every effort to conceal from Olga, "his
dear delightful actress," the fact that he too was ailing. He returned to Yalta but he allowed Gorky to persuade him to make a
two-week trip through the Caucasus with several friends.

They followed the famous "military road" through Georgia, visiting a number of monasteries though they were all unbelievers,
and stopped in Tiflis. In the train that was taking them to Batum,
Chekhov was surprised and delighted to encounter Olga, who had
gone to the Caucasus for a brief vacation with her mother; they
talked for six hours before they were separated again by a change
of trains. But not for long, for it had been agreed weeks earlier
that Olga would go to Yalta at the beginning of July.

Arriving there early in the month, she stayed with the Chekhovs until August 5. For the author and the actress these weeks
of continuing intimacy, their first in the two years during which
they had known each other, principally by letter, could result only
in the diminution of their reserve. Seeing Olga at all times of day,
growing more and more susceptible to her charm and her radiant
youth, Chekhov slipped almost without knowing it from the
lightly affectionate friendship to which he had thus far restricted
himself into love itself, blinding and passionate. Olga felt that at

last she was understood and knew that she was loved. They quickly became lovers.

For both of them these were splendid days of a rather mad passion, made the more delectable by the fact that they kept it jealously concealed. They had fallen into each other's arms one afternoon in the cottage in Gurzuf, to the soft music of the waves, or one evening in Chekhov's study. Thereafter, night after night, when Masha and her mother were sleeping upstairs, Olga came stealthily to Anton's study. She always wore the long white dress that he liked; playfully he let down her long black hair, allowing it to fall over her shoulders. Beyond the great arched windows they could see the garden, all black and silver and mysterious in the moonlight, as they talked quietly, Olga sang softly, and Anton, still the schoolboy, told stories. They embraced and spoke their love in whispers. Then, still without a sound, Olga would make delicious coffee and succulent jam sandwiches for him, and as they savored their clandestine *medianoche* they talked and laughed again in whispers like carefree students. When it was almost morning, Olga would go back to her room on tiptoe.

During this month of passion and intimacy they lived only for each other. Chekhov did no work, wrote only a few letters, resolutely barred friends and visitors. Were Masha and his mother, as he hoped, completely ignorant of what was going on or, as believed, had they soon guessed? In any event, they gave no sign and made no effort to interrupt the intimacy. There were only two false notes in this month of happiness: on July 22 Anton learned of the death of his friend Isaac Levitan which deeply grieved him, and, more comically, at the beginning of August he was unexpectedly visited by one of his former "sea gulls," Vera Kommissaryevskaya.

The beautiful actress, who had won the public's recognition and adulation, was on tour through the Crimea. She had never forgot the very gallant Chekhov who had told her one day, during the rehearsals for *The Sea Gull*: "My Nina had eyes like yours." Later she had made a subtle approach to him, sending him her photograph with a rather affectionate inscription taken from the play: "How good everything used to be. . . . What a bright, warm, joyful, pure life, what emotions like tender, graceful flowers." She and Chekhov met on August 3 in Gurzuf. It was a stormy day; they took a long walk on the beach, and then, in her beautiful deep voice that made audiences shiver, Vera recited Nina's monologue from *The Sea Gull* and some of Pushkin's poetry. She asked Chekhov to stay another day with her, and finally he promised to do so, but next morning she found that he had gone. He left her a photograph inscribed: "To Vera Kommissaryevskaya, August 3, a day of storm and noisy sea, from calm Anton Chekhov."

She preferred not to grasp what the adjective meant, and four days later she telegraphed: "I waited two days for you. We leave tomorrow for Yalta by boat. Your lack of perception saddens me. Will I see you? Please answer." Chekhov, on the contrary, was most perceptive, and his reply was a plea in estoppel: "It's very cold in Yalta and the sea is bad. Be healthy and happy. God keep you. Don't be angry with me." She sent him a final note: "I'm not angry, but when I think of your life, or what it is now, my heart aches." He did not reply.

Chekhov had of course been very careful not to let Vera Kommissaryevskaya know that he was in love, let alone in love with another actress. That he was very much in love with Olga, and was her lover as well, is convincingly enough demonstrated by the letters that he exchanged with her after her departure. By now he was using the intimate second-person form of address, dropping all reserve with her, and giving her pet names. On August 5 he had traveled with her by boat as far as Sebastopol, where he spent the night with her; then he put her aboard the train for Moscow. Three days later he wrote to her: "Hello, my dearest, my joy! . . . I am continually picturing the door opening suddenly and bringing you back. But you won't be back. . . . You are far from Yalta and me. . . . Good-bye, my good girl" (September 9, 1900).

In the beginning they wrote to each other several times a week. Neither of them could do anything without telling the other about it, and they were constantly repeating assurances of love. Chekhov wrote about the raging wind that was tormenting Yalta, his "prison," and about his work—he had gone back to it, proceeding with the draft of a play, *The Three Sisters*, begun a few months before—about his life, which was "neither gay nor sad but just so-so," about his unhappiness at the distance between them. And yet in spite of all these things how basically happy he was that he had found her! "My darling, glorious, magnificent actress, I'm alive, I'm well, I think and dream of you, and I feel absolutely alone without you. Take care of yourself and be happy, my wonderful little German. Don't be depressed" (October 13, 1900).

His little German replied by giving an account of herself: she had spent a weekend in the country, near Moscow, and it was a charming place: why could they not spend the next summer there? She reported on her successes: she had danced "until five-thirty, in a gold dress with a very low neckline." Both of them looked forward to an early reunion in Moscow. "When I arrive," Chekhov wrote, "we'll go to Petrovskoye-Razumovskoye again (a park just outside the city). But it will have to be for the whole day, and the weather will have to be right, good autumn weather, and you will have to be in a good mood and not tell me every minute that you have to dash off to a rehearsal" (August 20, 1900).

In Olga's eyes the relationship that had come into being between them could lead only to marriage. She had made up her mind that Chekhov belonged to her, and since in Russia it was often the woman who took the initiative in this kind of thing, she hoped to bring Chekhov round to making a proposal. On her return to Moscow she was so confident of her success that she talked to Nemirovich-Danchenko—who lost no time in retailing it to Stanislavsky—of her marriage to Chekhov "as a settled matter."

Meanwhile the weeks passed and Chekhov, who was already writing to her less often, still had not proposed marriage. He seemed indeed to be hesitating, not too convinced of the future of their sentimental adventure. Or did he already, perhaps, regret it? He showed no sign of jealousy when—undoubtedly with a purpose—she informed him that she had "sung and joked until two o'clock in the morning" in delightful company. In fact, he let it be clearly understood that he would find it almost normal of her to forget him: "I'm afraid of disappointing you," he wrote. "My hair is falling out terribly, so that—who knows?—in a week I may look like a bald old man. . . . My money is going as quickly, and my beard is turning white" (September 8, 1900). Would this affair not end like all the others? He was—or wanted to be—devoid of illusions. "By winter you'll have forgot what I look like. As for me, I'll be in love with someone else, I'll meet someone else just like you. And everything will go as before. . . ." No longer, as he had done earlier, did he mention going to Moscow soon to see her.

Besides, Chekhov was completely absorbed in something else at this time: he was working on a new manuscript. Urged on by Olga herself, who immediately on her return to Moscow had virtually issued an order—"Please write your play"—and dogged by Stanislavsky, who with his repertory in mind went to Yalta to discuss the subject with him, he had decided to develop the play about which he had been thinking for some time, *The Three Sisters*. In order to be able to work more consistently without intrusions, he had even gone alone to Gurzuf. But though he had his play well in mind and though he was being pressed to have it completed for the new theatrical season, he was not getting far in the writing.

Chekhov claimed to have been convinced by experience that a play should be written in a single inspiration, but this time it took him more than two months. Even he was surprised by the fact: "I'm writing slowly," he told Olga, "and this is something I hadn't anticipated" (August 30, 1900). No doubt there was good ground for his complaints about his visitors, who intruded on him constantly, but there was something else as well: he had absolutely no drive. There were days, he told Olga, when he was satisfied simply to sit for hours at his desk and think about his play, and then, when he could think of no lines, he was discouraged and picked up a newspaper. And before he could finish his play, he was beset by dangerous questions: was it perhaps too intellectual? Was it burdened with a plethora of characters? The most insidious problem of all was whether he might not be better advised to defer the writing of it for another year.

Frequently he asked Olga's forgiveness for not writing to her more often: she should not "be angry," because he was wrapped up in his play. Now Olga was in fact impatient and apprehensive. She made every letter a new assault: had he forgot his promise to come to Moscow? He replied with rather facile excuses: he had been ill for a week—"fever, coughing, a cold in the head"—and anyway was it not she was beginning to forget him? "You are damnably cold," he wrote, "as, I admit, an actress should be. Don't be angry, darling, I'm just saying that by the way" (September 15, 1900). Occasionally he was hard and almost cutting: for the moment he "had no desire to write to her," and in fact why should he go to Moscow? "To see you and go away again?" he asked sarcastically. "How delightful: make the journey, get a look at the audience in the theater, and leave" (September 22, 1900).

Chekhov had never liked rows and scenes, but Olga seemed not yet to have recognized this. So she was insistent: "Why don't you come, Anton? . . . What's keeping you? What's worrying you? I don't know what to think and I feel horribly uneasy. . . . I want to weep every day" (September 24, 1900). He was so hard and so cold with her, and she had the impression that he was concealing something from her. In an oblique fashion she reverted to her ideas of marriage and asked him what he had in mind: people were beginning to talk about them and openly hint at their future marriage.

Chekhov replied to these complaints with a mixture of irony and affection, though never addressing himself to their essence. "To judge from your letter," he wrote, "you want and expect an explanation, a long discussion with solemn faces and serious consequences. But I don't know what to tell you, except what I've already told you ten thousand times and what I'll undoubtedly go on telling you for a long time to come: and that is that I love you and that's that. If we aren't together at the moment, it's neither my fault nor yours but the Devil's: he's filled me with bacilli and you with the love of art" (September 27, 1900).

But too good-hearted as always, Chekhov was soon to give in. On October 16 his play was finished, for better or worse, and next day he telegraphed to Olga that he would leave "without fail" on the twenty-first for Moscow. His health was bad and his throat was giving him trouble, he had begun coughing again, and he wrote to Gorky: "In Yalta the weather is marvelous and healthy. . . . One doesn't want to leave here even for Moscow." But a few days later, as he had promised, he arrived in the capital and went to the Hotel Dresden in Tverskaya Street, in the heart of the city.

He planned to spend a maximum of two weeks in Moscow; he stayed seven weeks. He had rediscovered the urban life that he loved. He was a regular customer of the Art Theater, often with Gorky, and he attended rehearsals as well as performances. He saw several performances of *Uncle Vanya* and *The Sea Gull;* the ovations of the audiences made him smile. In November his portrait was painted by V. A. Serov. In addition he went out a great deal with Olga, Chaliapin, Gorky, and other friends, and since he enjoyed sitting late in restaurants like The Slavic Bazaar or The Hermitage, it was often well after midnight when he returned to his hotel. He paid for all this, of course, in higher temperatures, violent headaches, and accesses of coughing, but he no longer talked of going back to the Crimean coast.

Naturally, it was Olga most of all who kept him in Moscow. He saw her every day, first in the theater and then in the Hotel Dresden, where she joined him after the rehearsals. They no longer had to adopt the precautions of the previous summer in Yalta, and out of sight of Masha and his mother they could stay together as late as they liked. Olga pampered him, took every care of him, made his tea. And in a kind of role reversal, it was she who brought him candy and flowers and little tokens. For a few hours of every day no thought was given to "bacilli and the love of art."

Chekhov had brought the manuscript of *The Three Sisters* with him, and soon after his arrival Stanislavsky held a reading of it in the theater's green room, in the presence of the entire company. Initially extremely auspicious and, so to speak, electrified by the author's presence, the atmosphere turned hostile as the reading progressed, and when it had ended, Olga was to say later, "there was a kind of stupefaction, dead silence." To conceal his disquiet, Chekhov smiled, coughed nervously, and went to talk to one after another of the actors. Everyone's courage soon began to rise, and as the conversation became general Olga picked up bits of comment here and there: "It isn't really a play, it's just a skeleton . . . it would be impossible to act this, there are no characters, just profiles here and there." There was general uncertainty: was this a tragedy or a comedy? When one actor said, addressing no one in particular: "Even though in principle I don't agree with the author, still . . ." Chekhov walked out. No one except Stanislavsky was aware of his departure; the director, afraid that Chekhov might be ill, hurried to his hotel. He found Chekhov in an extremely vile humor. "That can't be possible!" he exclaimed. "Really: 'in principle'!"

But he soon saw Stanislavsky again, talked about the play more calmly, and promised to revise it. Methodical as always, he got down to this immediately, and he redid the first two acts completely during his stay in Moscow. But the reaction of the Art Theater's actors had discouraged him nonetheless. On November 13 he wrote to Vera Kommissaryevskaya, who wanted to perform *The Three Sisters* "as a benefit for herself" in Petersburg, and tried to dissuade her. "In the last analysis," he told her, "my play is boring, monotonous, and unpleasant."

His revision of *The Three Sisters* had not been finished when he finally decided to leave Moscow on December 11. Since he could not bare the prospect of another endless winter in his hermitage in Yalta, he had decided to go back to Nice. Olga was in tears when they parted. He broke his journey in Vienna, where, from the Hotel Bristol, he wrote her a charming letter that showed how deeply he too regretted the interruption of their seven weeks of intimacy in Moscow. "I still see the two beds in our room with the most eager desire; I'm going to sleep and think. But it's a shame that I am alone here, without you, my wicked child, my darling—an appalling shame" (December 12, 1900).

During Chekhov's stay in Moscow, Suvorin had resumed contact with him after months of silence and gone to visit him. Chekhov, who did not really feel that they had quarreled—he had said as much a few months earlier to his brother Misha—had been very pleased to see him, and shortly afterward he had sent Suvorin a pleasant note of congratulation on his daughter's marriage. He sent his warmest good wishes to the whole Suvorin family, "to whom," he said, "I feel bound almost as closely as to my own." Then, speaking of himself, he added a remark that would certainly have wounded Olga if she had known of it: "Have you heard that I am going to marry? It isn't true."

Even though his recollections of it were not too cordial, Chekhov went back to the Russian *pension* in the rue Gounod in Nice. It was really a bit of Russia, and nothing about it had changed since his previous visit: there were still the same French chambermaids "with the manners of duchesses," the amazing Russian cook and her Negro husband, and at mealtimes the same old ladies from Kharkov and elsewhere, those "dreadful scarecrows." It gave him more pleasure to rediscover his old card-playing companions, Yurasov, the Vice-Consul, Professor Kovalevsky, and Yakobi, the painter. But what was most important was the sun, the soft air— in short, spring in the middle of winter. "The roses are blooming," he wrote almost as soon as he arrived. "There are other flowers too. I can't believe my eyes." A day later he wrote: "I feel as if I were on the moon. It is hot, the sun is shining, the windows of my room are wide open, and so are those of my spirit. I am recopying my play and I'm amazed that I've written such a thing" (December 15, 1900).

His primary concern, in fact, was the completion of *The Three Sisters*, and the more so because the first two acts had already gone into rehearsal in the Art Theater. He worked with his usual speed. He made only minor changes in the third act, but he totally reworked the fourth; then he recopied both. Nevertheless he was able to send the revised manuscript to Stanislavsky less than a week after his arrival in France.

He was apprehensive, however, over the fate of *The Three Sisters*. It disturbed him that the rehearsals were being held without him. He was afraid that the actors would not fully understand their parts and that Stanislavsky might interpolate one or another of those details of naturalistic staging of which he was the master and that Chekhov loathed. "Describe even one rehearsal of *The Three Sisters* to me," he wrote to Olga. "Shouldn't something be added or subtracted? Are you acting well, darling?" Naturally this was followed by suggestions: "Look: in the first act don't seem sad. Annoyed, yes, but not sad. People who have carried a grief within them for a long time and grown accustomed to it are satisfied to whistle and often be meditative. Similarly, on stage, seem pensive often. You understand?" (January 3, 1901).

It was not only Olga on whom he lavished his counsels. For more than a month he was to be in continual communication with Stanislavsky, to whom he offered urgent suggestions on staging, and with the actors, to whom he explained how he envisaged their parts. He concerned himself with the most trivial details: he advised Vishnyevsky, who was playing the part of Kuligin, to wear evening clothes only in the first act. As for the actor playing Solioni, he was to make himself up "Lermontov-style."

There were several officers among the characters in the play. Afraid lest they become caricatures, Chekhov asked Stanislavsky to avoid this and, on the contrary, to show that in the little provincial town in which the play was laid they were really part of the local intellectual elite. With his great concern for details he even assigned a friend, Colonel V. Petrov, to attend the rehearsals and check on the authenticity of the uniforms and the behavior of these stage warriors. But he had not anticipated that the good colonel would take his mission so seriously that he would bitterly reproach Chekhov for allowing his hero, the married officer Vershinin, to seduce another man's wife: this was an immoral action in violation of the army regulations.

In spite of their weeks of intimacy in Moscow, his relations with Olga were still in a state of affectionate ambivalence. They wrote a great deal to each other, but they did not write the same language at all. She was importunate; he was charming but slightly skeptical, and he carefully avoided any promise of marriage.

Olga had wept copiously at his departure; the next day she wrote: "You know, Anton, I'm afraid to dream, or, rather, to tell my dreams aloud, but it seems to me that something beautiful and strong is going to grow out of our love. When I allow myself to believe that, I want to live and work, and the little things in life no longer bother me. I no longer wonder why I'm alive" (December 11, 1900). To this invitation to discuss the future of their love Chekhov replied without answering, with a kind of evasion. Yes, he loved her, he "kissed her affectionately," he embraced her "furiously," and yet: "I love you, but, to be honest, you don't understand it. You need a husband, or, rather, a spouse with an official's badge and side-whiskers, but what am I? Nothing very definite" (January 2, 1901). He wished her all possible joys for the new year and a love that would last for fifteen years. But he added, "Do you think there could be such a love? On my side, yes; on yours, no" (January 3, 1901). And, still the schoolboy, he signed his letters "Your Elder," or "Academician Toto," or "Anton, the Monk," or (in French) "ton Antoine."

He also asked Olga to write to him "often, often," and to send him Russian newspapers. For, as was to be expected with him, after the first few days of bedazzlement, Nice was already beginning to bore him. He soon had enough of playing the dandy in his summer topcoat on the Promenade des Anglais. Of course it was delightful to savor springtime in winter, to see so many flowers, beautiful ladies, and bicycles, but this was all out of a fashion drawing; it was wearying just as it was wearying to see his old friends, who were too many and too intrusive and who prevented him from working. But he could not manage to work because he was so devoid of drive. Was it because *The Three Sisters* had drained him, or had he grown old? "I don't know," he told Olga. "I ought not to write for five years but to travel for that time, and then come back and get down to work" (January 21, 1901).

He was thinking again of going to Algeria with his friend Kovalevsky, but in fact it was Rome for which they set out on January 27. He sent notes to Olga from Pisa and Florence: "Whoever has not seen Italy has not lived," he told her repeatedly. In Rome, under the guidance of a Russian professor and in the company of "two very pleasant ladies," he conscientiously toured the ruins of the ancient city. "I've bought an umbrella for Masha," he wrote to Olga, "but not the right one, I'm afraid. I've also bought handkerchiefs, probably not much better. . . . Rome is not Paris. . . ." Less casual with Kovalevsky, he told him bluntly one day: "As a doctor I know my life will be short."

It was in Rome, after a few days' delay as a result of his travels, that Chekhov learned that *The Three Sisters* had been performed on January 31. Telegrams from Olga and Nemirovich-Danchenko assured him that it had been a great success. This was not precisely the truth: as Stanislavsky was to acknowledge later, this first performance had been only moderately well received. Audience and critics alike had been perplexed by this almost static play, by its strange characters, by its often disjointed dialogue, frequently broken by silences, and by its uninterrupted counterpoint of symbols and realities. V. Lavrov was more honest, writing to Chekhov: "A success? Not so brilliant as that of *The Sea Gull*" (February 1, 1901).

In Rome the weather had abruptly turned cold: it was snowing.

Chekhov abandoned his plan of going on to Naples, and on February 7 he left by ship for Yalta by way of Odessa with the intention of "writing and writing."

During the ensuing weeks there, in fact, he was to write one of his finest stories: "The Bishop." The theme of it, he told Olga, had been "in his head for perhaps fifteen years," but undoubtedly it was even more in his heart. For in this revealing story, much more than anywhere else, Chekhov appears in filigree behind his character, that bishop who knows that he is soon going to die. Through him Chekhov tells us of the kind of disabused astonishment that he felt when he found himself in that zone between life and death, in what J. Reverzy has called "the corridor." Already his hero feels separated from the world of the living as if by a screen, he considers himself "more insignificant than anyone," and he has almost reached the bottom of that solitude into which he has been plunged for years. Before his surrender to death he would like to flee one last time, to "go abroad again." It is a sigh: "If at least there had been a single person to whom he could have talked, opened his heart. . . ."

There are works of art that take much time to come to maturity —to reach "the bottom of the filter," as Chekhov said—and this was particularly the case of *The Three Sisters*. This play was written in 1899 with the assistance of recollections of youth, some of which went back more than fifteen years. It brings back to life the world discovered by young Dr. Chekhov in Vosskressensk during his vacations in 1883 and the following years: a sleepy provincial town, where garrison officers and intellectuals are rotting with boredom and dreaming of escape. These recollections were blended with those of other vacations, spent a few years later in Luka in the Ukraine, in the dacha of the three Lintvaryeva sisters. Chekhov's fantasies and imagination brought the Luka girls and the Vosskressensk officers together, and the idea for the play was born.

But it was still to be written. "It was frightfully difficult for me to write *The Three Sisters*," Chekhov confided to Gorky. "Consider that there are three heroines—each has to have an individual personality, and all three are the daughters of a general! The action

takes place in a little provincial town, in the world of officers."
The three sisters are certainly alike, above all in their nostalgia for
Moscow, their stubborn and rather mad hope of escaping from
their provincial backwater, where "boredom stifles them as chaff
chokes off wheat," and returning to the metropolis of their
dreams. Moscow, alas, is at once as close and as unattainable as
Kafka's castle.

At the same time, too, as Chekhov intended, the general's three
daughters have individual personalities. Olga, the eldest, is a tall,
rather stiff, melancholy girl, certain that "everything in life happens against our wishes," already resigned to failing in life and
dying a spinster. She has become a teacher without a true vocation, and all she thinks about is getting out of her profession while
at the same time lacking the courage to embark on anything that
might help to fulfill her dream. Masha, the second sister, has made
a love marriage with a schoolteacher as stupid as he is pompous,
and, disappointed in this marriage, she projects her disillusion on
life as a whole: "What a foul life!" she says. "What a doomed life!"
She too takes refuge in dreams, but hers are sad and sullen. Irina,
the youngest, has not yet been scarred by "the erosion of life": gay
as a canary, she is at first concerned with nothing but love and
devotion. But she has already known the first disappointments,
her splendid courage withers, and she too elects the world of
dreams.

A random event is to awaken all three dreamers. A regiment is
posted to the little town, and at once everything is altered for the
three sisters. Their solitude is invaded, they lose their taste for
dreams, they begin to enjoy life again; some of the officers become
their assiduous visitors, and there is talk and flirtation; there are
dreams too, but these are now shared. Olga gets back her courage
and swears that she will do anything to get away from her school;
Masha rediscovers love in the person of Major Vershinin; Irina is
surrounded by adulation and finally accepts a proposal of marriage from another of the officers.

Life has apparently triumphed over dreams. But unfortunately
the illusion lasts no longer than the time of a garrison assignment.
After a few months the regiment is transferred, the officers make
their farewells to the young women, and as the military band's

music fades into the distance, silence and torpor recapture the town. For the three sisters it means rejection into loneliness and the end of a lovely dream that sends them back to their melancholy destinies. Olga's ardor wanes and she resigns herself to never being anything but a teacher and an old maid. Masha, whose passion was a mere chimera, remains with her husband, falls back into resentment, and prepares to grow old ungracefully. As for Irina, whose husband-to-be is killed in a duel, she will be a little provincial widow who has never been married. The horizon is dark and fogbound, and the three sisters no longer even dream of going to Moscow. . . .

Since its first performance by the Art Theater at the turn of the century this play has had a success that has never been tarnished. But one can be sure that the audiences who applaud it in every country in the world today do not have the same reasons or the same emotions as Chekhov's contemporaries. This is because plays that endure almost always have two themes, one of which, quite obvious and current, earns the play an immediate success, while the other, less apparent but also more permanent and susceptible of moving every audience, does not emerge for a long time. What made Russians flock to *The Three Sisters* in 1899 was the mirror that Chekhov held up to them and that showed them "the laziness, the indifference, and the boredom in which our Russia has too long indulged herself." As for today's spectator, if he still feels a fraternal complicity with the three sisters, it is because, just like them, he is still in search of "the meaning of life."

The deadly boredom of Russian provincial life presses down with all its weight on *The Three Sisters,* to the point of imbuing it with a climate of suffocation and disquiet that is almost intolerable. "This town has existed for two hundred years," Andrey, the sisters' brother, sighs; "it has a hundred thousand inhabitants, and there is not one among them who is not identical with all the others. . . . All they do is eat, drink, sleep—and then die." This "decomposition of boredom," which in the end overbears the strongest of characters, is composed of an immeasurable monotony that leads to inanity, laziness, and the vulgarity that makes poor Masha suffer so keenly. It is composed too of loneliness, because though one knows everyone there and everyone knows one-

self, there is no place where one feels more alone, more abandoned than in these narrow, these stifling little provincial worlds.

How did the rest, their neighbors, manage to avoid annihilation
by boredom? Andrey provides the answer: "They amuse themselves with malicious gossip, . . . cards, swindles, . . . *kvass,*
goose and cabbage, naps after meals. . . . " He himself, with his
rather weak character, employs defenses that are hardly more
lofty: he loafs, he plays the violin, he makes little frames for photographs, and when he has had enough of all this, he goes to his
club to get drunk and gamble—and lose. He is resigned to the fact
that his sole future is at best to become a city councilor, and he
consoles himself with nightly dreams "that he is a great scholar of
whom the nation is proud." His sisters, however, hold out better
against the quicksand: they believe in the value of work, and in
spite of their disappointments, they continue to interrogate themselves on "the meaning of life" and to hope that one day they will
learn it.

The meaning of life. . . . It is this question, continually stated
or implied but never resolved, on which the whole play is
founded. Around this central theme Chekhov built his drama like
a musical composition, a series of questions in many voices that
cross, harmonize, contradict one another, soar, or sink in despair.
The impatient inquiries of the three sisters are countered by the
more skeptical questions, often not even requiring responses, of
the officers—Major Vershinin, Lieutenant Tusenbach, Major Chebutikin. "But life does have a meaning, just the same?" Masha
cries. And Tusenbach replies: "What meaning? Look, see the
snow falling. What meaning does it have?"

The two older girls try to understand, but without much hope.
To Olga everything in life happens "against our wishes," and to
Masha it is not the vain knowledge that we have acquired that is
going to help see us through this "schoolboy farce." Little Irina
thinks that she has understood: "If we look darkly on life," she
says, "it is because we know nothing of work. . . . One must
work, work." But time erodes her ardor. Work does not bring her
the expected answer, and she sighs: "Time passes and it seems to
me that one draws always farther away from life, from life that is
beautiful, that one goes always farther toward a kind of abyss."

The chorus of the three sisters, as we have noted, is answered by the chorus of the officers of the garrison. The gloomiest is Major Chebutikin, who declares that he knows nothing, that no one knows anything, and who reaches the stage of doubting even his own existence. Life, he finds, goes by too quickly to embark on anything, and he cries: "Ah, if only one could not exist at all!" Tusenbach believes, as he does, that life has its own laws "that we shall never know." But it seems to him that in spite of everything man advances, he has "the nostalgia of work," and in addition a presentiment that "something enormous" is in preparation, a gigantic storm "that will soon rage over this old society and sweep away its laziness, its indifference, its prejudices against work, and the rot of boredom." As for Major Vershinin, he is wholly committed to a glowing vision of the future. To him the present is of no importance except insofar as our struggles and our sufferings lay the foundation for those beautiful tomorrows: "We suffer, yes, but we are creating the future, and that alone is the meaning of our lives, our happiness if you prefer."

At the end of the play there is a kind of general agreement in which it is the hope in the future that triumphs. "A day will come," Irina says, "when one will know the reason for all this, for all this suffering. There will be no more mystery. . . . Meanwhile one must live. . . . One must work, only work." Everyone promises to set to work, even the rich Tusenbach, even the skeptical Chebutikin, who swears that he will "change his life . . . to the very roots." But for all that, these fine dreams and splendid resolves have clarified nothing, and the last line is Olga's sigh: "Oh, if one could only know. If one could only know!"

But to summarize *The Three Sisters* by analyzing its themes, as we have just done, is to commit a treason against the play, which is beyond doubt the most Chekhovian of all its author's work. In none of the other plays are the light so filtered and changing, the action so everyday and at the same time static, the characters so constantly and subtly diluted, the silences so eloquent. Everything in this long dramatic poem is fluid. Here even more than in *The Sea Gull*, in which perhaps the poetry is somewhat too studied and the symbols too obvious, we see poetry take over the stage.

"When I write," Chekhov said in 1890, "I stake everything on the reader and expect him to be able on his own to add the subjective elements that are not in my story." In *The Three Sisters* he relied on the spectator, and it was because he was constantly appealing to that spectator's innermost "poetic" collaboration that he won his gamble. Chekhov did not call on the spectator to anticipate the course of the plot as it developed because there was no such course; he did not expect the spectator to become indignant or excited on behalf of others but to plunge into himself. Simply but in a very subtle, irresistible fashion, with half-finished sentences and questions left unanswered, he called on the spectator to ask himself in his turn what was the meaning of life, to remember and wonder whether happiness was anything but an illusion. This is how Chekhov's poetry insensibly glides from the stage into the whole theater.

When the play has ended and the final curtain has fallen, it takes time for the enchantment to dissolve. For certain lines are so simple—and so unsettling—so disturbing in their simplicity that unconsciously the spectator retains them. He leaves the theater, goes to a restaurant, and as he chooses what he is to eat, he remembers Andrey's utterly commonplace remark: "All they do is eat, drink, sleep—and then die," or that other observation of Chekhov's: "People are at dinner, simply at dinner, and while they are eating, their happiness is being built or their lives are being shattered."

"Bunin is here," Chekhov wrote to Olga shortly after his return to Yalta. "He comes to see me every day, and I am glad." Actually Ivan Bunin had been in Yalta for some time, and during Chekhov's absence he had already become an intimate of the family. At Masha's invitation he had stayed with her and her mother in the villa in Autka for several weeks. This slender young man of aristocratic origin and most elegant manners—who was both so convinced a Tolstoyan that he had "given up all his wealth to follow the master" and a writer who was beginning to be talked about —was a delightful guest. The Chekhov women had very quickly and affectionately adopted him and, indeed, the embryo of a kind of loving friendship had begun to grow between him and Masha.

When she had to go back to Moscow to resume her teaching, it was at her request that Bunin remained with her mother, to whom he gave great pleasure because he was an excellent and tireless storyteller.

Chekhov too was won over by Bunin's charm and they understood each other perfectly. Chekhov soon gave him one of those affectionate nicknames that were his specialty: to Chekhov, Bunin looked like a French marquis whose picture he had seen in the newspapers, and he called him Monsieur Bouquichon. Bunin, who was ten years younger than Chekhov and regarded the older man as his master in the art of writing, felt only admiring affection for him. Both men, too, had many tastes—and distastes—in common: they liked nature and simple living, scorned the new literary school of the "decadent" symbolists, and profoundly admired Tolstoy. They were constantly laughing like schoolboys, and they both delighted in practical jokes. One evening, as they were walking back to Yalta from the country, Chekhov suddenly began to shout at the top of his voice: "Bunin's been murdered!" Then he whispered to Bunin: "Tomorrow the whole town will be talking about your murder."

Bunin had an extraordinarily keen eye and he has left us an amazingly alive and colorful portrait of the forty-one-year-old Chekhov whom he had just come to know: he was tall, slender, always dressed with meticulous care—he would have died of shame if he had been seen without a necktie and a waistcoat—and though his voice was often stern, his warm smile, frequent, unpredictable, and fleeting, was that of a child. His hands were long, dry, and esthetically pleasing. "His eyes," Bunin wrote, "were so bright and so gentle when he was not wearing his usual pince-nez." This poet, who, it is true, was still a bachelor, had a mania for order in everything: he arranged things meticulously around him and he showed his irritation when vague or vulgar words were used in his presence. But with everyone—servant girls, gardeners, great ladies—he had an exquisite courtesy characterized by patience and a great gentleness.

Alexander Kuprin, who met him at the same time—when Chekhov was passing through Odessa—was to recount that on their first meeting Chekhov, with his innocent air and his eyeglasses on a ribbon, reminded him of a country doctor or a provincial professor. But he very soon discovered that Chekhov, with his irresistible smile and his brown eyes verging on blue—to the point that some people said that they were really blue—had "the most beautiful, the most sensitive, the most spiritual face that one could ever see."

His reserve was so remarkable that had it not been for his kindness, it might have been taken for coldness, and he had as well a fierce modesty. He rarely communicated his impressions and he never, even with his literary colleagues, spoke of his projects. According to Kuprin, furthermore, it was very seldom that his conversation "hinted at the artist, the writer." Similarly, he never complained about his health, mentioned it as little as possible, and even though as a physician he knew that he was inevitably doomed to a short life, he refused still to face the truth. "Even on days when he was suffering most," Bunin wrote, "no one could guess the fact." Finding him in his armchair with his eyes closed, his mother or his sister would ask: "Don't you feel well, Anton?" He would open his eyes and say casually: "Me? Oh, it's nothing, just a little headache." He appreciated this kind of reserve in others as well, and he shunned the pitiful, the violent, and the tragic.

He was very seriously ill; and he was alone, more alone than ever, in that kind of limbo that is the antechamber to death, but even if at a reduced pace, he continued to work and live as if nothing were wrong. Bunin has described one of his days: "Everything is silent in Chekhov's house except for the regular ticking of an alarm clock in Yevgenia Yakovlevna's room. Chekhov, without his glasses, is sitting at his desk and writing something methodically but without haste. Then he gets up, takes his overcoat, his hat, and his galoshes, goes out, and visits one of his mousetraps. He returns holding a live mouse by the tail, goes out again, crosses the lawn, and goes as far as the wall behind which the Tartar cemetery lies on a rocky hill. He carefully throws the mouse over the wall and comes back, at the same time carefully examining the saplings in the garden. He is followed by a tame stork and two little dogs. Chekhov sits down on a bench in the middle of the garden and pokes his cane at one of the dogs lying on its back at his feet. He smiles: there are fleas running along the dog's pink belly. . . . Then Chekhov leans back and looks toward Yalta in the distance, his head raised and his expression thoughtful. And so he remains for an hour, an hour and a half. . . ."

What was discussed in those long conversations with Bunin? There was often talk of literature, much talk of Tolstoy, and very little of politics. And yet public affairs were agitating many minds in Russia in that spring of 1901. As a result of his work on behalf of the persecuted sects, Tolstoy had just been excommunicated by the Holy Synod, and large crowds were demonstrating in his defense in both capitals. In Petersburg there were throngs waiting to view Repin's portrait of him. Student disorders had erupted, leading to the closing of the universities; in Kazan the Cossacks had charged into the demonstrators and many students had been killed.

The excitement had communicated itself to Gorky; he wrote to Chekhov that his "nerves were strained to the breaking point" in anticipation of some great event. "One feels that something is lurking near . . . a monstrous black beast waiting and wondering whom it is going to devour." But Chekhov himself was completely tranquil. He did not reply to Gorky's proposal of raising funds for the students.If Kuprin is to be believed, "the absurdity of Russian realities" wounded Chekhov and he gave it close attention, but he avoided speaking of it. His extreme reserve extended also to current problems, and lest he fall into theatrical postures and verbal violences, he preferred to say nothing.

One evening Bunin was in Chekhov's study, reading aloud his friend's "Gusev." When he had finished the story, which ends with a description of a sunset in the Indian Ocean, Bunin admitted that ever since childhood it had been his dream to travel over distant seas. He was interrupted when Chekhov suddenly said in a low voice: "Did you know I am going to marry?" But he immediately turned the matter into a joke: was it not better to marry a German rather than a Russian? a German would be more useful and would not allow their children to run through the house banging spoons against pots. "Of course I knew about his romance with Olga Leonardovna Knipper," Bunin said, "but I was not sure that it would end in marriage." He said nothing of his own views to Chekhov, but contemplating the world from which Olga came, her career as an actress, and the conflicts that would inevitably arise between her and Masha, he reflected that this was "really suicide, worse than Sakhalin!"

On his return to Yalta in mid-February, Chekhov had telegraphed to Olga: "Full of love and sad without my poodle." Next day he wrote to her: "My precious, my divine treasure, I throw my arms around you and kiss you passionately." He was eager to see her again and he suggested that they meet at Easter. In the letters that followed he was insistent: Olga must promise to come and join him after what had become the Art Theater's traditional spring visit to Petersburg. Would she prefer that he go to Moscow? Unfortunately he did not feel well enough to risk the journey.

He was most eager to see her, then, but since he still did not mention marriage, Olga finally became angry. Their friends were now openly talking about their marriage, but was he never going to make up his mind? Did he expect that she would always be satisfied to be his mistress and come to him on the sly at night, in his study? "You have so subtle a soul," she wrote to him on March 3, "and you ask for me. Is it possible that you don't understand?" She refused to go to Yalta for Easter. She did not want to expose herself again, as she had done the summer before, to his mother's pained expressions and Masha's shocked looks. "Do you remember how painful it was that summer, how torturing?" she wrote. "How long are we going to go on hiding? And why? It seems to me that you no longer love me as you used to and that all that you want is that I come to you and dance attendance on you. You don't think of me as someone close to you."

In the face of such pressure what could Chekhov do but give in? He detested scenes, but he wanted Olga badly and after all it was perhaps she who was right. Besides, he was no longer so desirous of fighting to maintain that freedom from all shackles that he had hitherto believed to be so essential for the artist and to which he had clung so fiercely. Moreover, even if he did give in to Olga, she could never succeed in gaining control of his deepest self, which had been made virtually impregnable by the long habit of se-

crecy. There was, of course, his precarious health, but Olga had
been forewarned of that, so why, when the happiness that he had
never believed in for himself was at last offered to him, refuse it
any longer? Why not try to be happy for the little time—he reckoned it at six years more—he still had to live?

Olga won, then, and completely. On March 6 he wrote to her
not only that he would go to Moscow at Easter to join her but also
that he accepted the idea of marriage. Nevertheless he issued a
mild warning: he was weary of running back and forth and his
health was that of an old man, so what she would get in him was
not a husband but "a grandfather." All that he now enjoyed was
gardening and solitude. "I've completely abandoned literature,"
he wrote to her, "and, once I've married you, I'll demand that you
give up the theater and we'll live together like planters. You don't
like that? All right, then, go on acting for, say, five years, and then
we'll see. . . ."

Meanwhile Olga was hugely enjoying her life as an actress forever surrounded by admirers and parties. On its visit to Petersburg at the beginning of March the Art Theater was given a triumphal reception: parties and dinners for the company were endless. At the Writers' Union dinner Olga held the place of honor,
"in a black velvet dress with a little lace collar, and a fresh treatment from the hairdresser." She and her colleagues enjoyed themselves like schoolboys on vacation: boatrides, skiing, trips to Finland, snowball fights. Did she have any pangs of conscience
when, sunburned and relaxed, she returned to Moscow? In any
event, just as Chekhov was preparing to leave for Moscow, she
unexpectedly arrived on Yalta on March 30.

She stayed two weeks. Undoubtedly one of the purposes of her
journey was the final resolution of the question of their marriage,
but when she went back to Moscow accompanied by Masha, she
was still uncertain as to Chekhov's real intentions. Hence she had
barely got home when she wrote to the lover whom she had just
left "with a bitter taste in her mouth." This letter was virtually an
order, and without equivocation: he should come to Moscow and
they would finally marry.

Weary of the struggle, Chekhov capitulated. But he did so
without enthusiasm, too ill to contemplate it otherwise than apa-

thetically: he was surrendering his destiny into Olga's hands. He promised to go to Moscow and marry her in May. "It's you," he wrote to her on April 22, "who will have to think of the future and run things in my place: and what you decide I'll do. Otherwise, instead of really living, we'll go on drinking little sips of life at the rate of a spoonful an hour."

Four days later he confirmed his promise to marry her, in spite of his aversion to ceremonies. "Olga, my poodle," he wrote, "I'm coming at the beginning of May. . . . If you give me your word that no one in Moscow will know about our marriage until after the wedding, I'll marry you the day I arrive, if you like. I don't know why but I have a terrible dread of the wedding ceremony and the ritual congratulations, the glass of champagne that one has to hold while one smiles off into the void. . . ." Let her have no fear: he would not forget to arm himself with the required documents. And he added a pathetic note: "Everything's in order here except one very minor detail: my health" (April 26, 1901).

In fact his health had grown steadily worse during the past few weeks. It was an effort for him to move, exhausted as he was by atrocious spasms of coughing. Early in May he wrote to Olga that he was spending his days sitting in his study and never leaving it, "thinking and coughing." But he would keep his promise: "We'll do everything you want. I am in your power" (May 2, 1901).

He arrived in Moscow on May 11 and moved into the Hotel Dresden. He was determined to keep his matrimonial plans secret to the very end. He did not mention them to either Masha or Ivan, both of whom were in Moscow. When his sister had gone back to Yalta to rejoin their mother, he wrote to her on May 17 to tell her that the specialist who had just examined him had found that his lungs had deteriorated further and had ordered a two-month kumiss* cure in the province of Ufa. But he continued to keep his plans secret, and suspecting that Masha might have guessed something, he even tried almost underhandedly to lead her astray. "To go there alone would be a bore," he wrote, "and to live on kumiss is equally a bore, but to ask someone to go with me would be selfish and unjust. I'd be glad to marry, but I don't have the necessary papers: they're in my desk in Yalta." This was a calcu-

* A fermented beverage with a mare's milk base.—TRANSLATOR.

lated lie, because, on Olga's advice, he had brought the papers
with him. Resolved to keep his secret to the end, he said nothing
to his brother Ivan either, when he ran into him on the wedding
morning itself.[4]

Chekhov's aversion to "ceremonies" and facile sentimentality
also induced him to hide his plans from his best friends until the
end. In order better to mislead them, he even thought of asking
Vishnyevsky, the actor, to arrange on his behalf a dinner for May
25—the wedding date—at which the guests would be his and
Olga's relatives and friends. And while their guests were waiting
for them, they were being married in a little church in the city.
Present at the ceremony were only the four witnesses required by
law: Olga's brother and uncle and, for Chekhov, two unknown
students. The couple then went to say good-bye to Olga's mother
and set off at once for the railway station to board the train for
Nizhni-Novgorod, the first stop on their honeymoon. Before they
left, Chekhov sent two telegrams, one to Vishnyevsky to announce
the marriage to him and the bewildered guests, the other to his
mother. "Dear Mother," he said, "give me your blessing. I'm married. Everything will be the same as before. I'm leaving for my
kumiss cure. Address: Aksenevo. . . . Health finest."

The newlyweds spent one day in Nizhni-Novgorod in order to
see Gorky, who was under police observation and house arrest.
Then they sailed down the Volga, up the Kama and the White
River, and landed at Aksenevo. It was in a sanitarium there that
they would spend their strange honeymoon.

Chekhov could not have been unaware that by marrying, and
even more by hiding the fact from her until the last minute, he
was deeply wounding Masha. Hence he wrote to her, in an effort
at self-justification, the day after his arrival at the sanitarium:
"That I'm married you already know. I don't think this in any way
changes my life or the conditions under which I've lived until
now." Their mother—but this was an indirect way of conveying
the message to Masha herself—was quite wrong in imagining that
there would be any alteration whatsoever in their lives. "I'll live
just as I have always done," he insisted, "and the same applies to

[4] As for Mikhail, he learned about the wedding from the newspapers.

Mother. My relations with both of you will be as unalterably affectionate as they have always been. . . . My wife and I will live apart: this is a situation, I might observe by the way, to which I'm already accustomed" (June 2, 1901).

The next day Chekhov received a letter from Masha that had been considerably delayed because of his departure. It was an answer to one that he had written her on May 20 in which he had alluded rather dishonestly to a possible marriage: "I'd be glad to marry, but I don't have the necessary papers." His sister made no secret of what she thought: "To me personally this line of conduct is shocking!" There was no occasion, however, to speak of sacrifice on her part or selfishness on her brother's. "You'll always be free to marry," she said. "Tell that to your Knipsgits.[5] First of all you ought to consider the state of your health. For God's sake don't go thinking that I am acting out of selfishness. You have always been the person closest and dearest to me, and your happiness is all I care about. . . ." But following this admirable profession of disinterested love, she added anxiously: "If you don't answer this letter right away, I'll be ill. Greetings to her."

If Masha had reacted so emotionally to the mere idea that her brother might marry, what would she say now, when he had just presented her with the accomplished fact without warning? Anton wrote her a long letter that for all its effort at persuasiveness, was in fact nothing but a piece of rather unsophisticated self-justification. He catalogued the reasons—quite out of character with his usual self—that had led him to decide on marriage: "First, I am now more than forty years old; second, Olga comes from a good family; third, if I have to be separated from her, I'll be able to act without hindrance, precisely as if I had not married: she is an independent person and she supports herself." He laid fresh emphasis on the fact that his marriage would make no change in his habits and that he would go on living "alone in Yalta." He endeavored to offer proof—rather surprising, it is true—of his good will: let Masha come and join them—in the middle of their honeymoon!—and they would all three take a trip on the Volga. And in order to hasten reassurance, he sent her at the same time a telegram in which he announced that his letter was on the way,

[5] This was one of Chekhov's innumerable nicknames for Olga Knipper.

once more repeating: "You are worrying without cause. Everything will stay as it was."

When at last Masha learned of her brother's marriage, she could not help crying out to him immediately her dismay, her distress, her profound perturbation. "What a frightful state I fell into when I heard of your sudden marriage!" she wrote. "Naturally I knew that sooner or later Olga would manage to get close to you, but the fact that you married her so suddenly has upset my whole existence and compelled me to think about you and myself and my future relations with Olga. These have changed abruptly, and that frightens me. I feel more alone than ever." Then she assured her brother that she wished happiness for him and Olga with all her heart, even though she was no longer certain what she felt about his wife. She ended her letter on a heartfelt plea: "You have to understand, Antosha, that I am very unhappy and demoralized, that I'm no longer fit for anything, and that everything revolts me. All I want is to see you, you and no one else" (May 28, 1901).

As for Anton's invitation to come and be the third party to their honeymoon, she had of course refused this curious suggestion. The she received a letter from Olga, who told her how much her letter had grieved the couple. Masha replied at once, though to her brother rather than to her sister-in-law, to apologize for having so unrestrainedly exposed her terrible shock. "That was the first time I had ever allowed myself so much frankness," she wrote, "and I'm sorry to have hurt you and Olga. If you'd married someone other than Knipsgits, I probably wouldn't have written to you at all because I would have hated your wife." But Olga was her friend, they were close to each other, and that was why this unexpected marriage had filled Masha with fear and doubt; perhaps exaggerated, but she had written what she felt. She was unhappy that she had hurt Anton and she would never repeat it. "So don't be angry with me," she concluded, "and remember that I love you both more than anything in the world" (June 16, 1901).

Broken-hearted but determined not to break off with the brother whom she loved so much, and who undoubtedly would still need her, Masha yielded. She never again referred to this painful subject in her correspondence with Anton. But the profound hurt remained, and she unburdened herself to Bunin, whose affection for her she knew. "I'm in a murderous mood and I continually feel my life is a shipwreck. The reason, in part, is my brother's marriage. It came so suddenly. . . . I was upset by it for a long time and even wondered why Olechka allowed a sick man to suffer such a defeat, and in Moscow to boot. But it seems the affair has worked out all right. . . ." In a kind of pitiful defiance she informed her dear Bouquichon that she too was now thinking of marriage and she asked him to find her a rich, generous husband. But her sorrow surged up again at the end of her letter: "Write to me a little more often. I'm very miserable because of Antosha and Olechka."

Her fantasies of marriage, of course, went no farther. For too many years—her best years—Masha had sacrificed herself utterly to her brother, and the habit had become a virtual reflex. She had had opportunity to marry earlier, and if she had refused it, it was undoubtedly because rightly or wrongly she believed that she was indispensable to her brother. She had been his loyal companion in everything: his office assistant as long as he had practiced medicine, his housekeeper in everything that had to do with domestic matters, his nurse untiringly preoccupied with his health. Hence she had come to believe that her indefatigable devotion had entitled her to a privileged place beside her brother, and this place had been brutally stolen from her—and by whom? by her own best friend. Anton told her repeatedly that nothing would be altered in their relations, but he said it too insistently, and she knew that, deliberately or otherwise, he was deceiving himself. His marriage to Olga had broken that bond of a private, total, selfless, and indefinable love that had linked him to Masha for so many years.

In the meantime Anton was sending good news from Aksenevo. He was continuing his *kumiss* treatment: he drank four bottles of the stuff every day, he was putting on a great deal of weight—more than eight pounds, he said, though he could not tell whether this was the result of *kumiss* or marriage—and he was coughing hardly at all. The sanitarium was most primitively equipped, but it was pleasantly situated between an oak wood and the steppe, which was dotted with wildflowers. But he admitted to his usual correspondents as much as to Masha that he was bored in this dead end of the world, which was hardly flattering to Olga. The wretched patients and the Bashkiri could not take the place of his friends. The newspapers, of which he was a greedy reader, were especially missed: those that he could find where he was were a year old. So although he had originally envisaged a two-month stay, he soon announced that he was going to "flee the fortress sooner," and in fact it was after barely a month that he left Aksenevo.

On July 9, after a three-month absence, he was back in Yalta.

XII

LIVING BY LETTER

Happiness that perpetuates itself from one morning to the next is
something that I could not endure. I promise to be an excellent
husband, but give me a wife who, like the moon, does not rise
daily over my horizon.

CHEKHOV in a letter to
SUVORIN, March 23, 1895

Traveling by boat from Novorossisk, Chekhov and his wife landed
at Yalta on July 8. For him there was not only the pleasure of
returning to its dry climate, his dogs, his accustomed ways, his
newspapers, and his properly ordered study, but also the apprehension at facing Masha and his mother after his sudden secret
marriage. The situation was even more delicate for Olga: naturally she would no longer have to endure the disapproving faces
of Anton's family, since she was arriving now as his wife, but
would she be able to make herself really accepted as such?

In relaxed moments Chekhov often called Olga "my little German." Perhaps she made the mistake of letting it be seen too soon
and too much that she was indeed a German. For she had barely
settled herself into the house in Autka when she began to take
over the management of her husband's life according to her own
lights. Masha and her mother, to whom Chekhov was still something of the erstwhile "Father Antosha," to be obeyed by everyone, had never interfered with his bachelor habits and had scru-
pulously respected his every idiosyncrasy: he took little care of

himself, was not fanatically clean, displayed a lofty indifference to meal schedules. So Olga decided, and rather forcefully, to bring some order into this bohemian arrangement: hereafter Anton was to have his suits and shoes cleaned regularly, brush his teeth, and shorten the intervals between baths and underwear changes. Furthermore, she pointed out, why should he be surprised at having stomach trouble when he ate as he did? So she revised his diet as well, set up a strict timetable for meals, and ordered special dishes cooked for him.

In addition she was quite attentive to her mother-in-law and she was trying to renew the closeness of her friendship with Masha. But her manner of disrupting the household's pleasant lack of order could lead only to resentment and friction. The kitchen was the sacred kingdom of the *Mamasha*, and this stranger had the gall to try to make changes in its output. Masha had hitherto taken care of Anton with untiring devotion, and now here was Olga daring to suggest that he try new medicines. There were reproaches and sulks and clashes: more than once Olga, who was single-minded and quick to get her back up, provoked disputes and threatened to clear out and take her husband with her. Anton, who had a horror of scenes, would try to soothe all sides, but he did not always succeed. He was beginning now to recognize that he had been a little premature in assuring his mother that "everything would go on as it had been."

When Olga left alone for Moscow on August 20 to begin rehearsals at the Art Theater, she was rather hostile to her in-laws. She wrote to Chekhov that she was jealous of his mother and Masha and that furthermore Masha would never become accustomed to treating her as his wife. Chekhov tried to reason with her and allay her anger. Perhaps she had some grounds for her jealousy, but how unlike her it was. "You exaggerate everything and fall into silly notions," he said, "and I'm afraid that before long you'll be fighting with Masha. Let me tell you something: be patient, and if only you'll just keep your mouth shut for a year, you'll understand everything. No matter what anyone says to you or what you imagine, be quiet, just be quiet. For everyone, man or woman, who is newly married, all the good part of life depends on non-resistance in the initial period. Do as I tell you, darling, be a clever girl!" (September 3, 1901).

They were already separated after barely three months of marriage, and both were suffering from it. Since they could not live together, they wrote to each other every second day. Chekhov pretended to joke by reproaching himself for turning into the typical middle-class husband who could not live without his "little wife," but it was the truth. His letters to his "Little Poodle," furthermore, were not written in his usual style of self-effacing casualness mixed with irony. They were overflowing with love and tenderness, sometimes to the point of sentimentality and gush, and with barely concealed desire. "I've had the gloomy, melancholy armchair in your bedroom moved into mine," he wrote. "Your room downstairs is silent and empty. Your mother's picture is on your table. . . . I love you very much, my sweet, very much. God bless you. . . . Write, write, write every day, otherwise I'll beat you. . . . I'm terribly lonely without you . . . ," he wrote on August 23. And a day later: "I've grown as used to you as if I were a little child."

Less than a month after his "sweet" had left, he hurried to Moscow to be with her without regard to the fact that he would be greeted as well by the cold, windy onset of winter. Olga and Masha had taken an apartment together, and that was where he stayed: it made him happy to see that the sisters-in-law seemed already to be on better terms. But if he had hoped to see much of his wife, he was disappointed. Olga, who was extremely ambitious and wanted to be the star of the Art Theater, was devoting herself entirely to her work. Obliged to rehearse daily, sometimes for as long as six hours or even into the middle of the night, and involved as well in performances and in her social life, she found little time for her husband, her dear "Russian Maupassant," whom, however, she loved passionately.

The Three Sisters was being given again that autumn by the Art Theater. Chekhov went with Olga to many of the rehearsals, as well as the opening night on September 21, during which the audience gave him "frenzied ovations." He wrote to a friend: "I gave some attention to the staging and made a few author's sugges-

tions, and I'm told that the play is doing better than last season."
What, in his unalterable reserve, he did not add was that his first
dealings at any length with Stanislavsky on the stage had not been
without conflicts, because Stanislavsky felt that the author was
encroaching more than he should on the domains of direction and
staging.

In his memoirs Stanislavsky had the courtesy to admit that if
these first encounters with Chekhov became all but confronta-
tions, it was the director's own fault. The famous author, in spite
of his initial great simplicity, made a considerable impression on
him, and since he did not want Chekhov to be aware of this, he
endeavored to impress him in his turn, to outdo him in intelligence. What was occurring between them was in fact nothing but
the eternal conflict between author and director, who, since each
of them saw the play from a different standpoint—one from
within, the other from without—could not arrive at an agreement
on how to stage it.

Chekhov was especially critical of Stanislavsky for carrying the
realism of his staging too far: he found it ridiculous to have the
cooing of pigeons accompany the rise of the curtain, and he had it
eliminated. To him an overly literal and labored presentation was
fatal to everything that made for the basic originality of his plays,
his discreet, allusive, almost suggested poetry. But this, it appeared, was beyond the understanding of the Art Theater's ebulli-
ent director.

When Alexander went to Moscow from Petersburg to visit his
brother in mid-October, he was shocked to see how very bad
Anton looked. After a month of very active city life, Chekhov was
really drained. He himself was aware of it, and on October 23 he
went to consult a doctor, who undoubtedly advised him to go
back south at once, because three days later he left for Yalta. He
went away in great sadness: when they were making their farewells, he saw Olga weeping, and he himself, once more accustomed to her presence every day, dreaded the solitude that was
waiting for him.

On his return to Yalta he felt that he was on "a desert island."
All that he could do was to resume his and Olga's grieving-lover
correspondence, embittered occasionally by separation and by the

cumulative effect of ungratified desires. Immediately after his departure Olga wrote: "I embrace you, Antonka, I kiss you lovingly, tenderly, gently. . . . How I wish I could throw myself into your arms!" Two days later she told him how she had stared at the emptiness of their bed: "I remember how it used to be, wonderful and warm." She asked whether he was making love to her in his imagination. But Chekhov's replies were ample evidence of that: "My sweet, my angel, my poodle, my darling," he wrote with the ardor of a twenty-year-old, "please believe I love you, I love you deeply. . . . I kiss you so hard, I hold you in my arms and kiss you again. My bed seems so empty, as if I were a miserable, unattractive old bachelor" (October 29, 1901). Before he knew her he had had no idea what loneliness was: "What joy it would give me now to talk to my wife, to touch her eyebrows and her shoulder, to laugh with her. Oh, darling, darling!"

In their uninterrupted correspondence of parted lovers that ranged over everything, they nevertheless meticulously avoided the one real question: why this separation when it made both of them suffer so cruelly? Instead they preferred to make and revise plans for meetings: when shall we see each other? Anton asked; just after Christmas, in Moscow? And Olga said that the idea delighted her, and besides Anton need not be afraid of the cold because the apartment would be well heated. Otherwise what they wrote was trivialities, but trivialities that to them were delicious: Olga wrote about her rehearsals, her social triumphs, her clothes, and the gossip of the literary world. Chekhov told her of his visitors, the weather, and, as a well-behaved husband, his diligent observance of her instructions: yes, he had changed his linen and taken castor oil.

For better or worse, then, they seemed to have settled into their strange existence as eternally separated spouses. It was not until December that Olga finally had the courage to raise the question that tormented both of them but that Chekhov would never have dared to introduce: should she or should she not give up the theater and come live with him in Yalta?

Olga had led Chekhov where she wanted: that is, into marriage. Probably she had no idea, since Chekhov himself had constantly

repeated that "everything would remain as before," that by the
very fact of this marriage that legitimatized them their relationship would again be distorted. As long as she was only his mistress she felt no obligation toward him; as his lawful wife she had
many, and if her husband was too tactful to remind her of them,
there were certainly others who would take the trouble. Now
Olga, who was not a Mediterranean, unquestionably did not conceive of marriage as entailing absolute, unqualified devotion to
her husband, and in addition she was younger, impulsive, ambitious, and greedy for pleasure, and she disliked sacrifices. It was
her hunger for living, her sensuality, her desire to please that had
enchanted Chekhov, but it was also all these things that now kept
her far from him in Moscow.

Nor had Chekhov ever asked her to give up the theater and her
career to live with him. The mere notion of demanding such a
sacrifice of Olga would have seemed almost monstrous to him.
Nevertheless the early months of marriage had already accustomed him to a certain pleasure in living as a couple—as if he had
been married twenty years, he said—and his eternal desire, so
characteristic of his illness, to be "elsewhere" and to believe that
this would improve his health was by now almost fixated on the
idea of being with his wife. He who had so rarely complained
could no longer prevent his letters from implying his longings, re-
current despite their reserve. He was bored without her, and how
lonely he was! "We are committing such a sin by not living together," he wrote.

Olga could not long hold out: her love for Anton had given
birth to a kind of remorse that was no longer bearable. At last she
wrote on November 6: "I want to be with you. I am angry at myself for not having given up the theater. Actually I don't know
what's happening to me, and that irritates me. Nothing is clear
any more. It makes me ill to think of you alone there, being sad
and bored, while here I keep going at a futile business instead of
devoting myself entirely to my love. What keeps me from it?"

What was Chekhov to reply? His reserve, his respect for others'
independence had restrained him thus far from even the most discreet allusion to Olga's possible renunciation of her career, but

now she herself seemed to be contemplating it. In one letter, even though a ray of hope pierced through it, he selflessly urged her to think carefully before making a decision. "Do you want to give up the theater?" he wrote. "Is this the truth? That's what I seem to grasp from your letter. Is it what you want? You ought to think it over seriously, my darling, very seriously, and not make up your mind until later. Don't forget that I'll be spending all next winter in Moscow." A few days later, when he himself had given it thought, he wrote self-sacrificingly: "It makes no sense for you to give up the theater for this dreary kind of life we have in Yalta now" (November 11, 1901).

Besides, after her first retreat before an access of guilt, Olga was turning to a more selfish view of the matter. Now she admitted that she had married "without thinking." She had always hoped that Chekhov's health would allow him to spend at least part of the winter in Moscow. "But it doesn't work this way, my Anton-chik!" she wrote on December 4. "Tell me what I should do." Nevertheless she was already virtually dictating his reply: what in fact would become of her away from the theater? "Without my work," she went on, "I'd be nothing but a bore to you. I'd drag myself from one place to another and everything would annoy me. I've completely lost the habit of living without working, and as for tearing down everything that I've built up with so much effort, that is unreasonable at my age." Could such an ambitious woman sacrifice her career to a seriously ailing husband?

For Chekhov's health was turning worse and worse. During the autumn he had cherished the notion of joining Olga in Moscow in January, but early in December he was forced to his bed by heavy hemorrhages that compelled him to abandon all travel. He informed Olga of this and at the same time, with his usual generosity, forestalled any possible offer by her to come to Yalta. "I don't expect you for the holidays," he wrote from his bed on December 11; "you mustn't come here, my dear. Take care of what you have to do; we'll still have plenty of time to live to-gether. Bless you, little girl." The most that he permitted himself was a quickly stifled complaint the next day: "Oh, my darling, how I envy you, if only you knew! I envy your energy, your strength, your health, your good humor, I envy you because no worry about spitting blood or anything else gets in the way of your drinking and living" (December 13, 1901).

One evening, however, his hemorrhages got the better of his stoicism, and he sent a frank cry of help to Olga. "I love you, Poodle," he wrote on December 18, "I love you very much, and I miss you terribly. It seems unlikely that we'll ever even see each other again. Without you I'm not good for anything. . . ." Olga could not be silent after this pathetic outcry. She wrote how deeply it grieved her that she could not be with him to take care of him, and she swore that now she had indeed vowed to give up the theater. This would be her final season, and in the new year she would devote herself wholly to him. "In your heart, undoubtedly," she wrote, "you reproach me for my lack of love, don't you? You blame me for not having given up the theater, for not being a real wife to you. I can imagine what your mother thinks of me. And she is right, absolutely right. Anton, my Anton, forgive me, brainless thing that I am, and don't think too badly of me. Perhaps you're sorry you married me? Tell me, don't be afraid to admit it to me honestly. I feel that I am being horribly cruel. Tell me what I ought to do" (December 23, 1901).

But Chekhov had already recovered his composure. He was quite determined to demand nothing of Olga, to stifle his own complaints, and to try to achieve a kind of complete detachment. "I have the habit of mastering myself," he was soon to write, "because it does not become a self-respecting man to lose control." Unquestionably the renunciation was not easy. He longed for all those things that were already eluding him, and increasingly for his wife, his health, the exciting artistic life of Moscow. But he exerted all his remaining vigor toward the goal of controlling himself and achieving detachment.

He even wanted to prevent Olga from knowing that he was battling himself: she must be reassured, gently encouraged along the road of her own selfishness, and even consoled for having disappointed him. "You're silly, my darling," he wrote. "Not once since our marriage have I reproached you about the theater. On the contrary, I'm glad that you're busy, that you have a goal in life, that you aren't dragging uselessly along behind your husband. . . . I strictly forbid you to be depressed and fall into melancholy attitudes. Laugh! I embrace you and I'm full of regrets, and that's all" (December 29, 1901).

That was all: the question, then, was settled, at least for a while. Their correspondence assumed a more serene tone; after the great dramatic exchanges of recent weeks there were now the pleasant, tender confidences and trivial or ridiculous bits of news that had formerly prevailed. Chekhov informed his "sweet" that since she would not be with him on New Year's Eve, he would not wait for midnight but would go to bed at nine o'clock. He was trying to make himself eat well, as his colleagues had advised, but he had virtually no appetite. So who could dare to say that he was doing nothing? He had trapped two mice. It was raining and cold. . . . What he did not write lest he frighten Olga, was that more and more often he had to remain in his chair for hours, unmoving, his eyes closed, his strength drained.

Olga's letters were all charged with the "air of Moscow." She remembered to ask about her Antonik's health before she went on to news of her theatrical world, to which, she admitted, she was devoted "like the idiot I am." She wrote about rehearsals, performances, parties. . . . A prominent actress, a pretty woman, the wife of the famous Chekhov, and therefore much sought after —and, with her greedy character, she was incapable of refusing an invitation—she was present at every big party, every concert, every celebration. With a kind of disarming innocence she told her husband that she had been drinking and dancing until eight o'clock in the morning. On January 11, somewhat like a daughter seeking her father's forgiveness, she wrote: "After the play we went to have dinner at The Hermitage and we had wonderful laughs. I flirted with Konstantin Sergeyevich [Stanislavsky]. All right? . . . Then, oh horrors, we went to a cabaret."

Masha, who was sharing her sister-in-law's apartment, was inevitably a witness to the spectacle of this carefree and rather dissipated life, and it often set her teeth on edge. In contrast to Olga, Masha was a puritan, a daughter of duty, who carried her devotion to her brother to the point of putting herself in service to

Olga, for whom she was something of a housekeeper and of whom she took care when Olga was ill. Masha continued to write regularly to Anton—who replied increasingly seldom—but she made it a point to avoid criticizing Olga. Yet from time to time her resentment erupted: one evening, for instance, she had tried to prevent Olga from going to a ball given by Morozov, the millionnaire, but Olga had attended nevertheless and had not got home until extremely late. Oh, how boring life in Moscow was, she added, and since she almost never saw Olga, how alone she felt there.

Chekhov, however, viewed matters much more tolerantly. Certainly there were times when he counseled his "sweet" to curb her pleasures, but he did it with a smile. "My prodigal wife," he wrote to her on January 7, for example, "stay home even for just a week and go to bed at a decent hour. . . . If you go on this way, you'll soon be a dried-up, evil-tempered old woman." Aside from this, he encouraged her to live a full life, enjoy herself, and be happy.

In love, indulgent, bewitched by Olga's youth, her body, and her vitality, Chekhov kept her in ignorance of his artistic and philosophical interests, eager as he was to have her living with him. Once and for all he had decided to behave toward her like a love-smitten, perhaps sometimes inane shopkeeper, and he stuck to this. It had not taken Olga long to become aware of this impenetrable screen that he had erected between his emotional life and his deeper artistic life, and she was beginning to be offended by it. She needed his "great soul, his thoughts, his originality," she wrote to him, and all that he told her about was his health, his mood, and his diet. Was it true, as Masha said, that he did not know what to discuss with her in his letters?

"You write to me about the weather, which I can read about in the paper," she wrote one day when she was so enraged that she forgot how important it was to him because of his health. Still tolerant, Anton replied that he was sorry and promised not to repeat the offense. But that did not mean that, as Olga hoped, he was promising to write only about "interesting things." In the letters that followed he still made only fleeting allusions to his literary projects or his meetings in Yalta with such eminent men as Tolstoy and Gorky. As for his inner life, as always he kept that enveloped in silence.

The most famous man of the time in Russia—and perhaps in the world—Lev Tolstoy, had been living on the Black Sea coast since the beginning of September. He was ill, and his doctors had ordered him to leave Yasnaya Polyana and travel by special railway carriage to the Crimea and settle in the little resort of Gaspra, a little more than six miles from Yalta. Countess Panina had offered him the estate that she owned there: it was a luxurious establishment in English neo-Gothic style, with turrets, high vaulted windows, and a marble staircase, and it was sumptuously furnished. From the terrace one looked out to the sea beyond over soft, beautifully kept lawns planted with cypresses and walnuts and oleanders. It was on this sun-bathed terrace that the old writer prophet —he had just turned seventy-three—often played host to Chekhov.

Tolstoy first invited him to Gaspra for September 12. Chekhov was so moved and excited at the thought of seeing his eminent friend again that Bunin, who was visiting Chekhov at the time, was struck by the amount of thought that he gave to what he would wear. He tried one suit after another, each time inspecting himself in the mirror. No, the trousers of this one were too tight, "he" would think Chekhov was a fop; but the others were too wide, "he" would take Chekhov for a "lout." The choice finally fell on a severe dark suit like a schoolteacher's and a modest soft hat. But Chekhov was wrong to have been so concerned for his appearance: Tolstoy, with the casualness of the true aristocrat, received him in a badly cut peasant blouse, knee boots, and a huge conical white felt hat that protected his head from the sun. This first visit, like those that followed, was most cordial and relaxed. Tolstoy, Chekhov wrote to Olga in a flattered tone, always seemed extremely pleased to see him, treated him with the utmost friendliness, and had long talks with him in which no holds were barred.

To be honest, most of the talking was done by Tolstoy. Sitting behind a cedar table on which a teapot was always within reach, the bearded old prophet, wrapped up in his loose blouse, expatiated, pontificated, perorated without restraint, his index finger imperiously thrust out at his companion. Shy, overwhelmed, balancing his soft hat on his knees, his eyes lowered, Chekhov either listened without comment or occasionally tried in a soft voice to

contradict Tolstoy or dam the torrent of his words. "Anton Pavlovich listened to my father in silence," Sergei Tolstoy was to write,
"and evinced respectful but skeptical attention for what he had to
say. He himself spoke little and avoided argument. My father felt
that Anton Pavlovich, for all the very genuine sympathy that he
felt for him, did not share his views."

That there existed for the two writers a strong reciprocal bond
of sympathy in spite of the differences in their ages and their
thinking was beyond question. It is touching to observe the considerate affection with which Chekhov, in all his letters during
that winter of 1901–1902, reported on Tolstoy's health and what
uneasiness he felt when it showed reverses. And Tolstoy held his
junior in the warmest regard. Gorky, who often saw them together
during this period, wrote later: "Tolstoy loved Chekhov, and
whenever he looked at him his eyes grew soft and seemed almost
to caress Chekhov's face. Tolstoy, that man full of emotion and
fierce pride, likened Chekhov to a quiet, modest young girl." Furthermore Tolstoy added: "And he walks like a girl. He is simply
marvelous." One evening, when all three had spent hours together, Tolstoy wrote in his diary: "I am so glad that I like Gorky
and Chekhov."

The dialogue between Tolstoy and Chekhov was not easy, however, because it was the dialogue of an impassioned participant
and a disabused observer, of a visionary prophet-preacher and a
skeptic, of a proud intransigent father and a son as meek as he was
tolerant. And so their sessions on the sunny terrace in Gaspra never
became true dialogue except when they talked shop—that is, literature.

They talked of Maupassant, of Pushkin, and of Shakespeare,
whom Tolstoy found especially repugnant and whom, Chekhov
was to report, he reproached for not having been a Tolstoyan. The
author of "The Steppe" found a great deal of pleasure in listening
to the old prophet thundering against the young Russian writers,
denouncing their Byzantinism and the futility of their work. He
hurled anathema at the novices of the new generation in literature, primarily and consistently because they were not Tolstoy-
ans, naturally, but even more because they had so little about
them that was Russian, either in their thinking or in their abstruse

fashion of expressing it. "But you," he would say, turning affectionately to Chekhov, "you are Russian. Yes, very, very Russian." And from Tolstoy, who had always been a Slavophile without being aware of it, this was the finest of compliments.

With a brutal peasant kind of frankness that deeply shocked Gorky, the genuine muzhik, Tolstoy also discussed Chekhov's work with its author. "Shakespeare's plays are bad," Tolstoy said summarily (according to the account given by his son, Sergei), "but yours are even worse. Shakespeare at least grabs the spectator by the collar and thrusts him toward a chosen end. . . . But where do your characters take us? From the couch where they have been lying to the storage room, and then back again." Tolstoy, as we know, believed that a dramatic work ought to pose a moral problem and provide its solution, and his younger colleague's "atmosphere" plays, crisscrossed with unanswered questions, could obviously only irritate him.

Even when Tolstoy told him that he "could not" read *The Three Sisters* and urged him to give up writing plays, Chekhov listened without a tremor, smiled softly, and lowered his head. How could one presume to argue with so distinguished an ancestor? One day Chekhov was to say to Ivan Bunin: "What I admire most in Tolstoy is his contempt for all of us writers. It's more than contempt, even; it's a feeling that he regards us all as less than nothing . . . as children."

It was with equal honesty, but this time with admiration, that Tolstoy talked to Chekhov about his stories. He read them over and over, and often, after dinner at Yasnaya Polyana; it was his custom to have one or another of his dinner guests read them aloud. He had the utmost admiration for this prose, in spite of its vast difference from his own in its velocity and its poetic limpidity, and he did not hesitate to compare it with Pushkin's.

Gorky reported that one day in Gaspra, in Chekhov's presence, the old man spoke rhapsodically of Chekhov's story "The Darling." "It's like lace made by a chaste young girl," he said. "There used to be such lacemakers, old virgins who infused their whole lives, all their dreams of happiness, into the patterns of their laces. They dreamed in visual forms of everything they loved; they wove their pure, inchoate love into their laces." Tolstoy was deeply moved and there were tears in his eyes. Chekhov, who had a fever that day, sat absolutely silent, his cheeks spotted red. He had listened with bent head to Tolstoy, carefully wiping his glasses, and he did not move for some time. Finally he sighed and said in a low, embarrassed voice: "It's full of printer's errors."

There were times, too, when Tolstoy tried to tease his guest. Having observed his excessive modesty and his avoidance of any talk of women, Tolstoy suddenly shot a question at him one day: "Did you fornicate much in your youth?" Disconcerted, Chekhov distractedly plucked at his beard and murmured something incomprehensible. Whereupon Tolstoy, more boastful than penitent, went into a lengthy dissertation on his own performances as a young man as an "indefatigable" lifter of skirts.

In January, just when he was feeling very much improved, Tolstoy was suddenly stricken with pneumonia. For weeks he was close to death. Anxious and unhappy to the point of anguish, Chekhov kept abreast of his condition through Altschuler, who was one of the physicians in attendance on Tolstoy. When Chekhov saw Tolstoy again in March, he was still in bed and very weak, and Chekhov was grieved by his "extremely aged appearance." But however physically impaired by his illness, Tolstoy had nonetheless retained all the keenness and spirit of his mental powers, his curiosity about all things, and his "remarkably intelligent eyes."

He had also retained his affection for Chekhov, the affection of an eminent elder aware always of serving as an example. One evening when Chekhov, about to leave, began to shake hands, Tolstoy pulled him close and kissed him; but at the same time he whispered: "But I still can't stand your plays. Shakespeare wrote badly but you're worse still!"

In their final conversation, on March 31, 1902, they talked for the last time about literature without reserve, as dedicated practitioners of their profession. Like every real writer, Tolstoy was still and always interrogating himself on the art of writing, and on this occasion he again raised the question of descriptive realism, of which he had been an incomparable master; and this desire, at the age of seventy-four, to look for new artistic forms aroused all of Chekhov's admiration. Pointing out how realistic literary techniques had been done to death, Tolstoy said: "One can no longer *describe* nature." This was an admission that Chekhov had long since been right to abandon the description of nature for the suggestion of it, the synthesis of it in a few poetic impressions cast into the reader's mind to awaken there a whole world of dormant images.

Tolstoy was also to acknowledge, after his friend's death, the contribution made by Chekhov as an innovator. In July, 1904, he told an interviewer: "He was an artist without equal . . . an artist of life. . . . His is a remarkable language. . . . Chekhov created new forms and, without any false modesty, I tell you that from the point of view of technique Chekhov is far superior to me."

During the autumn Gorky was often present at Tolstoy and Chekhov's meetings. He had arrived in the Crimea on September 12. After his arrest for revolutionary activities at the beginning of the year, he had been released but forbidden to live in Petersburg or Moscow, and although because of his health he had been given permission to go to the Black Sea, residence in Yalta was also prohibited to him. During the first week he had stayed with Chekhov, who had been extremely annoyed to find that a policeman had immediately been posted on guard outside his house; if Gorky went off somewhere, some impatient police official would at once telephone to ask where Gorky was. Then Gorky had found a house for rent in Oleiz, near Gaspra, and established himself there with his wife and their two children.

The two writers saw each other frequently, and the better they knew each other, the more highly they regarded each other. Gorky, Chekhov wrote to Olga, was still the same fine lad, intelligent, decent, and good: if only he would not drown himself in his horrible peasant blouses! Gorky himself was more and more drawn by Chekhov's charm: he admired this famous man for retaining such simplicity and such genuineness, for shunning conversations on "lofty matters," and above all for compelling those around him, through his own demeanor, to greater simplicity and sincerity. Gorky was astonished to see this man, undaunted by his sentence of death, still working, still loving life, still building, still planting new trees in his garden. He admired Chekhov most for

having been able to preserve complete intellectual freedom and
for his capacity to ignore totally what others expected or demanded of him.

Observation of Chekhov's way of living was such a marvel to
Gorky that often he made notes of the little scenes at which he was
present. In spite of his mounting exhaustion, Chekhov was always
unstintingly generous to the young writers who came to ask him
for counsel, and he was even more hospitable to the discouraged,
ailing teachers who visited him in great numbers. He comforted
them with words and often helped them with money. The situation of country schoolteachers in Russia in those days was abominable, and Chekhov, to whom popular education was the indispensable first step toward progress, was deeply disturbed by it.
"When I see a teacher, you know," he told Gorky, "I feel embarrassed in his presence by his shyness and his wretched clothes.
Somehow I feel I am responsible to a degree for that teacher's
suffering—seriously."

Always receptive to genuine people, Chekhov for all his gentleness was capable of being ironic and occasionally even savage
with those who were filled with their own importance. He loathed
pretense, smug stupidity, militant vulgarity. One day, according
to Gorky, three elegant ladies—magnificently dressed and over-
perfumed—went to visit him and persisted in besetting him, and
demanding the same in return, with "interesting observations" on
the current Greek-Turkish war: all that he talked about was jel-
lies. This was his way of getting rid of self-infatuated intruders. A
pompous prosecutor who was trying to lure him into a discussion
on judicial administration was politely asked whether he liked
gramophones. The worst victims were those ladies of fashion who
were determined at all costs—this had become something of a
convention—to hold "Chekhovian" conversations with him. When
one of them, with labored sighs, told him how gray and monotonous life was and what anxiety troubled her soul, adding "It's a
sickness," he retorted: "Of course it's a sickness! In Latin it's
called *morbus affectationis*."

Chekhov was more open and more intimate with Gorky than
with Tolstoy. Even though he did not pour out confidences, or
talk, for example, about his unhappiness at always being sepa-

rated from Olga, he did deal quite unreservedly with everything that was of interest to them both. Often they talked of Russia, the Russia they loved with equal fervor but whose future they envisaged so differently.

Gorky, a convinced Marxist, saw no salvation for his country except in a violent revolution that would destroy the existing structures and place the proletariat in power. Chekhov's trust was invested in a progressive evolution of the system in the direction of liberalism: in the end, he said, there would be fighting in the streets every week and after ten or fifteen years there would be a constitution. But in the interim he was dubious of the reliance that could be put on the virtues of his compatriots. "What an odd creature the Russian is!" he said frankly to Gorky. "He's like a sieve that can't hold anything. In his youth he is greedy to stuff his soul with everything he encounters, and then, once he's over thirty, all that's left is a grayish mishmash. . . . All of Russia is a country of people who are greedy and lazy at the same time. . . . We tell ourselves that everything will be better with a new Tsar, and better still in two hundred years, but no one does anything to make this 'better' come to pass tomorrow."

During the winter Chekhov also had frequent meetings with young Ivan Bunin, Kuprin, the novelist, and Balmont, the poet. He also came to know Leonid Andreyev, who was just beginning to acquire a name and whose strange stories, at once fantasy-ridden and precious, greatly impressed Olga. Chekhov did not much like the man, whose faults were precisely those Chekhov abhorred: the glaring absence of both simplicity and sincerity. But he had to admit to Gorky that Andreyev's "Thought" was "something pretentious, obscure, and apparently worthless, but written with talent . . . a talent (that) reminds one of a mechanical nightingale." Nevertheless he encouraged Andreyev to write for the Moscow Art Theater.[1]

Because he was far from Olga and Moscow, Chekhov felt very much alone in Yalta, and yet what a populous solitude his was! Kuprin described the horde of the admiring and the merely curious who were constantly forcing themselves on the sick man when

[1] Tolstoy, who shared Chekhov's view, said of Andreyev: "He wants to terrify me . . . and I'm not scared."

his only desire was to sit alone on a bench in the sun. "Toward noon or later," Kuprin wrote, "the house began to fill with visitors. Young people in broad-brimmed white felt hats spent hours with their noses pressed against the iron gates that separated the garden from the road. The most diverse kinds of people went to see Chekhov: scholars, writers, zemstvo politicians, officers, painters, admirers of both sexes, university professors, society people, priests, senators, actors, and God knows what else."

It is understandable that in such circumstances Chekhov found little time for writing. He managed somehow, but he still worked badly and arduously, and more out of habit and duty than desire, because the fine flame, the old irresistible rage to write had left him. Olga was urging him to write, and he replied with a certain vexation: "I'm writing, I'm working, but it is impossible to work in Yalta, darling, really impossible. One is so far from the world, one is bored, and worst of all it's cold" (October 17, 1901). All that he accomplished during the entire winter was to revise and finish "The Bishop," a story of some ten pages.

He was also contemplating starting another play, but aside from the title—*The Cherry Orchard*—his ideas were so vague that he had not written even a line. Having been incautious enough to mention it to Masha, he received a furious note from Olga, who resented having been kept out of the secret. "How foolish you are, darling!" he replied. "If I haven't written to you about the new play, it isn't because I don't trust you, as you say, but because I have no confidence in the play. . . . I myself don't know what it will be or what will come out of it, because it changes every day" (January 20, 1902). A few weeks later, moreover, he informed her that since there were already quite enough "damned playwrights," and writing plays had become a "vulgar, boring" job, he had abandoned the idea. But that was only a writer's renunciation. . . .

On the other hand, he was reading a great deal. Having nothing to do, he ran through anything that came to hand—magazines, newspapers, even theological publications. He read Bunin, Gorky —to whom he very frankly pointed out his defects—and Kuprin, for whose story "At the Circus" he felt particular admiration. He was also rereading Turgenev, and this resulted in vastly lowering his respect for the author of "Smoke." "An eighth or a tenth of what this man wrote will survive," he predicted. "All the rest will be filed away in the archives in the next twenty-five or thirty years" (February 13, 1902). And he remarked to Bunin how irritated he was by "the critics' idiotic insistence on finding 'traces of Turgenev' " in his own work.

Chekhov, then, was contemplating a new play. Without expending any imaginative effort, he could also have written a sequel, and a most "Chekhovian" sequel, to *The Sea Gull* on the basis of the news he had that winter from the woman who had been the inspiration of that play. What indeed had become of "the beautiful Lika," who was now wholly out of his life and of whom he would have known nothing if Masha, with her great kindness of heart, had not kept up their friendship?

For the past two years the poor "sea gull" had failed in everything she had undertaken: because she had little will-power, she had given up her ambition to become an opera singer, and she had also decided against opening the lingerie shop she had once mentioned to Chekhov. In recent months she had been acting with the Art Theater, but she had soon given up any thought of pursuing a career in the theater either. Now she was completely idle, and disoriented as well; she simply let herself go and was drinking a great deal. When Masha, out of pity for her, lent Lika her apartment for a night, she wrote to her brother, she found it next morning reeking of dead cigarettes and stale alcohol.

Olga showed less sympathy than her sister-in-law toward Lika. They had met at a party in December, and Olga had flatly—and perhaps with a certain malice—told her husband what she thought of his former "beautiful Lika." "Lika was drunk," she wrote, "and she kept insisting that I drink with her to *Brüderschaft*, but I didn't want to, because I loathe that kind of thing. I don't know her but I find her absolutely outlandish and I don't feel particularly drawn to her."

A few weeks later, in a tone of irony, Olga told her husband that Lika had married A. Sanin, the assistant director of the Art Theater. Though Chekhov had no great faith in the future of this marriage, he had the decency to defend it. "I've known Lika a long time," he wrote to Olga, "and no matter what might have happened, she's a good person, intelligent and honorable. She won't get along with Sanin, she won't listen to him . . . and in eighteen months, no doubt, she'll start being unfaithful to him. In short, it's all a question of luck" (March 12, 1902). This fatalistic prediction was the announcement of an ending: Lika was forever out of Chekhov's life and thereafter he was never again to mention her even once in his letters.[2]

Lydia Avilova's departure from Chekhov's life, as might be expected, was not to be so gracefully accomplished. A few weeks before his marriage, when the Art Theater was playing in Petersburg, she tried at first to meet Olga. Mrs. Avilova was later to insist that they had long known each other and that as children they had acted together in amateur theatricals in Moscow, but Olga, who could recollect nothing of the sort, assumed that her caller was some stranger looking for a free ticket and sent out word that she could not see her. Olga told Chekhov about this, but he merely laughed and threatened her with divorce before marriage if she emulated Mrs. Avilova by turning into a woman of letters and writing stories.

Obviously Mrs. Avilova could not have been unmoved by the news of Chekhov's marriage. When she learned of it from her sister, rather suddenly, she wrote in her *Recollections,* "a cold sweat covered my forehead and I fell into the first chair I could find." But she did not lose control to the extent that she missed hearing —in order to be able later to record them with a certain satisfaction—any of the petty remarks made in her presence on the subject of Olga Knipper either on that day or on subsequent days. Of course Olga had married for position, and they really must be a strange couple to see, she and that poor sick old man, Anton Pavlovich. And wherever Olga went she was trailed by her faithful *cavaliere servente,* Nemirovich-Danchenko. But for Lydia Avilova the real question, the important question was something else: should she or should she not congratulate Chekhov on his marriage?

[2] In contrast to her brother, Masha thought that Lika and Sanin made a rather well-matched couple. She must have been right, because Lika did not leave her husband but went into exile with him and lived with him in Paris until his death in 1937.

When, after great hesitation, she made up her mind to do so, she wrote, she naturally did it in her own way, which was romantic, sentimental, and, we might as well admit, highly contrived. Still convinced, in spite of his denial, that Chekhov's story "On Love" had been inspired by "their" romance, she wrote to him in the person of the story's heroine and as if that lady were addressing the man who was her lover in the story and congratulating him on his marriage to a rival. She was full of the warmest compliments, without reservations or rancor, and indeed she concluded by thanking him for all that he had given her. "Was our love a real love?" she wrote. "No matter what it was, real or imagined, how grateful to you I am for it! It showered my youth with a glimmering, perfumed dew. If I were capable of prayer, I would pray for you."

These congratulations and this reminder of a "real or imagined" love, if this particular "sea gull" is to be believed, evoked a reply from Chekhov that was grateful and without illusions. In addition to his thanks for her good wishes, he supposedly wrote: "You ask whether I am happy. In the first place, I am ill. And now I know that I am very ill. . . . Draw your own conclusions. I repeat, I am very grateful for your letter, very. . . . I have always wanted you to be happy, and if I could do something to assure your happiness, I would do so with joy. But I cannot." [3]

The "love story" of Chekhov and Lydia Avilova ended with this final exchange of letters. Or, to be more precise, it supposedly ended, for contrary to Ivan Bunin and Kyril Wilczkowsky, we must conclude that it never happened and that Mrs. Avilova was simply a new kind of "vindictive widow," the widow of a love that never existed outside her inflamed dreams. In her *Recollections*, written forty years after Chekhov's death, she made clever use of all the documents that had come to light in the interim in order to give her "love story" the color of truth. But to anyone who reads

---

[3] Mrs. Avilova discussed Chekhov's marriage and quoted their final exchange of letters in the last chapter of her *Recollections*. This chapter appears only in the latest edition of her book, published in 1960 after her death. The original of her letter has not been found, nor is there any trace of Chekhov's. According to Mrs. Avilova, his letter was stolen from her, along with other letters of his that she had refused to turn over to Masha Chekhova, on the ground that they were too private, when Miss Chekhova began assembling her brother's correspondence.

her book carefully and with full knowledge of all the facts the illusory premises and the fallacious conclusions are quickly apparent: it becomes obvious that with the assistance of quotations out of context, putative sources, and accounts of meetings for which there was no evidence, plus her excellent knowledge of the real biography of Anton Chekhov, Lydia Avilova embroidered the truth with an imaginary romance.

The epilogue to this remarkable fantasy is to be found in the letter that Lydia Avilova wrote on July 20, 1904, eleven days after Chekhov's funeral, to his sister, whom she did not know. In it she spoke of her grief and of her regret at not having met Masha at the cemetery, asked to be allowed to call Masha her "dear sister," and mentioned the letters from Chekhov that were in her posssssion. At this time, no doubt, she had not yet begun to think of manufacturing her romance, because she also wrote: "I don't mean to insinuate at all that I knew your brother well or that I meant anything at all to him. No, unquestionably I hardly knew him, but he had so great an influence on my life and I am indebted to him for so much. . . . I have many of his letters. But I don't know what he thought of me, and that is a great affliction to me."

Masha Chekhova did not attack Mrs. Avilova in her own book, *Out of a Distant Past,* but nonetheless she made it clear that while in part Mrs. Avilova's *Recollections* did recount facts, all the rest was imagined, pure invention. "Reading that part of her book," Masha wrote, "one might have the impression that Anton Pavlovich loved her, that their relation verged on the idyllic, and that he himself spoke to her of it. But nothing of the sort was the case."

Between Chekhov and Olga, however, the idyl continued, simultaneously impaired and as it were sustained and sublimated by separation. Chekhov, whom Altschuler had strictly forbidden to join his wife in Moscow, had spent the year-end holidays alone, as well as his birthday and then the long, monotonous month of January. The state of his health had declined still farther: he wrote to Olga that when he trimmed his rosebushes, he now had to stop and rest after each one.

Knowing how much he was suffering at Olga's absence, Masha prevailed on the management of the Art Theater to grant her a few days of vacation in February so that she could make a quick journey to Yalta. Olga announced that she was coming for "four days and five nights." But Anton, grown skeptical after so many broken promises, wrote back: "Are you really coming soon? I hope so, I hope so, I hope so. . . ." And this time he was not disappointed: on February 22 Olga arrived in Yalta.

She was to speak of this as a "second honeymoon," tender and passionate but too brief, like a lovers' excursion. They were hardly separated again when they wrote to tell each other how much they were suffering in the renewal of their respective lonelinesses. "Come back, darling, as quickly as possible," Chekhov wrote the day after Olga's departure. "I can't live without my wife. My room and my bed are now like a dacha deserted by its owners." To this his wife replied that she was almost haunted by the thought that he was stifling alone in Yalta "day after day, as if in a prison, thirsting for a different life, but with patience, with infinite patience."

The Art Theater had begun its Petersburg season, and Olga, who had gone there directly, was immediately caught up in the whirlwind of her professional activity. The Petersburg public was overwhelmed by Stanislavsky's company: the house was full every night, and there was a gala performance of *The Three Sisters* attended by the Tsar and his court. Olga was perhaps the most admired of all: the press had more praise for her than for her colleagues, and the baskets of flowers from admirers known and unknown piled up in her dressing room. She had never had such a triumph. And naturally it turned her head a bit. Swept off her feet, she accepted every invitation, every tribute, all the trappings of fame.

Nevertheless she suffered from attacks of remorse. At the height of her euphoria the sudden thought of Anton, alone and ill in his "prison," would sear her for a moment. Then she would write, trying to be tender and sympathetic but at the same time, undoubtedly without even being aware of it, seeking to justify herself. "There are moments when I violently detest the theater," she wrote; "there are others when I love it madly. It has given me life, much sadness, and many joys; it has given me you, and it has made me somebody." She insisted: Anton might think this was an artificial, illusory life, but in any event it was life, it was her life.

Chekhov was not asking her for justification; in fact he made no reproaches to her. He reassured her about his health: he was coughing less. Consistently fond and generous, he rejoiced at her successes and predicted that she would have a future like Sarah Bernhardt's. But, with a smile, he warned her that he would sue for divorce if she did not allow herself sufficient rest. He himself was already dreaming of the summer, and he told her that they would spend it together in a dacha near Moscow or in Finland. His letters also talked much and very lovingly of the "little Pamphilius" who had been much discussed since their wedding and who Chekhov hoped would soon be born.

But, unfortunately, there was to be no Pamphilius Chekhov that year. On March 31 Olga wrote in despair to her husband from Petersburg that she had just had a miscarriage that had compelled her emergency removal to a hospital. She had not been feeling right for several weeks, but she had not known that she was pregnant, and when she did learn that she was, it was too late. She was heartbroken, and although her friends in the Art Theater were doing everything for her, her only desire was to join Chekhov in Yalta as soon as possible and find shelter and strength in his arms. But she wrote a few days later: "Will you even want to have such a wretched wife? Send me a telegram, don't forget me, don't look down on me because of this."

As soon as he heard the news Chekhov sent a number of telegrams to Olga, but only to assure her of his love and of his concern for her health. And with good reason, because Olga was making a poor recovery, and when she arrived in Yalta on April 14, she was still very pale, feverish, and so weak that she had to be carried from the ship to the carriage that would take her to the house in Autka. A few days after her arrival Chekhov wrote to Korolenko that he simply could not enter into any discussion with him about the election of their friend Gorky to the Academy, and its subsequent invalidation by the government because he was too concerned with Olga's condition. "My wife has a high temperature," he wrote, "she is confined to bed, and she has lost much weight." He was so concerned for her that he could not eat, and he himself was ill for several days.

Chekhov, of course, had not said a word of criticism to the poor woman, but undoubtedly he and she alike sensed in his mother and especially in Masha—who knew whatever was to be known about the kind of life that her sister-in-law had been leading in Moscow and Petersburg—a kind of silent reproof. This would explain the fact that Chekhov did not wait for his wife to complete her convalescence before leaving with her for Moscow on May 25, even though there was no urgency for her to return, since the theatrical season had ended. Besides, Olga had to take to her bed again on doctor's orders as soon as they arrived in the capital. A few days later she suffered a serious relapse, and the doctors diagnosed peritonitis and recommended surgery.

Extremely anxious and distracted, Chekhov took care of his "sweet" with unremitting devotion and was at her bedside night and day. His self-control amazed Stanislavsky, who, like Olga's mother, did everything possible to help. Masha wrote from Yalta that she would come whenever Anton sent for her, and, perhaps with a certain guilt, she added that she was expecting him and Olga in Yalta as soon as Olga could travel. Then, on June 12, when surgery seemed unavoidable and Chekhov and his colleagues had just decided to move Olga to a hospital, suddenly "and in a totally unanticipated fashion," he wrote, "a change occurred and Olga felt better."

She continued to improve during the ensuing days to such a degree that Chekhov could occasionally leave her for a few hours in the evening and go to an open-air circus in the Arcadia Park. But he was exhausted, and on June 17, when he was completely reassured as to Olga's health, he entrusted her to her mother and left Moscow for Perm, in the Urals. He had rather curtly refused Masha's invitation to return to Yalta, and since he undoubtedly had rather bitter memories of their life together in April, he had also told her that it was highly unlikely that he would return to Yalta before the end of the year.

He had gone to the Urals as the guest of Morozov, the multimillionnaire. First by rail and then by water, traveling down the Volga and then up the Kama, they took more than a week to reach Morozov's huge estate at Vsevolodo-Vilva, beyond Perm. Chekhov maintained constant communication with Olga in affectionate telegrams and letters: the doctor declared that she was much better, she wrote, and he replied that he was spending his time sunning himself on deck and watching the landscape slip past.

In Vsevolodo-Vilva, Chekhov discovered the existence of a modern feudalism. Savva Morozov maintained a kind of baronial fief there, with a luxurious mansion, an army of flunkeys, a huge park, and a birch forest, as well as villages and chemical factories —in a word, a veritable miniature empire. Morozov was the archetype of those great pioneers of capitalism who were beginning to appear in large numbers in Russia: repulsive but almost likable, he was ostentatious with his weath and yet at the same time he displayed a certain genuineness in playing the Maecenas and the social reformer. He had just financed the Art Theater's new quarters, he sincerely admired Chekhov, and he was attempting to introduce certain paternalistic reforms in his factories.

As soon as they arrived, in spite of the fact that his guest was "gray with exhaustion," Morozov insisted on taking him on a tour of one of his factories. Chekhov talked with the workers with the utmost frankness, and afterward he did not hesitate to tell his host that he considered their twelve-hour working day too long; as a result, it was said, Morozov subsequently reduced it to ten and then to eight hours. The magnate also gave a great dinner for the local high society in honor of Chekhov, who, however, made no great show at it and for all the seven courses ate only a little soup and drank only mineral water. He was also invited to the dedication ceremonies of a school to which his name was given, but he could not attend because of his health.

The better he came to know Morozov, the more mixed and contradictory Chekhov's reactions to him became. While he had a certain respect for the Maecenas and the man of good will, he could not help feeling contempt, even though mixed with pity, for this wealthy man. Thinking that he was dazzling the world, Morozov impressed chiefly himself; he mistook obsequiousness for admiration, and with the simple-mindedness of all the newly rich, he had no idea that the aristocrats whom he invited to his dinners and who flattered his vanity took their revenge in ridiculing him as soon as his back was turned. One day Chekhov remarked to

Tikhonov, a young student employed by Morozov: "He's a rich merchant. .... He builds theaters and dabbles in revolution. ... But in his drug store there's no iodine; the pharmacist is a boozer—he's drunk up all the medicinal alcohol, and he treats rheumatism with castor oil. .... They're all the same: there you have our Russian Rockefellers." [4]

It was Tikhonov rather than Morozov—who was always hurrying back and forth and issuing orders—with whom Chekhov spent a part of every day. They took long walks through the magnificent birch forest, which excited Chekhov's admiration, and enjoyed fishing together. They also had long, intimate, and wide-ranging conversations on the student strikes, literature, Gorky, the Art Theater, and the "decadents."

While Tikhonov was overwhelmed by the writer's intelligence and extreme simplicity—Chekhov had treated him as an equal from the outset—he was also struck, and painfully, by his sickly appearance. Chekhov often had to stop to catch his breath during their walks. Thin, bent, his eyes almost hidden by a cap, his body wrapped in a black coat, his beard graying, how much older than his age he seemed at forty-two, and how near to death! On a strap over his shoulder was a leather-covered flask, like a hunter's, that hung at his left hip: on their first evening Tikhonov had seen him, when he was wracked by a long spasm of coughing, "unscrew the cap of the flask, turn his back in embarrassment, and spit some viscous reddish matter. . . ."

Tikhonov's bedroom was next to Chekhov's. One evening the student heard a sustained spasm of coughing, extremely violent and interrupted only by muffled groaning. Thoroughly frightened, he ran to Chekhov's room, where, in the flickering light of a candle, he saw the writer sitting up in bed and spitting quantities of blood into an enamel bowl. In his anxiety Tikhonov said something to Chekhov, who fell back onto his pillow and looked at him out of those big, childlike, desperate eyes, filled with tears—the first time that Tikhonov had seen them as it were naked, without their glasses. At first Chekhov seemed not to recognize him; then, with an effort, he whispered apologetically: "I've disturbed your sleep. Please forgive me, my dear boy."

[4] A. P. Tchekhov, *From the Recollections of His Contemporaries.*

Two days after his arrival at Morozov's, Chekhov had written that life there was "gray and uninteresting," and, contrary to his original plans, he went back to Moscow five days later, when he was feeling better. But he immediately left the city again. Olga and he had been invited by Stanislavsky's mother and they went to stay in her dacha at Lyubimovka, in a major Moscow suburb.

The area was wooded, picturesque, and, as Chekhov was quick to observe, watered by a river filled with fish. In the house—a big wooden chalet with a veranda—Stanislavsky's rooms were given to the Chekhovs, since the director was away. Chekhov liked Lyubimovka from the start, and a week later Olga wrote gratefully to Stanislavsky: "Our author . . . looks very well, is gaining weight, has a fine appetite, and is in excellent spirits. . . . He's a completely different man here, because here he finds nature to his liking."

Chekhov himself soon admitted that it was a long time since he had had so enjoyable a summer vacation. He was now completely certain of Olga's recovery—her doctor had just given her permission to go back to work in mid-August—and together they spent peaceful, almost bucolic days: they rested, "ate, and slept like archbishops"; Chekhov went fishing as often as five times a day: sitting on the river bank, he would drift into reverie or listen to the bells of the village church. For it was of himself that he was thinking when he observed ironically in his *Notebooks:* "He was a rationalist, but—who has no weaknesses?—he was extremely fond of listening to church bells."

Full of gratitude, he wrote to Stanislavsky: "Everything, in a word, is perfect. There's only one bad aspect: I'm loafing and doing nothing. I still haven't begun my play" (July 18, 1902). In spite of the urgings of Olga and his friends in the Art Theater, he really could not make himself get down to work. "I've become so lazy," he told Gorky, "that I find it unpleasant even to get out of bed."

This pleasant, lazy vacation lasted six weeks. On August 14 Chekhov left for Yalta. He was going back alone, leaving Olga in Moscow, where Stanislavsky's theater was about to resume rehearsals. But he and Olga had not separated without evidence of her resentment that Masha and his mother had not invited her to go with him, and there had been a rather bad quarrel. Anton took with him a letter from Olga to her sister-in-law that was to make matters much worse.

This letter, which was undoubtedly quite sharp, upset Masha, who gave it to her brother to read. He too became angry, and he let Olga know it at once: "Your letter," he told her bluntly, "is very, very unfair, and what is written with a pen can never be erased; there's nothing to be done about it. I tell you again, and I give you my word of honor, that Mother and Masha had invited both of us, not me alone, and that they've always had warm and affectionate feelings for you" (August 17, 1902). A few days later, when Olga sent a reply in which she continued to make accusations against Masha, he again counter-attacked by telling her frankly that she was wrong. "That just won't do, it really won't, darling," he wrote. "One should avoid unfairness. You must be above all reproach in this area, totally irreproachable, and all the more because you are good, very good, and understanding. Forgive me for criticizing, darling. I won't do it again, I dread doing it" (August 27, 1902).

He was right to dread it. For his reprimands, however cloaked in endearments, were not at all to the liking of the "very good" Olga. She was really angry, and she replied to her husband with the accusation that he was lacking in candor. Furthermore, was he not getting along quite well without her? "This can mean only one thing," she wrote acidly: "that we've lived together long enough. Has the time come for us to separate? Fine. . . ." Then she revealed what she was really thinking: in reality it was the problem of her career in the theater that was at the root of their conflict, that had made "a mess" of their lives. But was it worthwhile for her to give up her career in order to devote herself wholly to him when she had the feeling that his need for her was so minuscule? "There have been times," she concluded, "when I have felt in the way. I think you need me only as an enjoyable woman, but as a human being I feel alone and a stranger to you" (August 28, 1902).

How these postal battles wearied Chekhov! Eager to put an end to them, he wrote to Olga for the last time to confute, though curtly, her complaints and to warn her against those who would incite her against him. "As for the rest," he added, "I'm not going to try to undeceive you or convince you, because it's useless. . . . My sweet, good darling, you are my wife: please understand this once and for all. To me you're the person who is closest and dearest to my heart. I've loved you without measure, I still love you, but you stubbornly insist on writing to me about an 'enjoyable' woman who is alone and a stranger with me. Well, God bless you, do what you like" (September 1, 1902).

Having reassured her of his love, then, he was offering Olga a peace treaty: she accepted it. Yes, they had quarreled badly, but, she replied, since they were flesh-and-blood people, had they no excuses? As for herself, she had not been influenced by anyone, she had very simply suffered too much by being constantly separated from him. She admitted that she was wicked, truly wicked, but now, she wrote, "when I think of you, I always see myself on my knees before you, asking you to forgive me." She offered proofs of her good faith: since she was expecting Masha soon from Yalta, she was already putting flowers in her room. Subsequently, when Anton asked about her health—would she be able to have another child soon?—she replied that the doctor had assured her that she was completely recovered. "Are you pleased?" she wrote. "Next year I'll give you a handsome little boy."

Without the storms and calms of this marital correspondence Chekhov would have been quite happy in Yalta that summer with Masha and their mother. In contrast to Olga, who often disrupted his old-bachelor habits without a thought, these two women lovingly respected them. They allowed him to eat what he liked, and while they watched over his health with the utmost devotion, they never mentioned it because they knew how much he hated discussing it. Masha was also assiduous in shielding him from the importunate visitors whose number increased in direct proportion to the growth of his reputation. In addition, since she was the only member of the family with whom their brothers were in regular correspondence, she kept Chekhov informed about them, for in spite of geographical separation, he was much attached to them. Alexander, who had long been so unstable, had at last settled down and was beginning to acquire a name as a journalist in Petersburg, and Ivan, as steady as ever, was doing well in government service in Moscow. Anton was very pleased to learn that Misha had resigned from the editorial staff of *New Times*, whose reputation was growing steadily worse, in order to take over the management of the newsstands for which Suvorin possessed the monopoly throughout the Russian railway network.

Early in September, Suvorin visited Chekhov. They had not seen each other for months, and they were really happy to meet again—Suvorin, in fact, wept. They spent two days together, talking about many things and recalling the past. There was not much on which they were in agreement, but although Chekhov now had no reservations at all about denouncing the publisher's reactionary tendencies, he could still not forget what he owed Suvorin for good "memories of youth" and in simple gratitude. After Suvorin had gone Chekhov had the courage to defend him against Pervukhin, the editor of the local newspaper. When history had to pass judgment on Suvorin, Chekhov said, it would not be allowed to forget that he had been the first to raise journalists' salaries and to improve their working conditions, that he had given financial assistance to many young writers, and that while he had made use of the press to amass a great deal of money, he had also employed it as an instrument for the diffusion of culture.

Thus Chekhov was true to what he had written to this same Suvorin thirteen years earlier: "It is not for writers to judge and condemn." But at the same time he reserved all his admiration for those who had the courage to defend the oppressed and the innocent. On September 18 he wrote to his wife: "I am very sad today: Zola died. . . . I did not think too much of him as a writer, but on the other hand I respected him tremendously as a man, especially during those last years when the Dreyfus case was so important."

In order to satisfy his friends and admirers, who were always asking him for inscribed photographs, Chekhov frequently had his picture taken. Looked at in the sequence in which they were made between 1898 and 1902, these portraits reveal strikingly, even tragically, the accelerated changes in his appearance made by the illness that was devouring him.

During these few years the round cheeks, the curly hair, the smile in the eyes had vanished. Chekhov now—at forty-two—was an old man who looked like the sixty-year-old Zola: he was never without his glasses on their black silk ribbon, his face seemed sunken, his eyes were tired, his lips had receded, his hair and his pointed beard were gray. This premature senescence, which escaped the notice of his intimates, shocked his new acquaintance, Tikhonov, the student: he observed the ashen pallor, the gauntness, the stooped carriage, the alternation of febrility and a kind of torpor, the breathing that became gasping at the slightest effort, the leather-covered flask that was never absent from the hip.

The man was drained, doomed, at the end of his rope: he was outliving himself. He had just taken a long rest in Lyubimovka, and he was resting again in Yalta, but it made no difference, he was still going downhill. He had promised Olga that he would join her in Moscow, but soon he had to tell her that he did not feel well enough "to travel, write, or do anything." He put off the journey from week to week. His "brutal coughing" left him so weak that he could not even go from his house into town.

And yet what impatience was still seething within him! What a longing to be elsewhere! Like many tuberculars who develop an aversion to the place where they are and always think that they will feel better elsewhere—it was Katherine Mansfield, a victim of the same disease, who remarked on the phenomenon—he thought only of journeys and escapes. Why else would he have needed to undertake the wearing journey to Perm in the preceding June with a man who was not even a friend, except to gratify his insatiable desire for "blind flight"? But unfortunately he no longer felt well anywhere; he had left Perm after five days, he had spent only six weeks in Lyubimovka, he was already prepared to leave Yalta again. He thought of going to spend the winter in Africa or Ceylon. "You're always bored," his wife wrote to him; and it was true: as soon as he had established himself in one place, he began to long for sime unattainable "elsewhere."

He and Olga were photographed together. He was somewhat in the background, a cap on his head, his dark jacket buttoned high, his eyes enigmatic behind the glasses. She was leaning on a white umbrella and looking magnificent: her hair was luxuriant, her profile was smiling, her smooth cheeks were dimpled. Where had this strange couple arrived after more than a year of marriage? In reality, rather than husband and wife, they were still lover and mistress, a famous bachelor writer who was having an affair with a young actress. A profound shared desire made them miserable when they were away from each other and ecstatic when they were together, and unquestionably they loved each other, but they did not wholly give to each other.

During the critical period through which they had recently suffered, Olga had said: "It seems to me that if I lived with you all the time, you would turn cold toward me, or else you would take me for granted, like a table or a chair. Am I right?" To a great extent she was indeed right, and she knew it: she had seen her husband, for no good reason, leave for the Urals just when she was barely beginning to recuperate, and she had seen him go off again alone to Yalta after their bucolic visit in Lyubimovka. And she was right again when she told him that he felt no deep need for her, that all that he wanted of her was to be an "enjoyable" woman and in all other respects she was a stranger to him. On all these points, furthermore, Chekhov's only replies were evasions.

Far from changing him, age and illness had on the contrary accentuated and, as it were, hardened the features of his character as well as those of his face. He was still the withdrawn man, knotted up inside, who felt no need to explain himself to anyone and who at the same time had difficulty understanding that others might want to explain themselves. More than ever he kept his friends and relatives—and now even his wife—at a distance, and in spite of the kindness with which he behaved toward them, he regarded their lives with a certain indifference and detachment.

Bunin, who knew him well and liked him, later wrote: "What went on in the depth of his soul no one, even among those who were closest to him, could really know. His self-control never left him, even in our most intimate conversations. He was cordial always and with everyone, and occasionally, with some people, he was quite affectionate. But he kept everyone at a certain distance. . . . Had he at some time in his life known a blind, romantic, passionate love? I think not. And that is extremely significant."

To talk of "Chekhov the tender," then, as virtually all his biographers have constantly done, is merely to perpetuate a pious but empty lie. It confuses—deliberately or otherwise—the artist with the man. If exception is made for that sensual kind of tenderness that was manifested in his letters to Olga, there was nothing tender in Chekhov the man, and emotional impulses were not his nature. If evidence were required, one would have only to recall the manner in which he treated his sister at the time of his marriage to Olga, or to reread his letters to Gorky, in which he replied with polite phrases to the younger man's intense and spontaneous declarations of friendship. It was Gorky himself, moreover, who wrote, in connection with *Uncle Vanya*: ". . .You treat people with a diabolical coldness. You are as indifferent as snow or storm." And Sergeyenko, with whom Chekhov had gone to school, commented: "He is a solitary. He has many friends, but he is no one's friend. In fact no one attracts him to such a degree that he forgets himself." [5]

That this "lack of passion," of spontaneous tenderness, was compensated for by a continuous deliberate kindness and generosity is, however, undeniable. Chekhov had always been, and in spite of the lamentable state of health that might have enticed him into a certain egocentricity, always remained infinitely considerate. Worn out as he was, he went on seeing everyone who intruded on him, encouraging young writers, and providing moral and material support to those pariahs of the intelligentsia, the teachers. But, as Sophie Laffitte said so well, "in this universal solicitude . . . his deepest self was never involved."

"The enigma of his personality," to borrow Kuprin's expression, was actually that of many artists, who, endowed with an exceptional passive sensitivity capable of recording and understanding every shading of emotion in others, are still somehow lacking in human affection and active sensitivity. One has only to recall Jean-Jacques Rousseau, or, closer to our own time, André Gide or Jean

[5] It was Mme. Sophie Laffitte who deserved the credit for having first revealed this basic trait of Chekhov's character in her essay "Chekhov Alone." She cited the virtually unanimous opinion of Chekhov's friends on this point. But Ilya Ehrenburg, still worshiping at the ikon of the "tender Chekhov," countered by emphasizing the extreme sensitivity demonstrated by the writer's work. This, however, is only another manifestation of the eternal confusing of man with artist.

Cocteau. Perhaps it is because they always preserve a bulwark of indifference, and therefore of clearsighted disengagement, that such writers, through the very paradox of art, are often more capable than others of understanding and making us understand what men and women feel. Had he been more active and emotional, Chekhov might have devoted more of himself to his wife and friends, but then, beyond question, he would have given less to us, his readers.

Chekhov's sole real passion was and remained his art: literature. More than ever, as the end of his life drew closer, he was convinced that real art was conciseness, simplicity, precision. He told Gorky, whom he justly criticized for the intemperance of his language, that the finest description of the sea that he had ever read was in a school notebook: "The sea was huge." Since he was still working on the revision of his complete works for Marx—the sixth volume was to appear in that year, 1902—it was with this in mind that he was proceeding: he trimmed and pruned and lopped off whole sentences. One page proof shows that of the original twenty-five lines of type, he had retained only a dozen.

It was also a concern for sincerity that motivated him, for to him art and sincerity were inextricable. He elaborated on this one evening to Tikhonov—perhaps he would not have dared to make such a confidence to anyone but this unknown student—and this time he could not keep passion out of what he was saying: "What is good in art is precisely the fact that it does not permit falsehood. . . . One can lie in love, in politics, in medicine, one can lie to oneself or even to God—there have been such cases—but it is impossible to deceive in art."

He did not write to lie or deceive. He had been criticized—notably by Tolstoy—for having written about trifles, for not having chosen "positive heroes," or even, as Leskov did, "honest policemen." It was precisely because he did not wish to delude his reader that he portrayed only the world that he knew, the world of mediocre little intellectuals, brutal muzhiki, colorless provincials . . . and dishonest policemen. He was faithful to the prayer that he had inscribed in his *Notebooks:* "O Lord, do not allow me to judge what I do not know or understand, or even to speak of it."

It was Tikhonov again to whom he explained the meaning of his plays. He had not written them in order to evoke tears—that would be another way of defrauding the public, and possibly the most treacherous. It was Stanislavsky, he insisted vehemently, who had made such "weepy things" of his plays. He himself was seeking quite a different effect: he wanted to make his audience think. "I simply wanted to say to people in all honesty: 'Look at yourselves, see how badly and boringly you live.' The important thing is that people should understand that; and if they do understand it, they will surely build different and better lives for themselves. I shall not live to see it, but I know it will be completely different, nothing like what we have today." This idea was highly important to him; he believed in it, and he came back to it in his *Notebooks:* "Man will become better when we shall have shown him himself as he is."

For whatever he might have said on the subject, Chekhov in his last years had not altered his literary perspective. As a writer he was concerned always to "state the problem accurately" and to put it as it was before the public, which would find the solutions for itself. The author, who forbade himself to preach, hinted at none.

In spite of all this, the fact remained that Chekhov's skepticism had nevertheless lost its edge, that now he apparently believed that "men will build a different and better life for themselves." This remote, almost dreamlike hope recurs like a phrase in music toward the end of all Chekhov's late works. This hope for a humanity that will have been made better and happier by the sufferings of today's generation is synthesized in two sentences of *The Three Sisters:* "In two or three hundred years life on earth will be unbelievably beautiful, life will be marvelous . . ." and again, ". . . our sufferings will be transformed into joy for those who will come after us, peace and happiness will be established in the world, and those who will take our places will speak of us with affection and bless those who are living today."

But the distance was great, immeasurable, between this dream future and the reality of Russia at the beginning of the twentieth century. Although Chekhov as a matter of principle kept aloof from all political movements, and habitually refused any such discussion with his friends, Gorky and others, nevertheless he was far too clearsighted not to recognize the social and political reality of Russia for what it was—that is, radically unjust, harshly authoritarian, and, worse still, frozen into the most hopeless rigidity. What impressed and grieved him most was to see his beloved Russia, a country of nomads and movement, bound by laziness and resignation to the yoke of absolutism. "Russia is a bureaucratic country," he wrote in his *Notebooks*. "Nowhere does government have such crushing power as it does among us Russians, who are debased by our age-old enslavement and who are afraid of freedom."

It was as his resistance to this authoritarian and bureaucratic Russia, in which the writer by definition was suspect, that in 1902 Chekhov performed the one political action of his life. Early in the year his friend Maxim Gorky had been elected by his colleagues to membership in the Literary Section of the Academy of Sciences, and Chekhov was greatly pleased by this. But the Tsar was equally greatly displeased, and across the report on the election submitted to him by the Minister of the Interior the Little Father wrote in his own hand: "Extraordinary." Very soon the official government bulletin announced the invalidation of Gorky's election. Chekhov's friends pressed him to offer his own resignation from the Academy as a protest, and he at once sought to analyze the whole situation and ask the advice of others. Tolstoy, whom he consulted, replied with the jesting remark that although he was a member of the Academy, he did not regard himself as such. But Korolenko, who, like Chekhov, took the matter very seriously, made a special journey to Yalta in May expressly to discuss with Chekhov the position that they should adopt. Since the Academy itself had made obeisance and ratified the "act of the prince," both Korolenko and Chekhov decided to resign from it.

Chekhov sent his letter of resignation to A. Veselovsky, the Director of the Academy, on August 25. It was moderate and sober in tone. It began by pointing out that the Academy, and therefore he himself, had been guilty of self-contradiction in first electing Gorky and then setting aside the election; Chekhov continued: "I cannot accept such a contradiction, nor will my conscience permit it. After much deliberation, I have been able to arrive at only one conclusion, which I find most painful and regrettable, and that is that I must respectfully request that you relieve me of my title as an Honorary Academician."

Meanwhile, though he stood on the doorstep of death, Chekhov was still above all a writer, and it was as writer that he viewed for a moment, perhaps, his deepest drama. He had always written easily, with a kind of disconcerting eagerness, but as he told Grigorovich, the time when he could put together a story as a game, in a few hours and almost without thinking about it, was completely gone. During the past three years his creative atmosphere, so to speak, had grown steadily more rarefied—six stories in 1899, two in 1900, two and *The Three Sisters* in 1901, only one thus far in 1902—and now the spring seemed to have dried up completely. He still had ideas for plays and stories, but when he tried to sit down to write them, it was as if he were impeded by an agonizing paralysis. And his suffering was increased by the fact that from every quarter he was being pressed to furnish new works for the public that he had created for himself. Was he not a writer? was it not his function, his duty, to write?

It was Olga more than anyone else who gave him virtually no rest on this score. In almost all her letters, with the same note of command with which she ordered him to take castor oil and bathe more often, she bade him write. Had he finally begun a new story? above all, was he making progress with the writing of that play that he had been promising her for months? Poor Chekhov either did not reply at all or stammered the excuses of a schoolboy who has not done his homework: it was impossible to work in Yalta, his visitors gave him no peace, his health was bad . . .

It was not Olga alone who was pushing him: magazine editors, Gorky (who wanted to publish Chekhov in his own magazine), and in particular Stanislavsky and Nemirovich-Danchenko. As a result of Morozov's financial backing, the Art Theater had just moved into a new building that was the first of its kind in Russia with its revolving stage and its ingenious lighting, and the ambition of its two directors was to open their new season with a new play by Chekhov: success would be guaranteed. Since Chekhov had been foolish enough to outline the new play in detail to Stanislavsky, the directors not only harassed him constantly but enlisted Olga in their campaign.

Actually, Chekhov had tried in Lyubimovka to write this play, which had been in his mind for months, and then he had promised himself—and Olga—that he would finish it in Yalta. Almost as soon as he arrived there, he wrote to her that he was "installed at his desk." But a few days later he told her that he would not write the play that year, that his "heart was not in it," even though it had a "splendid" theme. So let Nemirovch-Danchenko stop nagging him. If he wrote anything it would be at most a little one-act sketch.

But he no longer had enough strength even for that. He did no more than work over *The Evils of Tobacco*, a monologue of a few pages written in 1885—oh, those wonderful days when he could work as if it were play!—which he had reread in connection with the preparation of his complete works. At first he had decided to omit this early piece; then he decided to rewrite it completely and include it in the Marx edition. The rewriting of these ten pages was his entire summer's work, and he apologized to Olga: "People come to visit without interruption and it's impossible for me to write" (September 5, 1902).

His physician and friend, Altschuler, had paid him a visit as soon as Chekhov had returned to Yalta, but whether out of his skepticism toward an art that he knew only too well or out of fear of Olga, who disliked the old doctor, Chekhov held out for several weeks against letting Altschuler make an examination, until he felt much better—toward the end of September. Then he was able to write to Olga, with perhaps a certain exaggerated optimism: "Altschuler found that my condition had improved substantially, and to judge by the change that has taken place since spring, my disease is on the way to being cured. He has even given me permission to go to Moscow: this is really marvelous! He says only that I should not go now but wait for the first frost" (September 22, 1902).

How happy Chekhov was at the thought of reunion with his "little crocodile," his "wonderful wife"! After those long weeks of solitude in Yalta he promised himself a sybarite's life in the capital: "When I come to Moscow I'll do nothing but eat, drink, make love to my wife, go to the theater, and, in my free time, sleep. I've made up my mind to become an Epicurean!" (September 24, 1902). Olga's reply to these enchanting plans was a cry of joy: "Antosha, my dearest golden boy, are we really going to see each other soon? Hurrah! . . . Oh, how I'll kiss you, how I'll look at you and examine every detail of my marvelous husband!"

So on October 12 the Epicurean set out for Moscow. His conscience was at rest: not wishing to leave his mother alone, he had sent her ten days earlier to his brother Misha in Petersburg. Winter had already begun in Moscow: Chekhov traveled in a heavy overcoat and galoshes, as he had promised Olga, who in her turn had promised to ply him on arrival with her customary remedies: cod liver oil and creosote, followed by beer and a good bath. Anton found her alone in her new apartment in Neglina Street; after their quarrels of the summer, Masha had found it better to remove herself and had gone to join her mother in Petersburg.

Like a reprieved exile who kisses his native soil on his return, Chekhov threw himself eagerly into the stream of Moscow's winter life. He went to every restaurant and every shop, visited the Art Theater's new premises, and saw a performance of Tolstoy's *The Power of Darkness* there, as well as *Uncle Vanya* and *The Three Sisters*, both of which, this time, he thought were magnificently done. He had planned—or hoped—to work: an endless flow of visitors prevented him. He saw Gorky, whose play *The Lower Depths* was in rehearsal, as well as Bunin and Suvorin. And he had the pleasure of encountering one of his old friends from the university, Dr. Rossolimo; in addition, he met Chaliapin and Sergei Diaghilev.

The days rushed past, the winter tightened its grip, and Chekhov wore himself out keeping pace with the swift tempo of the capital's intellectual life. Hence, after seven weeks, exhausted and again in the grip of coughing spasms, he was constrained to appeal for clemency. Already he must set out again on the road to exile, to Yalta the dull. But at least he had had a long period of happiness with Olga. Full of gratitude, he wrote to her as soon as he had returned to the Crimea: "I love you more tenderly than ever. To go to bed and get up without you is appalling, preposterous. You've spoiled me terribly" (November 30, 1902).

Another winter of unending, monotonous loneliness was beginning for him. December was gloomy and cold; he rarely left the house, even on the day when Nicholas II made an official visit to Yalta. Early in January he contracted pleurisy, which kept him in bed for days. Altschuler took care of him, prescribing hot compresses, and for once the patient did not resist. He had been invaded by a kind of apathy, which deeply shocked his visitors. From bed he wrote to Suvorin: "I'm leading an idle life, doing nothing, but against all my inclinations. The only activity I have is reading."

Now he was living only by proxy, thanks to Olga's letters, Stanislavsky's telegrams, and the news in the papers. In his "wilderness" he rejoiced in the success of Gorky's *Lower Depths* in Moscow, nor was he displeased to learn that at last *The Sea Gull* had had a triumph in Petersburg, in the Alexandrinsky Theater, on the same stage where six years earlier it had been so deplorably slaughtered by fools. Such news as he had to give to Olga was trivial, almost ridiculous: "There's nothing new and interesting" in Yalta, aside from the fact that his temperature had reached 101°. "My nails have grown long and there's no one here to cut them. I've broken a tooth. A button came off my shirt." He was hideously lonely for Olga, Olga's youth, Olga's healthiness, Olga's joy in living. Sometimes, as on Christmas night, he dreamed in ink of everything that might have been: "I feel that if I could spend only half a night lying with my face buried in your shoulder I wouldn't feel ill any more. No matter what you say, I can't live without you. . . ."

This was all that was needed to plunge Olga into guilt again when she learned that he was once more bedridden: her place was with him, not on the stage of the Art Theater. With the utmost kindness he tried to reassure her: "You always write, my darling, that your conscience torments you because you're living in Moscow instead of with me in Yalta. But what are we to do, my dear? Try to think rationally: if you spent the whole winter here with me, your life would be wasted, and I'd feel guilty, which would hardly be an improvement. I knew very well that I was marrying an actress and that that meant that once we were married, you would spend the winters in Moscow. I don't feel even minimally offended or cheated; on the contrary, it seems to me that everything is fine, the way it should be. So don't plague me any more, darling, with your problems of conscience" (January 20, 1903).

But he had his own feeling of guilt, which was always the same: he was not doing his job as a writer. Since his return from Moscow he had begun to work on a new story, "Betrothed," but it took him all of five months to complete this twenty-page story, and it was to take him four months more to correct it in proof. He was working slowly, yet not because his imagination had turned sterile—"I have a mountain of ideas in my mind," he wrote to his wife—but because his body was drained: writing was now literally beyond his strength. "I write six or seven lines a day," he told Olga, "and I couldn't do more even in my life depended on it. I have diarrhea every day" (February 5, 1903).

Were these six or seven lines a day worth the enormous effort that they demanded of him? And had he not already written twenty stories like "Betrothed"? There were days when the question beset him, times when, in the terrible temptation of abandoning himself to rest, he thought of putting away his pen forever. "Oh, darling," he wrote to his distant Olga, "I tell you very honestly it would give me a tremendous satisfaction to stop being a writer" (February 16, 1903).

It was so much simpler to sit quietly in his chair, his eyes closed, and "dream" his "stories" rather than write them and, as every writer knows by experience, thereby ruin them. As he had told his wife, he was not lacking in ideas for stories and plays. So he returned again and again in his mind to that possible play that he had discussed so enthusiastically the previous summer with his friend Vishnyevsky, the old Taganrog schoolmate whom he had met again as an actor in the Art Theater. The theme of the play was not only quite new but indeed unprecedented: the principal protagonist of the drama would never appear on stage. All through the first three acts the other characters would talk about him and his life, express their admiration for him, and wait most eagerly for his arrival. But in the last act they would receive a telegram announcing that he had died. This *Waiting for Godot*, the idea for which might have come to him from reading Maeterlinck's *The Blind*, which he much admired, was to remain only a dream as far as Chekhov was concerned and to be written fifty years later by someone else.

As for *The Cherry Orchard*, his friends would have had every reason to suppose that he had given up the thought of writing it: he had not mentioned it for months. On January 1, however, he informed Stanislavsky that he would start work on it in February and give him the completed play in Moscow in March, but all February went by without his having done anything. Then he suddenly wrote to Olga on March 1 that he had finally finished "Betrothed" and gone back to *The Cherry Orchard*. Three days later, when his wife criticized him for his laziness, he got his back up. "My laziness has nothing to do with it," he retorted. "I am not really my own enemy, and if I were strong enough, I'd write not one but twenty-five plays" (March 4, 1903). For the next few weeks he discussed the play and its characters with her, until his enthusiasm dwindled again. On April 9, he told Olga curtly: "I'll write the play in Moscow because I find it impossible to write it here."

He was still, however, reading a great deal. Habitual reading of large numbers of newspapers gave him the illusion of still being part of what was going on in the world. He went through all the literary reviews and also, more surprisingly, *The Missionary Review*, the organ of the Russian Jesuits, which he called "very interesting." He reread Turgenev's plays and advised the Art Theater to produce what he regarded as the best of them, *The Parasite* and *The Country Woman*. He also read and enjoyed Gorky's stories, which he still thought somewhat clumsy but nevertheless far better than Andreyev's. As for Tolstoy, Chekhov told a friend that he could no longer force himself to read the "sermons" that the old prophet was now publishing. It seemed to him that all these essays in which Tolstoy expatiated on the subject of God were in fact written against Him, out of a kind of "senile hatred."

Chekhov lived all winter on the dream of returning to Moscow in March; later he would rent a dacha not too far from the city and spend the spring there with Olga, and then in June he would go to Switzerland and Italy. But Altschuler was standing guard: when March came, he examined his patient and prohibited the journey to Moscow. Chekhov was miserably disappointed: Olga was the sole bond that still united him with life and the future, and he was strictly forbidden to go to her. He was the more exasperated because he felt death at his back. "We haven't much more time left to live together," he had written to Olga. "We ought to hurry, we ought to do the impossible in order to get something out of it." Then he asked her whether she could not get a leave of absence and spend Easter in Yalta. "I'm so miserable," he wrote to her on March 6. "I'm longing so to see you that I have no patience left. I beg you and beg you again to come." But again he was to be disappointed: Olga replied that at Easter she had to go to Petersburg with the Art Theater.

Good weather, meanwhile, had returned to Yalta, and with Altschuler's permission Chekhov might again walk the length of the promenade and go into town. But he rarely went much farther than his own garden gate, and he left it to his servant to trim his beloved rosebushes and plant the new iris bulbs that he had ordered from Germany and Japan. Most often he was satisfied to walk very slowly around his little property, followed by his two dogs, observe some of his trees, and then sit, exhausted, on his favorite bench looking out over the sea.

Bunin, who oftened visited him, found him motionless there, his cane between his knees, his eyes vacant: "I remember his silences, his coughing, his closed eyes, the thoughts that I could read on his face, which was serene and sad, almost solemn."

The spring brought not only Bunin but other friends back to the Crimean coast: Gorky, Kuprin, Fyodorov. They often went to see him, full of consideration and little attentions for him. But Chekhov, in spite of his former delight in being surrounded by his friends, no longer derived the same pleasure from their talk as before. They were full of life, arguing about literature and politics with enthusiasm; he emerged only very rarely from his semi-lethargy. It was as if nothing gave him pleasure any longer, as if everything were a burden to him. Thus, when he was told that Gorky was arriving in the Crimea, Chekhov showed no pleasure at all at the thought of renewing their animated conversations of the past, but rather complained that he would have to put up with Gorky's rather dull wife and their extremely active little boy. There was now a line in his *Notebooks*: "My motto: I need nothing." He might well have added: "and, except for Olga, no one."

Occasionally, however, he would revive briefly: his solitude was suddenly intolerable, he must talk to someone. Thus, one night in April, although it was quite late, he telephoned Bunin in Yalta. "My dear sir," he said in his low voice, "find a good cab and come and get me. . . . We'll have a ride." Bunin objected that it was almost ten o'clock and Chekhov might get a chill. "No arguments, young man," Chekhov replied with a laugh. Tractable and obliging, Bunin arrived at Autka a few minutes later, made his way through the dark, silent house, and went into Chekhov's study, which was lighted by two small candles. Chekhov, Bunin related, was waiting for him in the doorway:

" 'What a night!' he said, with a gentleness that was unusual even for him, greeting me with a kind of melancholy pleasure. 'Let's go to Oreyanda. If I catch cold, too bad!'

"It was a mild, quiet night, with a full moon and flimsy white clouds. The carriage rolled over the white road, we sat without speaking, and we watched the reflections in the sea. Then there was the forest with the outlined tracery of its shadows, then the black of the cypresses pointing straight at the stars. We got out of the carriage and began to walk among the cypresses, along the pale ruins of the palace, slightly blue in the moonlight. Suddenly he said:

" 'Do you know how many more years I'll be read? Seven.'

" 'Why seven?' I asked.

" 'Let's say seven and a half.'

" 'No, poetry lives a long time, and with constantly greater intensity. You're sad tonight, Anton Pavlovich,' I said, looking into that handsome, simple, kind face that seemed pale in the moonlight.

"He was looking at the ground, and contemplatively he disordered the pebbles of the path with the tip of his cane. When I told him that he was sad, he gave me a mocking look: 'You're the sad one, because you spent the money for the cab.' Then he turned serious: 'But it's true, I shan't be read more than seven years. And I have even fewer left to live—six years at the very most.' " [6]

A few days after these gloomy and doubly false prophecies—he was to die a year later; but on the other hand he is still read today, and more now than then—completely disregarding Altschuler's orders, Chekhov left for Moscow.

[6] Bunin.

XIII

THE AXE IN
THE CHERRY ORCHARD

> I often say to myself: suppose one could start one's life over again,
> but this time with full knowledge? Suppose one could live one's
> life as one writes a school composition, once in rough draft, and
> then live it again in the fair copy? Then, I think, every one of us
> would try above all not to repeat himself and to create different
> conditions of life for himself, for example a house of flowers, full
> of light. . . .
> VERSHININ in *The Three Sisters*

Long separations and brief reunions—ever since their marriage,
these were the alternations that had constituted the life of Chekhov and his wife. This time it was five months since Anton had
last seen Olga, and yet, when he arrived in Moscow on April 24,
he did not find her there: she was still in Petersburg with the Art
Theater and did not return until the next day. She had rented a
new apartment in Petrovka Street and Chekhov found it delightful, but there were three flights of stairs to be climbed, and this
was a martyrdom for him with his wheezing chest: it took him a
half hour to mount them all. But he was so overjoyed at being
with his "sweet" again that he barely noticed such things: he
brought new clothes and new plans, such as going to the public
baths, seeing his friends, and even accompanying the Art Theater
in its forthcoming tour to Kiev and Odessa.

Unfortunately, however, though the weather was already so
springlike in Yalta, it was still dank and cold in Moscow. Forced

to stay at home, Chekhov dispatched a mass of letters and telegrams to his friends, inviting them to come and visit him in Petrovka Street. Because he was so well liked, they came in force—
among others, Dr. Rossolimo, Bunin, Suvorin (who made a special trip from Petersburg). Word of Chekhov's presence had
spread quickly through literary circles, and so he was assailed as
well by the usual seekers of favors, the young writers in search of
publishers, the publishers in search of manuscripts, the unsuccess-
ful writers in search of help. And Chekhov, as always, exhausted
all his efforts to help them all. On the other hand, Tolstoy evi-
denced his esteem by sending a photograph of himself inscribed:
"To the beloved Anton P. Chekhov."

For all his increasing obsession with reforming the world
through non-violence, the eminent old writer was still interested
in literature in general and in Chekhov in particular. By way of
his son Ilya Lvovich he sent Chekhov a list of those of the latter's stories that he regarded as the best: among them were fifteen
that Tolstoy described as "first-rank." [1] In addition, Tolstoy had
made his own personal Chekhov anthology: he had had these favorite stories bound together into a book that he reread frequently
with consistently greater pleasure. "Chekhov is a prose Pushkin,"
he told Lazarevsky. "If there is an echo of his own experiences in
Pushkin's verse, the same thing is true of Chekhov's stories."

For more than a year Chekhov's friends, and especially Gorky,
had been urging him to renegotiate the publishing contract that
he had made with Marx and that was producing shocking profits
for the publisher. Further incited by a lawyer, Mirolyubov, Chekhov decided to discuss the matter with Marx in person, and for
this purpose he made a brief journey to Petersburg. One is obliged
to conclude, however, that he was a poor lawyer for himself, because on his return he wrote to Masha: "I spoke to Marx, but
nothing substantial came of it. He gave me a huge number of
books (about two hundred and seventy-five pounds of them), all
beautifully bound, and he also offered me five thousand rubles for
'medical expenses,' which of course I refused" (July 7, 1903).

---

[1] These were "The Urchins," "A Singer," "A Drama," "At Home," "Sorrow,"
"Escape," "In Court," "Vanka," "Those Ladies," "The Malefactor," "The Children," "Darkness," "Wanting to Sleep," "The Bride," "The Darling."

Since the winter, he had been contemplating spending part of the summer with Olga in Italy and Switzerland, but undoubtedly he recognized that in his present condition it would be sheer folly to undertake anything of the sort, and so he made up his mind to have a thorough physical examination. For this he returned to Professor Ostroümov, who had taken such excellent care of him six years earlier when he had had his most serious hemorrhages. Ostroümov said frankly that he considered Chekhov's condition extremely alarming: the right lung was heavily damaged and the emphysema had spread into the left. So when Chekhov posed the question of a long journey abroad, the physician countered with an official interdict: "You are an invalid," he said. Next day Chekhov sent an summarized account of this consultation to Masha, who was with their mother in Yalta, but he couched it in a very light manner. "He spent a long time plucking, palping, and auscultating me," he wrote. "He then wrote out five prescriptions, and above all he forbade me to spend the winter in Yalta because it is usually bad there; he ordered me to spend it in a dacha somewhere near Moscow" (May 24, 1903).

For Chekhov this ban on further winters on the Crimean coast was almost an adequate compensation for the disappointment of not being able to go abroad. He had begun literally to hate Yalta —undoubtedly because it reminded him too often and too forcefully of his illness—and since the illustrious professor was now virtually ordering him to do so, he made up his mind to spend winters hereafter in the vicinity of Moscow, which meant not too far from his dear "little horse," the restaurants, and the literary ambiance.

Rather strangely, far from depressing him, Ostroümov's ominous diagnosis seemed rather to have forced him out of his apathy. He was almost happy—but then hadn't having to change his place and plan of life again always made him feel better? He immediately wrote to Masha about selling Gurzuf and Kushukoy and sending their mother to Moscow for the winter; he was already beginning to look for a dacha. A few days later, when his sister expressed her concern over Ostroümov's diagnosis, he wrote to her quite ingenuously that he could understand neither her sorrow nor her pessimism.

What he did not tell Masha—though he did not conceal it from certain friends, especially Dr. Shredin—was that in spite of everything he had been quite surprised by Ostroümov's opinion and advice. He had accepted the doctor's prescriptions with his usual smiling skepticism toward miracle drugs, but in addition he admitted that he could not decide whether to abide by Altschuler's or Ostroümov's counsels. Which of his colleagues was right? After all, if it was Ostroümov, why had he been made to bury himself in Yalta through four interminable winters? And once he had become accustomed to living near Moscow, of course, some other physician would lose no time insisting on sending him back to the south, to the Crimea or perhaps even to Egypt . . .

Meanwhile one of Olga's friends, Marya Yakunshikova, an extremely wealthy society woman very much interested in the arts, insisted that the Chekhovs spend a few weeks on her estate in the Moscow area, and they accepted. When they arrived there, on May 25, they found that this regal property near Naroye-Fominskoye included, among others, a house "big enough for ten" that had been set aside for them. For Chekhov, who was once more eager to write as well as to rest, this was the ideal situation. Writing to Masha and reminding her to take care of his fruit trees, his rosebushes, and his Japanese irises in Yalta, he added: "There's a river here, plenty of ground for walking, an old chapel, and an abundance of fish."

But he also wanted to lose no time in finding a dacha for the autumn: as soon as they had arrived in Naroye-Fominskoye, he and Olga started scouting the area. This part of the country was all the more pleasing to him because it filled him with old memories; Vosskressensk and New Jerusalem, which in his youth had been his introduction to the delights of the Moscow countryside, were quite near. During these expeditions in search of a house he met some of his old vacation acquaintances; he also spent some time in the Zvenigorod Cemetery beside the grave of Dr. Uspensky, who had taught him in the rudiments of medicine twenty years earlier. In Vosskressensk itself he and Olga were invited to spend a few days with Savva Morozov, "the Russian Rockefeller," who seemed to have nursed no grudge against Chekhov for having rather abruptly abandoned his company at Perm a year earlier.

Olga relaxed in Naroye-Fominskoye and mingled with her hostess' many other guests: for the moment she had forgot the theater. Chekhov himself—like Trigorin in *The Sea Gull*—could never make himself forget that he was a writer. He had made up his mind to finish that *Cherry Orchard* he had been carrying about with him for more than a year, but first he had to correct the revised proofs of "Betrothed," and since he rather lacked confidence in himself at the moment, this task required considerable effort. Dissatisfied with what he had written, he redid whole passages. When at last he got back to *The Cherry Orchard*, he wrote to a friend: "I'm sitting in front of a large window and working a little." Unquestionably he was working on his play, but very painfully, without enthusiasm, almost without faith in it. He had confided to Mrs. Morozova that he was "profoundly disturbed by the fear that he had nothing more to say in literature," and this anxiety, combined with his tremendous weariness—and also, perhaps, with the fact that he had been carrying the embryo of the play in his mind too long—paralyzed his pen. Besides, he added, what was the use of writing plays in which the public would be interested for three or four years at the most?

One stormy day, when he had left the window beside his desk wide open, the wind scattered several sheets of his manuscript about the garden. They were found, but the rain had made them unreadable, even to their author. But of course, Chekhov was told by way of consolation, you'll remember what was in them. He smiled before he replied rather surprisingly: "Believe me, I don't remember any of it. I'll have to rewrite those scenes completely."

Infrequent storms of this kind were the only interruptions in the tranquil days and weeks at Naroye-Fominskoye, but such was certainly not the case for the rest of Russia during that summer. Right-wing gangs in Kishinev, with the support of the government and the protection of the police, had embarked on bloody massacres of Jews. The official press abstained from reporting them, and Chekhov, who wanted precise information, asked Suvorin to send him the latest issues of a clandestine Marxist newspaper, *Liberation*; his hard-core right-wing friend complied immediately. But regardless of his sympathies for those who were combatting oppression, Chekhov preserved his frankness of opin-

ion: when he had read the papers very carefully, he declared that
this revolutionary journalism was useful but much too lacking in
appeal, "as uninteresting as an encyclopedia." He also read sym-
pathetically Gorky's "open letter" on the Kishinev pogroms, but
once again, his critical sense unimpaired, he regretted that "it was
badly written, too long-winded, and lacking both the youthfulness
and the boldness of Tolstoy."

Nonetheless all his sympathies were on the side of the victims
of the pogroms. When Sholem Aleichem, the famous Jewish author of Russian origin, asked him to help them by writing something for a short-story collection to be published in Warsaw to
raise money for the Jews, Chekhov replied that he would be glad
to write something if his health permitted, but otherwise Aleichem should feel free to use any of his already published works.
"They are completely at your disposal," Chekhov wrote, "and
translations of them into Yiddish published in your anthology for
the relief of the Jewish victims of Kishinev would represent a real
pleasure for me" (June 19, 1903).

The sojourn in Naroye-Fominskoye would have been perfect if
it had not included Marya Yakunshikova and the endless procession of the visitors from Moscow whom she entertained in her luxurious white house. Olga seemed to enjoy the company of these
socialites, but Chekhov found them ridiculous and repugnant.
How could his actor friend Vishnyevsky lower himself to behave
toward them "as if they were gods," when they lived lives as useless as they were absurd and found their ultimate pleasure in being seen walking through the park with General So-and-So or a
minister or Prince Obolensky? To Chekhov a day of gabble from
all these fashionables was not worth an hour's talk with Maxim,
one of the estate's gardeners. Hence, having initially planned to
stay for two months, he had his fill of this *vie de château* at the
end of six weeks. Forgetting that Ostroümov had told him to
spend the whole summer in the Moscow district, he decided at the
end of July to go back to Yalta.

Still under the influence of Ostroümov's ominous diagnosis,
Masha had been impatiently waiting for him there for weeks. She
never told him so outright, but her descriptions of his garden, of
which she was the loyal keeper, were so tempting! She included

them in every one of her letters: the weather was marvelous, neither too hot nor too dry, and much-needed rains had transformed the little property into a fairyland of color and scent. His appetite aroused—and his suspicions as well—Chekhov wrote back that he had never heard of such splendid summers in Yalta. But when he arrived there on July 9 he saw that Masha had not exaggerated: his entire beloved garden was one great perfumed flower.

His luggage still contained the manuscript of *The Cherry Orchard,* which he had been hauling everywhere for so many months and which was still unfinished. Now, however, he was resolved to complete his play regardless of everything, and in order to make himself do so, he set himself a deadline: it must be ready in October for the new theatrical season. For weeks, then, at the cost of infinite exertion of will against inclination, against drugged imagination, against an exhausted body that cried for quarter, he was going to fight on, line after line, scene after scene, until he had made his plan a reality.

Nor did he allow himself to be distracted by the rather tense and vexing climate that prevailed round him. Relations were once more quite strained between Olga and her mother- and sister-in-law. As if to give her in-laws a lesson, his wife was constantly fussing over him, treating him like a child: she made him stick to the diet that she had prescribed and take a cold bath every day while she watched. All three women were constantly and jealously eyeing one another, but it was Olga who complained the most. She also accused her husband of not openly standing up for her. "Why are there always problems when I'm there?" she was to write to him immediately after she had gone back to Moscow. "Why do you torture me, and why don't you do anything?"

Indeed, even if Chekhov had wanted to drop the work that he had begun, he would have been unable to do so because of the terrible, exigent pressure imposed on him by everyone. With savage insistence, as if they really had no knowledge of the extent of his exhaustion, Olga, Stanislavsky, and Nemirovich-Danchenko repeatedly reminded him that the Art Theater was expecting his play for the autumn. The weeks went on and the two directors grew anxious, apprehensively questioning Olga: was her husband working again? To their way of thinking, the guilty man was Ostroümov: his alarming observations had robbed Anton Pavlovich of his good spirits and his peace of mind. Chekhov himself was then assailed by their inquiries, and with an embarrassed smile he tried to make excuses: he was lazy, the weather was too good, his theme was too difficult . . .

Stanislavsky finally became aware how unforgivable his importunities were, and he tried to make excuses to Olga. "Don't think badly of us," he wrote to her. "We're very concerned for Anton Pavlovich and those who are dear to him, and we think about the play only when we're worried about the future of our theater. Because our theater is Chekhov's theater, and without him things would go badly for us." Far from being angry at him, Olga made every effort to reassure him on the important thing: her husband was working every day now. "Yesterday and today, however," she wrote, "he was ill, and consequently he didn't write. . . . He sees very few people now, and if his health permitted, he would work more consistently." Then she broke off for a moment to verify her facts, and she added: "Don't worry, he's just started writing again" (August 3, 1903).

By the end of August, Olga was able to tell Nemirovich-Danchenko that her husband was "working well, with enthusiasm," and a few days later Chekhov himself confirmed this: if he could continue at this rate, he would soon be finished. Since Olga was going back to Moscow on September 15, he hoped that she would be able to take the play with her in its final form. But unfortunately he had not made allowance for illness: stricken by a fresh attack at the beginning of September, he was unable to write or even dictate for several days. On September 15 he was compelled to admit to Stanislavsky's wife that, although he felt better, he was still enduring such headaches that he had not yet returned to writing, so Olga would arrive in Moscow without the manuscript. He promised, however, that he would soon send the complete script—that is, all four acts. He added that the play was "not a drama but a comedy, and in places even a farce," and he wondered what Nemirovich-Danchenko would think of it.

After Olga had left he went through a brief period of discouragement: "I'm so far from everything," he wrote to her the next day, "that I'm beginning to lose heart. It seems to me that as a writer I've gone out of style, and every line I write seems worthless and totally useless." A day later, however, he recovered control of himself, and in spite of his extreme weakness, his headaches, his intestinal disturbances, and his vast weariness, he returned heroically to his task. Then, in almost daily notes, he kept Olga—and, through her, the directors of the Art Theater—abreast of his progress. He had promised to send her a telegram as soon as he had finished, and barely a week after her departure Olga did in fact receive the expected telegram: "The four acts are completely finished. Now recopying. Will send you play." The next day he wrote to her: "I have no idea what value the play has."

Nevertheless the writing of the fourth act had fleetingly fired him with enthusiasm, and indeed he had the feeling that he had accomplished "something new." But as he recopied the manuscript, his ardor diminished. He saw that there were many things in the play that he did not like, and he started to rewrite them. Meanwhile Olga was growing impatient and making no secret of her irritation: time was passing and there was no sign of the manuscript promised in the telegram. Like a schoolboy late with his assignments, Chekhov meekly apologized in his replies: if he was losing time, she must forgive him; it was because he was ill and because the coughing spasms had made him so weak that he could not write more than a couple of lines a day. He begged her not to be angry; it was really impossible for him to work faster. "Darling, forgive me about the play," he wrote. "Forgive me! I swear I've finished it and I'm only recopying it." He complained of the intrusions that prevented him from working, and he mocked at himself: "I drag and drag along," he write to Olga, "and simply because I drag, my play now seems something beyond measure, colossal, it frightens me, and I've lost all appetite for it." He also made excuses to Stanislavsky: "Don't be angry with me," he wrote to the director on October 10. "I'm making a fair copy of the play for the second time, and that's why I'm late. I'll send it to you in three days."

But it was only two days later that Olga received the confirmation for which she was so impatiently waiting: "Well, little horse,

hurrah! after all my long sufferings and yours. The play is finished, really finished, and tomorrow night, or on the morning of
the fourteenth at the latest, it will be in the mail for Moscow!"
And then there was a cry from the heart, from a heart that was
drained: "Oh, darling, how hard it's been for me to write this
play!" Two days later he sent a telegram confirming that he had
just mailed the mansucript.

Was he at last going to allow himself a more than earned rest
and forget the tortures of the past few weeks? Quite the contrary.
Once his play was in the mail, he was suddenly confronted by a
kind of spiritual vacuum, and he was besieged by doubts and regrets. He could not make himself stop thinking still and always
about *The Cherry Orchard*: oh, what he could not have made of
such a theme if only he had been in decent health! But instead of
writing his play in a single spurt, as he had always done, he had
dragged out his work and for that reason it seemed to him that his
play was lacking in spirit and pace. Hence he hoped that the directors of the Art Theater would read it quickly and equally
quickly liberate him from his doubts.

Now it was his turn to express impatience, an impatience that
was feverish and irrational, as if he really had no confidence in
himself and, dreading lest he had lost his creative faculties, was
waiting to be reassured as soon as possible. On October 19, which
was five days after he had sent her his manuscript—it could not
have arrived in Moscow for at least two days more—he wrote to
Olga that all day long he had been waiting for news with a pounding heart and total "terror." That evening, luckily, he received a
telegram from Nemirovich-Danchenko, and two days later there
was one from Stanislavsky.

Nemirovich-Danchenko's telegram, which came to exactly a
hundred and eighty words, was such as completely to reassure
Chekhov. This was his best play, the director said; it was new,
original, and poetic. He had only two reservations: the characters
were somewhat tearful and the second act dragged. Stanislavsky's
telegram was simply a shout of joy: "Overwhelmed, can't come
down to earth, swept away in admiration. Consider your play best
of finest things you've written. Deepest congratulations to a writer

of genius." In the ensuing days there were more telegrams from both directors, announcing that they had read the play to the Art Theater's actors: "Profoundly impressed. . . . Remarkable success, brilliant. . . . Every subtlety appreciated. . . . All wept at last act. . . . You wife absolutely in raptures, like everyone. No play has ever aroused such unanimous enthusiasm. . . ."

After such a concert of telegraphic adulation one might suppose that Chekhov would have been assuaged and even happy. He was not, and no doubt it was his isolation and above all his exhaustion, after the enormous effort of will that his play had cost him, that were responsible for the anxious, impatient, sometimes even nagging nervousness with which he continued to keep after both the directors of the Art Theater in the days that followed. First he became angry with Nemirovich-Danchenko, because for purposes of publicity he had summarized *The Cherry Orchard* for a reporter, who had of course at once printed a rather fantastic version of it that happened to come to Chekhov's attention. Without giving his friends time to catch their breath, he then complained that he was not kept informed of anything, that he did not know either whether his play would go on during the current season or how it would be staged. Though Stanislavsky attempted to answer his questions with minimum loss of time, Chekhov was only half satisfied. He was also worried about the casting, and fearing that Nemirovich-Danchenko might base his choices simply on friendship or policy, he sent a list of his own recommendations. Joint agreement on this matter was finally reached, and the first rehearsal was scheduled for November 10.

In spite of all the demonstrations of good faith by the directors of the Art Theater, Chekhov was nonetheless still uneasy over the fate of his play. He continued sending letter after letter, both to Olga and to Stanislavsky, in which he discussed settings, details of staging, or even certain psychological and physical aspects of his characters. In a letter of November 25 to Olga, again on the subject of *The Cherry Orchard,* there was a passage that synthesized all his unhealthy apprehensiveness: "We began with misunderstandings and that is how we shall end. That, it seems to me, is the destiny of my play.

This almost morbid impatience in a man who for so many years had been a model of self-control was the result of the terrible disease that had already almost devoured him. Since the end of August, Chekhov had been ill without interruption, his body wracked by unending spasms of coughing and unceasing intestinal disturbances. His life was such a Calvary that he confided to a friend that he regarded those long weeks as "time wasted and useless that should be torn out of the book of his life" (December 21, 1903). He was so exhausted that the mere act of dressing subjected him to an almost impossible effort.

On a number of occasions he had to send for Dr. Altschuler. The doctor told him bluntly that his health precluded travel of any kind; as for the cold baths insisted on by Olga, that was pure insanity. Chekhov, whose only desire was Moscow, resigned himself nonetheless to following—for the moment—the physician's instructions and waiting until his health had improved before going to join Olga. He consoled himself with the thought of spending the entire winter in Moscow, as Ostroümov had advised him to do. He discussed this idea with Altschuler, who was harshly critical of his big-city colleague. "He has begged me not to go to Moscow and not to live there," Chekhov wrote to his wife. "He told me Ostroümov must have been drunk" (October 2, 1903).

Quite consciously and most lucidly he was living the torturing paradox of the gravely ill man who has had enough of his illness and would like to stop thinking about it but whose disease itself consistently and cruelly compels his attention. He asked his wife whether he was not boring her with his "medicinal conversations," but what other subject of conversation was there for him? He himself would have liked to forget that he was merely a condemned man awaiting the expiration of his reprieve, but how could he not think about it? If he climbed five steps he had to stop, sweating and breathless; he began to write and a spasm of coughing constricted his chest and forced him to leave his desk and lie down. When he joined his family at meals, Masha immediately handed him a box of pills, and when he apologized for his lack of appetite, his mother reminded him that Altschuler had said that he must force himself to eat as many as eight eggs a day.

After Olga's departure he felt more alone than ever in Yalta, "like on a desert island." For he still loved his "sweet," his "little Hungarian horse," and it was because of her that this case-hardened bachelor had even become an apostle of marriage. When after several years during which they had lost touch with each other, he encountered a writer friend, V. Kiny-Dedlov, Chekhov said: "Haven't you married? Forgive me for asking, but why not? I've been married two or three years and it's made me very happy; it seems to me to have been a very fortunate change in my life. What is usually written about marriage is so much nonsense" (November 10, 1903).

His letters to Olga, however, no longer manifested either the gaiety or the almost overflowing tenderness of the past. What showed through quite often now was impatience, irritation, a more biting irony. But how could it have been otherwise when—except for the theater—their almost sole topic of conversation was now the one thing of which Chekhov wanted to hear no mention: his health? Justifiably anxious, Olga spoke of nothing else. She exhorted him to take care of himself, to follow his diet, and, good German that she was, she overwhelmed him with hygienic recommendations. She was a fanatic of cleanliness, baths, and body care, and her husband, who had allowed her to have her way with him for more than two years, was beginning to find that she was going too far. One day when she took up this subject again, he half-jokingly and half-angrily replied that she must be right, because since he had stopped taking baths on Altschuler's orders, his whole body had begun to sprout mushrooms and other fungi.

After the middle of October, when his play and his sister had gone off to Moscow, Chekhov felt even more lonely and abandoned. He had promised to write a story for a collection that Gorky was compiling, but he had neither the strength nor the wish to embark on it. During the summer he had become a reader for the magazine *Russian Thought,* and he killed time by reading manuscripts—extremely few of which he recommended—playing solitaire, and entertaining his very numerous visitors. He was still a polite and cordial host to everyone, but how many beggars and chatterboxes and pompous asses they included! One of them, a man named Shoposhnikov, was so extraordinarily boring that he forced Chekhov out of his automatic extreme courtesy and gave him the almost irresistible urge "to tear out his tongue."

He was so concentrated on the idea of going to Moscow that it became an obsession, but no matter how much time went by, his health did not improve, and Altschuler still forbade him to make the journey. Chekhov had made up his mind that as soon as he felt able to do so, he would leave without Altschuler's permission, but now Olga herself opposed his doing so. She insisted that he ought to consider his health above all, and that the weather in Moscow —as Masha confirmed—was still abominable. As soon as it improved she would ask him to join her.

But one day followed another, gray and endless, and the call for which he longed never came. His mood turned blacker, and in his bitterness—which, furthermore, he acknowledged—he now directed his anger at his wife, often on empty grounds. Why, he wrote to her furiously, had she not sent the boots that he had ordered for one of the servants, and the toilet paper? Why did she refuse to have a good fur-lined coat made for him in Moscow? Did she think it was too expensive and he had no right to wear a coat that cost three or four hundred rubles? She was simply a miser . . .

Moscow, Moscow! The pitiful, symbolic leitmotif of *The Three Sisters*—the Utopian hope that life must be more beautiful elsewhere—was now his own. He dreamed of Moscow when he sat on the bench in his garden—in Yalta the air was mild and bright—he dreamed of Moscow when he sat writing to his friends, and he remembered . . . "I'd like so much to go to The Hermitage," he wrote to Nemirovich-Danchenko, "and have a sterlet and a bottle of wine. One day I finished a bottle of champagne there alone, and I wasn't drunk; then I drank cognac, and I still wasn't drunk" (November 2, 1903).

In mid-November he informed Olga—in vain—that he was feeling better; she was not yet ready to give him the sign for which he was hoping. Then he got angry again and accused her of not wanting him to be in Moscow. If that was how it was, he would not write to her again, he would go abroad. Then he regained control and wrote more amicably: "I'm not writing anything because all I'm doing is waiting for your command to pack my suitcase and leave for Moscow. To Moscow, to Moscow! It is not *three sisters* speaking, it is *one husband*. I kiss my little goose" (November 21, 1903). Two days later he admitted to Stanislavsky how obsessed he was by the desire to be in the capital: "I sit in my study and never take my eyes off the telephone . . . and every second I'm expecting to be called at last to Moscow."

On December 1 the "little goose" finally made the so-long-awaited signal. Chekhov left Yalta next day, with all its "remarkable but . . . stale and useless weather," for Moscow and its rough winter. He had had enough of "feeling life pass by him" and he wanted plunge himself into it one last time even at the risk of dying of it.

He found Moscow as he preferred it to be: like a black-and-white drawing under its snow. In the icy air and the frozen silence, the Kremlin bells, which he loved, rang clearer than ever. It gave him pleasure to wear the fine fur-lined coat that Olga had finally decided to have made for him. A beaver cap covering his ears, he went walking with her through the center of the city; he loved to mingle with the crowd, to examine the windows of the elegant shops, to do his own buying of tea and herring and caviar. But such expeditions were infrequent: although he went every day to the Art Theater to watch the rehearsals for his play, and sometimes went back in the evening to see whatever play was being done, for the most part he preferred to stay at home in Petrovka Street. The winter had established a solid grip on the city, every day the air was colder, and if he went out each time he had to face the atrocious Calvary of the many flights of stairs to be climbed.

He had made it a rule that he would refuse all invitations, but friendship nevertheless compelled him at attend certain ceremonies and other events. One evening he went to the opera because it was a benefit performance for Fyodor Chaliapin, whom he liked immensely. He also considered it his duty to attend the funeral of his old school friend Dr. Altukhov, and to follow the hearse to the cemetery. During the journey he made jokes—of the ritual gallows-humor character that is almost obligatory among the members of the healing art—with another old fellow-student, Dr. Rossolimo: which of the two of them would be the first to see poor old Altukhov in the next world?

On New Year's night there was a celebration at the Art Theater that, according to Stanislavsky, was arranged for Chekhov's amusement, and he attended. The evening began with music-hall turns of which the main event was a mock boxing match between the gigantic Chaliapin, dressed as an Oriental prince, and the almost-midget Sulerzhitsky, which, after a great deal of sparring, gracefully evolved into a Ukrainian dance. After dinner, which was served in the lobby, the tables and chairs were removed and people in costumes, evening dress, and ordinary clothes danced for hours. Chekhov was sitting to one side, near a window, with Maxim Gorky. They were trying to sustain a conversation above—or below—the music and the laughter and the general confusion. In the end they abandoned all hope of verbal communication and merely exchanged winks: they were both coughing heavily. Finally Chekhov said with a gentle smile: "It might be said that we have had a highly interesting exchange of coughs."

Most of his evenings were spent in drearier fashion, in the solitude of the apartment in Petrovka Street. Bunin, knowing that he would be alone, often went to keep him company, barely getting a glimpse of Olga, who was preparing herself for an appearance at the theater or at some charity concert. Nemirovich-Danchenko would come to fetch her: he was always in evening dress, his beard freshly tended and smelling slightly of cigars and toilet water; she was young and fresh-looking in her splendid gown. They took hasty leave of Chekhov. "Don't be bored without me, darling," Olga would command him, on the run. "Anyway, I know you always like being with Bouquichon. Good-night. . . ." Bunin had barely time to kiss her hand before she was gone. This was always the beginning of a long, long vigil for the two friends, because Chekhov did not want Bunin to leave him until Olga had come home.

They talked without stopping. While he performed his various tasks such as washing his hair—Olga's beloved health rules were the law again—Chekhov would talk about his family and his youth. Then the conversation would drift into literary matters: he offered his younger colleague the affectionate but no less earnest counsel that he put aside his dilettantism and force himself to write every day if he wished to become a genuine writer. There were times too when in Bunin's presence Chekhov would dream aloud of his increasingly ardent desire to spend what was left of his life in flight from the world: like a true Russian he would take to the roads and go from one place of pilgrimage to another until he had come to the monastery lying between a forest and a lake where at last he could halt and sit on a bench at the gate in the long summer evenings. "About four in the evening, sometimes later," Bunin was to write, "Olga Leonardovna would come home, in an aroma of wine and perfume. 'Aren't you asleep yet, darling? That isn't good for you. And you're still here, Bouquichon? Certainly he wasn't bored with you!' I would immediately get up and leave."

Chekhov's great concern, however, was still his play. Its first performance was scheduled for January 17, and in spite of the state of his heath, he was attending every rehearsal. But it was without the slightest eagerness that he would go to the Art Theater, and in fact, as the rehearsals progressed, he was filled with growing dissatisfaction and resentment, because exactly what he had dreaded from the start was taking place: Stanislavsky's staging proved that he had understood nothing of *The Cherry Orchard!* Sitting alone in the dark, empty theater, shivering and trying not to cough, Chekhov watched as his play became the opposite of what he had conceived, of what he had "seen" as he was writing it.

"The directors and the author never understood each other or reached any agreement," Olga later wrote. As Stanislavsky saw matters, Chekhov was exceeding his rights as an author when he criticized staging and direction; from the day of his arrival in Moscow he had "knocked everything to pieces." This time, in fact, the disagreement between them was basic: it had to do less with the way in which *The Cherry Orchard* should be presented as with the way it must be understood, with its essential character. Chekhov—he had said the same thing a dozen times since the summer—had conceived his play as a gay comedy, "in places even a farce," whereas Stanislavsky saw it as a social drama, the drama of the minor rural nobility compelled to give way to the "new rich," who for all their vulgarity were stubborn and hence victorious. Even before Chekhov's arrival in Moscow, furthermore, Stanislavsky had persuaded the actors to his point of view, and it was thus that he had evolved his whole presentation.

Author and director stood their respective grounds and, confronted by Stanislavsky's obstinacy, Chekhov at last abandoned the effort to make his own views prevail. But he did not hesitate to criticize the director and broadcast his disapproval. "I can't get it clear in my own mind," he told a visitor one day. "Either the play is no good or the actors don't understand me. . . . As it's being done now, it's impossible to put on my play." Hence he was fearful of the audience's reaction, and a few days before the opening, he confessed that he was not expecting a success.

Was that why he refused to attend that first performance of *The Cherry Orchard* on January 17? Unquestionably; but no matter what Masha was to say about it, it was also because he suspected that his friends were planning a spectacular celebration for him for the same evening because it was his forty-fourth birthday and his "silver jubilee" in literary life.[2] In any event, Chekhov had made up his mind to stay at home, and the performance did indeed begin in his absence. But as the second act was ending, Stanislavsky sent him an urgent note: the audience and the actors were screaming for him.

He arrived at the theater as the third-act curtain was falling. He was dragged on stage, where all the actors, the two directors, and the leaders of the major literary and dramatic groups of Moscow were already waiting for him. He was thrust into the foreground; the audience was at first taken by surprise, for there had been no announcement that he was coming, but then it broke out into a thrilling ovation that seemed incapable of ending.

The rite of tribute was about to begin. Gifts, wreaths, baskets of flowers piled up on stage. These were followed by speeches—

---

[2] Chekhov himself was to be the first to point out that this jubilee was somewhat premature, since his entrance into letters, with a short piece printed in *Alarm Clock,* had been made only in March, 1880.

grandiloquent, flowery, flat. Journalists, actors, officers of literary societies, everyone had to speak his piece and create his own glory in honor—or at the expense—of the jubilarian. Emaciated, deathly pale, blinking in the harsh lights, not knowing what to do with his hands, Chekhov listened in unbelief and agonized embarrassment to all the fine things that were being said about him and that he was the last to credit. He forced himself not to cough, and he seemed about to faint. Was he overcome by emotion? Or more likely, with that sense of humor that never left him, was he not remembering how often he had mocked that Russian passion for jubilees and the heartfelt lies that were part of them, and how he had always refused to have anything to do with them, even when it came to honoring his "discoverer," Grigorovich? At one point he could not help smiling: someone in the audience, obviously perceiving how exhausted Chekhov was, shouted, "Sit down, for heaven's sake!" and everyone on stage scurried about looking for a chair and finding none.

The speeches went on and on, equally solemn and all fully interchangeable, but interrupted by the reading of dozens of telegrams of congratulation from every part of Russia. Stoically still on his feet, Chekhov went on listening and smiling. Almost hiding in the darkness of her box, Masha observed her brother's triumph: this evening, all these testimonials of admiration and affection that poured in on her Antosha rewarded her in a single surge—in her heart—for twenty years of total and unseen devotion, and she wept unashamed in joy and pride. Her emotion was shared by the entire throng when Nemirovich-Danchenko, in his fine passionate voice, concluded his speech to Chekhov with an admirable scorn for whatever of the ridiculous might be read into his words and his act: "What you see here is only a token of the unbounded affection in which you are held by the whole elite of Russia. Our theater owes so much to your talent, to the tenderness of your heart, to the purity of your soul, that in all justice you can say: this is my theater."

This remarkable manifestation of homage before a standing, excited audience lasted for more than an hour. It ended in a final ovation; then Chekhov, who had not spoken a single word of thanks, withdrew. But this time the affection that had been lavished on him had got the better of his skepticism. Two days later he was still paralyzed by his emotion, and he wrote to his friend Batyushkov: "They honored me in so magnificent, so joyous, and so unexpected a way that I have not yet got over it."

Nevertheless this staggering personal triumph had not blinded him to the reception of his play. It had been better received, perhaps, than he had feared, but nonetheless this first performance had been only a *succès d'estime*, a manifestation of personal affection and loyalty. This was confirmed in the next few days by the press, which tended indeed to a certain severity of criticism—not so much of the play, it is true, as of the actors and their style. Because Stanislavsky had described *The Cherry Orchard* as a kind of social drama, the critics were thrown off balance by the frankly comic aspect of certain characters. And this must not have displeased the author too much.

For Chekhov still believed that his director had committed a major error of interpretation: the author stood his ground, his play was a comedy. He was to go back to this point, and with poorly masked irritation, months later in a letter to Olga: "Why do they insist on calling my play a drama in their advertisements and posters? Nemirovich-Danchenko and Stanislavsky see in my play something entirely different from what I wrote, and I'm willing to bet that neither of them has read the play carefully even once. Forgive me, but I am certain this is the case" (April 10, 1904).

Critics who always want to "read between the lines" have a wonderful time with Chekhov's fluid dialogue punctuated by question marks and silences. In the case of *The Cherry Orchard* they are almost unanimous in tracing the filigree of its "message," and even, since this was his last play, its author's "final message." This one word, "message," and this pretension to extrasensory exegesis would indeed have amused Chekhov, who had no love for critics and who told Gorky one day that after twenty-five years of reading what they had written about him, he could not find in all of it "one worthwhile comment or a single piece of good advice."

In actuality *The Cherry Orchard* offers no message, in code or in clear, and Chekhov, true to himself right to the end, no more utilized this play to give lessons, political, social, or moral in character, than he did his earlier works. The very most that one can say, as Gorky did, is that here again, by holding up this new dramatic mirror before us, he told us once more, in his own way, "with a sorrowful smile, in a tone of gentle but deep reproach, with a desperate nostalgia in his eyes and in his heart: 'Gentlemen, how badly you live your lives.' " This time, however, the smile is much more open and the melancholy is much less somber than in *The Three Sisters* or *Uncle Vanya.*

Chekhov did something quite different, in his last play, from sending us a final message: with exemplary reserve—it is so distasteful, he said, to die in public—he was making his farewells to life and men. Just as his heroine, Lyubov Ranyevskaya, gives a last party in her beloved birthplace, which she knows is doomed, so he invites us for the last time to a Chekhovian party. As we look on he recalls, in a series of "living tableaux" rather than in a continuing play, everything that he has loved in life, even if, often, without knowing that he loved it; but now he knows it, now when he is taking his leave: the old family house, commonplace and unique, the flowers of spring "that make one want to do silly things," a bird-woman, beautiful, laughing, and charmingly incoherent, an ardent adolescence, word-drunk, in love, and a little mad.

Even more than Chekhov's other plays, *The Cherry Orchard* has "no fixed structure" and tells no story. Jean-Louis Barrault, who has staged it with admirable devotion, summed it up in a few lines: "Act I: the Cherry Orchard is in danger of being sold. Act II: the Cherry Orchard is going to be sold. Oct III: the Cherry Orchard is sold. Act IV: the Cherry Orchard has been sold. As for the rest: life."

It is, however, precisely because it has no action, because nothing happens in it, that paradoxically the play is "full of suspense" and basically highly dramatic. *The Cherry Orchard* is a marvelous example—one of the first in the history of the theater—of drama in reverse, of drama in which the peaks of action are replaced by the successive impediments set up against the unleashing of action. The audience that goes to see classic theater expects ups and downs, hopes for "sensations," constantly wonders "and now what's going to happen?" The miracle of *The Cherry Orchard* is that it succeeds in reversing this suspense in the audience, which very quickly, as soon as it has fallen under the spell, fears rather than wants action and hopes that nothing will happen, that the Cherry Orchard will not be sold.

An old family residence, a place of magic steeped in the sorceries of memory, has to be sold. Handled in the realistic or naturalistic style, this theme would have been almost unbearably pathetic —or would have foundered in melodrama—and one very soon senses how a Zola or a Bècque, for instance, would have got his big dramatic effects out of it. We know that Chekhov, in complete contrast, wanted to make it a light comedy, that he constantly insisted on this point, and that he sharply criticized Stanislavsky for having turned it into a "tear-jerker" through his direction. For Chekhov wanted his "farewell to life" to be said almost casually, without any pathos, with a smiling, slightly disenchanted amiability.

He invites us to laugh at Uncle Gayev making his solemn farewells to the wardrobe "that has been in the family a hundred years," but while we smile, our hearts are moved nonetheless, and this Chekhov well knew. "It always seems to me," he wrote, "that I fool people with my face, which is either too gay or too serious," and this time he fools us more than ever, deliberately, because although what he is dealing with is touching, he himself is smiling more than usual, if indeed not frankly laughing. The tone of *The Cherry Orchard* is often that of a rather frolicking humor—one has only to recall Gayev's incoherences or Charlotte's buffooneries —that is not to be found in the earlier plays and that recalls the unreined laughter of the young Chekhov when he was simply "the man without spleen" or Chekontey.

Immediately on seeing the title of the play—on which Chekhov was most insistent—we know that in contrast to his other plays, all of which derive their titles from one or several of the characters, the center of gravity of this one is to be not one of its heroes but the site of the drama itself, that old country house that is called the Cherry Orchard. Ever since the day when as an adolescent he had seen his father's house in Taganrog sold out from under him, Chekhov had known the nostalgia for a "family nest, and, as soon as his means had made it possible—first at Melikhovo and then in Yalta—he had moved as quickly as possible to create a new one for himself and his family. In *The Cherry Orchard* it is this lost and regained family home, now definitively abandoned because he is leaving it to die, to which he is saying farewell.

One is irresistibly reminded of that moving ceremony with which, until not very long ago, Russians accompanied every departure from home. Even if they were going away for only a few days—but can one ever be certain that one will not die somewhere and not come home?—they all came together at departure time, formed a procession behind the ikon, and made the circle round the house; then, having closed all the shutters, they all stayed a little time together in the drawing room. Thus Chekhov, before the great journey, made the tour of *The Cherry Orchard* for the last time, closed the shutters, and stood awhile with all his luggage before at last abandoning the empty house.

Under questioning by Stanislavsky, who was always intent on constructing realistic settings, Chekhov confined himself to saying: "The house should be large and solid—wood or stone, it makes no difference. It is very old and very spacious, one of those houses that summer people refuse to rent for the summer; one of those houses that are torn down so that their materials can be used again." What difference indeed did it make to him whether it had stone columns or a fretworked wood veranda, as long as the house was properly there on the stage? Whether it was beautiful or ugly, it would suffice to let his characters talk in it and it would be transmuted by their memories into an enchanted realm.

The other country houses in Chekhov's plays are all a kind of prison in which everyone is dying of boredom and that one longs to leave; the Cherry Orchard is a privileged place in which one dreams of taking refuge and that one will leave only under duress, heartbroken. This is so much the case that while Chekhov's last play is again—and more than ever—an atmosperhic play, the atmosphere this time is wholly different from that in which *Uncle Vanya* and *The Three Sisters* are steeped. The stifling climate of

entrapment in provincial life, of "the horror of living in the country," is supplanted here by the enchanting climate of a certain
pleasure of living withdrawn into the family.

The major characters of *The Cherry Orchard* are again and always "dreamers," but when they are compared with those who
preceded them in Chekhov's plays, it is clear that their dream has
changed its direction, that instead of being projected into the future, it is turned toward the past, that it is no longer the dream of
what might be but the nostalgic dream of what has been. Lyubov
Ranyevskaya and her brother too must often have been lethally
bored in the country, but they no longer remember that, and what
they love to recall is their mother's glowing recollections and the
rooms they occupied as children. Their Cherry Orchard bloomed
only two weeks in the year, but in their memories it is always
quivering in a dazzling whiteness.

This nostalgia for a time that will never return and for a familiar setting that is about to crumble under the axes of the wreckers
must not be allowed to slip from restrained emotion into tearful,
common sentimentality. Chekhov had the ability to avoid this
snare, as we have said, by giving his play a general atmosphere of
humor, in this instance the humor of hyper-modesty. But there is
more: this particular comicality, light and rather imaginative, is
also, with its passwords, its scapegoats, and its veiled allusions, a
family humor. And perhaps the most astonishing accomplishment
of the play is the fact that from the start it initiates us into the
game, it makes us participants in this humor in spite of its rather
secret quality, something for the initiate, and that thus the play
succeeds in establishing a kind of complicity between characters
and audience, a much deeper intimacy than would have been created by a sentimental style.

One always feels a bit of a pedant when setting out to define the
themes of a work by Chekhov—one can see him starting to smile
—and one knows in advance too that if one limits oneself to only
two or three of them, one will be not only inadequate but unjust.
Yet why not confess that in this amazing evocation, this marvelous
"epitome" of all Chekhov's work that *The Cherry Orchard* is,
among all this interlacing of themes dropped as soon as hinted,
there are two that have especially struck us? Never so sharply as

here, first of all, did Chekhov condemn man's blindness to the beauty that he destroys; and never did he speak so serenely, with so much indulgence, of that kind of casual and lazy fatalism that always makes us put off for tomorrow not only our plans but our thoughts and our happiness.

Like Dr. Astrov, Chekhov loved beauty and went in search of it, and he suffered when he saw it destroyed by those who were blind to it. Like the English poet, he believed that "A thing of beauty is a joy forever." In *Uncle Vanya* his hero cried out his anger at the massacre of the forests and the woods; more softly he pitied the beautiful Yelena for sacrificing her beauty and her youth to her old husband. At the heart of *The Sea Gull* Chekhov had put the symbol of the beautiful bird "stupidly butchered" because of a hunter's bad shot. But in *The Cherry Orchard* the theme is taken up again more broadly, and all the characters are offenders against beauty.

Lopakin is of course the man who murders the Cherry Orchard with his axe. But he, who is blind to its beauty and who, because he has never lived in it, is in addition ignorant of its magic, is less guilty with respect to it than the other characters. The real murderers of the Cherry Orchard's beauty are its owners, who, by loading themselves with debts, have made its loss inevitable. While, in the moment of leaving it, Lyubov Ranyevskaya weeps over her "dear, her frail, her marvelous garden," it is nonetheless she and her brother who, through their indifference, have doomed it to destruction. As for little Anya and the student, Trofimov, they are so enrapt in the future, in what they think will be a "new life," that they too are blind to the beauty that lies quivering before their eyes, and they rejoice at the demolition of the Cherry Orchard. "All Russia is our orchard," Trofimov announces rather pompously. "There are many marvelous places in Russia. . . ."

The Cherry Orchard is also—saving the presence of those who now want, in their own expression, to "derussify" it on the pretext of making it more universal—an unbroken series of variations on an essentially Russian theme, the eternal theme of *Nechevo?*— What's the use? All its characters with the exception of Lopakin are people who always put off for tomorrow whatever decisions are to be made, who let things drift and look to events to solve problems, who lack the will to resolve. Lyubov Ranyevskaya does not even take the trouble to go and see that rich aunt in Kharkov who might still be able to save everything, and Gayev, as he waits for disaster, plays billiards. The indifference, furthermore, is universal, and it erupts in laughing farandoles during the impromptu party in the third act, which takes place just when the fate of the Cherry Orchard is being decided. What does tomorrow matter—*nechevo!*—if tonight we dance, we flirt, we drink, and we forget!

It has too often been said of Trofimov the student that he foreshadows the future, that tomorrow he will surely be a revolutionary. His words are indeed golden when he proclaims: "If we want to begin to live, we must first redeem our past." But then he adds: "One can't buy anything without an appalling, stubborn effort . . ." and such an effort in fact frightens him, he seems unready to attempt it. As Lopakin reminds him, he has been a student now for ten years, and though he never misses the chance to give other people lessons, he forgets to give them to himself. Will his desire to struggle go beyond his ringing declarations of principle? The answer, it is very much to be feared, is No, and in all probability a few years later he will be still and always a student, having deserted Anya and learned to speak more effectively than ever about the future and work, "the sole solution for all the ills of Russia."

Lyubov Ranyevskaya is the very incarnation of indifference, though with grace and charm as well. "It isn't hard to play the part of Ranyevskaya," Chekhov wrote to his wife. "All that's needed is to find the right note at the start. You must invent a smile and a way of laughing, and have excellent clothes sense. . . ." A gay, trivial, impulsive, beautiful, perfumed woman, "absent-minded and affectionate with everyone," she is the archetype of the kind of woman whose company Chekhov always enjoyed and whose final portrait, by way of farewell, he sketched in this play. That his own wife, who in so many aspects —her "little German" aspects—was so unlike her should have been chosen to bring Ranyevskaya to life on the stage must have seemed, to Chekhov, a final subtle irony of fate.

Dreaming, incoherent, refusing to desire the means of their own happiness, the weak heroes of *The Cherry Orchard* arouse our sympathy nevertheless, and even, the more we see them come alive before us, our affection. Their shallowness—of character, of course, but of soul as well—is so great, they have so much grace and detachment, that in the end one prefers them to the realists that they would have to be if they wanted to save their Cherry Orchard. In his leavetaking from his irresolute, weak heroes, re-united for the last time in *The Cherry Orchard*, Chekhov had the capacity to make us see, even if through laughter that blushes, but much more clearly than elsewhere, that in spite of it all he loved them.

When Chekhov left for Moscow, Altschuler told him that he was committing suicide; paradoxically, however, his health improved after he arrived there. He himself wrote to a friend that he felt better than during the previous winter, and at the same time he reproached himself for not working enough. He neglected to men-tion that he was revising—and with considerable energy—the proofs of *The Cherry Orchard* and also reading and annotating a mountain of manuscripts. He was also seeing a great many people —too many for his own liking—but sociable and helpful man that he was, how could he have barred the door either to friends or to favor-seekers?

Besides, he still had his eager curiosity about everyone and everything. One evening, when he was entertaining a number of writers, he asked Konstantin Balmont, the young poet, to read some of his work aloud. Chekhov listened carefully and patiently, although he had little affinity for this new poetry, and while the young symbolist was reciting, he murmured to the man beside him on the couch that if someone suddenly began reading aloud some of Lermontov's poetry, "there would be nothing left of Bal-mont's."

When it was not his favorite theme, literature, that he discussed with his friends, it was the war that had just begun between Russia and Japan. This was of course the universal topic at that time, and Chekhov, carried away like the great majority of his fellow citizens by the vast wave of patriotism that surged over the country, had no doubts as to either the legitimacy or the ultimate victory of the Russian cause. But the war took up a great deal of his attention, and soon he was to write to Olga: "At the moment all of us are interested in nothing but the war, and that's all we think about" (March 18, 1904).

He complained of the invasion of his privacy by visitors. "There's such a flood of people here," he sighed, "that I don't have a minute to myself. I am constantly seeing people in and out, and I talk without stopping for breath, so that when there is a rare moment of freedom, I begin dreaming of going back to my *Penates* in Yalta, and I have to confess that the thought of it gives me pleasure" (January 20, 1904). Actually a few weeks had been enough to drain the pleasures of Moscow to the bottom, and now that his play had opened, he was once more in the grip of the desire to be somewhere else. There was no reason why he should leave Moscow, and still less why he should dream "with pleasure" of Yalta, which normally he detested, but by now he was constantly haunted, to the point of obsession, by a pathetic need for "headlong flight." If he remained in a given place for even a few weeks, he unfailingly developed an aversion to it and had only one thought—to go elsewhere. Tuberculosis, as it so often does, had turned him into a kind of nomad pursued by death.

He seemed to have no further regard for the advice of either Altschuler or Ostroümov. Just before going back to the Crimea, however, he remembered that Ostroümov had urged him to spend the summer in the Moscow district, and he and Olga went to look at a dacha near Tsaritsino, about twenty miles outside the city. While the trip back to town in an open sleigh through sun-bathed snow was not what was prescribed for him, he thoroughly enjoyed it. When he and Olga got home that evening, he began packing the various gifts that had been presented to him on the occasion of his jubilee, when he was interrupted by the arrival of a letter from Lydia Avilova.

This time the fevered young woman's mind had fixed on repentance as the best means of capturing Chekhov's attention: she apologized for her previous behavior and expressed the hope that at last she would be "understood." "Please forgive my unasked frankness, Anton Pavlovich," she wrote. "Although I was not looking for it, I am taking advantage of this opportunity. I was afraid I might die without ever having been able to tell you that I have always had the highest respect for you and that I have always looked on you as the finest of men. And what is there to say if I have devalued myself in your eyes? This had to be. This has been the great grief of my life. The time has come to tell you so. . . . I do not ask you to forgive me, but what I do ask of you is to understand me" (February 9, 1904).[3]

The "finest of men," naturally, had no desire to plunge himself afresh into long postal explanations with this "sea gull" whose unbridled passion for complications he knew only too well, and he immediately replied with an evasive note, which was in fact rather curt in spite of its fatherly tone, that put a kind of full stop (though in the shape of a question mark) to their correspondence. "Forgive me: I am frozen because I have just got back from Tsaritsino," he wrote. "My hand can barely write and I still have to pack. . . . Be happy and take a less complicated view of life; very probably, in actuality, it is much more simple. Does this life about which we know nothing really require all these torturing cogitations in which our Russian brains wear themselves out? That is still and always the question" (February 14, 1904).

Chekhov boarded the train for the Crimea the next day. In Yalta he was surprised to find his brother Alexander, who had rented a house near Anton's for a month on the coast with his wife and son. Anton was still apprehensive for the future of this elder brother, who was not only unstable but fond of drink, but he observed with pleasure—and lost no time informing Masha—that Alexander seemed finally to have opted for sobriety. Altschuler, who was one of the first to visit Chekhov as soon as he had returned, was stunned to find his patient looking so well. Chekhov's spirits too seemed to have risen: it amused him to show the doctor the remarkable collection of objects presented to him for his jubilee which ranged from an eighteenth-century silver inkwell to a twentieth-century fishing rod. This, by the way, was the gift that

---

[3] Mrs. Avilova did not quote this letter in her *Recollections*. It was published for the first time in Moscow in 1960 in the fourth edition of *A. P. Tchekhov, From the Recollections of His Contemporaries*.

he most appreciated. The silver inkwell, which Altschuler seemed to admire very much, was to be bequeathed to him in Chekhov's will.

But these high spirits—undoubtedly the result of the change of scene—soon dropped again. As in Moscow, his innumerable visitors—whom he did not have the courage to throw out and whom in a kind of self-contradiction he often sought out as well—very soon wearied him, sometimes to the point of exasperation. A day after his arrival he was already complaining to Olga: "Visitors, visitors without end, who keep me from writing and depress my mood. There was one man who spent the entire day sitting in my study." Yalta had looked attractive to him when seen from Moscow, but almost as soon as he was back there it seemed drearier than ever, this "lower-middle-class town that smells of perfume factories." It was again to Olga that he voiced his griefs: "Life is dull and devoid of interest," he wrote to her on February 27. "The people here are revoltingly uninteresting, they have no desire for anything, they are apathetic to everything."

Actually Yalta had restored Chekhov to his old background, life, and habits of illness, and it was chiefly this that galled him. In Moscow it had been possible for him to get away from his illness, almost to forget it; here everything reminded him of it. This made him angry, and it was often Olga on whom he vented his resentment. She attempted, for her part, to distract him with the latest news of literary and theatrical circles, and she hoped that he would be pleased by the fact that she had found a new apartment in a building with an elevator, but too often his replies were criticisms and petty quarrels. Why did she not want to take a summer lease on the dacha that they had visited in Tsaritsino? Why did she not write to him more frequently? Angry when there was no word for two days from Olga, who was ill, he sent her a furious note: "Why, oh, why couldn't you send me a single telegram about your health? Why? Obviously I don't matter to you, I'm simply excess baggage. In a word, it's revolting" (March 12, 1904).

Olga also annoyed him by her questions. Had she not yet been able to understand that she was not supposed to play the Chekhovian heroine with him or try to know his innermost thoughts? " 'What is life?' you ask me," he wrote to her. "It's exactly as if you were to ask me: 'What is a carrot?' A carrot is a carrot, and that's all there is to know about it" (April 20, 1904).

These flashes of irritation, however, did not mean that he no longer loved his wife. Even if endearments had become less frequent in his letters, still he often reassured her of his love. He loved everything about her, he told her affectionately, except her insistence on "spending so much time washing." She was still his "little horse," his "wonderful little half," his beloved "great actress," and if she should fall into depression, she should emulate him and think about the wonderful summer that they would soon spend together. There were even times when he still hoped that they might have a child: "At this moment I'd give ten thousand rubles to have a child. I feel sad without some living being to comfort me. But you'll do everything you can about that, I leave that to you" (April 20, 1904).

He was still driven by the desire to write, but because his physical exhaustion made it impossible, he unconsciously sought excuses for himself. At first, as in Moscow, there had been that endless flood of visitors that prevented him from working, and there was also the war in the Far East, which, Altschuler later reported, really preoccupied him more and more. "I'm working," he told Olga, "but without any results. It always seems to me that no one will read us because of the war." He closely followed the battlefront news in the papers, and like almost all Russians, he was deeply depressed by the defeats inflicted on the Tsar's army by the Japanese. He worried about what was happening to Olga's two uncles, both of whom were at the front, and he himself often spoke of enlisting in the medical corps during the summer.

But he was not blinded by patriotism. When certain friends suggested that he write a play about the war, he refused on the ground of what had always been his major concern as a writer: objectivity. "Don't you see," he argued, "it would need a lapse of twenty years first. It's impossible to write about it now. The mind must first recover its serenity; it is only then that a writer can be impartial." [4]

He was no longer strong enough to work, but what he had done continued to live and to win him a wider and wider audience,

[4] Stanislavsky, *My Life in Art.*

both at home and abroad. Translations of his stories were published successfully in France and Germany, his plays were performed in Prague. Editions of his books in Russia poured out one after another and Marx was making a fortune at Chekhov's expense, to the indignation of his friends. As soon as it had been performed and even before its publication, *The Cherry Orchard* was a tremendous success everywhere; already it was being presented in a number of provincial cities. A Sebastopol company even went to Yalta to perform it there one evening, but Chekhov could not leave his bed and did not attend. This was just as well, because what his friends told him about the performance led him to believe that "those abominable actors had murdered the play."

It was beyond question that no one understood *The Cherry Orchard*. Chekhov devoted one evening to a long explanation of it to Karpov, the director of the theater in Petersburg that belonged to Suvorin, and again he complained bitterly that Stanislavsky's staging of it—which was the model for all the provincial productions—had completely distorted the spirit of his play. "Is that really my *Cherry Orchard?* Are those my characters? Except for two or three of the parts, none of that is mine. I describe life. Granted, it's dreary, middle-class life, but it isn't hateful, tearjerking life. They start by turning me into a weepy writer and then just a bore. Whereas I've written plenty of books full of happy stories. . . ."

He wrote bluntly to his wife: "I can tell you one thing: Stanislavsky has butchered my play." Nevertheless he added: "But God be with him! I'm not angry at him for it" (March 29, 1904). Indeed, even though he was frank in his sharp reproaches, this in no way prevented him from doing full justice to the Art Theater and its two directors for their contributions to the rejuvenation of the theater in Russia. On the assumption that she would want to repeat it to her friends in the Art Theater, he wrote to Olga in connection with the vicious attacks that were being made on them in the press: "No matter what they do, it is beyond anyone's power to destroy you. As artists you have already attained the goal that you had set for yourselves, and hence you can contemplate the present and the future almost with indifference" (March 31, 1904). A few days later, too, his confidence was rewarded: the Art

Theater had just initiated its traditional spring season in Petersburg and scored a tremendous success there with *The Cherry Orchard*. Nemirovich-Danchenko, who at once informed Chekhov of it by telegram, added that never in his long career had he known an audience to react so spontaneously to the most subtle shadings of a dramatic text.

If Chekhov had been strong enough he would have written more plays, but he had to be content to dream about them endlessly and sometimes, in the excitement of conversation, to allow himself the indulgence of saying something about them to his friends. Thus, during a talk with Orelnyev, an actor who was about to go abroad with his company, Chekhov said that he was much tempted to write a play for him that would be intended for production abroad and hence would not first have to be submitted to the Russian censor. He offered to write it, and even promised that it would be finished in September. He also spoke soon afterward to Stanislavsky about an idea for a new play: the story of a scholar whose wife had let him down—either through indifference or through infidelity—and who in desperation goes to the Far North. In the last act he would appear alone on the deck of a ship caught in the ice; in the majestic total silence of the Arctic night he would see the specter of the woman he loved seeming to glide across the sky . . .

Chekhov was doing virtually nothing now but dreaming: of plays and stories to be written, of trips to be taken, of vacations with Olga, and also, no doubt, of death, which he knew was so near but which he never mentioned to anyone. Visitors often found him in a rocking chair in his study, his hands empty and his eyes fixed on the distance. At the very end of his strength, he was writing nothing. In order to keep himself occupied, he read manuscripts sent to him by Goltsev, the editor of *Russian Thought,* and sent them back with brief comments. He admitted to Olga that he was spending hours rereading old letters and outdated newspapers. Out of lack of employment—or, as often happens, out of a kind of unconscious need to put his papers in order before he died —he also was attempting to recopy in ink the penciled contents of his *Notebooks,* which were in danger of becoming illegible. And as he did these things, he dreamed still, musing over the countless stories—enough to take care of his family for life, he joked to a friend—that he might have written from those notes.

There were moments of exceptional clarity of mind in which he doubted whether he had any future left, even the briefest. Discussing plans for the summer, he wrote to Olga on March 3: "After all, these are dreams, dreams!" More often, however, his will to live gained the upper hand and enabled him to forget his unshakable conviction—as both patient and physician—of imminent death. Like his own heroes, the old professor in "A Dreary Story" and "The Bishop," he refused to let himself yield to the fascination of death—whereas Tolstoy, on the other hand, had been absorbed in it for more than twenty years—and in fact, with smiling courage, he went on playing at the game of living. He asked Olga, who was on tour in Petersburg, to go to the boat show there and buy him a light, attractive fishing boat for the summer. On April 18 he wrote to her: "I'm dreaming of the summer. I'm hungry to be alone, to write, to think."

For more than two months, "solitary as a comet," he had been eating his heart out in Yalta, that city "that I love and despise at the same time, as one loves and detests women who are good but ugly." In mid-April he was attacked again by intense coughing spasms and violent intestinal disturbances, but was not this deterioration in his condition actually the product of the Crimean climate? Once more he could not sit still, and on May 1, having been cautious enough not to ask Altschuler's opinion, he set out for Moscow. "I'll arrive during the morning," he wrote to Olga. "Poodle, my darling poodle, how lonely I've been for you!"

In those days the journey from Yalta to Moscow took a long time—more than two days—and Chekhov became ill during the trip. As soon as he arrived in Moscow he went directly to Olga's new elevator-equipped apartment in Leontyevsky Avenue and was at once ordered to bed. Olga sent for her family doctor, J. Taube, a German, who could establish only that Chekhov's condition was critical: he diagnosed a relapse into pleurisy complicated by an "intestinal catarrh," which seemed to indicate that the tuberculosis had spread into the intestines.

Chekhov's temperature remained high for several days. It was extremely difficult for him to breathe, and he also complained of sharp pains in his arms and legs that prevented him from sleeping and, as he was later to confess, almost convinced him that his spinal column had been infected. In order to ease the burden on his heart, Dr. Taube was giving him morphine injections. When at last he began to feel better, Chekhov was placed on a very strict diet and ordered to remain in bed. Taube said that as soon as Chekhov was sufficiently improved, he was going to send him to Germany to be examined by a Berlin tuberculosis specialist.

"My wife is taking care of her ailing husband—she is a marvel," Chekhov wrote to his and Olga's friend Dr. Shredin. "I've never seen such a nurse. That means it's a good, a very good thing that I'm married; otherwise I have no idea what state I would be in now" (May 22, 1904). But he was not an easy patient, and for all his recognition that Dr. Taube seemed extremely competent and dedicated, he fretted and fumed. "I now lie all day on a couch," he wrote to Altschuler, "and since I have nothing else to do, I rail constantly against Ostroümov and Shurovsky. This gives me considerable pleasure." This vindictive reference to the two doctors who a year earlier had made recommendations diametrically opposed to Altschuler's was certain to please the Yalta physician, who was also amazed that it had not occurred to Dr. Taube to consult his two Russian colleagues, both of whom were familiar with his patient's case.[5] Making every effort to reassure Masha, Chekhov wrote to her that lying in bed all day long was enough to make him "roar with boredom"—that boredom as incurable as his tuberculosis, and as persistent.

But for Chekhov there was more than boredom and the impossibility of simply "doing nothing." That sense of duty that he had always possessed had not been overpowered by his illness, and rather than give in, he wanted to carry on the struggle. Until the very end he wanted to "serve," to serve others and to serve literature. So from his bed he continued to listen to everyone who wanted something from him, to read and annotate manuscripts, to

[5] In his *Recollections* Altschuler did not hesitate to assert that by subsequently deciding to move Chekhov to Germany in the condition in which he then was, Dr. Taube was responsible for his premature death.

write letters of recommendation, and to order shipments of books sent to the public library in Taganrog. It was his wish that if he was destined to vanish soon, life should nonetheless continue to be as good as possible, and he sent Masha detailed instructions for the care of his rosebushes and fruit trees in Yalta, in spite of his reasoned skepticism whether he would ever see them again.

Knowing how ill he was, his friends were hesitant now to intrude on him, but it was he who wrote to them to insist that they come. He apologized for lying on a couch in dressing gown and slippers when they arrived, and he made a special effort to make them forget his waxen complexion and hollow cheeks by being the delightful host, forever, smiling and interested in everything. He never even alluded to his health, except occasionally—on a semiprofessional basis—with his medical colleague Rossolimo, who was disturbed to note that like almost all tuberculars Chekhov talked of his illness with optimism in spite of his burning palms and flushed temples. Much more often than in the past, however, he enjoyed reviving old recollections. He talked about his youth, he recalled his days at the university, he asked what had become of this or that classmate.

With Vladimir Gilyarosky, the poet who had once been his guide through the jungle of journalism and whom he had not seen for some time, he talked at length about the happy, carefree days of their first appearances in the little satirical weeklies of the 1880s. Chekhov grew more animated, remembered the broad jokes that they had had together, and laughed freely. Gilyarosky, who had only recently returned from a long period of wandering over the steppes, described his adventures, his picturesque encounters with Cossacks and vast herds of horses. "Ah, the steppes, the steppes!" Chekhov exclaimed. "What a lucky man you are! That's where one finds poetry and strength. Everything there is bronzed by the sun, it's not like here." Then, his lips relaxed in a genuinely happy smile, he closed his eyes and let his head fall back on the pillow. "I suppose he was picturing the steppe," Gilyarosky said.

Chekhov was as enthusiastic about the theater as ever. Much impressed by Maeterlinck's plays, he devoted months to persuading Stanislavsky to include his favorites among them—*The Blind, Interior,* and *The Intruder*—in the Art Theater's repertory. When he learned that this decision had finally been made and actual preparations were going forward, he asked the director and the actors of the Art Theater to come and talk about the project with him. It interested him so much that he even had them make models of the sets and the costumes for him.

Meanwhile poor Masha, who had to remain in Yalta with their aged mother, was miserably apprehensive for her beloved Antosha. "I beg you to write more often about your health," she wrote to him, "because it makes me terribly anxious when I get no news. Especially at night. . . ." Antosha had actually been writing to her very seldom since his arrival in Moscow, speaking of his health only in the vaguest terms and assuring her merely that he was being very well taken care of. Masha's appeals that he return to Yalta—the spring was magnificent, the garden was a fairyland of flowers, she would soon be starting to make preserves—went ignored.

After three weeks, finally, he informed his sister that he was in much better health and, indeed, had not "felt so well in almost twenty-five years." Nine days later, on May 31, he proudly announced greater news: for the first time in a month he had put on street clothes and taken a carriage ride in town with Olga. Now there was no further obstacle to his accepting Taube's urgent advice and leaving for Germany. He had already made reservations on the Berlin train for Olga and himself; they would leave Moscow on June 3.

Among the friends who came to say farewell was one who had shared the happy period in Melikhovo, the "little *astronomka*," Olga Kundassova, as well as another very old friend, Teleshov the writer. He visited Chekhov the day before the departure; he had not seen him since the winter and was painfully shocked by the changes in his appearance. Chekhov looked like a different man: lying back on his pillows, his face sunken and almost translucent, he was as if compressed into himself, a little old man with hunched shoulders. Teleshov had no doubt that this was the last time that they would meet, especially because Chekhov greeted him by saying: "I'm leaving tomorrow. Good-bye. I'm going away to . . . die." [6]

Teleshov was so upset that he could barely speak. "By now," he wrote later, "I was afraid to start speaking aloud again, I was afraid even of making any noise with my shoes. A certain loving silence was essential, his few words had to be spoken to a receptive heart, because . . . they would be the last that would come from the pure and noble heart of Chekhov."

But Chekhov talked only of others, not of himself. He reminded his guest to remember him to the members of The Tuesday Club, a literary group of which Teleshov was president; he wished them happiness and success. Teleshov saw in Chekhov's eyes a kind of conscious, serene acceptance. But his voice grew warmer when he began to talk about Ivan Bunin: "Tell Bunin that he should write and write and write. There's a great writer in him. Yes, tell him that from me, don't forget." [7]

Chekhov and Olga arrived in Berlin on June 5 and took a room in the Hotel Savoy. The eternal wanderer in him immediately came back to life, stirred, and felt better. Reading his letters, Masha could have thought that a genuine miracle had taken place, as if being abroad were enough to enable him to wear his street clothes every day. He was enjoying himself immensely, he was on the run all day long, visiting the shops and walking in the Tiergarten. It was a long time since he had eaten with so much appetite, and he was even beginning to put on weight. He was also looking over the women, but unfortunately they dressed "abominably" and he had yet to see a single pretty German. Overflowing with optimism, he announced that he would be back in Yalta in August at the latest.

Such optimism, however, was not shared by those who saw him in Berlin. Professor K. Ewald, the tuberculosis specialist to whom Dr. Taube had referred Chekhov, subjected him to a lengthy examination and left him without a word, as if he knew that any further treatment was useless. G. B. Illos, the Berlin correspondent of *The Russian News,* who obligingly made himself com-

---

[6] The word that Chekhov used was much stronger than "die," but in his *Memoirs* Teleshov admitted that he preferred not to repeat it.

[7] A. P. Tchekhov, *From the Recollections of His Contemporaries.*

pletely available to Chekhov during this visit, wrote to his editor later: "I had the feeling that Chekhov's days were numbered. He seemed critically ill to me; he was appallingly thin, he was coughing, and he had to struggle for breath after the slightest exertion; and his temperature was consistently high."

Three days later, when Chekhov left Berlin for the Schwarzwald, Illos accompanied him to the Potsdam station. It grieved him to see how the climbing of a few stairs compelled Chekhov to sit and rest for several minutes, looking completely bewildered, before he could catch his breath. Nevertheless Chekhov had no difficulty during the train trip, in spite of its length: he had to cross the whole of Germany in order to reach Badenweiler.

This little watering place on the edge of the Black Forest, about twenty-five miles from Basel, seemed at first to Chekhov to be the refuge of which he had dreamed in spite of the utter characterlessness of its little hills and its middle-class houses. He spent the first two days in a family *pension* and then moved into a private residence that accepted paying guests, *Haus Frederika*. He made his choice on the basis of its large tranquil garden with excellently arranged flower beds from which there was a fine view over the distant mountains. From morning until seven o'clock in the evening he spent every day in a comfortable armchair in the sun, which, he wrote to Masha, did not burn but, rather, caressed. Under excellent care from a local physician, Dr. Schwöhrer, he agreed for the first time in his life to submit to the treatment that his condition required: absolute rest and proper food. His very rigorous diet—"stupid" cocoa and oatmeal—amused him, but, he wrote, while "there is a good deal of charlatanry in all this, there is at the same time a good deal of tonic."

His early letters from Badenweiler were bursting with optimism and good spirits. The place was delightful and quiet, he was eating and sleeping splendidly, he no longer had pains in his legs; in sum, he would be himself again in short order. In fact, he told Rossolimo, there was only one thing about him that was incurable, and that was his laziness. He wrote to his mother (and it was not merely a lie born of love): "My health is improving so much that I can say I'll be absolutely fine in a week." Once more the future was his, and he made wonderful plans: soon he would go to

Italy and then he would return to Yalta by ship via Constantinople. He had already ordered a white flannel suit.

After a week of rest, however, Chekhov was again seized by his
anxiety, his boredom, and that torturing need to be elsewhere that
more and more quickly made him suddenly find it impossible to
endure the place where he was and the people whom he found
there. Now he no longer mentioned the quiet charm of Badenweiler, but its climate of invincible boredom. "I cannot accustom
myself to German calm and placidity," he wrote to Masha on June
16. "Here there is not a single drop of talent, not a single drop of
taste, but there are orderliness and honesty to high heaven. Our
Russian life is much more full of talent, to say nothing of the Italian or the French." Even the good Dr. Schwöhrer, with his daily
visits and his weakness for cocoa, was beginning to irritate him.
Though he could not leave the little watering place so soon, at
least he could desert *Haus Frederika,* which had become "too
common" for his taste; and on June 21 he moved into the Hotel
Sommer, the best in the resort.

This time too—it was the last time—the change of scene and
company was enough to revive his suffering spirits for a few days.
He was quite pleased with his new room. He spent hours on its
balcony, from which—again for the last time—the observer that
he had always been could watch life go by and could be diverted
by the traffic in the street, which was especially heavy in front of
the post office situated opposite the hotel. He was still making
plans: he had not yet had his fill of traveling, he wrote to Masha.
He reckoned on returning to Yalta by sea, but he was not yet sure
whether he would sail from Trieste or Marseilles. He asked to be
informed by telegram of the sailing dates and accommodations of
the various ships. Reassured by the good news that she was receiving from Anton, Masha and her brother Ivan left Yalta on
June 28 for a short vacation in the Caucasus. Just before her departure she wrote to Chekhov: "Take good care of yourself, dear
Antosha, try not to cough but to eat more, get back your strength,
and come home."

Poor Masha had no way of knowing that on the same day when
she was offering this ingenuous, affectionate counsel, her dear An-

tosha was addressing a much less optimistic medical bulletin to her. "I eat really delicious food," he wrote in great discouragement, "but it does no good, because my stomach is completely out of order. . . . It's obvious that my stomach is hopelessly ruined, and it's impossible to keep it functioning except by fasting—I mean eating absolutely nothing, and that's it. As for my lack of breath, that too has only one remedy, which is not to move a muscle" (June 28, 1904).

No food, no movement . . . but even these feeble ruses could no longer avail against his disease. On June 29 there was a severe attack, and in order to keep his heart beating, his doctor had to resort to morphine injections and oxygen. For two days the fears for his survival were at their peak. Two Russian newspaper correspondents who had rushed to Badenweiler telegraphed medical bulletins to their papers. Chekhov himself still preserved all his serenity, his clarity of mind, and also his thoughtfulness. He notified a bank in Berlin to send all future remittances in his wife's name, and when Olga asked him why, he gave her an evasive answer: "Oh, just like that, just in case."

The Russian reporters were able to file more hopeful stories on July 1: Chekhov's heart was holding out, and the patient had had a rather good day. He himself felt much better, and late in the afternoon he insisted that Olga, who had not left his bedside for three days, go for a walk in the huge park belonging to the hotel. When she came back, Chekhov, still more concerned with others' welfare than with his own, asked her why she did not go downstairs to dinner. She told him that the bell had not rung—this was not true, but neither of them had heard it—and she stretched out on a little couch near his bed. Unhappy and fearful although, she was to say later, she had not the slightest suspicion "that the end was so near," she lay there without speaking. Seeing that she was preoccupied, Chekhov began telling her a story in order to distract her. His voice was weak at first, but then, as he was carried away by what he was telling her, it grew stronger, and he smiled: it was his last story.

The story took place in a watering place much more fashionable than Badenweiler, a haunt of overfed bankers and red-cheeked

English and American tourists bursting with health and doting on
fine food. After an afternoon's outing, or a long walk, all this fine-
fleshed high society came back in the evening with voracious ap-
petites and delight at being so hungry. What a sumptuous,
what a royal repast they would have. But when they returned,
what news was awaiting these gluttons? The accomplished chef
had unexpectedly vanished, and with him all hope of a sumptuous
or even a respectable dinner. How would these expert lovers of
fine food react to this frightful frontal attack? That was what
Chekhov, amusingly describing each one's particular disappointment, undertook to tell Olga, who, rolled into a ball on her
couch, was now laughing without restraint.

In spite of the extremely oppressive heat the patient went to
sleep early that night. There was every reason for his wife to suppose that he would have a restful night but shortly after midnight
he awoke and asked her to go find a doctor. It was the first
time in his life that he had ever made such a request of her.
Extremely disturbed, and frightened at being so alone and
helpless in this huge hotel filled with nothing but strangers, who
furthermore must all be asleep at such an hour, Olga at first did
not know what to do. Then, remembering that she had met two
Russian students who were staying in the hotel, she awakened
them, and one of them ran to get Dr. Schwöhrer. "I can still," she
wrote afterward, "hear the sound of his footsteps on the gravel
path diminishing in the silence of that suffocating July night."

Chekhov's fever was so high that he was half delirious: he was
raving about some unknown sailor and expressing fear of the Japanese. But when Olga came to put an icebag on his chest, he
abruptly came to himself and gently pushed it away. With a sad
smile, he explained: "One doesn't put ice on an empty heart."

Although the big windows were opened wide, he had great difficulty breathing. When Dr. Schwöhrer finally arrived, at about
two in the morning, Chekhov sat up in bed; well bred to the end,
he said aloud in German (which he spoke badly), with a certain
solemnity: "*Ich sterbe.*" The doctor immediately gave him a cam-
phor injection; but there was no heart reaction, so he said that he
would send for oxygen. But Chekhov, who amazed Schwöhrer by

remaining absolutely calm, said: "Everything's useless now. I'll be a corpse before it gets here." The doctor then ordered a bottle of champagne.

Chekhov took the glass that was offered to him, turned toward Olga, and said with his wonderful smile: "It's a long time since I've had champagne." He drank it off slowly, then stretched out quietly on his left side. A few minutes later he died—as he had lived: tactfully, without fanfare, without excitement.

A great black moth had flown in through the open window. When the doctor had gone and Olga was alone in the sudden, crushing silence, she heard the moth blindly hurtling against the lamp and the walls. Suddenly there was a sound like a holiday firecracker: the cork, replaced in the champagne bottle, had just flown out. The moth finally made its way back to the open window and disappeared in the hot darkness. Then it was silent again, until the sounds of birds and the rustling of leaves signaled the dawn. Olga watched as Anton's face slowly came out of the darkness: it was at peace, serene, illuminated by a smile that seemed to say that at last he had discovered that "meaning of life" in which, even so, he had never believed.

In "The Lady With the Pet Dog" Chekhov had written: "In every human being real life, in its most interesting elements, is lived under the cover of secrecy as if under the cover of night. Every individual existence is founded on secrecy." But he had taken his own secret with him into death. He had closed his eyes on that world of which he had never been more than an observer, certainly a most attentive and warm-hearted observer, but also utterly disenchanted, having never offered any explanation of his "lack of passion" for living. Was it his childhood without childhood, his lonely adolescence, or his premature tuberculosis that had thus impelled him to hold himself aloof from life?

The major and almost obsessive theme of his plays is that of the frustration of every human destiny. Was it not because he was so convinced of this that he had refused to throw himself body and soul into the battle of life? Only the story of Chekhov's life, followed step by step, with love, can make it possible, perhaps, to know the answer. Perhaps . . .

Mikhail was the first of the Chekhov family to learn that "dear Antosha" was dead. As he was arriving in Yalta on July 3 to visit his mother, he saw his cousin Georgi waving his hat to him; then Georgi made a trumpet of his hands and called: "Anton's dead!" He immediately sent a telegram to Masha and Ivan, who were finishing their tour of the Caucasus, but he was afraid to tell his mother. It was Masha who assumed this grievous task two days later, when she returned. Then came a telegram from Olga, saying that she was taking Chekhov's body back to Moscow, where he would be buried on July 9; the entire family left for the capital, arriving on the day of the funeral, when Chekhov's few dozen friends who had gone to the Nikolaev station to receive the coffin were already accompanying it through the city to the Novodyevichy cemetery.

Gorky was at the station when the coffin arrived. What he saw outraged him so deeply that he wrote next day to his wife: "I am so destroyed by that funeral that I doubt whether I can even tell you about it and make sense. . . . My heart aches and I could howl, bleat like a calf, lash myself with anger and fury." Such an outburst of indignation would undoubtedly have made Chekhov smile: everyone, obviously, Gorky as much as Stanislavsky, saw nothing in life—and death—but dramas, whereas for him it was all comedy.

Chekhov's funeral might have been the last of his own ironically sad stories, called "The Great Writer's Bungled Funeral." The coffin containing the writer "so tenderly beloved" by Moscow arrived in the station in a greenish freight car bearing, in large letters, the legend OYSTERS. Then, while a military band blared its brasses on the platform and a funeral procession began to form, some of the few people who had come to greet the writer's remains began to follow the music and the marches. It took these friends and admirers of Chekhov some time to become aware that they were following the coffin of General Keller, who had been killed in Manchuria; it had arrived at the station at the same time. This gave rise to smiles and what Gorky called "sniggers."

Chekhov's mourners—a hundred people—left the station behind a fat police officer perched on a monumental white horse. Olga walked alone behind the coffin, which was carried by students. As the procession moved through the sunshine and the clouds of dust raised by the marchers' feet, a lady in a purple dress, sheltering under a lace parasol, was the only person to mention Chekhov. To her neighbor, a little skeptical-looking old man with a constant cough she said: "Oh, he was so exceptionally kind, and so intelligent!" The other mourners were wondering what they would do after the funeral: some suggested going to a café together, others wanted to visit friends. In front of Gorky—who was tense and grief-stricken and furious—two lawyers, dressed "like young bridegrooms" in new shoes and loud neckties, were making small talk: one of them, V. Maklakhov, was boasting about the intelligence of his dogs and the other was touting the comforts of his new house.

All vehicular traffic had been interrupted and the intersections were blocked. A rather large crowd was kept back by a line of students with linked arms. The curious pointed out Gorky and Chaliapin, who were walking side by side, and tried to get close to them. There was a short pause before the Art Theater, and then Chekhov's mother, sister, and brothers, all of whom had had difficulty establishing their identities, joined the procession.

As it proceeded, the crowd behind it increased, following all the way to the Novodyevichy Monastery. There the crowd clotted at the rather narrow gates, and in the spectators' haste to reach the grave site as quickly as possible, there was a great deal of rough pushing and shoving. Surrounded on all sides, the pallbearers, the family, and the friends of the dead man could barely enter the cemetery. Shouting, complaining, the crowd pressed behind them —breaking crosses, overturning headstones and fences, and trampling flowers—and overran the cemetery.

Chaliapin was weeping and cursing. "That's the scum he lived and worked and taught for!" he said to Gorky. There was no formal speech; this was Chekhov's funeral oration.

When Chekhov's coffin was lowered into the grave that had been dug beside his father's, the crowd chanted the old liturgical melody "Eternal Memory." Then, when there was silence again, Olga and Chekhov's family and friends stood one by one before the open grave and dropped their ritual handfuls of earth, which rattled on the coffin. The grave was then covered. Almost incoherent with grief, Masha mechanically counted the wreaths that were laid on the grave: there were more than a hundred.

Chekhov had already written the epilogue to his funeral on the day when he scribbled in his *Notebooks:* "Watching from a window as a funeral went by, someone said: 'You, you're dead and they're taking you to the cemetery; me, I'm going out to lunch.'"

BIBLIOGRAPHY

The author has felt obliged to restrict himself to listing those works he actually consulted during his research. There is a huge Russian-language bibliography, but only the essential works are included here, under their original titles.

I. RUSSIAN WORKS

1. ANTON CHEKHOV'S WORKS:

Polnoye sobraniye sochinenyi i pisem A. P. Chekhova (Moscow, 1944–51; twenty volumes).

Pisma A. P. Chekhova, edited by Marya Pavlovna Chekhova (Moscow, 1912–16; six volumes).

Perepiska A. P. Chekhova i O. L. Knipper, edited by A. B. Derman (Moscow, 1934–36; two volumes).

M. Gorky i A. Chekhov, Perepiska, edited by N. I. Gitovich (Moscow, 1951).

Literaturnoye Nasledtsvo, Chekhov (Moscow, 1960), Volume LXVIII.

2. BIOGRAPHY, MEMOIRS, AND ESSAYS:

B. I. Alexandrov, *Seminaryi po Chekhovu* (Moscow, 1957).

E. Balabanovich, *Dom v Kudrinye* (Moscow, 1961).

G. P. Berdnikov, *A. P. Chekhov, Ideiniye i tvorcheskiye iskaniya* (Moscow, 1961).

I. A. Bunin, *O. Chekhova. Nyezakonchennaya Rukopis* (New York, 1955).

Mikhail Chekhov, *Vokrug Chekhova* (Moscow, 1959).

Marya P. Chekhova, *Iz dalyokovo proshlovo* (Moscow, 1960).

A. B. Derman, *Tvorchesky portret Chekhova* (Moscow, 1929).

V. Ermilov, *A. P. Chekhov* (Moscow, 1954); *Dramaturgiya A. P. Chekhova* (Moscow, 1948).

N. I. Gitovich, *Letopis zhizni i tvorchestva A. P. Chekhova* (Moscow, 1955).

I. I. Levitan, *Vospominaniya i pisma* (Moscow, 1950).

V. I. Nemirovich-Danchenko, *Iz proshlovo* (Moscow, 1938); *Teatralnoye naslediye* (Moscow, 1952).

Z. Panerny, *A. P. Chekhov. Ocherk tvorchvestva* (Moscow, 1954).

N. A. Sisoyev, *Chekhov v Krimv* (Simferopol, 1960).

A. S. Suvorin, *Dnyevnik,* edited by M. Krichevsky (Moscow, 1923).

K. S. Stanislavsky, *Moyazhizn v iskustve* (Moscow, 1954 [translated as *My Life in Art,* New York, 1948]).

M. N. Stroyev, *A. Chekhov i Khudozhevstvyenny Teatr* (Moscow, 1955); *Tvorchestvo A. P. Chekhova. Sbornik Statey* (Moscow, 1956).

A. P. Chekhov v vospominaniyakh sovremennikov (Moscow, 1960; 4th edition).

B. Zaitsev, *Chekhov. Literaturnaya biografya* (New York, 1954).

II. WORKS IN FRENCH

1. ANTON CHEKHOV'S WORKS:

Oeuvres complètes d'Anton Tchékhov. Translated by D. Roche (Paris: Plon, 1922–34; eighteen volumes). Volumes I–XIII include the stories, Volumes XIV–XVI the plays, Volumes XVII–XVIII the correspondence. Volumes XIX (correspondence) and XX (notebooks, biographical and critical documents) are forthcoming.

Oeuvres complètes d'Anton Tchékhov. Published under the direction of Jean Pérus. Translated by M. Durand, E. Parayre, and E. Triolet (Paris: Éditeurs Français Réunis, 1962; nineteen volumes). Volumes VI and XIX are devoted to the plays.

Collection Anton Tchékhov. Published under the direction of Georges Haldas. Translated by M. Durand and E. Parayre, and, for the plays, E. Triolet, A. Adamov, and G. Arout (Lausanne: Éditions Rencontre, 1964–65; twelve volumes).

Quatre nouvelles. Carnets de notes. Translated by G. Cannac (Paris: Calmann-Lévy, 1958).

Théâtre. Translated by A. Barsacq, A. Vitez, G. and L. Pitoëff, and J. J. Jouve (Paris, Donoël: 1958).

Théâtre. Translated by A. Adamov (Paris: Le Club Français du Livre, 1958).

Théâtre complet. Translated by P. Quentin, N. Gurfinkel, J. Mauclair G. Cannac, and G. Perros (Paris: L'Arche, 1958; three volumes).

Correspondance Gorky-Tchékhov. Edited by Jean Pérus (Paris: Grasset, 1947).

Tchékhov. Edited by Roger Grenier. Translated by C. N. Thomas (Collection L'Essentiel, Paris: J'ai Lu, 1963).

Les vingt meilleures nouvelles de Tchékhov. Selected by M. and D. Gillès, and L. Verviers (Éditions Gérard, 1964).

2. BIOGRAPHIES AND ESSAYS:

Pierre Brisson, *Tchékhov et sa vie* (Monte Carlo: Sauret, 1955).

Cahiers de la Compagnie Madeleine Renaud–Jean-Louis Barrault, VI. *Anton Tchékhov et la Cérisaie* (Paris: Julliard, 1954).

Rose Celli, *L'art de Tchékhov* (Paris: Del Duca, 1958).

Léon Chestov, *Pages choisies* (Paris: Gallimard, 1931).

Daniel-Rops, *Carte d'Europe* (Paris: Perrin, 1928).

Charles du Bos, *Journal*, Volumes I–IV (Paris: Corrêa, 1921–28).

Henri-Bernard Duclos, *Anton Tchékhov, le médecin et l'écrivain* (Paris: Grasset, 1927).

Ilya Ehrenburg, *À la rencontre de Tchékhov*, Translated by E. Brobowsky and V. Galande (Paris: John Didier, 1962).

Europe, Nos. 104–105, dedicated to Chekhov (Paris, 1954).

Maxim Gorky: *Trois Russes: L. N. Tolstoï, A. P. Tchékhov, Léonid Andreyev*, Translated by Dumesnil de Gramont (Paris, Gallimard: 1935).

Maxim Gorky, Olga Knipper-Tchekhova, Korney Tchukovsky, and Vladimir Ermilov, *Essais sur Tchékhov* (published in various languages in Moscow, 1960).

Edmond Jaloux, *Figures étrangères* (Paris: Plon, 1925).

Sophie Laffitte, *Tchékhov par lui-même* (Paris: Éditions du Seuil, 1955); *Tchékhov, 1860–1904* (Paris: Hachette, 1963); *Léon Tolstoï et ses contemporains* (Paris: Seghers, 1960).

Ettore Lo Gatto, *Histoire de la littérature russe des origines à nos jours*, Translated from the Italian by M. and A. M. Cabrini (Paris: Desclée De Brouwer, 1965).

André Maurois, *Destins exemplaires* (Paris: Plon, 1952).

Serge Michelson, *Les grands prosateurs russes* (Paris: Éditions de la Jeune Parque, 1946).

Irène Nemirovskaya, *La vie de Tchékhov* (Paris: Albin Michel, 1946).

Ossip-Lourie, *La psychologie des romanciers russes du XIXe siècle* (Paris: Alcan, 1905).

Serge Persky, *Les maîtres du roman russe contemporain* (Paris: Delagrave, 1912).

Quentin Ritzen, *Anton Tchékhov* (Paris: Éditions Universitaires, 1962).

Claude Roy, *Descriptions critiques, IV: La main heureuse* (Paris: Gallimard, 1958).

Marya Tchekhova, *Le musée Tchékhov à Yalta* (Moscow, foreign-language edition, 1959).

Elsa Triolet, *L'histoire d'Anton Tchékhov. Sa vie, son oeuvre* (Paris: Éditeurs Français Réunis, 1954).

Henri Troyat, *Sainte Russie, souvenirs et réflexions* (Paris: Grasset, 1956).

III. WORKS IN OTHER LANGUAGES

Anton Cechov, 1860–1960. Some Essays. Edited by T. Eekman (Leyden: E. J. Brill, 1960).

T. Eekman, *Anton Tsjechov en de russische intelligentsia* (Arnhem: Van Loghum, 1951).

Oliver Elton, *Chekhov* (Oxford University Press, 1952).

William Gerhardi, *Anton Chekhov, A Critical Study* (London, 1923).

David Magarshack, *Chekhov, A Life* (London, 1952); *Chekhov the Dramatist* (London, 1952).

Thomas Mann, *Nachlese* (Frankfurt, 1956).

Ernest J. Simmons, *Chekhov, a Biography* (Boston: Little, Brown, 1962); *Introduction to Russian Realism* (Bloomington: University of Indiana Press, 1965).

Maurice Valency, *The Breaking String* (Oxford University Press, 1966).

❧ INDEX ❧

A. P. Tchekhov, From the Recollections of His Contemporaries, 132, 359, 407n., 416
A. P. Tchekhov in My Life (Avilova), 132n., 165, 170n.
Abbazia, 202, 203, 205
"About Love," 269, 279
Abramov Theater, 125
Academy of Sciences, 103, 293, 369
Aksenevo, 328–332
Alarm Clock, 31, 41, 49, 396n.
Albertini, Tanya, 215n.
"Album, The," 63
Aleichem, Sholem, 384
Alexander I, 5n.
Alexander II, 62, 87
Alexander III, 62, 87
Alexander Nevsky (ship), 137
Alexandrinsky Theater, 109, 125, 221, 373
Alexandrovsk, 143–147
Altschuler, Dr. Isaac, 266, 278, 279, 346, 354, 371, 373, 376, 378, 382, 390–392, 406–409, 412, 413
Altukhov, Dr., 393, 394
Amusement, 58
Andreyev, Leonid, 349, 375
Anna Karenina (Tolstoy), 83
Annals of Surgery, 216
Antokolsky, Mark, 258
Anton Chekhov Sanitarium, 289

Antony and Cleopatra (Shakespeare), 154
Arkhangelsky, Dr., 56
Art Theater, *see* Moscow Art Theater
"At Home," 248, 380n.
"At the Circus" (Kuprin), 350
L'Aurore, 251, 252
Avilova, Lydia Alexeyevna, 132, 133, 165, 169–170, 210–212, 218, 219, 223, 226, 233, 237, 238, 244, 249, 250, 268, 269, 270, 273, 279, 406, 407

Badenweiler, 417–422
Bakunin, Mikhail, 19, 47
Balmont, Konstantin, 262, 349, 405
Barrault, Jean-Lewis, 399
Batyushkov, 398
"Beggar, The," 128
Belle Hélène, La (Offenbach), 23, 52
Berdyaev, Nikolai, 114
Berlin, 416–417
Bernhardt, Sarah, 49, 247, 356
"Betrothed," 374, 375
Biarritz, 244, 245–246
Bilibin, V., 73, 74, 77
"Bishop, The," 316, 350, 412
"Black Monk, The," 195, 196
Blind, The (Maeterlinck), 243, 375, 415
Bourget, Charles, 119, 130
Braz, 257

"Bride, The," 380n.
Bunin, Ivan, 303, 304, 321–324, 330–331, 345, 349, 350, 351, 353, 372, 376–378, 380, 394, 395, 416
Buryenin, V., 72, 95, 104, 154
"Busybodies, The," 170

Calas, Jean, 253
Century Illustrated Monthly Magazine, The, 144n.
Cervantes, Miguel de, 31, 41
Ceylon, 148–149
Chaliapin, Fyodor, 262, 311, 372, 393, 394, 423
"Chameleon, The," 63
Chekhov, Alexander, 3, 5, 6, 11, 14–17, 21, 22, 26, 27, 32–37, 41, 45–47, 50–58, 76, 81, 83, 86–90, 93, 96, 102, 111, 112, 117–120, 134, 140, 149, 177, 178, 187, 199, 210, 212, 224, 254, 255, 273, 274, 300, 362, 407, 423
Chekhov, Anton Pavlovich
    and Avilova, Lydia, meeting of, 133
    birth, 9
    childhood, 3–29
    death, 421
    as Doctor of Medicine, 59ff.
    European trips, 155–159, 202–205, 244–258, 312–315, 416–421
    and Knipper, Olga, meeting of, 261
    and Leikin, meeting of, 53
    marriage, 328
    and Mizinova, Lydia, meeting of, 116
    and Moscow Art Theater, 258ff.
    at Moscow School of Medicine, 46ff.
    awarded Pushkin Prize, 103
    trip to Sakhalin Island, 137–149
    first story published, 48
    and Suvorin, meeting of, 72
    and Tolstoy, meetings with, 214–215, 219, 343–347
    contacts tuberculosis, 59
Chekhov, Ivan, 11, 26, 28, 34, 37, 46, 51, 52, 78, 102, 137, 177, 187, 212, 241, 267, 328, 362, 422, 423
Chekhov, Mikhail (brother), 11, 22, 28, 34–40, 44–51, 78–80, 85, 92, 98, 133, 137, 140, 149, 152, 159, 161,

168, 169, 176–178, 195, 198, 212, 218, 222, 328n., 363, 422, 423
Chekhov, Mikhail (cousin), 32, 33, 36–41, 45
Chekhov, Mikhail (uncle), 10
Chekhov, Mitrofanos, 7, 10, 11, 21, 28, 32, 59, 75, 83, 84, 201, 202
Chekhov, Nikolai, 5, 11–23, 26, 27, 33–37, 42, 45–47, 50–53, 56, 70, 78–82, 102, 112, 118–122, 140
Chekhov, Pavel Yegorovich, 3–17, 20, 22, 26–28, 30–38, 41, 45, 46, 50, 52, 102, 143, 169, 176–177, 186, 187, 262–263
Chekhov, Yegor Mikhailovich, 9–11, 22, 27, 28, 37, 42
"Chekhov by Himself" (Laffitte), 366n.
Chekhov Museum, Yalta, 12n.
Chekhova, Marya (Masha), 11, 24, 28, 33, 35, 46, 51, 70, 71, 77–80, 83, 89, 96, 103, 109, 116, 117, 134, 137, 140, 143, 161, 168, 169, 176–181, 186, 188, 202–212, 223–225, 238, 241, 249, 262–273, 278, 281, 285, 300–306, 321–322, 328–334, 341–342, 422, 423
Chekhova, Olga Leonardovna Knipper, 261, 265, 280–290, 300–315, 324–423
Chekhova, Yevgenia Yakovlevna, 4, 11–16, 22, 28–38, 43–50, 80, 137, 140, 143, 149, 169, 170, 176, 177, 182, 187, 263, 264, 267, 271, 278, 283, 285, 306, 321, 328, 333–334, 423
Chekhov's Correspondence, 211n.
Cherry Orchard, The, 66, 295, 350, 375, 383, 385, 388, 389, 395–405, 410, 411
Chertkov, Count A. D., 10
Chertkov, Vladimir Grigorievich, 10n., 214
"Children, The," 380n.
Chopet, 20
"Chorister, The," 182
Coachman, The (Grigoryev), 25
Cocteau, Jean, 367
Colombo, 149
Constantinople, 149
Cooper, James Fenimore, 21
Cosmopolis, 250

"Cossack, The," 128
Country Woman, The (Turgenev), 375
Crime and Punishment (Dostoevsky), 204
Crimean War, 11, 15

"Darkness," 380n.
"Darling, The," 279, 345, 380n.
"Daughter of Albion, A," 63
Davydov, 88, 109
"Death of an Official, The," 63
"Death of Ivan Ilyich, The" (Tolstoy), 124
"Decoration, The," 63
Diaghilev, Sergei, 132, 372
Diakonov, 19
Disciple, Le (Bourget), 119, 130
Dr. Pascal (Zola), 192
Dostoevsky, Feodor, 47, 63, 73, 92, 104, 193, 242
"Drama, A," 380n.
Drama of the Chase, A, 49
"Dreary Story, A," 121–124, 127, 129, 171, 228, 412
Dreyfus, Capt. Alfred, 251–255, 363
Dreyfus, Mathieu, 251, 258
Drossy, Andrey, 24, 25, 32, 38, 39
Drossy, Marina, 39
Drumont, 251
"Duel, The," 151, 153, 158–160, 171, 172
Duse, Eleanora, 154

"Echoes of Moscow Life," 69
Efros, Evdosya (Dunya), 77, 78
Ehrenburg, Ilya, 366n.
Einsame Menschen (Hauptmann), 288n.
Encyclopaedia Britannica, 193n.
Ermak, 142
Ermilov, 194
Ermolova, M., 49
"Escape," 380n.
Esterhazy, Major, 251, 253
European Messenger, The, 92
Evils of Tobacco, The, 371
Ewald, Professor K., 416

Fantasy for Orchestra (Rachmaninov), 262
Faraway Princess (Rostand), 218
Fathers and Sons (Turgenev), 185
Faust (Goethe), 199
Florence, 156–157, 315
Fyodosia, Aunt, 140, 164, 376

Galkin-Vrasky, M., 135
Garbunov, 214
Garshin, Vsevolod, 95, 196
Gavrilov, I. E., 36, 41
Gavryushka, 274
Gay, 219
General Flirt, 150
Genoa, 204
Gide, André, 366
Giliarovsky, Vladimir, 50, 58, 414
Girgorovich, Dmitri V., 72–76, 79–81, 84, 86, 94, 103–105, 121, 128, 286, 370, 397
Glinka, Mikhail, 189
Glivanov, 25
Gnedish, P., 292
Goethe, Johann Wolfgang von, 19, 199
Gogol, Nikolai, 23, 47, 62, 95, 104, 119
Golden Ass (Apuleius), 192
Goltsev, 411
Goncharov, Ivan, 119
"Good People, The," 128
"Gooseberries," 260
Gorky, Maxim, 266–268, 276–279, 281, 286–292, 295, 296, 300–305, 311, 324, 328, 342–350, 356, 367, 369, 370, 372, 376, 377, 380, 384, 391, 394, 398, 399, 422, 423
Grasshopper, 31, 48, 49
"Grasshopper, The," 180, 209
Green, Julien, 287
Grigoryev, 25
"Gusev," 149, 151, 324

Hamlet (Shakespeare), 23
Happy Man and Other Tales, The (Avilova), 218, 219
Hauptmann, Gerhart, 288n.
Hedda Gabler (Ibsen), 303
Hermitage Theater, 260

Herzen, Alexander, 19
History of Medicine in Russia, The, 58
History of Sexuality, A, 55
"Holiday," 103
Hong Kong, 148
Hugo, Victor, 31
"Hunter, The," 72, 75

Ibsen, Henrik, 112, 291
Illos, G. B., 416, 417
"In Court," 380n.
"In the Cart," 248
"In the Ravine," 286, 293
In the Twilight, 96, 103, 138
Inspector General, The (Gogol), 23, 24
Institute of Fine Arts, Moscow, 34
Interior (Maeterlinck), 415
Intruder, The (Maeterlinck), 415
Island of Sakhalin, The, 132, 144–147, 160, 188, 192, 193, 212
Ivanenko, 243
Ivanov, 66, 87–91, 103, 107–115, 118, 121, 124, 125, 217, 227, 228, 294

Jókai Mór, 49

Kabilin, 10, 25
Karatinga, 120
Karpov, 221, 410
Keller, General, 422
Kennan, George, 144
Kharkeyevna, Varvara, 262
Kheifels, Josef, 287n.
"Kholstomir" (Tolstoy), 173
Khotyaintseva, Alexandra, 252
Khudekov, Sergei, 133, 165
Kiny-Dedlov, V., 391
Kishinev pogroms, 383, 384
Kisselyev family, 68–71, 76, 78, 83, 85, 86, 94, 96, 110, 141, 161, 179
Kisselyevsky, 89
Knipper, Olga, *see* Chekhova, Olga
Koch, Robert, 174
Kommissaryevskaya, Vera, 222–227, 234, 306, 307, 312
Kononovich, General, 143, 144, 145
Konovitser, E., 78n.

Kony, Judge, 234
Korff, Baron, 144, 145
Korolenko, Vladimir, 79, 80, 83, 90, 93, 95, 110, 154, 196, 293, 369
Korsch, 86–90
Korsch Theater, 108
Kotov, A., 132n.
Kovalevsky, 247, 254, 256, 313, 315
Kramsakov, 19
Kravstov, Petya, 30, 37, 85
"Kreutzer Sonata, The" (Tolstoy), 129, 150
Kruglov, 58
Krylov, Ivan, 99, 103
Kundassova, Olga, 117, 137, 415
Kuprin, Alexander, 303, 322–324, 349, 350, 366, 376
Kushukoy, 263, 264, 274, 381
Kuvshinnikova, Sofia Petrovna, 180

"Lady with the Pet Dog, The," 284, 286, 421
Lafitte, Sophie, 194, 366
Lavrov, V., 47, 136, 315, 316
Lazare, Bernard, 258
Lazarevsky, 380
Leikin, 53–60, 69, 72, 76, 77, 79, 82, 83, 86, 165, 169, 199, 210, 211, 238, 242, 246
Lenin, Nikolai, 194
Lenin Library, Moscow, 145n., 161n., 191n.
Lensky, 125, 180
Lentovsky Theater, 56
Léon Tolstoï et ses contemporains (Lafitte), 194n.
Leontyev, Ivan, 126
Lermontov, Mikhail, 405
Leskov, Nikolai, 52, 95, 110, 277, 367
"Letter, The," 128
"Letter from a Don Landowner to His Scholarly Neighbor," 48
Levitan, Isaac, 51, 70, 71, 78, 79, 94, 137, 158, 161, 162, 179–180, 209, 213, 217, 236, 243, 249, 281, 286, 305, 306
Levkeyeva, 223, 224
Liberation, 275, 383
Libre Parole, La, 251

Life, 275, 276, 293
"Life in the Seminary," 41
Lintvaryev family, 98, 99, 101, 118, 126, 160, 164, 167, 178, 179, 201, 316
Literary Heritage, The, 165n.
Little Russian Izba, The, 262
Living Dead, The (Tolstoy), 291n.
Lower Depths, The (Gorky), 372, 373
Luka, 98–100, 101, 119–120

Maeterlinck, Maurice, 230, 243, 414
Makar, 42, 45, 47
Maklakhov, V., 423
"Malefactor, The," 380n.
Maly Theater, 49, 108, 120, 124, 289
"Man with the Case, The," 19, 260
Mansfield, Katherine, 364
Marriage Proposal, The, 108
Marx, A. F., 64, 271–274, 278, 302, 367, 371, 380, 410
Marx, Karl, 87, 99
Maupassant, Guy de, 243, 344
Mauriac, François, 299
Medical Institute, Moscow, 40
"Meeting, The," 128, 129
Memoirs (Kovalevsky), 254
Memoirs (Teleshov), 416n.
Merezhkovsky, Dmitri, 92, 104, 156
Meyerhold, 261, 289
Mikhailovsky, 47, 110, 116, 124
Milan, 203
Mirolyubov, 380
Missionary Review, The, 375
Mizinova, Lydia Stakhievna (Lika), 116, 117, 137, 162, 179, 181, 182, 189–192, 200, 201, 204, 205, 207, 213, 216, 217, 223–225, 241, 243, 249, 256, 257, 268, 270, 351–354
Monastery of the Holy Mountains, 85
Monastery of the New Jerusalem, 58
Monte Carlo, 157–158, 256–257
Morozov, Savva, 243, 249, 257, 342, 357–360, 370, 382
Morozova, Fedosya Yakovlevna, 33
Morozova, Yevgenia Yakovlevna, *see* Chekhova, Yevgenia Yakovlevna
Moscow Art Theater, 235, 258, 264–266, 279–291, 298, 301, 303–305, 311– 313, 318, 325, 326, 334–336, 349, 351–360, 370, 372, 375, 376, 379, 385–389, 393, 394, 410, 415, 423
Moscow Gazette, The, 90
Moscow News, 253
"Moscow Notes," 54
Motley Tales, 73, 76
"My Life," 220, 221
My Life in Art (Stanislavsky), 409
"My Wife," 182

Naples, 157
Naradin, 47
"Neighbors, The," 182, 211
Nemirovich-Danchenko, Vasily, 125, 206, 217, 218, 235, 258–261, 265, 282, 291, 305, 308, 315, 352, 370, 371, 385, 386, 388, 389, 392, 394, 397, 398, 411
Nemirovskaya, Irina, 112
Nevsky Prospekt, 92
New Athos, 101
New Times, 72–76, 81, 82, 88, 90, 95, 97, 117, 135, 137, 139, 140, 142, 151, 154, 160, 163, 168, 170, 186, 203, 212, 233, 252, 253, 254, 276, 277, 363
News of the Day, 49
Nice, 204–205, 246–258, 312–315
Nicholas I, 92n.
Nicholas II, 220, 276, 355, 369, 373
Niva (The Field), 220
Northern Echo, The, 123
Northern Messenger, The, 93, 95, 242
Notebooks, 157, 207, 235, 236, 260, 281, 360, 367–369, 377, 411, 424
Novodyevichy Monastery, 241, 422, 423
"Nude Courtesan" (Semiradsky), 110

Obolensky, L. E., 83, 199
Obolensky, Dr. N. V., 237
Odessa, 120, 147, 149, 202
Old Believers, 52n.
Onegin, Evgeny (Pushkin), 106
"On Love," 260, 353
"On the Road," 262
Orlov-Davidov, Count, 184
Orphan Girl, The, 41

Oskolki, see Splinters
Ostroümov, Dr., 237, 238, 381, 382, 384, 386, 390, 406, 413
Ostrovsky, Alexander, 95
Out of a Distant Past (Chekhova), 354

Palmin, Lyodor, 50, 51, 53, 58, 164
Panina, Countess, 343
Parasite, The (Turgenev), 375
Paris, 158–159, 205, 245–246, 258
Patti, Adelina, 247
"Peasants," 235, 237, 241–242, 284
"Pechenyeg," 248
Pegorov Congress, 298
Pélléas et Mélisande (Maeterlinck), 230
People's Art Theater, Moscow, 258; *see also* Moscow Art Theater
Pervukhin, 363
Peter the Great, 8, 18, 258
Petersburg (ship), 147, 148
Petersburg Gazette, The, 69, 72, 75, 94, 133, 233, 273
Petersburg News, The, 266
Petrashesky revolutionary group, 92
Petrov, Colonel V., 314
Pisa, 315
Pisarev, 19
Platonov, 49, 64–67, 111, 294
Platov, M. I., 10
Platova, Countess, 10, 22
Pleschev, Alexei, 92, 95, 97–99, 106, 117, 119, 122, 128–130, 141, 241
Pobyedonotsev, 62
Pokrovsky, F. P., 19
Postscript to "The Kreutzer Sonata" (Tolstoy), 173
Potapenko, Ignatyi, 189, 190, 192, 196, 198, 200–207, 213, 217, 218, 221–227, 250, 256–257
Powers of Darkness, The (Tolstoy), 372
Proudhon, 174
Pushkin, Alexander, 19, 106, 307, 344
Pushkin Prize, 92, 103, 104, 121

Rachmaninov, Sergei, 262, 303
Rayevsky Institute for Girls, 51, 71, 116, 212

Recollections (Altschuler), 413n.
Recollections (Avilova), 238, 249, 273, 352–354, 407n.
Recollections (Potapenko), 207
Recollections From the House of the Dead (Dostoevsky), 193
Repin, Ilya, 92, 196, 324
"Requiem, The," 73
Resurrection (Tolstoy), 214, 239, 271, 292
Reverzy, J., 316
Revolution of 1917, 18n.
Romance of Nina Zarechnaya, The (Grossman), 191n.
Rome, 157, 315
Rossolimo, Dr., 61, 372, 380, 394, 414, 417
Rousseau, Jean-Jacques, 87, 366
Rumyantsev Library, 134
Russian News, The, 50, 244, 252, 416
Russian Thought, 136, 186, 192, 208, 211, 241, 249, 252, 268, 391, 411
Russian Writers' Mutual Aid Society, 276

Sakhalin Island, 127, 131–152, 153, 154, 159, 160, 161, 170–173, 186, 236, 245, 294
Saltykov-Shchedrin, Mikhail, 95
Samkovich, 38
Sanin, A., 291, 351, 352
Savelyev, D. T., 42, 45, 47
Savina, Marya, 222
School of Fine Arts, Moscow, 26
School of Medicine, Moscow, 46
Schopenhauer, Arthur, 31, 98
Schwöhrer, Dr., 417, 418, 420, 421
Sea Gull, The, 67, 180n., 200, 203, 216–234, 243–244, 258–260, 264–266, 280, 283, 289, 291, 293, 303–307, 311, 315, 320, 351, 373, 383, 403
Sealed Angel, The (Leskov), 52
Selivanov, 28, 29, 30, 37, 84
Semiradsky, 110
Sergeyenko, P., 51, 58, 59, 201, 207, 271, 272, 366
Serov, V. A., 311
Shchepkina-Kupernika, Tatiana, 179, 182, 189, 192, 206, 209, 217, 218

Shakespeare, William, 19, 23, 292, 344, 345, 346
Shapovalov, L. N., 264
Shavrova, E. M., 154
Shcheglov, 4, 102, 133, 136, 165
Shekhtel, F., 20, 236
Shishkin, 196
Shredin, Dr., 284, 382, 413
Shurovsky, 413
Sinani, Isaac Abramovich, 262
Singapore, 148
"Singer, A," 380n.
Sitin, 208
Slavophiles, 345
Smagin, Alexander, 119, 167, 178, 179
"Smoke" (Turgenev), 351
Sobolevsky, 244, 246
Socrates, 106
Solovtsov, N., 125
"Sorrow," 380n.
Spectator, The, 49
Spiro, 17
Splinters, 53, 54, 55, 58, 77
Stammerer, The, 26, 27, 31, 32
Stanislavsky, Konstantin, 258–261, 265, 290, 291, 304, 308, 311–315, 336, 341, 355, 357, 360, 368, 370–375, 385–389, 393–395, 398, 410, 412, 415
"Steppe, The," 23, 95, 344
Stock Exchange, Moscow, 34
Stories and Tales, 208
Stories Drawn From the Lives of My Friends, 121–122
Stowe, Harriet Beecher, 23, 41
Strempf, Dr., 26, 40
Strulev, Isaac B., 31
Struve, Peter, 275
Sukhotin, 215
Sulerzhitsky, 394
Sumbatov-Yushin, Alexander, 249
Suvorin, Alexis, 39, 72, 75, 76, 78, 91, 92, 96–137, 141, 150–160, 165–173, 186, 187, 194, 195, 200–204, 212–225, 233, 234, 237, 240, 245, 249, 252–258, 264, 271, 272, 276, 277, 301, 312, 363, 372, 380
Suvorin, Alexis (son), 101, 154
Suvorina, Anna Ivanovna, 79–80, 96, 100–101, 109, 196, 224–225

Svobodin, 125
Swan Song, 86
"Swedish Match, The," 63
Symbolists, 219

Table of Ranks, 18
Taganrog, 3–43, 44–47, 55, 57, 58, 61, 84–85
Tales of Melpomene, The, 57
Tatarina, Fanny, 305
Taube, Dr. J., 412, 413, 416
Tchaikovsky, Peter, 126, 189
Teleshov, 415, 416
That Crazy Platonov, 64n.
Theodosia, 100–101, 201–202
"Those Ladies," 380n.
"Thought" (Andreyev), 349
Three Sisters, The, 56, 66, 67, 111, 307, 309, 311–313, 315–321, 335, 345, 355, 368, 370, 372, 379, 392, 399, 401
Three Years, 208
Tikhonov, 359, 364, 367, 368
Tit for Tat, 41
Tolstoy, Alexei, 261
Tolstoy, Countess, 219, 272
Tolstoy, Ilya Lvovich, 380
Tolstoy, Lev Lvovich, 186, 215
Tolstoy, Lev Nikolaevich, 5n., 10n., 61–63, 83, 87, 95, 99, 101, 104, 106, 124, 128, 129, 136, 144n., 150, 164, 166, 173, 174, 184, 194–197, 213–215, 219, 234, 235, 238–239, 241, 242, 254, 271, 278, 279, 282, 286, 291–293, 324, 342–349, 367, 375, 380, 384, 412
Tolstoy, Masha, 219
Tolstoy, Sergei, 344, 345
Tolstoy, Sofia, 79
Tolstoy, Tatiana, 215, 219, 279
Treasure, The, 83
Tretyakov, Pavel, 257
Tretyakov Gallery, 257
Trieste, 203
Tsar Fyodor (Tolstoy), 261
Tuesday Club, The, 416
Turchaninova, Anna, 213

Turgenev, Ivan, 41, 63, 104, 185, 196, 220, 242, 286, 350, 351, 375
"Tutor, The," 63

Uncle Tom's Cabin (Stowe), 23, 41
Uncle Vanya, 66, 111, 176, 227, 268, 285, 287, 289–291, 294–300, 303–305, 311, 366, 372, 399, 401, 403
University of Moscow, 61, 94, 247
Urban, 19
"Urchins, The," 380n.
"Useless Victory, The," 54
Uspensky, Gleb, 110, 154
Uspensky, Dr., 382

"Vanka," 380n.
Venice, 155–156, 203
Veselovsky, A., 369
Vienna, 155, 202, 203, 312
Vilar, Jean, 64n.
Vishnyevsky, 24, 290, 314, 328, 374, 384
Vladivostok, 148
Voltaire, 106, 253
Vsevolodo-Vilva, 357–360
Vutchina, Nicholas, 16, 17

Waiting for Godot (Becket), 375

War and Peace (Tolstoy), 174
"Ward Six," 182, 193, 194, 195
Wedding, The, 125
"What Is Art?" (Tolstoy), 239n.
Why the Hen Cackles, 41
Wilczkowsky, Kyril, 353
"Wish to Sleep, The," 94, 380n.
Wood Demon, The, 109, 124, 127, 216, 218, 289, 294
Writers' Union, Moscow, 326

Yakobi, 247, 313
Yakunshikova, Marya, 382, 384
Yalta, 120–124, 199–200, 262–278, 285–310, 316–327, 333–357, 360–378, 385–393, 407–412
Yasinsky, 234
Yassensky, 170
Yavorskaya, Lydia Borisovna, 191, 192, 206, 217, 219, 226
Yegorov, E., 164, 166
Yurasov, 247, 313

Zankovyetskaya, Marya, 166
Zembulatov, Vassily, 38
Zola, Émile, 192, 196, 252, 253, 254, 363, 364
Zvenigorod, 58